Sikkim Development Report

सत्यमेव जयते

Planning Commission
Government of India

Sikkim Development Report

सत्यमेव जयते

PLANNING COMMISSION
GOVERNMENT OF INDIA
NEW DELHI

Published by

ACADEMIC FOUNDATION
NEW DELHI

First Published in 2008 by
Academic Foundation
4772-73 / 23 Bharat Ram Road, (23 Ansari Road), Darya Ganj, New Delhi - 110 002 (India).
Phones : 23245001 / 02 / 03 / 04. Fax : +91-11-23245005. E-mail : academic@vsnl.com
www.academicfoundation.com

Published under arrangement with :
Planning Commission,
Government of India,
New Delhi.

Sikkim Development Report
ISBN 13: 9788171886685
ISBN 10: 81-7188-668-X

Designed and typeset by Italics India, New Delhi
Printed and bound in India.

Core Committee

Constitution of the Core Committee for preparation of SDR, Sikkim (2003)

1.	Shri N.K. Singh, *Member, Planning Commission*	Chairman
2.	Smt. Adarsh Mishra, *Secretary, M/o DoNER*	Member
3.	Shri S.W. Tenzing, *Chief Secretary, Govt. of Sikkim*	Member
4.	Smt. Reva Nayyar, *Adviser (NE), Planning Commission*	Member Secretary

Members of the Core Committee underwent a change over a period of time as below:

Chairman:

1.	Shri B.N. Yugandhar, *Member, Planning Commission*	Chairman
2.	Shri B.K. Chaturvedi, *Member, Planning Commission*	Chairman (*present*)

Members:

1.	Smt. Suman Swarup, *Adviser (NE), Planning Commission*	Member Secretary
2.	Shri A.N.P. Sinha, *Sr. Adviser (NE), Planning Commission*	Member Secretary
3.	Smt. Jayati Chandra, *Sr. Adviser (NE), Planning Commission*	Member Secretary (*present*)
4.	Shri Lakshmi Chand, *Secretary, M/o DoNER*	Member
5.	Smt. Gauri Chatterjee *Secretary, M/o DoNER*	Member
6.	Smt. Sushma Singh *Secretary, M/o DoNER*	Member
7.	Smt. Veena Sreeram Rao *Secretary, M/o DoNER*	Member (*present*)
8.	Shri N.D. Chingappa *Chief Secretary, Govt. of Sikkim*	Member (*present*)

List of Contributors with their Affiliations

N.J. Kurian

Director, Council for Social Development,
New Delhi (formerly, Senior Consultant,
National Institute of Public Finance and Policy, New Delhi)

Mahendra, P. Lama

Vice Chancellor, Central University of Sikkim, Gangtok
(formerly, Professor, School of International Studies,
Jawaharlal Nehru University, New Delhi)

Simanti Bandyopadhyay

Senior Economist, National Institute of Public Finance and Policy, New Delhi.

Saumen Chattopadhyay

Associate Professor, School of Social Sciences,
Jawaharlal Nehru University, New Delhi

Anuradha Bhasin

Consultant, National Institute of Public Finance and Policy, New Delhi.

एम. एस. आहलुवालिया
MONTEK SINGH AHLUWALIA

सत्यमेव जयते

उपाध्यक्ष
योजना आयोग
भारत
DEPUTY CHAIRMAN
PLANNING COMMISSION
INDIA

FOREWORD

One of the important Tenth Plan initiatives of the Planning Commission was to sponsor the preparation of State Development Reports with much of the work being done by reputed national level institutes. This exercise was undertaken in recognition of the fact that economic circumstances and performance in individual States varied considerably and it was necessary to examine development challenges for individual States in the light of State specific constraints and circumstances. The basic idea is to produce quality reference documents on development profiles of individual States and the possible strategies for accelerating growth, and reducing poverty and inequality.

The Sikkim State Development Report reviews Sikkim's experience and highlights issues critical for the State's development in the years ahead. I hope its publication will stimulate debate on growth strategies appropriate for Sikkim. I am sure the road map indicated in the Report will stimulate a broader awareness of the critical policy issues facing the State and will assist the State to move to a higher growth path and to achieve all round human and economic development.

(Montek Singh Ahluwalia)

योजना भवन, संसद मार्ग, नई दिल्ली – 110001 दूरभाष : 23096677, 23096688 फैक्स : 23096699
Yojana Bhawan, Parliament Street, New Delhi : 110001 Phones: 23096677, 23096688 Fax : 23096699 E-mail : dch@yojana.nic.in

Pawan Chamling
(Honoris Causa)
Chief Minister of Sikkim

03592-202575 (O)
03592-202304 (R)

Tashiling
Gangtok-737103
Sikkim

MESSAGE

Sikkim State's Development Report has been prepared by the National Institute of Public Finance and Policy in collaboration with the Planning Commission. I would like to convey my sincere thanks and gratitude to these august institutions. I also appreciate the vision provided by Dr. N.J. Kurian and Prof. Mahendra P. Lama in this endeavour.

The peace and tranquility in the State has been a catalyst resulting in development of Tourism, Horticulture, Floriculture, Power, Industrial Growth and expansion of Infrastructure. The data on several fronts on literacy, birth rate, death rate, growth rate and per capita income all are indicative of the progress made by the State, especially during the last decade.

We are conscious of the need for a sustainable development duly dovetailing the need to preserve the Ecology and Environment, so as to ensure that the fruits of development reach the poorest of the poor. The strengths, weaknesses and potential of our State have been dwelt upon in detail in the report. We shall not leave any stone unturned in meeting the challenges ahead of us.

We accept the need for environmental sanitation and the benefits provided by the CNG in controlling vehicular pollution, as evidenced in our National Capital Delhi. We hope that the Central Government provides CNG facilities to our State also. We are consciously promoting Eco-Tourism, Horticulture and Floriculture in our State where we have a comparative advantage. We are committed to optimal utilization of our Hydel resources in an environmentally friendly manner, without causing undue hardship to our people

In order to put Sikkim in the path of sustainable development with all round improvement in human indices, we have taken a number of measures, which we are confident, would meet the economic growth rate of 8 %

prescribed by the Planning Commission in the current plan period. We aim at rationalizing revenue expenditure and increasing investment in areas leading towards more capital formation.

Our economic strategy focuses upon areas like, poverty alleviation, creation of employment opportunities and income generation through self-employment and our thrust sectors are Agriculture, Horticulture & Floriculture, Tourism and Human Resource Development. It is also our endeavor to create congenial atmosphere for promotion of business infrastructure and bringing of private investment in industries, especially services oriented sectors like tourism, IT and border trade etc. We are also actively encouraging public private partnership in the State.

Our vision is to ensure complete literacy, quality education and skill development to increase and enhance the scope of employment together with adoption of new technological devices in rural management and agriculture.

I am confident that the report would open new vistas of development for the State.

(Pawan Chamling)

सत्यमेव जयते

बी. के. चतुर्वेदी
B.K. CHATURVEDI

सदस्य
योजना आयोग
योजना भवन
नई दिल्ली–110 001
MEMBER
PLANNING COMMISSION
YOJANA BHAWAN
NEW DELHI-110 001
TEL: 23096594
e-mail: bkchaturvedi@nic.in

MESSAGE

Preparation of State Specific Development Reports is a recent initiative of the Planning Commission with States Concerned. The objective of the State Development Report is to identify critical development issues of the State and suggest strategies for accelerating development process of respective states. The report prepared mainly by experts and specialized institutes with the cooperation of the State Government would be of immense value to the Centre and the State which would assist in the setting of the agenda for higher and more equitable growth of states.

A Core Committee under the Chairmanship of Shri N.K. Singh, former Member, Planning Commission, was constituted in October 2003. The Core Committee worked out the modalities for preparing the State Development Report for Sikkim and decided to assign the job to National Institute of Public Finance and Policy(NIPFP) and Prof. M.P.Lama of Jawaharlal Nehru University, keeping in view their involvement in preparation of "*People's vision*" on Sikkim and "*Sikkim Human Development Report, 2001*" and their interest for the job. The Government of Sikkim was also actively associated in this process.

The report has taken into account the historical evolution of the indigenous people and the state, its sensitive and fragile environment, biodiversity and natural resources, poor connectivity, underdeveloped infrastructure, shortage of skills, expertise and the role of government at the centre-stage of development while analyzing the development profile of the state. The report highlights all critical policy issues, State economy, development performance of the State Government and suggests sustainable developmental`strategy through strengthening of social and physical infrastructure and proactive role of the government. The directions and strategies suggested in the report will go as a long way in achieving a higher growth rate.

I would like to record my appreciation of the work done by NIPFP and Prof. Prof. M.P.Lama for their effective contribution in preparing the report. I am thankful to he Government of Sikkim for rendering full cooperation and support to NIPFP in preparation of the report. The efforts done by the State Plan Adviser (NE) in liaising with NIPFP, State Government Deportments is noteworthy. I would like to appreciate the work done by officers of the State Plan Division in providing all necessary help to the Core Committee.

(B.K. CHATURVEDI)

Contents

...CONTD. ...

...CONTD. ...

List of Tables, Figures, Boxes and Annexures

Tables

Figures

Boxes

Annexures

Acknowledgements

The State Development Report for Sikkim has been prepared with generous contributions of many individuals and organizations. The Planning Commission, Government of India, entrusted the task of preparing the Report to National Institute of Public Finance and Policy (NIPFP), New Delhi. Professor Mahendra Lama, Vice Chancellor, Central University of Sikkim, Gangtok (formerly, Professor, School of International Studies, JNU, New Delhi), was taken as a collaborating partner. We are grateful to all authors, experts and peer reviewers for their timely contributions.

Shri N.K. Singh, the former Member, Planning Commission, Government of India, Shri B.N. Yugandhar, and Shri B.K. Chaturvedi, Member, Planning Commission, Government of India, served as the chairpersons of the Core Committee for different periods during the preparation of the Report. We are grateful to them for their interest and initiatives. They, in addition, gave valuable suggestions on different drafts of the report. Smt. Reva Nayyar, and Smt. Suman Swarup, Advisers (NE), Planning Commission, Government of India coordinated the review of various drafts of the Report and gave useful comments. All these have gone into improving the quality of the report. Special thanks are due to Shri S.N. Brohmo Choudhury, Director (NE), Planning Commission, Government of India, for his untiring efforts for overall coordination since the very beginning.

We are extremely grateful to Mr. Pawan Chamling, Chief Minister of Sikkim, for his extensive help and cooperation at different phases of our study and field visits to Sikkim. We would like to thank N.D. Chingapa, Chief Secretary, Government of Sikkim, G.K. Subba, Principal Secretary and Development Commissioner, Planning and Development Department, Government of Sikkim, T.T. Dorji, Principal Secretary, Finance Department, Government of Sikkim, R.S. Basnet, Principal Secretary to the Chief Minister of Sikkim, Government of Sikkim and S.W. Tenzing, Advisor, Government of Sikkim (formerly, Chief Secretary, Government of Sikkim) for their support and help in building up the necessary database which was critical for preparing the report.

We have interacted with various departments in the Government of Sikkim and also the organizations working on different aspects of development in Sikkim. We would like to thank V.B. Pathak, Secretary, Rural Management & Development Department, Alok Srivastava, Secretary, Department of Tourism; G.K. Gurung, Secretary, Department of Animal Husbandry; C.Cintury, Secretary, Welfare Department, B.K. Rasaily, Secretary, Department of Buildings; Pratap Basnet, Secretary, Department of Roads and Bridges; O.P. Singhi, Secretary, Department of Science and Technology, K.G. Bhutia, Commissioner Cum Secretary, Department of Animal Husbandry; Jaishree Pradhan, Special Secretary, Department of Urban Development and Housing Development; T.K. Pradhan, Special Secretary, Department of Tourism; Suresh Chand Varshney, Additional Secretary, Department of Buildings; Kuber Sharma, Additional Secretary, Food and Consumer Affairs; T.N. Dhakal, Additional. Secretary, Land Revenue Department, Govt. of Sikkim; S.P. Subba, Additional. Secretary, Land Revenue Department; Dawa Sandop, Additional Secretary, Land Revenue Department; Sonam Lepcha, Deputy Secretary, Planning and Development Department; A.D. Mishra, General Manager, State Tourism Development Corporation; Anil Mainra, Additional Chief Commissioner, Forests; S.B.S. Bhaduria, Conservator of Forests; Gopal Pradhan, Senior Scientist, Environment

& Pollution Control, Department of Forests, Environment & Wildlife, Sonam Tshering, Director, Directorate of Economics and Statistics, Planning and Development Department; Rajesh Verma, Director, Department of Information Technology; Jyotsna Shubba, Joint Director, Planning and Development Department, Usha Lachungpa, Senior Research Officer (Wildlife), Forest Department, L.S. Srivastava, Indian Council of Agricultural Research, Gangtok; Annapurna Alley, Under Secretary, Panchayat, Rural Development Department, Ramesh Subramaniam, Senior Project Officer, AUSAID; Sandeep Tambe, Project Manager, The Mountain Institute, Sikkim; Renzino Lepcha, Executive Secretary, Ecotourism and Conservation Society of Sikkim (ECOSS); Peter Zoller, Program Manager, Gangtok, Shillong and South Asia Regional Water Supply and Sanitation Program, Sally Rynveld, Consultant, Gangtok, Shillong and South Asia Regional Water Supply and Sanitation Program; P.D. Rai, Independent Consultant for their initiatives at different stages of preparation of the report which have led to its successful completion.

We would also like to thank Arindam Banerjee, Sayantan Bera and Vimal Khawas for their excellent research assistance. We thank Rita Wadhwa, NIPFP, for editorial inputs and Amita Padhwal, NIPFP and Kavita Issar, NIPFP for their assistance in formatting the report.

M.G. Rao

Director, NIPFP,
New Delhi

Executive Summary

Situated on the northeast border of the country, Sikkim is a uniquely positioned mountainous state having international borders along three-fourths of its boundary. The planning process in the state was initiated in the 1950s, but it was only in 1975 after it joined the Indian union, that Sikkim's developmental agenda was placed on a fast track. Although overall social development is relatively high in the state, its small size, poor connectivity with the rest of the country, and shortage of skills and expertise have kept per capita incomes low, and poverty high.

The *Sikkim State Development Report* attempts to assess the main strengths and weaknesses of the state in achieving a high level of development. Based on the analysis of the economy's fundamentals, it recommends a development strategy that takes into account the state's potential and builds on its strengths: a peaceful environment, diverse agro-climatic topography, supply of cheap labour and vast potential in tourism, hydro-power, and horticulture. The sustainable developmental strategy recommended will seek to (i) empower people by strengthening the social infrastructure, in the form of education and skill formation and easy access to good health systems, and physical infrastructure, such as a good connectivity and communications network, quality energy supply, and (ii) vastly changed role for the government as an enabler rather than a direct participant in the production–distribution processes.

Economic Growth, Structural Change and Employment

Even though nominal growth has been 15.5 per cent per annum since the 1980s, real growth in the economy decelerated from 11 per cent in the 1980s to 9 per cent in the 1990s. Per capita income grew at around 6 per cent per annum. This period has seen a structural change in favour of services at the cost of the primary sector, while the share of the secondary sector in GSDP remained somewhat constant. Disappointingly, while secondary sector grew at about 12 per cent in the 1990s, manufacturing growth was only one per cent, and the 13 per cent growth in services was driven mainly by the expansion of public administration and 'other services.'

Any development strategy in Sikkim has to focus on an expansion of new avenues for employment. Recent estimates indicate a worsening unemployment situation in the state with an increasing number of educated entering the job market, and shrinking of employment within the government. The government's role has to shift from direct job creator to facilitator. It has already taken steps towards shifting from low-quality employment to high-quality employment by increasing avenues for skill formation and provision of seed capital. New avenues for employment will have to be found in tourism and horticulture, which if developed appropriately can also deal with another of the issues plaguing the state—the rapid urbanisation, and environmental and infrastructural incapacity of urban centres to deal with the influx. The proposed promotion of industries such as agro-processing, knowledge-based services, and the state as a hub for healthcare and education is expected to spawn demand for different levels of skills and expand the employment base in the state.

Social protection can be ensured by enforcing labour laws, but this cannot be done at the expense of labour market flexibility and industry competitiveness.

Natural Resource Management and Sustainable Development

Any strategy for development has to be sensitive to the fragile environment of the state. Sikkim is one of the richest states in India in terms of biodiversity and natural resources. With fragile mountain ecology threatened by landslides and floods, it is difficult to strategise development priorities maintaining the environmental needs of the state.

More than 80 per cent of the population, directly or indirectly, depends on the natural resources of the state. Since land is very scarce in the state, food security is the prime issue of concern. With growing population, unemployment in the state is becoming unmanageably high, a direct consequence of which is poverty. These fundamental issues can partly be tackled with proper planning in natural resource management.

There is an immediate need to take proper measures for land, soil, and water conservation. This will ensure sustainable growth in agriculture, forestry and animal husbandry, and improve livelihoods of the masses. By widening the protected area network, introducing regulations in trekking and other tourist activities and training programmes for registered porters and tourist guides, the state can ensure sustainable tourism. Restricting biopiracy and developing a good patent information centre in the state would restore resources drained in the absence of patents. With proper planning in disaster management and mitigation, the state can minimise unplanned losses. NGOs and CBOs should be given more autonomy to sensitise people and build awareness regarding the major environmental hazards in the state.

The garbage disposal system in the state needs to be reformed thoroughly. The 'no plastics' policy of the state has not been fully successful. The new moves in the Action Plan for municipal solid waste management are in the desired direction. There should be a separate plan of garbage disposal for the tourist destinations to attract high value tourists.

Vehicular emission is the major source of air pollution in the urban areas and tourist destinations of the state. New improved standards like 'Bharat Stage 2' should be proposed to control excessive vehicular pollution. Exploring the options of CNG in terms of cost-benefit analysis in the state might provide new solutions to the problem.

Ambient air quality is in line with national norms, but drinking water especially in rural areas needs attention. There have been some major moves in maintaining water quality. Water treatment plants and water testing laboratories have been proposed for all districts; the water-testing laboratory in the east district has started functioning. There are plans to involve schools in the water quality improvement programmes by testing water quality in their laboratories with the spillover benefits of raising awareness among children.

Fiscal and Financial Management

Fiscal consolidation will have to focus on ensuring a healthy growth of revenues, diversifying the resource base and ensuring expenditure efficiency and accountability. Despite a relatively small own-revenue base, typical of most hill states with their limited industrial activity, both own-tax and non-tax revenues were on the upswing till recently, buoyed by receipts from lotteries, state income taxes and sales taxes.

The Tenth Plan projected outlay at Rs. 1656 crore is higher than the Ninth Plan outlay by 47 per cent. Of this, state's own resources are projected to be Rs. 95.5 crore. Sikkim is one of the three northeastern states that could make a positive contribution in financial resources towards the Tenth Plan. The flow of grants from North East Council (NEC) and Ministry of Development of North Eastern Region (DONER) are already showing signs of rising.

Though the state's dependence on central transfers has shown a decline, it still constitutes about 80 per cent of revenue receipts. On the expenditure side, capital outlays are a high 20 per cent of GSDP, based on a larger plan size and the state's positive contribution to plan financing, unlike many other northeastern states. However, the rapid growth of the wage and pension bill has put the state under fiscal stress, and an increase in debt servicing on account of repayment of loans and interest, is pushing the state towards a debt trap. With a debt-to-GSDP ratio of around 80 per cent, the crucial question is whether the present fiscal regime is sustainable.

To push forward the development strategy, the state needs more resources, but it also has to decrease its dependence on the centre. Fiscal reforms need to aim at augmenting revenues and more effective management of public expenditure for better delivery of public services and restructuring to release resources for developmental projects envisaged in this report. Reform measures initiated by the state under the Memorandum of Understanding (MoU) and the Medium Term Fiscal Restructuring Programme (MTFRP) have been satisfactory. The state has begun to initiate fiscal reforms and has initiated measures to spread the awareness of imperatives of reform to the electorate. However, realising the full development potential will require overhauling the entire system, as piecemeal attempts will not be sufficient.

As own revenue constitutes a small percentage of state's revenue, the state should explore new avenues of resource generation. The vast revenue potential from hydel power is virtually untapped. Other revenue-augmenting measures include phasing out power subsidies, raising vehicle registration fees and making state income tax more progressive. The state needs to take some quick decisions on state public sector enterprises as closed enterprises have been draining resources over the years. With regard to local bodies, the state is advised to follow the recommendations of the State Finance Commission. Steps taken so far to consolidate and strengthen the functioning of the rural local bodies have been exemplary. However, state may ensure a corruption-free system where there is no room for patronage and political affiliation.

Education

Education in the state received a tremendous boost with the state's merger in 1975, in terms of infrastructure and training. There has been a notable decline in school dropout rates especially in the lower grades, and the gender gap in school enrolment has fallen between 1981 and 1991, and the state has one of the lowest teacher-pupil ratios in the country. The state has since witnessed a marked improvement in its effective literacy rate (69.7 per cent in 2001), although female literacy is still lagging substantially behind.

The quality of education particularly in the government system has been a major concern. The declining quality of teachers is attributed to the recruitment process, which is based on the 'sons of the soil' policy. More recently, the state has been encouraging an exchange of goods, knowledge, skills and institutions from other parts of the country (such as the Sikkim Manipal University set up in 1998) and abroad.

Reforms in the education system are needed in areas such as rationalisation of the functional powers and composition of the education department, proper planning, effective monitoring and evaluation, teachers' training and making *panchayats* responsible for the functioning of primary schools. Unproductive manpower in the education department should be phased out gradually and redeployed in terms of locations and functions.

Massive institutional revamping is required which should include the setting up of Board of Secondary Education, University Management Board and Private Institutions Regulatory Board. Teachers' training should be made compulsory with every five years cycle at all levels in both government and private schools. All the teachers must be exposed to other schools and institutions within and outside the state. Capacity building of *panchayat* members for effective management of primary schools should be steadily carried out.

Primary schools with thin enrolment should be closed down. Students could be brought to nearby boarding schools. Teachers released should be redeployed. School maintenance rather than expansion in numbers and upgradation should be the major thrust. At least 25 per cent of the education outlay should be devoted to maintenance for at least next 8-10 years.

Indiscriminate subsidies in education have been counterproductive; subsidies need to be better targeted and preferably merit-based, which will allow the release of funds that can be put to better use, such as, school maintenance. There is also an urgent need for a proper database and information network in the state's education system.

Most of the central projects including the Sarva Shiksha Abhiyan (SSA) have been extended to Sikkim. However in many cases, there is little dissemination of information about the programmes, involvement of agencies other than the government has been limited and there is a conspicuous absence of monitoring and evaluation mechanisms. In many cases, the distribution of benefits are unbalanced both geographically, and demographically.

The state should have a very clear higher education policy. With the massive expansion of facilities at lower levels, the numbers qualifying in the higher secondary examination are rising steadily. There has been considerable enthusiasm and a growing need for expanding access to higher educational institutions. Having its own university will impart a 'completeness' to the state's education system and provide a new thrust to research and academic activities.

Sikkim requires an array of technical institutions related to IT, tea, tourism, health, horticulture-floriculture, biotechnology, engineering, mountain ecology, mass media, management and fashion technology. Opening of one good technical and professional institution could make a huge difference in the quality of human resources, local economy and future orientation of its people. All these institutions also have direct links with the tourism industry.

The Investment Policy 2003 is promoting the state as an educational hub, which should have employment-generating benefits. Sikkim's comparative advantages in the social, geo-climatic and economic spheres can be leveraged to make it a major destination for the educational and professional institutions, attracting students from neighbouring states and countries as also from the non-resident Indian population.

Health

Government efforts to increase access to health services took off after 1975, and today Sikkim's health indicators are above national averages. Crude birth rate was 21.8 in 2000 (against 25.8 for India) and crude death rate was 5.7 (against 8.5 for India). By 2002, 90 per cent of infants were immunised against the six killer diseases. However, even though the share of people below the poverty line has steadily decreased, malnutrition continues to be an issue.

The changing nature of health requirements and the pressure on health amenities are the major challenges in the health sector. Health problems arising from environmental pollution, improper sanitation, and contaminated water persist in both the urban and rural areas, and there is a gradual emergence of coronary diseases, AIDS, and diabetes in urban areas. These, and the re-emergence of diseases like tuberculosis will place enormous pressure on the public facilities.

Even though the state has a higher number of doctors and nurses than the national norm, the health system suffers from inadequacies and lack of appropriate planning. There is a shortage of necessary infrastructure, quality of health staff and availability of medicines.

The management and maintenance of the massive infrastructures and deployment of the health manpower are major concerns. This will be heightened by the increase in the incidence of diseases arising out of both poverty and stress factors. This is where the role of non-governmental organisations comes into the fore. All the primary health centres should therefore, be handed over to the *panchayats* who could run with the support of reputed NGOs which are already involved in providing health education awareness in hygiene and other communicable diseases.

The mountainous terrain hampers the timely and efficient delivery of health services in the interior regions. Interventions like those provided by AUSaid and the Sikkim Manipal University could improve efficiency in health management. Health insurance could be considered as an option to the indiscriminate provision of treatment to patients referred outside state hospitals. The 15 per cent gap in male and female literacy rates has had serious implications on women's health. The emphasis naturally should be on preventive health, through very specialised and focused efforts to increase awareness and through education.

Sikkim is the land of faith healers. There has been a long-felt need to record traditional systems of medicine (TSM)–related knowledge and to examine whether natural biodiversity components are being used effectively for healthcare. In the absence of any systematic study, it is very difficult to assess their vanishing traits on the population.

The state needs to upgrade and rationalise the health information system. The lack of institutionalised monitoring and evaluation mechanisms for health-related projects has made the system slow, tardy, insensitive, and inefficient.

The health sector can be promoted as a potential avenue for investment, which would have revenue-enhancing and employment-generation benefits. The health insurance as a second-generation reform measure must be encouraged both to make the health amenities more sustainable and efficient use of health and financial resources.

Infrastructure

Economic progress is intrinsically linked to connectivity. For Sikkim, in the absence of rail or air services, roads are the only life line. But the slow pace of expansion and poor maintenance of the road network is worrisome. The construction of road network should receive high priority and it should no longer be used to serve short-term goals such as employment-generation. Professional firms have to be involved in the mechanised construction of roads, which should be sanctioned only after conducting a thorough environmental impact assessment.

A good telecommunications system could help overcome some of the geographical and locational disadvantages of the mountainous state, and compensate for the lack of a good road network. Information Technology has made a promising start with the establishment of several CICs across the state, some in relatively remote villages. The full potential quality of life of people in remote areas needs to be explored.

Sikkim's hydelpower potential of 8,000 MW remains largely unharnessed, and the state contributes only 0.2

per cent to the total installed hydelpower capacity in the country. Energy sources have been used inefficiently and imprudently. Power generation and its supply continue to remain a state monopoly. Energy prices have been kept low, revenue collection is unsatisfactory and transmission and distribution losses abound. Further, the distribution network is inefficient and technically unsound, management of the utilities is poor, the utilities are overstaffed and the employees lack adequate training and discipline.

A majority of the people are willing to pay a higher tariff for ensured regular supply of quality power. But this calls for the time-bound restructuring of the power sector. Rural electrification has been the most daunting task in Sikkim. The state has announced full rural electrification, but the use of electricity in villages is still very limited.

Investment in the power sector in the state must be made more broad-based and competitive. For this the state has to make its investment policies and enabling laws attractive as well as investor friendly. The thrust on power development in the state should be in power trading and export. A serious and institutionalised machinery should be set up for this purpose urgently. The possibilities of power trading with other states and the neighbouring countries should be explored. Neighbouring Bhutan is an apt example of how hydelpower potential can transform the entire economy and development orientation.

The environmental impact assessment studies for the power projects should be carried out in a more transparent, open, and all encompassing manner particularly in terms of involving the local stakeholders. This is rather a necessity.

The harnessing of opportunities generated by the reopening of the Nathu La trade route in 2006 would largely depend upon the development of infrastructure. The Nathu La Trade Study Group has stated that the preparation on the Chinese side is being done on a massive scale whereas it is not to be found so on the Indian side. The most crucial 143 kms road link between Siliguri and Nathu La *via* Gangtok requires significant upgradation. The highway is also expected to act as a vital link to the old trade route between India and Tibet/China through the Nathu La pass. Efforts to improve the highway and link it with the pass are being looked after by Sikkim Industrial Development and Investment Corporation Limited (SIDICO). Future plans for the highway include linking it with the east-west corridor and with the golden quadrilateral, so that the state becomes better integrated with the other parts of the country.

Given the expectation, the nature and composition of trade through Nathu La and the topographical constraints on the existing Jawaharlal Nehru Road from Gangtok to Nathu La, the search for alternative roads to reach this pass is already on. The multiple routing to reach Nathu La should be explored both to avoid congestion and minimise the uncertainties caused by weather/climatic conditions. This would also reduce environmental degradations. Given the extent of infrastructure required and the likely gains in the long run, the Nathu La Trade Study Group has recommended a one time Infrastructure Development Package of Rs. 1650–1700 crore. This would greatly facilitate the development of the trade route both within Sikkim and its periphery areas in Darjeeling district.

Agriculture, Horticulture and Animal Husbandry

The vital role that these sectors play in the state's economy makes it imperative that development strategies are focused on them. Around 64 per cent of the working population is dependent on agriculture for a living, and 89 per cent is rural based. Productivity has been low and declining across all these sectors, and while agriculture and animal husbandry are conducted as subsistence vocations, horticulture, especially large cardamom and ginger and flowers have great potential for commercial production. However, the absence of strong marketing links and storage facilities, and high transport costs have given farmers little incentive to increase production.

Overall strategy should involve a shift from providing free inputs to farmers to improving vital infrastructure such as irrigation, strengthening marketing links and promoting private initiatives in areas like animal health, feed and fodder supply, nurseries and storage facilities. The application of scientific and more technologically advanced farming methods is becoming imperative. A basis for this can be laid by promoting better-directed, state-relevant research in the many research institutes located in Sikkim, and better dissemination of successful outcomes.

No agri-based value addition is done within the state, and oranges, once made into juices and jams within Sikkim, are now exported to Bhutan for processing. There is tremendous potential for value addition in the form of fruit processing, cardamom-oil extraction, ginger-preserving, etc., which needs to be tapped for its employment and revenue-generation potential. The agri-export zones proposed for some horticultural products are expected to strengthen the horticulture supply chain from the farmer to the market, and create jobs, but this initiative has been slow to take off.

The government intends to declare the entire state 'organic' by 2009. However, given the high transition costs, large scale research and extension into organic practises and methods appropriate for Sikkim and creating organic marketing links, the preferred option should be to promote organic farming in a selective manner.

Industry and Trade

Despite positive real growth in the state, industry has been lagging in terms of employment and output. The Industrial Policy, 2003 identifies and announces incentives for areas such as agro-based industry including tea and medicinal plants, tourism-related industry, knowledge-based industry, and developing Sikkim as a hub for education and health. However, it is questionable whether financial concessions alone can attract entrepreneurs, without adequate infrastructure and requisite skills and expertise among the working population.

In view of the fragility of the environment and lack of comparative advantage for many industries, only selected industries ought to be promoted. The strategy for industrial development should have both micro-level and macro-level components. Micro-level policy will provide inputs and information to individuals, expand the scope of the CICs, and use local bodies to identify households capable of initiating businesses in agro-based industries, handicrafts, and tourism. Macro-level policy will focus on setting up growth centres, to circumvent constraints related to availability of land and infrastructure, formation of an investment board, developing a marketing network and strengthening infrastructure, especially power, transport, and communication.

The reopening of the traditional trade route between Sikkim and Tibet Autonomous region of China in 2006 is to transform the entire development process in and around Sikkim into a robust and flourishing system. For Sikkim, its geographical location has been the main constraint in its development. However, the Nathu La trade route has made the same geographical location the most advantageous location.

There are indeed very distinct advantages. The Nathu La Trade Study Group has estimated that on the higher side projection, trade flow through Nathu La will be $ 48 million (Rs. 206 crore) by 2007, $ 527 million (Rs. 2266 crore) by 2010 and $ 2.84 billion (Rs. 12,203 crore) by 2015. On the lower side projection, trade volume passing through Nathu La route will be Rs. 353 crore in 2010, Rs. 450 crore in 2015, and Rs. 574 crore in 2020.

Besides generating a huge revenue for the state in terms of license fees, toll taxes etc, trade-related activities could lead to direct employment of 4000 to 10,000 persons per annum (including drivers, cleaners, mechanics, loaders, warehouse keepers) and other major cascading impacts like income and employment through opening of restaurants, shops, petrol pumps, telephone booths, banking, hotels and other civic and administrative amenities on the roadside.

There is marked potential of investment activities on both sides of the border in Sikkim and Tibet Autonomous region of China in the aftermath of the reopening of Nathu La trade route. Despite so many concessions extended by the Government of Sikkim, very few investors have come to the state in the past. One of the main reasons attributed to the shyness of investment in the state is the high transport cost and limited market options. Therefore, once the Nathu La trade route is reopened, Tibet and mainland China will act as additional marketing outlets. This is bound to encourage and trigger investment activities in Sikkim and surrounding areas.

Tourism

The state's rich natural and cultural resources have not been developed to their full tourism potential. Efforts by the tourism department and travel operators and hoteliers have slowly begun to impact on the pattern of tourist traffic. If developed in a sensitive manner, tourism can be one of the main avenues to create employment to the youth and accelerate sustainable development.

The government has a clearly enunciated commitment to promoting alternate forms of tourism which are also the new leisure time activities across the world. More relaxed permit systems and the opening up of the Nathu La pass are expected to boost tourist traffic. The World Tourism and Travel Council has predicted that travel and tourism demand in India will grow by 8.8 per cent per annum, in real terms, between

2004 and 2014. Sikkim is in a good position to take advantage of this growth.

To be in line with the overall development paradigm for the state, tourism development will have to be sustainable—environmentally, culturally, and economically—with a focus on 'non-mass' segments, such as eco-tourism, adventure tourism, village tourism. This will entail a shrinking role for the government in the active provision of tourism services and the increasing participation of private providers. Rural communities and village-based NGOs will play an important part in making a success of rural tourism, spreading environmental awareness, training local people and ensuring a more equitable dispersion of the benefits. The government in turn needs to be actively involved in providing enabling infrastructure, preserving natural habitats, promoting the state as a whole, enabling the involvement of other agencies and, most important, regulating tourism services and initiatives.

The Nathu La Trade Study Group has recommended integration of trade with tourism between Sikkim and Tibet Autonomous region of China by 2012. For this a fresh bilateral legal framework needs to be set up to facilitate the movement of tourists across the border. The Group also recommended that by 2018, these tourism linkages should be extended to *SAARC* tourism thereby integrating tourism activities of third countries of the region including Bangladesh, Bhutan and Nepal. This would mean opening up all the SAARC tourists to cross the border through Nathu La.

A modern museum that would house all the artefacts, archival materials, memoirs and other objects related to various missions, agreements, and physical exchanges regarding Nathu La trade may be set up at Nathu La.

Rural Development

Sikkim's economy is basically rural. The vast majority of the population (around 90 per cent) is rural-based. Agriculture is the most important occupation. Mixed farming with animal husbandry is also common. Poverty and unemployment are the twin blocks of rural development. Most of the poverty alleviation programmes have failed to generate the expected levels of income and employment in the state.

The pattern of growth in rural employment over the last decade is not very healthy. A fall in the proportion of main workers and a drastic rise in the proportion of marginal workers accompany the rise in the proportion of total workers. East and south, with relatively greater concentration of industries and tourism opportunities have witnessed a slightly better pattern with a rise in the proportion of main worker. In the north the proportion of total workers has risen, with the most pronounced rise (in terms of percentage points) in the proportion of marginal workers mostly because of migration. West recorded a rise in the proportion of non-workers, which is even worse.

Rural connectivity is one of the biggest challenges for policy making in Sikkim, and progress on building rural roads has been slow. Housing and access to basic amenities such as electricity, drinking water and toilets, however, have improved for rural households which, indicates an improvement in the standard of living. Given the stagnancy in employment generation, some of this improvement can be attributed to housing and other policy initiatives. However, a superficial growth of houses has resulted from the model village schemes, the sustainability of which is questionable.

Sikkim has a strong two-tier *panchayat* network with four *zilla panchayats* and 166 *gram panchayat* units, with two traditional *zumsas* still operating as self-governments in the north district. From 2003 onwards decentralisation of financial power to the *panchayats* has been effected. Efforts are on to make the process a success by effective capacity building of the elected representatives to suit the changing scenario of panchayati raj institutions.

Development of Forest Resources

Deforestation is a critical issue for the state's fragile environment. Despite its many traditional forest laws, steady deforestation took place in the past, mainly because of energy needs, land diversion for development activities, commercial deforestation, forest fires, grazing and natural calamities.

Forestry, if linked to the rural development, could benefit a large number of people. If afforestation were made part of the rural development schemes, and part of people's livelihoods, this would naturally lead to forest protection. One way would be to link afforestation with the 'food for work programme' so as to match generation of income, employment, and environmental protection.

The poor coordination, low productivity and dismal usefulness of most of the central institutions working on forest, agriculture, and environment located in Sikkim should be put to a halt urgently. They should be made more purposive and useful.

The state has a wide and undiscovered development frontier in the scientific and commercial harnessing of its medicinal plants. To explore this to its full potential, it is important to: i) develop a well-planned strategy to explore medicinal plant-wealth of the state; ii) explore methods of propagation; iii) encourage sustainable harvesting of plants from the wild; iv) involve small farmers and communities in their cultivation; and v) conduct phyto-chemical, pharmacological and pharmacognostic studies on commercially exploitable species.

The TRIPS requirements under the WTO will have major relevance for a biodiversity rich state like Sikkim, which will have to address issues varying from patenting to livelihood. A national institute for natural resources management should be set up as a centre of conservation techniques, and one of its first tasks will be to develop a biodiversity data bank and status report of plant species. Scientific monitoring of biodiversity should be initiated largely based on participatory process at the grassroots level. NGOs have begun playing a role in environmental management. However, there needs to be an independent, non-governmental mechanism to promote and regulate NGO activities in the state.

Urban Development

Although Sikkim is still primarily an agrarian state, its urban areas have begun to experience the pressures of urbanisation mainly because of growing migration. Migration is likely to continue in the medium term. Rapid urbanisation has not been matched by appropriate planning and management, investment in urban systems, or improvements in service delivery. Haphazard, unplanned growth has put unsustainable pressure on the environment as it has led to spiralling pollution and congestion, construction which puts the landscape at risk, and overburdened urban service networks, leading to water and soil contamination.

The absence of any elected municipal bodies, non-implementation of any of the master plans and a general apathy towards vehicular congestion, unauthorised construction, and disregard for urban aesthetics are fast making the growth of Gangtok, and other towns, unsustainable. Growth needs to be regionally balanced and future development initiatives need to be located in other towns, besides Gangtok, which today is the centre of all activity—administrative, commercial, cultural, tourism, education and health-related. The explosion in vehicular traffic calls for an immediate reduction in taxi licenses and government vehicles, supplemented by a minibus system within the city.

Scheduled Castes and Scheduled Tribes

Sikkim has an interesting history of evolution of the ethnic groups in the state. *Lepchas* are considered to be the original inhabitants of the state. In 1642, the *Bhutia* rule started in Sikkim under the influence of Tibetan theocracy. It was the first attempt of racial assimilation by *Bhutia* immigrants.

With the signing of the Anglo-Chinese convention at Calcutta in March, 1890, Sikkim became protectorate of British India. British contact brought in a new type of administration, revenue system, forest conservation rules and development of the area by improving the communication network. Nepali immigration was encouraged, as labour was needed for construction of roads and extension of agriculture. The ethnic composition of Sikkim changed rapidly as the Nepalese multiplied in number and has increased the latter's present share to more than 80 per cent of the population

Lepchas and *Bhutias* got the constitutional status of scheduled tribes (ST) after Sikkim's merger with India. The scheduled castes (SCs) and other backward classes (OBCs) are from Nepali community. Very recently two Nepali communities, *Limbu* and *Tamang* have been included in the ST category. STs constitute 20.6 per cent, SCs 5 per cent and the OBCs 40 per cent of the total population.

Among the four scheduled castes in Sikkim, *Kami* as a caste has the highest proportion followed by *Damai*, *Sarki* and *Majhi*. *Kami* and *Damai* constitute more than 95 per cent of the community of ST population. Among the tribes in Sikkim, *Bhutias* have a greater proportion than the *Lepchas* within the tribal community. However in the north district, the *Lepchas* outnumber the *Bhutias*.

Unlike the rest of India, in Sikkim there is not much difference between the development indicators of the ST, SC, OBC communities and those of the others. Among the STs, *Lepchas* are weaker of the lot. Among the SCs, *Damais* are the most progressive followed by *Kamis*, *Majhis*, and *Sarkis*.

A critical assessment of the policies designed for development of these communities reveals that often the beneficiaries are not from the most deserving sections of these communities. Policies aiming at poverty alleviation and employment generation should be formulated and implemented to ensure that the benefits percolate to the lowest strata of the communities. Education and skill development programmes for these communities need to be strengthened. Sensitising the masses regarding the amendment of the land alienation law in the state is an immediate need as such an amendment is expected to minimise many distortions in the economy.

Ensuring Governance

A major hindrance to the formulation of appropriate policy is the severe lack of reliable statistics in almost all the sectors. It is difficult to target poverty alleviation programmes when accurate poverty figures are not available for the state, and estimates for Assam are used as a proxy for the State. Similarly, the severe downward revision of estimates of agricultural and horticultural output along with areas and yields in 2001 after the re-estimation based on full enumeration means a break in the trend, with no plausible explanation. Even when official data exist, different sources provide contradictory data as in the case of tourist arrivals into the state.

The quality of governance is another major issue. Many of the centrally sponsored programmes, especially those dealing with rural poverty alleviation and employment generation, show high degrees of leakage. Transparency and widely disseminated information and data will reduce avenues for corruption, expose project delays and programme flaws, and improve programme monitoring and functioning. Governance is also a crucial issue in improved expenditure management. There should be a halt to the regularisation of muster roll and daily wage workers, and moves should be made to eliminate 'ghost' workers from the rolls. Downsizing the government will be possible if all new employment is made on contractual basis. Enforced car-pooling will help reduce car maintenance expenditures and decongest the capital. Local participation in budget-making and spending would ensure transparency and plugging of leakages, a prerequisite for better delivery of public services.

Chapter 1

Sikkim: Development Profile and Future Directions

Sikkim, which was a protectorate, became a state of the Indian Union in 1975. It is the smallest state of India in terms of area and population. It is a landlocked state nestled in the Himalayas with Tibet to the north and northeast, Bhutan to the east, Nepal to the west, and Darjeeling district of West Bengal to the south. Though the state started late on its road to development, it has caught up with others rather quickly.

Sikkim is gifted with a rich biodiversity and a variety of natural resources. The state has been aiming to pursue an eco-friendly sustainable development process during the last 30 years. With over 500 species of orchids, 28 mountain peaks, 21 glaciers, 227 lakes and wetlands, one national park and six wild life sanctuaries, Sikkim is emerging as a popular tourist destination in India. Sikkim is also the largest producer/exporter of large cardamom accounting for about a half of the total world production. However, a stagnant agriculture and steadily declining industrial activity have severely hampered the development process. The government has been at the centre stage of development and has been involved in every sphere of activity. Since non-government employment opportunities are minimal, the government has become the principal employer. This has put the government under severe fiscal stress.

1.1 Sikkim's Performance at the National Level

The growth rate of state domestic product (SDP) of Sikkim during the IXth Plan at 8.3 per cent per annum was the highest among the Indian states. Only two UTs, *viz.*, Chandigarh and Puducherry and the National Capital Territory (NCT) of Delhi experienced higher growth rates. However, since Sikkim was a relatively poor state to start with, even after this impressive growth performance, the rank of the state in per capita income terms was 11 at the beginning of the Xth plan. The projected growth rate of SDP for Sikkim during the Xth plan is 7.9 per cent per annum against the national target of 8 per cent. The decomposition of the projected growth rate sectorally is agriculture (5 per cent), industry (5.2 per cent) and services (10.4 per cent). In comparison to the national target of agriculture (4.0 per cent), industry (8.9 per cent) and services (9.4 per cent), the state is expected to perform much better in agriculture and services.

1.2 Development of Social and Economic Infrastructure

In terms of income poverty, Sikkim's position is ever more worrisome. The latest available estimates for 1999-2000 indicate that the share of population below the poverty line in Sikkim is 36.6 per cent. Even the projected level of poverty in the state at the end of the Xth plan at 33.8 per cent is significantly higher than the national average of 19.3 per cent. One major limitation of the poverty estimates for the state, however, is the fact that they are based on the household data for Assam. The only Sikkim factor is the adjustment for price differentials based on prices prevailing in Sikkim. This is an anomaly, which needs to be corrected.

In terms of human development, Sikkim is far better than majority of the states. According to census 2001, Sikkim's level of literacy at 68.8 per cent is the 9th highest among the states of India. In terms of female literacy also, the state fares much better than most of the states. The state has achieved spectacular improvement in universalising literacy over the last quarter century.

The important health indicators also show that Sikkim has made impressive progress. The total fertility rate of Sikkim at 2.75 in 1998 was well below the national average of 3.2. The fertility levels of 17 states are above that of Sikkim. Again, the infant mortality of Sikkim at 52 per 1000 live births in 2001 was well below the national average of 71. In terms of access to safe drinking water, the position of Sikkim is significantly better than most states. The latest available data for 2001 indicate that 81 per cent of Sikkim households had access to safe drinking water as against the national average of 62.3 per cent. In urban areas of Sikkim access was as much as 97 per cent as compared to 81.4 per cent at all India level. While 78 per cent of the total households has electricity in Sikkim, it's share in urban household is as high as 97 per cent.

Sikkim, however, suffers from a huge disadvantage in terms of access and infrastructure. The state is land-locked and mountainous. The state has neither air link nor rail link with the rest of the country. The long-standing efforts to build the first airport of the state at Pakyong have been delayed due to the problems of acquiring the requisite land and capacity to commit funds. Indeed, flat land is very scarce in the state. The lifeline of the state connecting it to the rest of the country is highway 31A running parallel to Teesta river which links Gangtok to Siliguri in West Bengal. Even this link road which is maintained by the Border Road Organisation (BRO) is subject to frequent landslides, especially during the monsoon season. Within the state also, the road connectivity is inadequate for essential movements and economic activities of the people. Road density in Sikkim measured in terms of road length per 1000 sq. kms of area is the lowest among all the states in the country.

One of the most valuable resources of the state is its hydel potential which is estimated to be over 8000 MWs. However, only a minuscule share of this vast potential has been exploited so far. As a result, Sikkim has very low availability of electricity. Per capita consumption of electricity in the state in 1999-2000 was just 192 kwh against the all India average of 355 kwh. This position is likely to improve significantly when the ongoing hydel projects on Teesta river are commissioned in 2007. This is likely to drastically improve the power situation and the sale of power also fetch a handsome revenue for the state.

1.3 Sikkim's Development Profile in the Regional Context

Sikkim was included as a member of the North-Eastern Council in 2002. The Council functions as a planning body for the overall development of the north-eastern region comprising of 8 states including Sikkim. All the 8 states are characterised as special category states (SCS). And except for Assam came into existence much after the states' reorganisation in 1956. They are mostly hilly and inhabited by tribal people. Poor infrastructure and connectivity are a common problem for all (N.E.) states of them. All the 8 north-eastern states have sensitive international borders. Sikkim is one of the most peaceful states in the country.

A comparison of the development profile of Sikkim *vis-à-vis* other N.E. states will place the needs of Sikkim in the correct perspective. Table 1.1 presents the

TABLE 1.1

Per Capita Income and Poverty

States	*Per Capita NSDP* (Rs.)*			*Percentage of Population Below Poverty Line*		
	1990-91	*1999-2000*	*2000-01*	*1973-74*	*1993-94*	*1999-2000*
India				54.88	35.97	26.1
Sikkim	**7375**	**10250**	**NA**	**50.86**	**41.43**	**36.35**
Arunachal Pradesh	6927	8521	9575	51.93	39.35	33.47
Nagaland	8313	8726	NA	50.81	37.92	32.67
Manipur	5393	6873	6573	49.96	33.78	28.54
Mizoram				50.32	25.66	19.47
Tripura	5026	7967	9397	51	39.01	34.44
Meghalaya	6928	9003	9427	50.2	37.92	33.87
Assam	5574	5785	5867	51.21	40.86	36.09

Note: *: Per capita NSDP at constant prices (1993-94).

Source: Indian Public Finance Statistics, 2003-04 and Poverty figures from the *Tenth Five Year Plan: Volume III.*

comparative picture in terms of per capita income and the level of poverty. In 1990-91, Sikkim had the second highest average income after Nagaland. By 1999-2000 Sikkim had overtaken Nagaland. The income estimate for Sikkim in 2000-01 is not available. However, it is safe to assume that Sikkim maintained the first position in that year also in view of the very high growth of NSDP during the IXth plan period.

Because of the low level of incomes, the incidence of poverty in the N.E. states is higher than that for the country as a whole. The state-wise estimates of poverty for three time-periods presented in Table 1.1 reveals this. There, however, is a limitation to the poverty estimates of the N.E. states. They are all based on the field data relating to Assam. Only the price variations and the rural-urban population shares influence the state specific estimates. Because of the high cost of transport and the relatively low share of urban population the level of poverty is higher in Sikkim compared to other N.E. states. Indeed Sikkim's poverty level was the highest among N.E. States in 1993-94 and 1999-2000.

The relative development of Sikkim and other N.E. states in terms of infrastructure development is presented in Table 1.2. In terms of per capita consumption of electricity which is a good indicator of development, the position of N.E. states is far below the national average. Sikkim's relative position in the N.E., however, is better.

In terms of road density, the situation in N.E. is generally poor and Sikkim's position, even worse. As compared to the national average of 749 km per 1000 sq. km of area, Sikkim has only 258 km per 1000 sq. km. Among the N.E. states, the density of road in Sikkim is better than only Arunachal Pradesh and Mizoram.

The density of post offices measured in terms of population per post office in higher in Sikkim than all other N.E. states, except Mizoram.

The comparative picture of access to safe drinking water in N.E. states for 1991 is somewhat dated. The relative position of Sikkim, however, is quite good. At 73 per cent Sikkim has the highest level of access to safe drinking water in north-east and the state betters the national average of 62 per cent.

Index of social and economic infrastructure for 1999 worked out by the Eleventh Finance Commission placed Sikkim ahead of all the other N.E. states and above the national average as is given in the last column of Table 1.2.

Sectoral composition of plan expenditure of N.E. states at three different points of time is presented in Table 1.3. Social sector expenditure in Sikkim was one of the lowest among N.E. states in 1981-82. Thanks to consistent effort by the government, by 1997-98, the social sector expenditure in the State was one of the highest among the N.E. states. Even as the share of social sector in plan expenditure in all the N.E. states has been increasing in the 1980s and 1990s, the growth of social sector spending in Sikkim has been distinctly higher. Indeed, this has resulted in better performance in terms of human development indicators in Sikkim.

TABLE 1.2

Infrastructure and Development

Infrastructure	*Per Capita Consumption of Electricity,1999-2000 (in kwh)*	*Road Length Per 1000 sq. km of Area in 1996-97*	*Population under One Post Office, 1999-2000 (2001 Population)*	*Access to Safe Drinking Water in per cent of Households, 1991*	*Index of Social and Economic Infrastructure, 1999*
India	354.7	749	6639	62.3	100
Sikkim	**192.4**	**258**	**2647**	**73.19**	**109**
Arunachal Pradesh	68.6	168	3627	70.02	69.7
Nagaland	84.7	1107	6623	53.37	76.1
Manipur	69.5	490	3123	38.72	75.4
Mizoram	120.7	229	2221	16.21	82.1
Tripura	95.5	1405	4464	37.18	74.9
Meghalaya	160.3	278	4721	36.16	75.5
Assam	95.5	872	6776	45.86	77.7

Source: Planning Commission. *Tenth Five-Year Plan 2002-2007: Volume-III.*

TABLE 1.3

Sectoral Composition of Actual Plan Expenditure

States	*Social Sector*			*Infrastructure*		
	1981-82	*1991-92*	*1997-98*	*1981-82*	*1991-92*	*1997-98*
Sikkim	**19.83**	**28.09**	**45.38**	**41.42**	**47.07**	**32.9**
Arunachal Pradesh	24.59	25.9	29.65	45.66	47.07	46.37
Nagaland	26.65	24.38	36.73	39.33	30.42	19.87
Manipur	29.07	24.58	32.44	29.93	37.31	38.57
Mizoram	26.54	25.68	30.35	45.93	35.38	41.1
Tripura	28.69	30.16	43.18	27.53	26.11	22.34
Meghalaya	28.97	29.32	37.83	45.09	38.99	33.58
Assam	17.97	34.31	45.89	52.56	29.97	22.12

Source: Planning Commission. *Tenth Five Year Plan 2002-2007: Volume-III.*

A few important demographic and health indicators for different N.E. states and all-India are given in Table 1.4. The sex ratio at 875 is the lowest for Sikkim among N.E. states. It is also well below the national average. This is surprising as in terms of child sex ratio, Sikkim stands to be better than all India average of 963 though still below most of the N.E. states.

Total fertility figures presented in column 4 indicate that Sikkim has the lowest figure among N.E. states except for Arunachal Pradesh and this is well below the national average. Infant mortality figures in column 5 show that N.E. states except Assam are better off than the country. At 52, infant mortality for Sikkim is better than that of only Assam in the N.E. region.

The N.E. states including Sikkim have been devoting a fairly high share of plan expenditure on infrastructure during the first two time periods. The worrisome fact is that for majority of N.E. states including Sikkim, infrastructure share in plan expenditure came down sharply by 1997-98.

Table 1.5 presents the state-wise literacy levels in N.E. states and at all-India level. Except Arunachal Pradesh, Meghalaya, and Assam, the level of literacy is higher in other N.E. states as compared to the national average. Mizoram, Tripura, and Manipur have literacy levels higher than that of Sikkim. The gender gap in literacy in the region is significantly lower than that of the country. In terms of gender equity, Sikkim fares better than four of its neighbours. But the state has to go a long way to catch up with Mizoram in gender equity in literacy.

TABLE 1.4

Sex Ratio, Total Fertility and Infant Mortality

States	*General*			
	Sex Ratio	*Sex Ratio (0-6) yrs*	*Total Fertility 1998*	*Infant Mortality 2004*
India	933	927	3.2	71
Sikkim	**875**	**963**	**2.8**	**52**
Arunachal Pradesh	893	964	2.5	44
Nagaland	900	964	3.8	NA
Manipur	978	957	3	25
Mizoram	935	964	2.89	23
Tripura	948	966	N.A	49
Meghalaya	972	973	4.6	52
Assam	935	965	3.2	78

Source: Planning Commission. *Tenth Five-Year Plan 2002-2007: Volume III.*

TABLE 1.5

Literacy and Gender Gap

States	*General*			
	Literacy Rate			*Gender Gap in Literacy*
	Persons	*Male*	*Female*	
India	64.8	75.3	53.7	21.6
Sikkim	**68.8**	**76**	**60.4**	**15.6**
Arunachal Pradesh	54.3	63.8	43.5	20.3
Nagaland	66.6	71.2	61.5	9.7
Manipur	70.5	80.3	60.5	19.8
Mizoram	88.8	90.7	86.7	4
Tripura	73.2	81	64.9	16.1
Meghalaya	62.6	65.4	59.6	5.8
Assam	63.3	71.3	54.6	16.7

Source: Planning Commission. *Tenth Five Year Plan 2002-2007: Vol. III.*

TABLE 1.6

District-wise Key Indicators: Sikkim

Indicators	*Total*	*North*	*West*	*South*	*East*
Area (sq. kms.)	7096	4226	954	750	1166
Districts (no.)	4	1	1	1	1
Sub-divisions (no.) (2001)	9	2	2	2	3
Zilla panchayat wards (no.)	100	20	25	24	31
Gram panchayat units (no.)	166	20	51	45	50
Gram panchayat wards (no.)	886	103	255	255	273
Revenue blocks/villages (no.)	454	54	122	145	133*
Towns (no.)	8	1	2	2	3
Households (no.) 2001	114223	10921	23244	25477	54581
Population 2001	540851	41030	123256	131525	245040
Urban Population (%)	11.1	3	1.5	3	21.6
Rural Population (%)	88.9	97	98.5	97	78.4
ST population (%)	20.6**	53.1	19.3	15.6	18.5
SC population (%)	5	2.1	4.7	4.8	5.8
Decennial growth rate 1991-2001	33.1	31.3	25.6	33.4	37.3
Population density (per sq. m)	76	10	106	175	257
Literacy rate 2001	68.8	67.2	58.8	67.3	74.7
Males	76	75.7	66.8	74.3	81.2
Females	60.4	55.4	50.1	59.7	66.8
Total main workers (%) 2001	39.4	42.8	36.8	43.6	37.8
Marginal workers (%) 2001	9.3	14.6	6.4	9.4	9.8
Non-workers (%) 2001	51.4	42.6	56.8	47	52.4

Note: *: 2 uninhabited villages; **: This is likely to go up sharply after the census of the two newly included scheduled tribes is carried out in 2005.

Source: Census 2001; No. of towns according to *Economic Survey of Sikkim, 2003-2004*.

1.4 Intrastate Development Trends

Sikkim is divided into four districts and 9 subdivisions for administrative purposes. While north district accounts for about 60 per cent of the geographical area of the state, east district accounts for over 45 per cent of the population. In terms of most of the developmental indicators, east district which has got Gangtok, the state capital, is ahead of the other three districts. A few key indicators are given district-wise in Table 1.6.

Table 1.7 presents district-wise health infrastructure in 2001. While in terms of number of primary health centres and sub-centres, the coverage of east district is poorer compared to the others, in terms of hospital beds situation it is far better in east district. This is principally owing to the fact that the state referral hospital is located in Gangtok.

District-wise sex ratio and child sex ratios are presented in Table 1.8. Sex ratio varies considerably across districts. While the west and south have much more favourable sex ratios, north has abysmally low sex ratio. When it comes to child sex ratio the differences narrow down considerably. While low sex ratio in east district can be explained in terms of male migration in search of employment, the very low sex ratio in north district is rather difficult to explain

TABLE 1.7

Health Infrastructure

State/ District	*PHC Nos.*	*Population Per PHC*	*PHSC Nos.*	*Population per PHSC*	*Total Beds Nos.*	*Population per Bed*
East	8	30630	48	5105	480	511
West	7	17608	41	3006	120	1027
North	3	13677	19	2159	80	513
South	6	21921	39	3372	160	822
State	24	22535	147	3679	840	644

Note: Population figures correspond to 2001 Census; Total beds include beds in PHCs, State Referral Hospital, and Community Health Centers.

Source: Dept. of Health, Govt. of Sikkim.

TABLE 1.8

General and Child Sex Ratio

State/District	*General*	
	Sex Ratio	*Sex Ratio (0-6) yrs*
Sikkim	875	963
North	752	995
West	929	966
South	927	969
East	844	950

Source: Census of India, 2001.

TABLE 1.10

District-wise Literacy Rate in Sikkim

State/District	*Literacy Rate*			*Gender Gap in Literacy*
	Persons	*Male*	*Female*	
Sikkim	68.8	76	60.4	15.6
North	67.2	75.7	55.4	20.3
West	58.8	66.8	50.1	16.7
South	67.3	74.3	59.7	14.6
East	74.7	81.2	66.8	14.4

Source: Census of India, 2001.

Tables 1.9 and 1.10 present the district-wise distribution of educational institutions and the level of literacy. It is clear that east has an edge over the other districts in terms of institutions and the literacy outcomes. Gender gap in literacy is highest in the north district. An unfavourable sex ratio coupled with high gender gap in literacy qualifies north district to be characterised as the gender insensitive district of Sikkim.

1.5 Objectives of State Development Report

The Sikkim Development Report attempts to draw a roadmap for the social and economic development of the state for the next 15 to 20 years. As already noted, the state has achieved a relatively high level of social development, but despite high growth seen in recent years, the level of per capita income is still relatively low and, poverty remains relatively high.

The state has several strong points for achieving fast growth. It is a peaceful state. It has an ideal climate and natural beauty. The state has great potential for tourism. There is substantial hydelpower potential. The state is rich in herbal and medicinal plants. The horticultural potential is only partially exploited. Its location and international borders offer great potential for trade-led growth. It has got cheap labour which adds to its competitiveness. The principal weaknesses or handicap of the state are its small size, fragile ecology, poor connectivity, underdeveloped infrastructure and shortage of skills, expertise, and enterprises.

TABLE 1.9

Number of Government Educational Institutions: 2005

Categories	*East*	*West*	*North*	*South*	*Total*
LPS	35	62	21	48	166
PS	110	95	39	92	336
JHS	48	36	16	47	147
SS	30	23	11	28	92
SSS	19	10	3	9	41
Total	242	226	90	224	782

Note: LPS: Lower Primary School; PS: Primary School; JHS: Junior High School; SS: Secondary School and SSS: Senior Secondary School.

Source: Data supplied by Human Resource Development Department, Government of Sikkim, 2005.

The development strategy should build on the strengths of the state, to overcome the handicaps and to convert the handicaps into strengths. International experience shows that achieving the goals in social development is more difficult than economic goals. The state has already solved the more difficult problem by achieving a fair level of social development. Now the state will have to turn to the less difficult task of economic development to ensure higher and sustainable incomes to all households in the state.

The proposed strategy of development concentrates on empowerment of people by education and healthcare, infrastructure development, harnessing of natural resources and fiscal consolidation. The development strategy should build around both the government and the private sector, NGOs and CBOs.

Human development should continue to get priority. Universal literacy and universal healthcare should be ensured at the earliest. Higher education and skill formation will be given highest priority. Food and nutrition security have to be ensured. Infrastructure development will focus on three areas, *viz.*, power, roads and transport, and communication. Concentration will be on three driving forces, *viz.*, governance, resource mobilisation and people's participation.

Fiscal consolidation will have to get high priority. Healthy growth of revenues will have to be ensured, revenue base should be diversified, allocative and technical efficiency in public spending must be ensured, and accountability must be enforced.

The great potential of reopening of Nathu La trade route should be fully exploited. The requisite infrastructure should be in position at the earliest. Appropriate policies have to be evolved to ensure optimum benefit to the state which will be widely shared by the people.

Sikkim has to evolve itself as an important regional player in the north-eastern region. The state has to ensure full benefit as the eighth member of NEC. Sikkim has to position itself to benefit from trade with neighbouring states as well as neighbouring countries.

The benefits of development of the state should be equitably distributed among all Sikkimese. To achieve this goal, the growth strategy should be an inclusive one. This can be ensured only by employment and incomes to all. Government should facilitate rather than create employment. Development and growth should be regionally balanced. Promotion of eco-tourism in the remote areas will ensure this to an extent. Other activities with great employment potential to be promoted are agro-processing and knowledge-based industries. Further, with appropriate policies Sikkim can be offered as a hub for education and healthcare.

Chapter 2

Natural Resource Management and Sustainable Development

Sikkim is one of the richest states in India in terms of biodiversity and natural resources. Endowed with varied eco-regions covering a wide range of altitudes, the state is gifted with innumerable species of flora and fauna. A large number of glaciers feed many water bodies in the state with a good potential for hydroelectric power generation. At the same time, fragile mountain ecology characterised by landslides and floods poses significant challenges. Sikkim is a peaceful state amidst the insurgency and law and order crisis in the Northeast.

In Sikkim where 80 per cent of the people depend on natural resources, designing and implementing policies for management of natural resources without compromising on the developmental goals becomes particularly difficult. The chapter attempts to integrate the developmental issues of various sectors with the issues in management of natural resources, pollution and wastes, after studying thoroughly the sectoral interdependence pattern. The thrust would be on identifying the conflicting issues related to sustainability linkages of natural resources and environmental management. The chapter also intends to give some useful recommendations.

The chapter is organised as follows:

2.1 gives an account of the resources of the state in the light of the measures taken so far by the state to manage their degradation and identifies the main issues;

2.2 gives an account of the wastes and pollution generated in the development process and the measures taken so far to manage wastes & pollution efficiently and identifies the main issues;

2.3 gives an account of the bodies involved in the participatory approach to sustainable development, their desired role and contribution in the process: Government, NGOs, army and the civil society;

2.4 gives a critique of the State Biodiversity Strategy and Action Plan;

2.5 suggests some recommendations on how to strategise the development priorities without disturbing the environmental balance of the state.

2.1 Resource Base

2.1.1 Diverse Resource

According to 1958-60 Survey Operation and the Gazetteer of Sikkim, the land area under different utilisation categories is 7299 sq. km. Detailed break-up is given in Table 2.1.

The state is gifted with abundant natural resources, like agricultural crops, fodder and forests, non-wood forest produce like sand, boulders, and other material

TABLE 2.1

Land Area under Different Utilisation Categories

Land Use Pattern	*Area in '000 ha*	*Per cent of Area*
Barren Land	209.01	28.28
Land put to Non-agricultural Use	69.96	9.58
Permanent Pastures and Grazing including Cultivable Waste	102.49	14.40
Land under Miscellaneous Tree Crops and Grasses	4.17	0.57
Forest Land	265.21	36.34
Land under Operational Holdings	79.06	10.83
Total	729.90	100.00

Source: Annual Administrative Report. Forest Department, Sikkim.

minerals like copper, iron, lime, dolomite/limestone, coal, quartzite, talc, silicate and graphite. Garnet is abundant; Mica is also found at places. Large cardamom production is very high in the state. There is a vast potential for hydroelectric power generation as well.

TABLE 2.2

Natural Resources in Sikkim

Species	*Approx. Numbers*
Flowering Plants	4500
Orchids	500 +
Rhododendrons	36
Bamboos	20
Ferns and Ferns Allies	362
Tree Ferns	9
Primulas	30
Oaks	11
Mammals	144
Birds	550
Butterflies	600 +
Fishes	48
Mountains & Peaks	28
Glaciers	21
Lakes and Wetlands	227
Rivers and Streams	over 104

Source: Annual Administrative Report. Forest Department, Sikkim.

BOX 2.1

The Main Constraint

Sikkim is a state with predominantly hilly and mountainous terrain. A large proportion of the area is under forests. Therefore, there is very little scope for increasing the area under agriculture to augment the food production in the state. The main problem therefore, is how to provide food and other resources to the growing population

Forestry is the major land use in the state with 80 per cent of the total geographical area of the state being controlled by the forest department. The forested area of the state is 3129 sq. km, which is 44 per cent of the total geographical area. This figure is one of the largest in the country. There is one high altitude national park cum biosphere reserve and six wildlife sanctuaries, which together constitute over 30 per cent of the total geographical area of the state. Table 2.3 gives an account of the Wildlife Protected Areas (WLPA) in Sikkim, district-wise:

TABLE 2.3

District-wise Legally Gazetted Wildlife Protected Areas in Sikkim

Wildlife Protected Areas	*District*	*Area in Sq. Km*
Khangchendzonga National Park	North and West	1784
Shingba Rhododendron Sanctuary	North	43
Barsey Rhododendron Sanctuary	West	104
Kyongnosla Alpine Sanctuary	East	31
Wildlife Protected Areas	District	Area in sq. km.
Fambong Lho Wildlife Sanctuary	East	51.76
Pangolakha Wildlife Sanctuary	East	124
Maenam Wildlife Sanctuary	South	35.34

Source: Annual Administrative Report. Forest Department, Sikkim.

2.1.2 Diverse Eco-regions

Sikkim is also blessed with diverse eco-regions specified according to their heights.

The tropical eco-region extends roughly from the foothills of the outer Himalayas to an altitude of about 1200 m.

The subtropical eco-region extends up from about 1200 m to 3000 m with heaviest rainfall in the zone and humid climate throughout the year.

Most of the human population of Sikkim resides in these two zones

The temperate eco-region extends from 3000m to 4000m.

The alpine forests and scrub extends to 4500 m with small crooked trees and large shrubs interspersed with fur and pine.

The trans-himalayan eco-region extends from 4500 m to 5500 m with cold desert vegetation and is confined to the north district of the state.

Table 2.4 attempts a SWOT analysis of these eco-regions in Sikkim in terms of the resources they are endowed with and their sustainability potential.

2.1.3 Main Issues

More than 80 per cent of the population, directly or indirectly, depends on the natural resources of the state. Since land is very scarce in the state, food security is the prime issue of concern. With growing population, unemployment in the state is becoming unmanageably high, a direct consequence of which is poverty. These issues can partly be tackled with proper planning in natural resource management.

TABLE 2.4

Eco-region-wise SWOT Analysis

Eco-region	*Strengths*	*Weaknesses*	*Opportunities*	*Threats*
Tropical	Better communication, accessibility, longer growing season, climate is very mild, land is stabilised, specially in east Sikkim. Rice, ginger production, orchids, teak, sal, giant bamboo	Higher population density, solid waste disposal, drinking water scarcity, high influx of migrant population	Hydel power, ecotourism, Kitam bird sanctuary is under the process of being notified; proposed butterfly park, NHPC dams—operational and also under construction. Industrial belt for eco-friendly industries, Educational hub, gobar gas	Forest fire, polluting industries, deforestation, solid waste, loss of indigenous varieties of crops, erosion of knowledge of traditional farming systems
Subtropical	Large cardamom, orange, squash, peas, rice production, Broom grass, mild climate, better communication, temi tea, good forest cover	Heavy rainfall, landslides, moderate population density	Gobar gas, village tourism, educational hub; Tourism potentials in and around two protected areas as Fambong Lho Sanctuary in east and Mennam Sanctuary in the south. Potential for large cardamom, tea, naturalised exotics markets.	Soil erosion, reduced natural regeneration of oakforests, loss of indigenous varieties of crops, erosion of knowledge of traditional farming systems.
Temperate	Trekking destinations, Snow, high Altitude lakes, Conifer forests hemlock, spruce, pine, fur, junipers, rhododendron; Wildlife, red panda, himalayan black bear, blue magpie, reptiles, amphibians	Connectivity, extreme climate, short growing period	Animal husbandry, dairy farming, trekking tourism, Wildlife Tourism, Potential for medicinal plants, dyes; Trouts in lakes; Tourism in an around four wildlife sanctuaries *viz.* Shingba rhododendron sanctuary, barsey rhododendron sanctuary, kyongnosla alpine sanctuary, and pangolakha wildlife sanctuary & khangchendzonga national park (shared with the alpine region); Education hub; Health resorts	Soil erosion, unregulated grazing
Alpine	Rhododendron, medicinal plants; Musk deer, himalayan tahr; livestock like yak; rivers	Connectivity	Potential for Trouts in rivers; Medicinal plants; tourism in an around four wildlife sanctuaries and national park shared with the temparate eco-region; education hub; Health resorts	Poverty, unemployment
Trans-Himalayan	Kiang, nayan, tibetan gazelle, snow leopard, Tibetan wolf, etc.	Connectivity Not included in the protected area network; short four-month growing season; existence of feral dogs; landmines	Tourism potential, trekking, proposed "Tso Lhamu cold desert conservation reserve" Is under active onsideration. This will represent the transhimalayas in the protected area network	Most threatened eco-region in terms of endangered species; vanishing tribes like dokpas.

Source: Sikkim Biodiversity Strategy and Action Plan; Annual Administrative Report. Forest Department, Sikkim.

There is an immediate need to take proper measures for land, soil and water conservation. This will ensure sustainable growth in the key sectors of the economy *viz.*, agriculture, forestry, and animal husbandry; livelihoods of the masses will be improved. By widening the protected area network, introducing regulations on trekking and other tourist activities, and training programs for registered porters and tourist guides, the State can ensure sustainable tourism, which in turn will generate employment and income. Restricting biopiracy and developing a good patent information centre in the state would restore resources drained in the absence of patents. With a proper planning in disaster management and mitigation, the state can minimise unplanned losses. NGOs and CBOs should be given more autonomy to take necessary actions and sensitise people and build up awareness regarding environmental sustainability in the state. The government should act as a facilitator in the process.

2.2 Waste and Pollution Management

The findings of some of the studies conducted by the State Pollution Control Board (SPCB) of Sikkim to assess the waste and pollution management status of the state indicate that in spite of the presence of fewer industries in Sikkim the problem of waste management arises due to lack of proper handling, treatment and management of the wastes.

2.2.1 Biomedical and Municipal Solid Waste Management

Two studies in 2002-03 *viz.*, Management and Handling of Biomedical Wastes and Management and Handling of Municipal Solid Wastes reveal very interesting trends and problems. The focus of bio-medical wastes was the Gangtok town area. The data was collected from Hospital areas, Primary Healthcare Centres, Urban Development and Housing Department and from the sites of disposal of the plastic bags and materials. The study records an amount of 320 kg per day disposal from STNM Hospital, Gangtok alone. The wastes generated are classified into nine categories and treatment methods are suggested in Table 2.5.

Municipal Solid Wastes consist of garbage, refuse and other discarded solid materials from industrial, commercial and agricultural operations and from community activity. Sikkim generates 0.45 kg per capita of municipal solid waste per day. The total quantity of municipal waste generated is about 42 tonnes per day and the problem is mainly of the urban areas. Table 2.6 summarises the main sources and average composition of solid waste in Gangtok town.

TABLE 2.5

Categories and Methods of Treatment of Biomedical Wastes in Sikkim

Categories of Biomedical Wastes	*Treatment and Disposal*
Human Anatomical waste	Incineration/deep burial
Animal Waste	Incineration/deep burial
Microbiology & Biotechnology Waste	Local autoclaving/microwaving/ incineration
Waste Sharps	Disinfection/autoclaving/ microwaving/shredding
Discarded Medicines and Cytotoxic Drugs	Incineration/destruction and drug disposal
Solid Waste	Disinfection/autoclaving/ microwaving/shredding
Liquid Waste	Disinfection/discharge
Incineration Ash	Disposal in municipal landfill
Chemical Waste	Chemical Treatment and discharge

Source: *Assessment of Pollution Action Plan*. Report published by SPCB, Sikkim.

TABLE 2.6

Sources and Composition of Solid Waste in Gangtok

Main Sources of Solid Waste	*Percentage*
Domestic	34.19
Commercial	28.1
Institutional	19.2
Agricultural	3.17
Industrial	0.12
Others	15.22
Average Composition of Solid Waste	*Percentage*
Food Waste	51.50
Grass	13.80
Paper	10.80
Plastic	0.50
Metal	0.60
Glass	0.40
Misc. degradable	10.80
Misc. non-degradable	10.00
Inorganic substances	1.60

Source: *Assessment of Pollution and Formulation of Action Plan*. Report published by SPCB, Sikkim.

2.2.2 Present System of Waste Disposal

Collection of wastes by Urban Development & Housing Department (UD&HD) is through bins placed at different locations and street sweeping. After collection, the wastes are transported through trucks to the disposal sites on a daily basis and are dumped in open dumps. Some closed dumps have been constructed recently. Dumping sites are located near rivers. UD&HD has initiated a project on the treatment of municipal solid wastes with modern plants in Gangtok.

2.2.3 Pollution Management

Tables 2.7, 2.8 and 2.9 summarise the results of some experiments done by SPCB in Gangtok to monitor the pollution levels for different media.

Noise Pollution

The ambient noise level is measured by sound level 2031A (cygnet). The measurements were taken for seven consecutive days in each of the sites in three slots, morning (8-10 am), afternoon (2-4 pm) and evening (6-8 pm). The noise was monitored thrice in 2001, in the months of January, April, and July and an annual average is given. Lmax and Lmin are respectively the maximum and minimum sound levels measured in decibel units; Leq is the average sound energy of the total time of monitoring. The results show that the standards are violated for evening category in all the areas and in the commercial areas the standards are violated in the mornings also.

Air Pollution: Ambient Air Quality

SPCB has also done some useful experiments to assess the levels of main air pollutants in and around Gangtok. A comparison of the levels of air pollution with the National Ambient Air Quality Standards (NAAQS) show that in most of the experimental sites except the hospital point (for SPM, SO_2 and NOx), and zero point for SPM, the air quality satisfies the norms.

Vehicular Emissions

Vehicular emission is the main source of air pollution in Gangtok. In 2001, periodic monitoring of vehicles were done. Table 2.9 summarises the main findings of a study by SPCB in Gangtok in 2002.

TABLE 2.7

Status of Noise Pollution in Gangtok

Types of Area	*Monitoring Locations*	*Time*	*Lmax*	*Lmin*	*Leq*	*Standards*
Residential	College Valley, Tadong	Morning	74.2	34.3	51.6	55
		Afternoon	78.4	42.2	60.8	
		Evening	76.3	39.5	58.4#	45
	Deorali Govt. Qtr.	Morning	71.5	35.1	55.3	55
		Afternoon	76.3	39.9	61.4	
		Evening	73.4	36.2	57.2#	45
	Development Area	Morning	78.4	35.5	51.6	55
		Afternoon	85.3	41.7	65.8	
		Evening	71.5	34.6	50.7#	45
Commercial	Bazar, M.G. Marg	Morning	97.1	58.4	70.4#	65
		Afternoon	105.2	61.0	74.3	
		Evening	85.4	56.2	62.1#	55
	Indira Bypass	Morning	93.0	52.0	68.5#	65
		Afternoon	97.0	57.4	73.2	
Silence Zone	Hospital Point	Evening	88.0	43.8	69.4#	55
		Morning	74.3	38.2	50.1	50
		Afternoon	84.2	40.8	62.5	
	District Court	Evening	85.1	41.6	63.2#	40
		Morning	68.1	34.2	47.1	50
		Afternoon	72.5	38.6	49.2	

Note: #: Figures exceed the standards.

Source: Assessment of Pollution and Formulation of Action Plan. Report published by SPCB, Sikkim.

TABLE 2.8

Status of Air Pollution in Gangtok (mg/m³)

Name of Sites	*Category*	*NAAQS SPM*	*SPM*	*NAAQS SO_2*	*SO_2*	*NAAQS NOx*	*NOx*
Deorali	Residential	140	118	60	18.6	60	16.1
Tadong	Residential	140	108	60	16.2	60	15.7
Indira Bypass	Commercial	360*	137	80*	17.4	80*	22.6
Bazar (near Metro point)	Commercial	360*	145	80*	22.3	80*	20.4
Hospital Point	Sensitive	70	122#	15	19.6#	15	18.6#
Zero Point	Sensitive	70	98#	15	10.2	15	12.3

Note: *–Standards for Industrial Areas; #–figures exceed Standards.
Source: Assessment of Pollution and Formulation of Action Plan. Report published by SPCB, Sikkim.

TABLE 2.9

Status of Vehicular Emissions in Gangtok

Type of Vehicle		*No. of Vehicles Monitored*	*No of Vehicles*	
			Complying Standards#	*Not Complying Standards*
Petrol (CO emissions)	Two-wheelers	54	48 (88.88%)	6 (11.11%)
	Four-wheelers	161	132 (81.98%)	29 (18.01%)
	Total	215	189 (83.72%)	35 (16.27%)
Diesel (smoke Density)	Four-wheelers	90	78 (86.66%)	12 (13.33%)

Note: #–Standards specified in Section 115(2) of the Central Motor Vehicle Rules, 1989.
Source: Assessment of Pollution and Formulation of Action Plan. Report published by SPCB, Sikkim.

BOX 2.2

Action Plan for Municipal Solid Waste Management: New Moves

- **Segregation and Storage of Wastes**: door-to-door collection including shops and offices
- **Primary Collection**: adequate number of bins, community bins, NGOs encouraged to participate
- **Transportation**: covered vehicles, manual loading to be avoided
- **Processing and Disposal**: composting, latest and appropriate technology to be used, recycling encouraged
- **Availability of land**: for construction of dumping sites and installation of composting plants
- **Administration and Financial Management**: UD&HD proposed to be declared the nodal agency, master plan for solid waste management

Water Pollution

Drinking water quality is monitored at various points in Gangtok from where it is used for consumption in 1998-99. It is clear from the analysis that quality of drinking water is reasonably good in Gangtok. Table 2.10 below summarises the results of the experiment. Only the magnesium content in water in 'Old Market' area has exceeded the standard.

2.2.4 Main Issues

In the light of the above evidences and the first hand experience of visits to the state, we can sum up the main issues of concern in wastes and pollution management in the state. The garbage disposal system in the state needs to be reformed thoroughly. The new moves in the action plan for municipal solid waste management are in the desired direction. In pollution management the studies are mostly Gangtok centric. We find that noise pollution in Gangtok is excessive. Ambient air quality in the hospital point does not satisfy the national norms for important air pollutants, which is a matter of concern. A small sample of vehicles shows that a good proportion of vehicles comply with the standards, but the standards are old. The general perception after visiting the state is that vehicular emission is the major source of air pollution in the urban areas and tourist destinations of the state. Drinking water scenario in Gangtok according to the experiment cited above though gives positive results, first hand experiences of visits to the rural areas are pathetic although no quantification can be provided. The fact can be justified by the incidence of water-borne diseases in the state.

TABLE 2.10

Status of Drinking Water in Gangtok

*Zones**	*Pollutants Concentration (mg/lit)*											
	BOD		*Nitrates*		*Calcium*		*Magnesium*		*Chlorides*		*TDS*	
	Max	*Min*	*Max*	*Min*	*Max*	*Min*	*Max*	*Min*	*Max*	*Min*	*Max*	*Min*
1	2.2									105		
2												
3												26
4				26		54		23				
5							35#					
6		1.8	41		68				127			
7		1.8									43	
Standards		30		45		75		30		250		500

Note: # - Standard violated. Zone 1: Deorali, Zone 2: Lall Market, Zone 3: New Market, Zone 4: Old Market, Zone 5: Hospital Point, Zone 6: Development Area, Zone 7: Balwakhani Area.

Source: Assessment of Pollution and Formulation of Action Plan. Report published by SPCB, Sikkim.

BOX 2.3

Environmental Acts/Laws in Force in Sikkim

Indian Forest *Act*, 1927

Wildlife Protection *Act*, 1972

Water Prevention and Control *Act*, 1974

Water Cess *Act*, 1977

Forest Conservation *Act*, 1980

Air Prevention and Control of Pollution *Act*, 1981

Environmental Protection *Act*, 1986

Sikkim Forest, Water Courses and Road Reserve *Act*, 1988

Public Liability Insurance *Act*, 1991

Environmental Tribunal *Act*, 1995

Biological Diversity *Act*, 2003

2.3 Participatory Approach to Sustainable Development

Sustainable development needs community participation. This section enumerates the present and prospective future roles of the NGOs, army, local people and government in strengthening the sustainability linkages of the development process in the state.

2.3.1 NGOs: Main Activities

Conservation Education

To develop ecological ethics through workshops, fairs, street plays and model demonstrations; involving students actively in conservation activities; Conducting seminars and quizzes in schools and also training school teachers on how to impart conservation education to school children. Combined conservation activities in collaboration with agencies (like Singapore International Foundation, WWF, TMI) are also on the agenda.

Training

Different skill development training at a very basic level for porters, vegetable farmers, cooks, pack animal operators and local guides. Training and Capacity building of NGOs and stakeholders involved in Ecotourism and Conservations.

BOX 2.4

List of Important NGOs Involved in the Process

1. Khangchendzonga Conservation Committee (KCC)
2. Ashoka Trust for Research in Ecology and Environment (ATREE)
3. Concerned Citizens of Sikkim (CCS)
4. Ecotourism and Conservation Society of Sikkim (ECOSS)
5. Sikkim Paryavaran Sanrakshan Sangh (SPSS)
6. Green Circle
7. Chungthang Welfare and Sporting Association (CWSA)
8. Sikkim Lepcha Youth Association (SLYA)
9. Gharelu Samaj
10. Drishti
11. Uttarey Tourism Development Association

Micro Planning

In order to ensure a more holistic approach to development, micro planning is carried out jointly with various government departments, specially the Forest department.

Advocacy with Government Agencies

Advocating and lobbying with the government agencies for appropriate policies in tourism sector for sustainable development, which would benefit the community to conserve the natural resources.

Monitoring

Monitoring the use of natural resources in and around the Khangchendzonga Biosphere Reserve. This includes monitoring the tourism enterprises that are operating trek in the area to control illegal extraction of herbs, incense and other medicinal plants as well as proper disposal and management of waste. Strengthening the monitoring of wildlife and poaching with the help of porters, cooks, tourists, and guides.

Promoting Alternate Livelihoods

Different skill development trainings at a very basic level for vegetable farmers, use of biogas, energy efficient *chulahs*, bamboo propagation, NTFP promotion, etc.

Rehabilitating Tendong

Afforestation activities, water source conservation, reducing forest and wildlife offences.

Grassroot Institution Building

Formation and capacity building of *Pani Panchayats* around Tendong Nature Reserve.

Appropriate Technology Intervention

Introducing eco-friendly interventions to reduce the dependence on natural resources, e.g. GI wire mesh in lieu of branches and poles for cultivation of squash (vegetable).

2.3.2 Issues Relevant for participation of Army in Sikkim

- Biomonitoring by Army in the remote high altitudes of North and East Sikkim.
- Army support for joint patrolling in high altitude areas of North and East Sikkim.
- Reduce damage due to developmental activities by GREF/BRO.
- Sensitising the armed forces towards sustainability issues.
- Reducing animal casualties due to land mine in border areas of China.
- Eliminating feral dogs around army establishments in North and East.

Table A-3 in the Annexures gives the details of the roles and initiatives of the main bodies needed to be involved for the participatory approach to Sustainable Development.

2.4 Sikkim Biodiversity Strategy and Action Plan (SBSAP): A Critique

The state has recently come up with a comprehensive strategy and action plan for biodiversity conservation. The methodology adopted in the SBSAP for formulating the Action Plan is described in brief and a critical evaluation is attempted thereafter. The main issues related to sustainability addressed in SBSAP are extracted in Table A-2 in the Annexures.

2.4.1 Community Strategy and Action Plan (CSAP)

The first step in formulating the SBSAP was to organise public hearings for the local people eco-region-wise to collect information and opinion on important issues on biodiversity.

Table 2.11 presents the list of public hearings conducted eco-region-wise.

TABLE 2.11

Eco-region-wise Public Hearings for SBSAP

Eco-region	*No of Public Hearings*	*Sample CSAP*
Trans-Himalayas	2	Chho Lhamo–Lashar (North)
Temperate	2	Lachen (North)
Subtropical	27	Hee Patal (West)
Tropical	8	Kitam (South)

Source: Sikkim Biodiversity Strategy and Action Plan (SBSAP).

BOX 2.5

Uttarey: A Success Story

The Shingalila trek, on the razor sharp Shingalila Range traverses through some bewildering oak forests, rhododendron forests and alpine meadows of the Khangchendzonga National Park in West Sikkim. It is a 18 days trek with 12 camping sites and average altitude being 12000 ft. It is fast catching up with foreign and Indian tourists as a trekking destination.

In order to ensure that the community benefits from this tourism and the multiplier ratio is high the villagers organised themselves into the Uttarey Eco-Tourism Development Society

150 porters, 10 naturalist guides, 16 pack animal operators are registered with this association. They have also framed operational guidelines to ensure that everyone gets an equal opportunity and the tourists get good service. A rotation system is in place to ensure that the porters get their opportunity in time and there is no competition amongst themselves leading to undercutting of the wage rate. The association also provides basic facilities like good footwear for its members. This has resulted in a total of Rs. 9 lakh income for villagers in 2003 from 400 tourists.

In order to promote the natural medicinal plant wealth of the region, UETDA is also planning to create a herbal interpretation center (HIC) at Uttarey which shall not only interpret the medicinal plants diversity of KBR but also more importantly make the visitor aware of the code of conduct. This will reduce the threat to the biodiversity values of KBR. The design of the HIC shall be traditional and the construction would be done using local materials to make it ecofriendly. A live herbal section shall also be maintained here with adequate interpretation. In order to increase the number of visitors to this HIC, linkages with the Tourism Department and TAAS shall be made. Details about the services provided here and the fees charged shall be advertised through the local newspapers, radio, and other media. Sale of local handicrafts and souvenirs would be initiated. There are also plans to have group insurance for the trekking support staff and provide them with solar lanterns and warm clothing. The Mountain Institute, NGO, is also assisting in providing training for the trekking service providers and homestay operators.

BOX 2.6

List of Important Programmes Undertaken by NGOs in Sikkim

- Gangtok School Sanitation and Environmental Programme in collaboration with HDFS
- Village Tourism activities in Khedi in collaboration with KEEP
- Training Capacity Building and Participatory Planning with Forest Department-FDA project
- Village Tourism and Community Development activities in collaboration with FRHLT (INGO)
- EDP Training on Ecotourism Enterprises with collaborating Institutions
- Entrepreneurship Training for unemployed youth-CMSES Programme
- Ecotourism initiatives in West Sikkim

2.4.2 *CPI Model: Methodology*

- The CSAPs obtained from the 39 public hearings were segregated eco-region-wise and the aspirations of the local community listed out as "Biodiversity Conservation Issues".
- These issues were broadly classified into five categories namely, conservation issues, livelihood issues, infrastructure development, culture conservation and negative outside influences. Similarly the necessary actions against these issues were also listed down. Then these eco-region-wise CSAPs were clubbed into one matrix.
- At each CSAP level the issues which were raised were given one point and the issues which were not raised were given zero point
- These rankings at CSAP level were clubbed eco-region-wise and their rankings averaged to obtain the CPI score. This CPI is an indicator of the priority given to that particular issue by the villages in that eco-region.

2.4.3 *CPI Model: Limitations*

The model has serious limitations.

Firstly, the numbers of public hearings differ from one eco-region to another. There is no mention of the basis on which the numbers are chosen.

Secondly, though it is mentioned that appropriate weights have been assigned/given to make representations of all the eco-regions uniform, the methodology for assigning weights is not clear. The simple average for attaining CPI is faulty.

Thirdly, the range of indices specified as:

0.00-0.15 low

0.16-0.50 medium

0.51-0.75 high

0.76-1.00 top

in the document is not very useful as none of the issues appear to be in the top priority range.

2.5 Recommendations

It is claimed that the state has been consciously following a growth path, which is ecologically sustainable. However, the allocation figures of the 9th and 10th five year plans of the state (Tables A-5 and A-6) show that there is a decline in both the absolute and percentage allocations for all the sectors contributing to natural resource and environment management, except for the sector ecology and environment where increases are marginal.

The main issues related to sustainable development are summarised in the annexure to Table A-2 for a clear idea about the priorities of the state. Table A-4 summarises the steps which have already been identified by the government. A set of recommendations is given in this section to fill up the gaps, which still exist.

Conservation of Land, Soil and Water Resources

- Revival of rotational collection and non-destructive harvesting of medicinal plants & wild edibles by local JFMCs, EDC.
- Carrying capacity based rotational grazing with rest periods for the proposed cold desert conservation area in north Sikkim.
- Firewood and fodder plantations on private and community land, and degraded forest land by JFMCs and NGOs; forest dept. as facilitator.
- Reduction in *jhum* cultivation.
- Improvement of catchment areas through plantations by villagers.
- Protection of water source through prevention of grazing and firewood collection by forest, RDD and PHED, and
- Minimum and controlled dynamiting by GREF.

Protected Areas

- No building construction inside protected or forest area: only tenting and camping facilities in designated areas (outside forest areas/near potential Ecotourism sites).
- Fuel requirement (kerosene, biogas) should be ensured for trekkers: No trees and bushes to be used as fuel wood in the national parks.
- Awareness programmes for villagers on biopiracy issues by forest dept., Science & Technology Dept. and NGOs.
- Eco Development Committees should be strengthened and empowered for development of sustainable ecotourism.
- Conservation of wild citrus in subtropical belt by declaration of species as protected.
- Organic cultivation in community nurseries around protected areas in collaboration with citrus Dieback Research Station, Darjeeling.
- Organic tea plantation and wool cottage industry as private enterprises facilitated by eco-development programmes of the government

Disaster Management

- R&D programmes for pilot studies of landslide affected areas using bioengineering and bio-technological interventions.
- Modification of unsustainable land use practices in landslide affected areas.
- A separate head for grants on landslide control to be created by the Centre for states having frequent landslides.
- Proper disaster management and mitigation plans by forming a Disaster Management Cell in the state, and
- The Relief Commissioner should be involved in the state's planning process.

Biodiversity

- Setting up a Sikkim Biodiversity Conservation Board.
- Army to keep up effective and proper fencing of mined areas to reduce casualties through watch and other preventive measures.
- No restrictions on rotational grazing in traditional areas (outside land-mined sites).
- Trans-himalayan eco-region to be included in the state's protected area network.
- Establishing State Gene Bank: value addition through appropriate marketing in the long term (e.g. 'Jewel Orchids' of Sikkim), and

- Biodiversity Strategy and Action Plan (BSAP) should be revised as it suffers from short-sightedness in the method of indexation.

Pollution and Waste Management

- Environmental Impact Assessment for all visitors' destinations.
- Relocation of food-stalls to a distance of at least 2 kms from the spots.
- Planned parking spaces at distances from the spots.
- Vehicles checked for pollution.
- Water supply to food stalls.
- Building infrastructure for waste and garbage management (litter cans, bins, etc).
- Frequent disposal of garbage: according to the intensity of tourist traffic.
- Involvement of local community;
- Apply user charges to maintain civic amenities in the visitors' destinations and stopovers.
- Raising of road plantations of bamboos, etc. as dust and noise sinks.
- Effective clean-up of local *Jhoras.*
- Garbage disposal system needs improvement. Areas of tourist interest particularly needs proper planning in this regard.
- Separate bins (green) for biodegradable and (blue) for non-biodegradable wastes.
- Separate dumping structures for wet and dry garbage.
- Detailed studies on pollution in the rivers as a consequence of industrial development to be done by SPCB.
- Assessment of rural drinking water quality by local schools and SPCB.
- Vehicular pollution to be contained: Use of cleaner fuels to be enforced.
- Vehicles to conform to *Bharat Stage 2* norms: eventual phasingout can be proposed.
- Safe drinking water and treatment plants in rural and urban areas, also around all PAs to be ensured by RDD, forest and PHED.
- Improvement of drinking water source through recharge of underground aquifers.
- CNG option to be explored: cost benefit analysis can be proposed.
- Punishment and penalty schemes to be made more effective and strict.

References

Community Information Center (n.d.). *Facts and Figures about Sikkim.*

Das, B.S. (1996). *The Sikkim Saga.* New Delhi: Vikas Publishing House.

Dasgupta, Manas (1992). *Sikkim: Problems & Prospects of Development.* New Delhi: Indus Publishing Company.

Dept. of Forests, Environment & Wildlife. *Annual Administrative Report 1999-2000.* Govt. of Sikkim.

———. *Annual Administrative Report 2002-03*. Dept. of Forests, Environment & Wildlife.

———. *Joint Forest Management.* Govt. of Sikkim.

———. *Sikkim Biodiversity Strategy and Action Plan (SBSAP)*. Govt. of Sikkim.

Dept. of Information Technology. *Annual Administrative Report 2001-02*. Govt. of Sikkim.

———. *Annual Administrative Report 2002-03.* Govt. of Sikkim.

Directorate of Economics & Statistics. *Economic Survey of Sikkim 2003-04.* Govt. of Sikkim.

ENVIS Centre. *Environmental Status Report*. Sikkim.

Govt. of Sikkim. *Background Notes for Discussions of Annual Plan 2003-04.*

———. *Sikkim-A Statistical Profile.*

———. *Sikkim State Annual Plan 1999-2000.*

———. *Sikkim State Annual Plan 2000-2001.*

———. *Sikkim State Annual Plan 2001-2002.*

———. *Sikkim State Annual Plan 2002-2003.*

———. *Memorandum of Works under Natural Calamity—1996-97, 1997-98, 1998-99, 2000-01.*

Information & Public Relations Dept. *Our Natural Resources, Our Responsibilities.* Govt. of Sikkim.

Khanchendzonga Conservation Committee. *Annual Report 2001-02: Conservation of Sustainable Livelihoods.*

Lama, Mahendra P. (ed.) (1994). *Sikkim: Society, Polity, Economy, Environment*. New Delhi: Indus Publishing Company.

———. (2001). *Sikkim Human Development Report, 2001*. Delhi: Social Science Press.

Planning & Development Dept. *Ninth Five Year Plan 1997-2002.* Govt. of Sikkim.

———. *Tenth Five Year Plan 2002-2007.* Govt. of Sikkim.

Rai, Suresh Chand, *et al.* (eds.) (1998). *Sikkim: Perspectives for Planning and Development.* Sikkim Science Society.

Sikkim Pollution Control Board (SPCB). *Pollution Status Report of Sikkim.* Dept. of Forests Environment & Wildlife, Govt. of Sikkim.

———. *Assessment of Pollution Action Plan.* Sikkim.

———. *Report on the Assessment of Pollution & Formulation of Action Plan.* Dept. of Forests, Environment & Wildlife. Govt. of Sikkim.

Singh, O.P. (1985). *Strategic Sikkim.* Delhi: B.R. Publishing Corp.

State Council of Science & Technology. *Commemorating Five Years of Existence—A Report*. Department of Science and Technology, Govt. of Sikkim.

United Nations. *Millennium Developmental Goals.*

Chapter 3

Economic Growth, Structural Change and Employment

The most important indicator for assessing the performance of the state economy is the pattern of income growth. Furthermore, it can shed light on the relative contribution of the sectors which are driving the economy. In view of this, an assessment of the growth potential of the state economy needs to be made which would constitute the basis for formulating a sector-specific development strategy. This is because the development strategy needs to be situated in the context of the past profile of growth and its potential. Linked with this is the issue of sector-wise workforce participation. An analysis of the workforce participation and employability of the workforce in the context of the dynamics of growth will set the stage for discussions on policies for employment generation.

3.1 Growth: Trend and Composition

As per the new GSDP series, the state economy grew at the rate of 9.3 per cent during 1993-94 to 1999-2000, down from 11.0 per cent achieved during 1980-81 to 1992-93. However the nominal growth rate remained unchanged at around 15.5 per cent during the 1980s and the 1990s indicating higher inflation rate during the latter period. Per capita income grew at the rate of 11 per cent in nominal terms during 1993-94 to 1999-2000. However, in real terms it grew at 6.3 per cent per annum.

Primary Sector

The fall in the growth rate of the primary sector during 1993-94 to 1999-2000 to as low as 0.2 per cent from 8.3 per cent in the earlier period is worrisome for a state where people are mainly dependent on agriculture and related activities for their livelihood. However, nominal growth rate of 8.7 per cent during the same period indicates price rise to an extent of 8.5 per cent compared to 5 per cent in the earlier period. Within the primary sector, agriculture and mining witnessed negative growth rate. However, forestry and fishing with small shares in GSDP experienced positive growth.

Secondary Sector

Secondary sector as a whole grew at a reasonably high rate of 12 per cent during the 1990s, up by nearly 4 percentage points compared to the 1980s. Manufacturing nearly stagnated. However, higher growth rates attained by construction and electricity, gas and water supply pepped up the tempo of growth of the secondary sector (Table 3.1).

Tertiary Sector

Real growth rates of transport, trade and commerce, banking and real estate slumped during 1993-94 to 1999-2000 in comparison with the respective growth rates in the earlier period. There was a marginal fall in the tertiary sector growth rate. The tertiary sector grew at an impressive rate of around 13 per cent during the 1990s, driven mainly by high growth rates attained by public administration and 'other services.' Hotels and restaurants grew at a lower rate, causing its share to fall.

3.2 Structural Change

The sectoral change is reflective of the undergoing structural change that the state economy is experiencing. In nominal terms, the share of the primary sector has declined from nearly 49 per cent in 1980-81 to 28 per cent in 2001-02 whereas at constant process, the fall in the share has been steeper. During 1997-98 to 1999-2000, the fall in the share nearly by 11 percentage points was due to a sudden spurt in the share of the tertiary sector. This was caused by a

TABLE 3.1

Sectoral Growth Rates

	1980-81 to 1992-93		1993-94 to 1999-2000	
	Nominal	*Real*	*Nominal*	*Real*
Gross State Domestic Product	15.6	11.05	15.5	9.3
Primary	13.3	8.26	8.7	0.14
Agriculture	13.38	8.37	8.6	-0.2
Forestry & Logging	12.3	-1.00	11.6	4.8
Fishing	23.4	8.01	4.3	3.1
Mining & Quarrying	20.1	8.65	-6.5	-9.3
Secondary	10.61	8.6	17.0	12.2
Manufacturing	10.6	8.98	8.1	1.3
Construction	13.6	11.6	20.5	15.7
Electricity, Gas & Water Supply	NA	NA	16.7	15.7
Tertiary	19.8	14.9	19.1	13.4
Transport, Storage and Communication	27.9	25.5	19.1#	3.5#
Trade, Hotels and Restaurants	19.6	18.18	10.0	6.8
Banking & Insurance	26.1	23.72	22.6	17.4
Real Estate	12.9	7.76	11.4	2.9
Public Administration	18.9	11.74	22.1	16.3
Other Services	22.6	13.96	25.0	21.4

Note: # Refers to transport by other means only. NA: Not available.
Source: CSO, GoI.

sudden growth in public administration. The swelling of the wages and salaries bill on account of implementation of the sixth pay commission recommendations which raised the contribution of the public administration in the tertiary sector.

TABLE 3.2

GSDP Sectoral Shares

	Primary	Secondary	Tertiary	Primary	Secondary	Tertiary
	(at current prices)			(at constant prices)		
1980-81	48.9	20.7	30.4	48.9	20.7	30.4
1983-84	48.2	19.3	32.5	50.2	20.9	28.9
1985-86	47.6	19.4	33.0	45.1	21.3	33.6
1990-91	42.8	14.5	42.6	40.9	18.0	41.1
1992-93	36.4	15.1	48.5	35.7	19.8	44.5
1993-94	35.1	19.0	45.9	35.1	19.0	45.9
1995-96	35.7	20.3	44.0	33.2	21.2	45.6
1997-98	33.5	21.5	45.0	30.0	23.6	46.4
1999-2000	26.8	18.9	54.4	22.8	20.4	56.8
2001-02	28.2	18.0	53.7	NA	NA	NA

Source: CSO, GoI.

The share of secondary sector at constant prices has remained the same during the period under consideration after reaching nearly 21 per cent during 1997-98. Since then it has declined. If we consider the 1980s, the share has in fact stagnated. The rise in 1997-98, was spurred mainly by construction activity in the state. The share of tertiary sector witnessed a steady rise both at constant prices as well as current prices since 1980-81. In real terms, the rise in the share has been greater. This explains the steep jump in the share witnessed during 1998-99 by more than 10 percentage points as mentioned earlier. Public administration and 'other services' have contributed to a rise in the share of tertiary sector on a sustained basis.

A decline in the primary sector share associated with a rise in the tertiary sector share is similar to the experiences of almost all the economies in transition. What makes this pattern a little different from the most other developing economies, is the stagnant share of secondary sector, in particular, a fall in the share of manufacturing.

3.3 Employment

If development means income growth with equity, generation of employment opportunities remains a formidable challenge for the state and arguably the main objective of development. It is only through employment generation that economic well-being of the people would be ensured and poverty reduced on a sustained basis. Though the size of the population is rather small, the fact that a growing number of educated youths are entering the job market every year cannot be ignored. Employment generation is all the more challenging particularly in the context of ongoing economic reform, which seeks to redefine the role of the government as more of a facilitator rather than an employer, and a greater emphasis is placed on efficiency and competition coupled with integration with the global economy.[1] Low quality employment should be gradually substituted by high quality employment.

The issue of employment generation cannot be divorced from issues related to expansion of economic

1. The employment elasticity of the labour force in the era of post reform has been considerably low. (*Report of the Task Force on Employment Opportunities*, Planning Commission, Government of India, July, 2001).

activities. What needs to be developed is an employment-oriented development strategy rather than devising a strategy for the sake of employment generation alone. In this chapter, we deal with issues related to employment generation indicating policy directions the state may consider.

3.3.1 Data Sources: Confusions Galore

An analysis of employment related issues require an understanding of the existing workforce in the state. While a detailed analysis of workforce participation and its composition based on Census (2001) is dealt with in chapter 11, this chapter focuses mainly on outlining an employment-oriented policy. This chapter refers to employment data based on NSSO survey (55th round on employment and unemployment) and census data. However, the data on employment and unemployment from these two sources are not strictly comparable. Both these sources are useful for understanding the employment situation of the state. The state does not have a Directorate of Employment.

3.4 Pattern and Composition of the Workforce

3.4.1 Sectoral Distribution of Workers

Sectoral distribution of the workforce depends on the factors that drive the sectors of the economy, manpower skill and most importantly the adoption of the extent of labour-intensive technology.

Based on the results of 55th NSS Round (1999-2000), the percentage employed in the tertiary sector (urban) at nearly 82 per cent is relatively high for Sikkim, next only to Tripura among the north-eastern states (Table 3.3). Even in the rural economy, the tertiary sector employment at 29 per cent is second highest next to Tripura. This shows the importance of the public sector and trade-related activities in the services sector in comparison with the secondary sector. On the other hand, workers employed in the primary sector in the rural areas is second lowest at 60.8 per cent followed by Tripura among the north-east states. This indicates that the employment share of services sector in the rural areas is relatively high among the north-eastern states.[2]

3.5 Workforce Participation and Trends in Employment

The percentage of main workers[3] in total population continued to fall during the 1970s and the 1980s. However, during the 1990s, it started rising again and by 2001, the level became the same as it was in 1981. This may be partly attributable to the trend in economic activity as well as due to the labourers migrating from outside the state. What is worrisome is the substantial rise in the percentage of marginal workers during the 1990s. However, this has been the trend in other north-eastern states and India as well (Table A-10) as the percentage of marginal workers in

TABLE 3.3

Distribution of Workers

	Rural			*Urban*		
	Primary	*Secondary*	*Tertiary*	*Primary*	*Secondary*	*Tertiary*
Arunachal Pradesh	83.4	7.5	9.0	8.7	13.4	77.9
Assam	67.7	6.2	26.2	6.0	13.5	80.5
Manipur	75.3	8.9	15.8	28.3	15.6	55.9
Meghalaya	86.5	3.0	10.5	1.3	14.6	84.1
Mizoram	88.5	2.4	12.2	30.3	14.7	55.0
Nagaland	79.7	2.2	18.1	8.4	12.1	79.5
Sikkim	**60.8**	**9.9**	**29.3**	**2.1**	**16.1**	**81.8**
Tripura	45.7	12.0	42.3	2.7	8.0	89.3
All India	76.3	11.4	12.4	8.8	32.0	59.2

Source: Census, 2001.

2. Rural urban demarcation among the North-eastern states is not strictly comparable.

3. Main workers are defined as those who have work for at least 6 months or more during the reference period. Marginal workers are those who did not have work during the major part of the reference period.

TABLE 3.4

Employability of those Seeking Work (percentage)

	Seeking Work			*Never Worked Before*		
	Total	*Male*	*Female*	*Total*	*Male*	*Female*
Illiterate	35.1	12.8	22.3	27.0	9.5	17.5
Below primary	16.8	8.9	7.9	15.2	8.3	6.9
Primary	11.9	6.4	5.5	12.6	6.7	5.8
Middle	14.2	8.3	5.9	15.7	9.3	6.5
Matriculation/ secondary	12.9	7.8	5.1	17.2	10.3	6.9
Higher secondary	4.0	2.2	1.8	5.6	3.0	2.5
Diploma/certificate (non-tech)	0.0	0.0	0.0	0.0	0.0	0.0
Diploma/ certificate (tech)	0.1	0.1	0.0	0.1	0.1	0.0
Graduate degree (non-tech)	3.9	2.6	1.3	5.6	3.6	2.0
Post graduate degree (non-tech)	0.6	0.5	0.1	0.4	0.3	0.1
Graduate/PG or diploma (tech)	0.0	0.0	0.0	0.0	0.0	0.0
i. Engineering	0.3	0.2	0.1	0.4	0.3	0.1
ii. Medicine agriculture and dairying veterinary teaching	0.0	0.0	0.0	0.0	0.0	0.0
iii. Others	0.2	0.2	0.0	0.3	0.3	0.0
Total	100	50	50	100	52	48
Memo: Number of respondents	1118	559	559	756	391	365

Source: Census, 1991.

2001 is higher than that of 1991 for all the states. It may be noted that though the state economy suffered a marginal fall in the growth rate during the 1990s, real growth rate was reasonably high at 9 per cent per annum. As discussed earlier, this was associated with a steady change in the sectoral shares in favour of services and away from the primary sector.

With regard to the composition of the workers, there has been a fall in the share of cultivators as well as agricultural labourers. What calls for attention is the rise in 'other workers.' It also shows people were moving out of agriculture and opting for other employment options as opportunities were diversifying in the process of development. Since Sikkim is pre-dominantly an agricultural state, the percentage of workers employed in the household industry is rather small.

We can also use the sample data as given by the NSS 55th Round Survey to supplement our understanding of the situation. Quite expectedly, a little less than half of the workforce is engaged in trading followed by hotels and restaurants and manufacturing (Table A-11).

3.6 State no Longer a Major Employer

The job aspirants continue to look forward to the government for employment opportunities. Public sector employment is pretty high compared to the population of the state. At present, the total number of employees in the government remain one of the highest amongst the north-eastern states.[4] Expectations for government jobs may vary with respect to the development of a region, particularly in terms of education and job opportunities available in that region. This is important because job aspirants, mainly educated urban youths are keen to be employed in the public sector. This puts pressure on the government and consequently, rightsizing of the public sector is delayed.

Since 1975, the government has emerged as a major employer for carrying out the development activities in the state. In 1974, the total strength of the government was 4000, up from 38 in 1918.[5] Nearly 7 per cent of the population are employed in the public sector, regular and temporary combined together (Table A-7). What is laudable of course, is the initiatives taken by the government to encourage self-employment through various schemes in the recent times. The government is also seriously contemplating rightsizing of the government.

3.7 Ensuring Livelihood to All

The major objective of development should be to ensure livelihood for all as emphasised in the *Vision Document*[6] of the state. It means freedom to pursue what one desires and therefore, self-esteem is duly respected. This requires the government to facilitate job creation, empower people to become capable of fending not only for themselves but also creating job opportunities for others as well. The concept of 'capability' therefore, becomes crucial for designing the strategy. Therefore, fostering economic expansion and creation of 'capability' would be mutually reinforcing each other. Government might play the role of a

4. The size of the government in terms of employment cannot be compared with the population of the state. The state has to provide basic minimum services irrespective of the population. Small size of the population sparsely distributed over the state, habitats scattered in the inhospitable difficult terrain entail greater services rather than less.

5. In 1918, the government department was reorganised for the first time. The government had seven departments manned by three secretaries, one superintendent, six head clerks and twenty-eight clerks (*Sikkim Manpower Review, 2002* by S.D. Tshering).

6. *Sikkim: The People's Vision, (2001).*

facilitator by providing training and creating jobs in the comparatively backward regions.

3.8 Ensuring Regionally Balanced Growth

In view of regional imbalances in the state in terms of opportunities and handicaps, development strategy should seek to ensure that regional imbalances are eliminated through designing of region specific policies. The policies should, therefore, be framed in the context of advantages and disadvantages of the four districts of the state. Owing to the altitude, climate and remoteness, the population density of the north district is rather low. The prospect of industrialisation is also limited. The focus should be on self-employment in tourism and agro-processing suitable for the north district. The south and west districts are more or less evenly balanced. However, location of the state capital, Gangtok has tilted the balance in favour of the east district.

3.9 Assessing the Growth in the Labour Force

It was estimated that around 6500 jobs per annum need to be created to ensure jobs for jobseekers. Policy mix suggests 2000 jobs in agriculture and service sectors, 1000 in animal husbandry and 1500 in industry (SHDR) need to be created.[7] However, a conservative estimate based on preliminary calculation puts the figure at around 5900. Around 42 per cent of the population was in the age group of 15 to 29 as per 1991 census. If we assume that the age composition of the population during the 1990s has remained the same and further, we assume that population in this age group grows at the rate of 2.5 per cent per annum, conditions have to be created for absorbing almost 6000 job aspirants every year. If we consider the backlog, we will be very close to the estimate given in the SHDR 2001.[8]

3.10 Growing Unemployment: Migration to Urban Centres

Given the percentage of people below the poverty level, the quality of employment is generally low. The unemployment figures are often misleading as different definitions have different connotations. In fact, the definitions capture varying degrees of widespread under-employment. Moreover, the definitions of unemployment refer to the period of time that a worker recollects to have worked without referring to the income earned or productive nature of employment.

Though the estimates of employment and unemployment are not strictly comparable, indications suggest that the unemployment situation in the state has been worsening. This has created discontentment among the people. There has been an increase in the unemployment rate from 0.80 per cent in 1993-94 to 3.1 per cent in 1999-2000 for the rural areas based on the results of 55th NSS Round (1999-2000). For the urban areas, it has increased from 2.90 per cent to 8.4 per cent during the same period. The incidence of unemployment amongst youth (aged 15 to 29) on current daily status[9] (CDS) basis increased from 5.1 per cent to 17.5 per cent during the same period. Based on usual status, the rate of unemployment among the educated youths went up from 4.6 per cent to 12.3 per cent in the rural areas and 4.9 per cent to 12.1 per cent in the urban areas. With regard to current weekly status (CWS) and CDS, unemployment in Sikkim is close to 4.5 per cent, which is next to Assam and Nagaland (Table A-12).

There are various estimates of the extent of unemployment in the state. The census 1991 provides the number of job seekers in the state. However, this may tend to underestimate the extent of under-employment in the state.

From the census, 1991, we get an alternative estimate of unemployment in the state. Only 1864 (which is less than one percentage of the state population) respondents admitted to be looking for jobs including the new entrants, which seem to be an underestimate. However, Table 3.4 reveals employability of those who are looking for jobs. Almost one-third of those who are looking for jobs, are illiterate. As we move up the scale of education, the incidence of unemployment falls. However, the extent of unemployment is higher among the non-technical aspirants.

3.11 Strategies for Employment Generation

What we need to be concerned about is the stagnation of the primary sector when a large share of the population earns its livelihood from this sector. With a huge forest cover in a mountainous state with fragile ecology, use of land for expanding the scope of

7. A detailed calculation will be made after the age composition of the state population is made available as per 2001 Census.

8. Lama, Mahendra P. (2001). *Sikkim Human Development Report 2001*. New Delhi: Social Science Press.

9. CDS gives more realistic estimates of unemployment at least directionally. Usual and subsidiary status underestimate the volume of unemployment since these definitions exclude a large number of underemployed or unemployed people.

economic activities has to be judicious. Low productivity of agriculture results in low per capita income of the people dependent on agriculture. The increase in the share of marginal workers (census, 2001), high share of tourism and repair services (NSSO 55th round) reveal that there has been an increase in the labour employed in the unorganised, informal activities. The growth of 'other services' is also supportive of this. The stagnation of manufacturing and very limited organised industrial activity (chapter 9) corroborates this. In the absence of labour legislation, poor enforcement of *Minimum Wages Act*, wages remain low in this sector. Employment in the public sector had been on the rise till recently when the onset of fiscal reform halted this. The absorptive capacity of the public sector has, in fact, been reduced.

One aspect of the strategy should, therefore, be on promoting high value activities in agriculture through diversification, agro-processing, adoption of productivity enhancing measures, and identifying areas with potential for growth. This will reduce migration from rural to the urban areas and would lessen pressure on government for creation of jobs in the public sector. The focus should also be on identifying some of the potential areas in the service sector, such as, tourism sector, promoting education and healthcare industry and information technology (IT). Some of the elements of an employment-oriented strategy are discussed below.

Information, awareness about capacity, rights and capabilities and organisations are the crucial elements of such a strategy, which requires institutional support. Promotion of entrepreneurship is merely the first step. The government should marshal its expertise and in case it is required, should seek outside help to identify areas where, say for example, floriculture can be developed, identify the persons and train them accordingly with initial provision of loans. Employment generation should be intricately linked with industrial strategy.

3.12 Elements of an Employment Oriented Strategy

3.12.1 Vocational Training for Skill Development

Skill formation and manpower development are crucial for fostering development of human capital and to equip the labour force to take up the challenges of employment opportunities that will come in their way, as Sikkim develops and becomes a vibrant economy with the private sector enterprise being at the core of such a development. Therefore, training is required to enhance their skills, ensuring higher productivity of both the new entrants and the existing workers. While imparting training programmes, accountability must be ensured. In the area of technical education, the state has to play a major role. The state plans to introduce vocational courses at the secondary level to equip the students for gainful employment. Computer education within the regular curricula at the secondary level is being introduced. The Directorate of Technical Education is in the process of implementing the World Bank assisted *Third Technician Project* under which two polytechnics have already been established in the state. Four more polytechnics are to be set up. The Industrial Training Institute (ITI) imparts vocational training in eight trades under the craftsmen training scheme of NCYT. Apart from this, the Sikkim Manipal Institute of Technology offers courses in BE/BCA/MCA. Training imparted by the private sector polytechnic institutes is likely to be more market responsive. These institutes design and offer courses in accordance with the emerging demand for skills. However, strengthening basic education should be assigned top priority.

3.12.2 Social Protection

One of the main attractions of the organised employment is the social security associated with it. There is a need to extend the main benefits to the workers of the unorganised sector as well, which include healthcare, pension, and old age security. As the government is already providing security in many of these areas, there is scope for further improvement. With the growth in industrial activity, the labour laws, labour security, labour related disputes and issues deserve more attention from the government. So far only 13 labour laws are in force in the state; notable ones being *Industrial Disputes Act, Trade Union Act, Industrial Standing Order Act*. Factories Act, Maternity Benefits Act. Though the problem of child labour and bonded labour are nonexistent, the labour department, the NGOs, and rural local bodies may work together for elimination of any kind of exploitation of labourers, that may exist in the state.

To ensure low unemployment, labour market flexibility should be maintained to begin with subject to the compliance of minimum wage rate. To create a high wage, high employment economy with primacy being assigned to education and training, may improve productivity and quality of products. The possibility that higher wage eroding competitiveness and therefore robbing the state of its attractiveness to the investors should not be a stumbling block as market will settle at a higher level of equilibrium. The fear that the gains will accrue to those who are employed at the expense of those who remain outside the job market should not undermine the importance of training and skill formation.

3.13 Employment Generating Schemes

Employment generating schemes will continue to play an important role notwithstanding our renewed emphasis on strategic sectors geared towards employment generation. The schemes will still be needed where the impact of aggregate growth on employment is alleged to be weak. The schemes, which are under operation in the state are discussed below.

Swarna Jayanti Gram Swarojgar Yojana is a self-employment programme. The key elements of this programme are training, technology, infrastructure, and marketing. This scheme in its earlier incarnation known as IRDP, provided assets and inputs to target groups through the provision of bank credit and government subsidy and encouraged formation of self-help groups (SHG). The performance during the Ninth FYP was not impressive as achievement fell far short of the target in most of the cases. However during 2000-01, the coverage increased substantially to 2000 families. Apart from this, individual *Swarozgaris* are to be targeted in the hilly areas where formation of SHG is difficult. Already 158 groups have been formed.

Employment Assurance Scheme seeks to create employment opportunities for the unemployed living in the rural areas particularly during the lean period. This is a centrally sponsored scheme on cost-sharing basis with the state providing for 25 per cent of the project fund. The performance has been impressive. During the Tenth Five-Year Plan period, the target is 149.9 lakh mandays as against 31.58 lakh mandays during the Ninth FYP. Since the population share determines the state's allocation, north-eastern states' shares are alleged to have fallen below the requirements. This has been replaced by a new scheme of wage employment known as *Sampoorna Grameen Rozgar Yojana* (SGRY) with effect from 2001.

A centrally sponsored scheme *Swarna Jayanti Shahari Rozgar Yozana* for generating employment opportunities and removal of urban poverty is also under operation. State's share is 25 per cent and the remaining is funded by the centre. There are three major components of the scheme, urban self-employment programme (USEP), urban wage employment programme (UWEP) and the community structure (CS). Under the three components, USEP, UWEP and CS, Rs. 66 lakh, Rs. 50 lakh and Rs. 79.6 lakh respectively were disbursed in 2003-04. While the schemes are varied and making satisfactory progress, given the need and rise in workforce, the amount sanctioned seems to be small. Under the USEP loan, there was a significant jump in the 2003-04 to 84 beneficiaries from 58 beneficiaries in the year before. For skill development and training under USEP there was also a jump from 310 beneficiaries during 2003-04 from 104 in the previous year.

Under *Entrepreneurship Development Programme* (EDP), educated unemployed youths are also trained. This training programme is carried out in batches in select areas in collaboration with the state and central government department. Small Industries Service Institute (SISI) at Tadong, Sikkim Consultancy Services (SICON), SIDICO and SABCO, banks and financial institutions participate in this programme. During 2003-04, 65 training programmes were conducted.

Creation of an Employment Cell

In view of serious data problem pertaining to the extent of unemployment in the state, the government may consider formation of an employment cell under the Bureau of Economics and Statistics so that a database for unemployed youth can be generated. The information may be gathered from the district headquarters and compiled to generate the database. The data on availability and non-availability of skilled manpower will help in designing region specific policies by targeting those who are in need of jobs.

3.14 Recent Initiatives of the Government

Among the recent initiatives of the government to promote self-employment, the Chief Minister's Self-employment Scheme (CMSS) deserves appreciation. In view of the limited organised sector activity, priority should be given to promote self-employment to encourage private sector initiatives. It is more so, when industrial activities are generally of the types of small-scale enterprises or household.

BOX 3.1

CM's Self-employment Scheme

In the presence of limited industrialisation, employment generation should primarily be self-employment based which entails development of entrepreneurship and necessary skill formation. Launching of CMSS is an initiative in the right direction. The scheme constitutes formation of self-help groups to initiate self-sustaining economic activities with special emphasis on vocational training. Sikkim Industrial Development and Investment Corporation (SIDICO) has been identified as the lead agency. During 2002-03, 41 training programmes of one week duration were conducted and 1491 were trained in various trades like grocery, *manihari*, dairy and poultry farming, tourism related activities, beautician and manufacturing ready-made garments. Loans disbursed were in accordance with the educational qualifications of the entrepreneurs. Those with class X qualification were given Rs. 50,000 and graduates and above were given Rs. 1 lakh. The performance is being monitored and recovery has been satisfactory. The government started off with a fund of Rs. 5 crore to create employment for 800 people. Skill development fund of Rs. 2 crore has also been set up to tackle the problem of limited availability of skilled manpower.

Source: State Budget 2003-04.

BOX 3.2

SIDICO: A Success Story

SIDICO has been playing a lead role in providing credit to the potential entrepreneur. The major difficulty being faced by SIDICO is that the loans are non-competitive because of the high cost of borrowing. If SIDICO can access cheaper funds, it would be possible to disburse loans at a cheaper rate. The cost of funds is around 10.5 per cent. It may be noted that SIDICO is not a bank. Cheaper loans are absolutely necessary in Sikkim to overcome its infirmities.

TABLE

Loans disbursed by SIDICO (Rs. Lakhs)

	2002-03		*2001-02*	
Purposes/trades	*No*	*Amount*	*No*	*Amount*
Hotel/restaurant	62	65.45	98	134.31
Compostie/SSI	22	17.60	35	42.80
Personal computer	294	156.25	164	81.10
Motor vehicle	10	20.10	2	3.50
CMSES	1491	931.50		
Total		1190.90		261.71

Source: SIDICO Annual Report 2002-03.

3.15 Conclusions and Recommendations

The tardy growth of employment opportunities has not been in consonance with reasonably high growth rate the state has achieved. An employment oriented strategy based on private initiative needs to be designed. The continued preference for regular wage employment particularly in the public sector should be discouraged in view of public sector restructuring. This requires ensuring social security for the workers in the presence of a facilitating intervention by the government. 'Son of the soil policy' towards the employment seekers often attract the Sikkimese to return to the state for an assured job, *albeit*, more often than not, in a position lower than what they deserve. This leads to a wastage of talent.

To reiterate, success in generating employment opportunities would crucially depend on the growth of industry and trade. The employment oriented strategy needs to be viewed in the context of the new measures for encouraging industrial development that this report is suggesting (chapter 9).

The state has to ensure employability of the growing workforce to match the emergent demand for skills and to promote self-employment. Low quality jobs with low emoluments need to be phased out with high quality, high wage jobs without sacrificing the competitiveness of the industries arising out of cheap labour as high quality skilled labour, raises productivity and produces better quality products.

Stagnation of agriculture and manufacturing resulted in an increase of marginal workers and those who are employed in unorganised informal activities without any social protection. Measures should be taken to improve their productivity and incomes through skill upgradation and enforcement of Minimum Wages Act.

Migration to urban areas, especially to Gangtok, in search of employment from backward regions of the state is a matter of concern. Ensuring regionally balanced growth of the four districts of the state should be an important part of the public policy. This will generate self-employment and wage employment opportunities in the remote regions of the state.

Chapter 4

Fiscal and Financial Management

Sikkim being a mountainous state with very limited industrial activity has a narrow base for fiscal resources. Like other north-eastern states, Sikkim is a special category state (SCS) which entitles the state to a favourable treatment in terms of dispensation of plan grants from the Planning Commission. This is effected in two steps. Out of total plan assistance, 30 per cent is supposed to be kept aside for the SCS. Out of this, 90 per cent is given as grants and 10 per cent as loans as against 30 per cent grants, and 70 per cent loans for the non-SCS.

The state like other SCSs has come to depend heavily on transfer of resources from the centre. However, in view of overall deterioration in fiscal health, various reform measures have been adopted by the state to ensure fiscal consolidation. While reform initiatives are yielding positive results, there is an urgent need for expediting the reform process at a much wider scale to improve upon the fiscal situation. This is critical, as supporting developmental activities and financing of projects to realise the desired goal being envisaged in this report need more resources.

In this chapter, we present a broad picture of the fiscal situation and financial management of the state. To begin with, we discuss the various sources of state's revenues. This is followed by a discussion on resource utilisation, i.e., state expenditure and the importance of good governance in expenditure management. The outcome of resource generation, central transfers and expenditure are reflected in deficit and debt profile of the state. This is followed by an account of the state's progress in setting up the Panchayati Raj institutions and fiscal decentralisation. The chapter concludes with an account of state's reform initiatives and suggests ways to overcome the dependency on centre by diversifying revenue sources, improved expenditure management and expenditure restructuring.

4.1 State's Own Resources: Tax Revenues

Sikkim has broadly three major sources of resources, (a) own revenue from taxes and non-taxes; (b) transfer from the Centre comprising plan grants and non-plan grants, state's share in central taxes and resources dispensed by the ministries for financing of projects (partly or wholly), including North-east Council (NEC) and the Ministry of Development of North-East Region (DONER), special area programmes such as Border Area Development Programme (BADP) and centrally sponsored schemes (CSS); and (c) borrowing from the centre, financial institutions, and small savings and provident funds.

The share of own tax revenue in GSDP witnessed a fall during the 1990s from around 7.8 per cent in 1989-90 to 5.8 per cent in 1999-2000. However, it turned around and by 2002-03, the ratio was nearly 10 per cent of GSDP. This was mainly on account of higher collection from income taxes (under the state laws) on lotteries and impressive collection from sales tax. However, as per the latest budget for 2004-05, own tax ratio fell to 7 per cent in 2003-04 (revised estimate). It was the slump in taxes collected from state's own income tax and sales tax, which pulled the ratio down in 2003-04.

The changing relative importance of sources of own tax revenue is noteworthy. The share of state income tax has gained importance over the years as noted above. The tax rates have never been revised upwards with exemption limit remaining unchanged despite growth in the number of taxpayers at the lower income level as GSDP continued to grow at a reasonably high rate. This has possibly made the tax structure highly regressive as the effective tax rate rises at a declining rate with the growth in income (Table 4.1). However, the tempo in income tax collection has slowed down considerably in the recent past, though, the shares of stamps and registration fees and sales taxes has continued to rise. In contrast, the shares of state excise, land revenue, and tax on vehicles have shrunk.

To assess the individual performance of the different sources of tax revenues, one should look at the growth in revenue associated with the rise in respective tax bases (proxied by GSDP) as measured by buoyancy. It is evident from the buoyancy estimates (Table 4.2) of all the major taxes during the period 1996-97 to 2002-03 compared to an earlier period of 1989-90 to 1995-96 that there has been a satisfactory improvement in resource mobilisation from state income tax, sales tax, state excise duties, and stamps and registration duties. However, collection from land revenue and taxes on vehicles have not been commensurate with the GSDP growth.

Additional revenue mobilisation: The effort by the state government in garnering additional resources has been laudable. The Appendix Table A.15 shows measures adopted to mobilise additional tax revenue during 1997-1998 to 2001-02. One of the factors behind impressive performance in tax collection is the collection of arrears. The arrears in tax collection have been brought down significantly in the recent years.

4.2 State's Own Resources: Non-tax Revenues

The state, like own tax revenue, also witnessed a fall in the share of non-tax revenue in GSDP during the 1990s. The share declined nearly by 3.8 percentage points during 1991-92 to 2001-2002 (Table 4.3). However, the improvement in the share thereafter has been spectacular. The share rose to 13 per cent during 2002-2003 from 7.3 per cent in the previous year. Collection from online lottery and dividends[1] are responsible for this sudden spurt. However, it is being apprehended that increasing competition and mounting number of cases of litigations from private operators might dampen the growth of this promising source of revenue. This is evident if one looks at the State Budget for 2004-05. The budget shows a fall in this specific source of revenue of around 5 percentage points. This is likely to have serious implications on the health of state finances. The state's effort in raising user charges in various spheres of public delivery of services deserves attention.

TABLE 4.1

Composition of Own Tax Revenues (Percentage Share)

	1990-91	*1994-95*	*1998-99*	*2002-03*
Income Tax Levied under State Laws	26.00	27.34	39.19	30.84
Land Revenue	1.81	0.57	0.26	0.38
Stamps & Registration Fees	1.16	1.23	1.09	3.26
State Excise Tax	42.05	36.39	25.36	21.19
Total Sales Tax	20.10	27.03	27.94	39.09
Tax on Vehicles	2.40	3.28	3.24	2.22
Other Taxes on Commodities & Services	6.48	4.17	2.92	3.04
Own Tax Revenue	100.0	100.0	100.0	100.0

Source: Finance Accounts, Budget Documents and CSO estimates of GSDP.

TABLE 4.2

Buoyancy Estimates

	1989/90-1995/96 *1*	*1996/97-2002/03* *2*	*Improvement (+) = (2-1)*
Own Tax Revenue	0.60	1.81	1.20
Income Tax Levied under State Laws	0.60	1.98	1.38
Land Revenue	0.75	0.52	-0.22
Stamps & Registration Fees	0.73	2.67	1.95
State Excise Duty	0.35	1.12	0.78
State Sales Tax	0.95	2.33	1.38
Tax on Vehicles	1.30	0.79	-0.52
Other Taxes on Commodities & Services	0.02	1.63	1.61

Source: Estimates by the team based on data available in the *Finance Accounts* and CSO, GoI.

The unrecovered dues from the sick and closed industries has been a major area of concern. Transport and power are the two major areas where the state spends more than what it earns indicating large sum of explicit subsidy. The state is incurring substantial amount of losses due to subsidised power tariff, and T&D losses. In 2002-03 and 2003-04, the losses amounted to Rs. 34 crore and Rs. 27 crore respectively. Similarly for transport, losses amounted to Rs. 4.1 crore and Rs. 4.5 crore in 2002-03 and 2003-04, down from Rs. 9 crore in 1999-2000.[2]

4.3 Transfers from the Centre

Trends in Transfer

Total transfer from the centre comprising plan and non-plan and the state's share in central taxes

1. There was an increase of Rs. 67 crore in the collection.
2. Interim memorandum submitted to the *Twelfth Finance Commission*, Vol. I, 2003, GoS.

TABLE 4.3

Revenue Sources: 1985-86 to 2003-04 (Select Years) (As a Percentage of GSDP)

	1985-86	*1991-92*	*1993-94*	*1995-96*	*1997-98*	*1999-2000*	*2000-01*	*2001-02*	*2002-03*	*2003-04 (R)*
Revenue Receipts	75.04	70.31	59.59	72.57	63.38	63.55	70.15	76.75	85.14	81.91
a. Own-tax Revenue	4.67	5.95	5.53	5.67	5.61	5.84	7.22	8.28	9.95	6.85
b. Non-tax Revenue	8.86	11.04	7.30	7.23	6.61	7.71	7.20	7.28	13.36	10.03
c. Share of Central Taxes	10.44	9.83	9.55	9.37	12.27	11.85	7.88	8.63	7.21	8.22
d. Grants from the Centre	51.08	43.50	37.21	50.30	38.90	38.15	47.84	52.57	54.63	56.81

Source: Finance Accounts, various issues and *Budget Documents*, select years.

declined from nearly 57 per cent in 1980-81 to 50 per cent in 1999-2000 to rise again to nearly 62 per cent in 2002-03. State's share in central taxes continued to rise from merely 0.5 per cent of GSDP in 1980-81 to 12.27 per cent in 1997-98 (Table 4.4). The share declined in the recent years mainly on account of a tardy growth in tax collection by the Centre. In fact, SCS with heavy dependence on their share in Central taxes suffer more. In terms of Sikkim's share in total central transfers, the percentage share has risen from 0.27 (as recommended by the Eighth Finance Commission (1985-1990) to 0.38 as recommended by the Eleventh Finance Commission (2000-2005).[3] However, the decline in the share of non-plan grants led to a fall in the share of total grants during 1997-98 and 2002-03. It may be remembered that for a SCS like Sikkim, where central transfers constitute a major proportion of total revenue, declining share in central taxes is destabilising for managing state finances.

The importance of central transfers for the state can also be understood from the profile of revenue composition. In 1980-81, central transfers constituted nearly 92 per cent of revenue receipts while the rest came from own taxes and non-tax sources. The dependence on central transfers has, in fact, gone down unlike many other north-eastern states. In 2002-03, 27 per cent of revenue receipts came from own sources, tax and non-tax combined in contrast with 18 percent in 1985-86 due to improved performances in tax and non-tax collection in the recent years (Table 4.4). As per the Budget estimate for 2004-05, a rise in the allocation of plan grants due to release from NEC would lead to a rise in the share of central transfers to nearly 80 per cent.

Trends in Grants

Plan grants in terms of GSDP fell marginally from 37 to 35 per cent during 1980-81 to 2002-03 only to rise again in 2004-05 (Budget estimate). Despite a fall in non-plan grants, during the same period, the total grants witnessed a marginal rise.

TABLE 4.4

Central Transfers: Select Years (As a Percentage of GSDP)

	1980-81	*1985-86*	*1991-92*	*1995-96*	*1997-98*	*1999-2000*	*2002-03*	*2004-05 (R)*
1. (2+3) Total Transfers	56.8	61.5	53.3	59.67	51.17	50.00	61.8	65.0
2. Share of Central Taxes	0.5	10.4	9.8	9.37	12.27	11.85	7.2	8.22
3. Total Grants	56.3	51.1	43.5	50.30	38.90	38.15	54.63	56.8
Plan Grants	37.1	38.2	35.9	39.63	33.24	36.23	34.6	41.9
Non-plan Grants	19.2	12.9	7.6	10.68	5.66	1.92	20.1	14.9
Memo: Transfers/Revenue Receipts*	91.9	81.9	75.8	82.2	80.7	78.7	72.6	79.4

Note: *Only profit from lotteries has been considered in estimating revenue receipts rather than gross collection from lotteries.

Source: Finance Accounts and *Budget Documents* (GoS).

3. This has happened only to Sikkim among the North-eastern states, apart from Jammu and Kashmir among the SCS.

State Plan

Tenth Five-Year Plan

The approved outlay for the Ninth Plan was Rs. 1600 crore. However, the state was able to draw Rs. 1265 crore, i.e., 79 per cent of the approved plan size due to lower utilisation of plan funds. Only under the head of rural development, the state spent Rs. 70 crore, substantially more than the agreed plan outlay of Rs. 49 crore. For all other items, the actual expenditure fell short. In the aggregate, the actual plan expenditure was 76 per cent of agreed plan outlay of Rs. 1257 crore.

The approved outlay for the Tenth Plan was Rs. 1655.74 crore, an increase of only 3.5 per cent under the guidelines of the Planning Commission compared to that of Ninth Plan outlay. However, the state government submitted an ambitious proposal amounting to Rs. 3062.7 crore for the Tenth Plan.

An attempt has been made to ensure that the major observations and recommendations of the two reports prepared by the state government, the *Human Development Report, 2001* and the *Vision Document* are considered while formulating the Tenth Plan. The shares in approved outlay have increased in transport, rural development, social services, and general services (Table 4.5).

TABLE 4.5

Plan Outlay: Approved and Actual

	Ninth Plan Outlay		*Tenth Plan Outlay*	
	Approved (in Rs. crore)	*Share (per cent)*	*Approved (in Rs. crore)*	*Share (per cent)*
Agriculture and Allied Activities	205.4	12.84	174.99	10.57
Rural Development	54.4	3.40	74	4.47
Special Area Programme	—	—	30	1.81
Irrigation and Flood Control	41	2.56	31	1.87
Energy	343	21.44	242.9	14.67
Industry and Minerals	70	4.38	62	3.74
Transport	160	10.00	265	16.00
Science, Technology and Environment	11	0.69	11	0.66
General Economic Services	53.75	3.36	40.4	2.44
Social Services	616.35	38.52	666.25	40.24
General Services	45	2.81	58.2	3.52
Grand Total	1600	100	1656	100

Source: Tenth Five-Year Plan Documents.

The Annual Plan outlay for 2002-03 was Rs. 350 crore, which was 21 per cent of total outlay under the Tenth Five Year Plan. The size of the Annual Plan for 2003-04 marks an increase of 62 per cent.

Out of which, states' own resources is projected to be Rs. 95.5 crore and the remaining would be in the form of central assistance. Among the north-eastern states, Sikkim is one of the three states, which is expected to make a positive contribution towards the Tenth Plan size (Table A-14). However, the scheme of financing shows overwhelming dependence on net market borrowings (SLR based) to the tune of Rs. 201 crore and Rs. 67.5 crore of negotiated loans to offset Rs. (-)51.25 crore from balance on current revenue (BCR) and miscellaneous capital receipts of Rs. 194.35 crore among other items.

Plan expenditure as a percentage of GSDP for the state during the Eighth and Ninth FYP was 36.5 and 33.8, next only to Arunachal Pradesh among the SCS.[4]

Given the size of the Plan for a relatively small state like Sikkim and the imperatives of plan financing, there are serious implications of higher plan size for the state finances. The important concept in this context is balance on current revenue (BCR), which measures state's contribution towards plan financing out of own resources after meeting the current expenditures. The overall improvement in the fiscal situation is reflected in an improvement of BCR as per the latest available data (Table 4.6). However, in 2003-04, there has been a deterioration in the balance mainly because of the slump in non-tax collection.

TABLE 4.6

Balance from Current Revenues (BCR)

(in Rs. crore)

	1999-2000	*2000-01*	*2001-02*	*2002-03*	*2003-04 Pre-actuals*
1. Own Tax	49.07	65.39	80.38	105.53	106.77
2. Share in Central Taxes	99.54	72.2	84.83	77.2	111.87
3. Non-tax Revenues	64.79	65.53	71.12	143.36	93.72
4. Revenue Receipts=1+2+3	213.4	203.12	236.33	326.09	312.36
5. Non-plan Grants	10.8	147.71	139.32	213.9	150.33
6. Non-plan Revenue Expenditure	397.41	383.99	414.49	462.11	474.65
7. BCR=6-4-5	-173.21	-33.16	-38.84	77.88	-11.96

Source: Latest data provided by the Department of Finance, GoS.

4. *Tenth Five-Year Plan, Vol. III*, p 14.

Since the north-eastern states are allowed to debit the committed liabilities of previous plan schemes to the extent of 20 per cent under the plan account, plan size gets affected. The inability of the state to utilise plan funds resulting in actual expenditure falling short of approved outlay has been an issue of concern.

Centrally Sponsored Schemes and Departmental Transfers

Over and above the plan funds agreed upon between the Planning Commission and the state government, there are three additional channels of resource transfers, namely, funds given under additional central assistance (ACA), funds released by the NEC, and the DONER under the scheme of non-lapsable central pool of resources.

Additional Central Assistance (ACA)

The state government gets one time project specific grant as ACA. During March, 1998 to December, 2002, there were eight schemes amounting to nearly Rs. 15 crore.

Among the schemes, worth mentioning is the Border Area Development Programme (BADP). The objective of the programme is to cater to the special needs of the people living in the remote and inaccessible border areas. Special central assistance is provided as 100 per cent grants. The share of the state is determined by the length of the border, area and population of the border blocks (all assigned equal weightage).

NEC and DONER

NEC: Sikkim was inducted into the North-East Council as the eighth member in September 2003. NEC has been recognised as a regional planning body. During the current financial year 2004-05, Rs. 32 crore (up from Rs. 0.90 crore in 2003-04) is expected to be released by the NEC.

DONER: In the central budget for 1998-99, the setting up of a non-lapsable pool of resources (NLCPR) was mooted. Earlier, in 1996-97, it was decided that each central ministry or department should earmark 10 per cent of its budget for the north-eastern region. In the event of actual allocation falling short of 10 per cent of budget allocation, the resources to the extent of this shortfall should be transferred to this pool for development purposes for north-east out of an approved amount of Rs. 3103.60 crore, Sikkim's share is 7.5 per cent. During 1998-2003, out of Rs. 1868.66 crore, Rs. 158.30 crore (8.5 per cent) was released to the state. The project-wise performance of Sikkim has been satisfactory, as NLCPR commitments have generally been complied with for the DONER projects.

Finance Commission Transfer

For non-plan grants, there has been a very steep rise to 16.3 per cent of GSDP in 2000-01 from 1.9 in the previous financial year. This is because the Tenth Finance Commission required the state to bridge the non-plan revenue gap by the end of 1998-99 through ARM and therefore no funds were made available to finance the deficit in the non-plan revenue gap (Table 4.8).

Under the assessment of the Tenth Finance Commission, non-plan revenue expenditure was grossly under-assessed, particularly for 1998-99. The state finances got derailed on account of a sharp jump in the

TABLE 4.7

Releases from BADP and NLCPR BADP: Allocation/Releases during the Ninth Plan

(in Rs. lakh)

	1998-99		*1999-2000*		*2000-01*		*2001-02*
	Allocation	*Release*	*Allocation*	*Release*	*Allocation*	*Release*	*Allocation*
Sikkim	400	400	550	550	572	463	572
Total	19500#	19152	21000	21000	21000	21000	21000@

	Releases of Funds from NLCPR (in Rs. Lakh)			
	1998-99	*1999-00*	*2000-01*	*2001-02*
Sikkim	1000	3201	2378	4971
Common to North-east & Sikkim	—	900	946	—
Total	12195	41992	31304	49181

Note: # 1997-98: Rs. 400 lakh were left unallocated for Myanmar border states. @ Actual: Rs. 24,000 lakh.

Source: Tenth Five Year Plan, Vol. III, p. 94 and 99.

TABLE 4.8

Assessment made by the Tenth Finance Commission

(in Rs. crore)

	1995-96	1996-97	1997-98	1998-99	1999-2000	Total
Receipts*						
Assessed	35.04	39.31	43.59	48.57	53.92	220.33
Actual	55.54	61.05	82.35	71.38	96.02	366.34
Non-plan revenue expenditure						
Assessed	151.07	163.57	175.53	188.30	201.73	880.20
Actual	179.65	203.69	255.07	357.83	397.41	1393.65
Non-plan revenue deficit after devolution**						
Assessed	-48.05	-37.45	-15.06	-5.13	7.89	-97.80
Actual	-72.45	-61.10	-83.71	-166.35	-184.01	-567.62
Non-plan revenue deficit grants						
Assessed	48.05	37.45	15.06	5.13	0.0	105.69
Actual	48.05	37.45	15.06	5.13	0.0	105.69
Overall surplus or deficit						
Assessed	0	0	0	0	7.89	7.89
Actual	-24.40	-23.65	-68.65	-161.22	-184.01	-461.93

Note: *–Includes tax revenue (excluding state income tax), non-tax revenue and non-plan grants.

**–Devolution includes state income tax.

Source: GoS (2003). "Interim Memorandum" submitted to the *Twelfth Finance Commission*.

wages and salaries bill, which was not accounted for. Actual receipts exceeded assessed receipts, otherwise the situation would have been worse. During the initial years of the Eleventh Finance Commission assessment, state's performance in revenue collection from own sources, particularly, in non-tax revenue have been better than predicted. This has contained the extent of slippage as reflected in the overall improvement in the fiscal health.

4.4 Borrowing Requirements

The borrowing requirements of the state governments are primarily determined by the plan size and various other schemes (like CSS), which entail counterpart funding on the part of the state. As mentioned earlier, Sikkim, being a SCS, is entitled to 90 per cent of plan size as grants and the remaining as loans. Notwithstanding, the borrowing as a percentage of plan size, comprising state plans and centrally sponsored scheme (CSS) has risen over the years (Table 4.8).[5] A detailed calculation may churn out a lower percentage, but the message remains loud and clear. The component of borrowing even for a SCS is pretty high compared to the plan related grants from the centre. In the absence of a commensurate return from investment on borrowed resources compared to the cost of borrowing (which is unlikely and often not warranted given the high component of social expenditure in total plan expenditure) debt conditionality indicates that the state would gradually slip into a debt trap.

One of the major attributes to this increased borrowing is to be the underassessment of resource requirements by the Ninth, Tenth and the Eleventh Finance Commissions under-assessed resource requirements which led to an increase in borrowing by the state.

4.5 Utilisation of Resources: Trends in Expenditure

Though the state is spending more towards revenue expenditure in terms of GSDP, the share of capital outlay has increased. However, the composition of net aggregate expenditure has moved in favour of revenue expenditure, committed liabilities arising out of plan financing at the end of the plan period are treated as non-plan expenditure. Therefore, higher plan size inevitably leads to mounting non-plan expenditure. In terms of the size of the economy, revenue expenditure has gone up by 13 percentage points during 1985-86 and 2002-03 (Table 4.3). The share of net lending has remained stagnant.

The growth in the interest payments has also been steep. The ratio of interest payments rose from 4.1 per cent of GSDP to 9.4 per cent during 1985-86 to 2002-2003. As argued earlier, not only has the state been borrowing more, it has been doing so at a higher cost. During the 1990s, the effective interest rate on borrowing went up, pulling up the effective interest cost on total borrowing to nearly 15 per cent. Only in the recent years the rates have mellowed down. As per the budget estimate for 2004-05, the effective interest rate on outstanding debt is likely to fall to 11.1 per cent. However, there is a scope for further reduction in the effective rate of interest, if the state resorts more on debt swap.

Within revenue expenditure, the share of social services in terms of GSDP has increased from 18.2 per cent in 1985-86 to 22.4 per cent in 2002-03 whereas the share of economic services has witnessed a fall

5. The percentage shown here is higher than what it should be if loans were shown as a percentage of aggregate plan resources. The estimates given in the Table 4.8 needs further refinement. The estimates by the state government indicate that the loans constitute one-fifth of aggregate plan resources.

TABLE 4.9

Loan Component of Plan Financing

	Market Loans	*Loans for State Plan Schemes*	*Loans for CSSS*	*Small Savings & PF*	*Total Loans*	*Plan Grants*	*Grants for CSS*	*Total Grants*	*Loans as per cent of Plan Grants*
1989-90	576	608	91	385	1659	5465	969	6434	25.8
1990-91	654	681	98	466	1898	6233	1246	7480	25.4
1991-92	729	873	101	574	2278	7858	1407	9265	24.6
1992-93	712	984	158	787	2640	8850	1739	10589	24.9
1993-94	719	1088	144	979	2930	9863	2289	12152	24.1
1994-95	1165	1255	77	1180	3676	11822	2092	13914	26.4
1995-96	1603	1866	139	1238	4845	16235	2719	18955	25.6
1996-97	1783	1702	134	1464	5083	15426	2199	17625	28.8
1997-98	2000	2151		1848	5999	19304	2117	21421	28.0
1998-99	4200	2438	54	9510	16202	21828	3947	25775	62.9
1999-2000	6999	2882	25	5680	15587	26855	3502	30357	51.3
2000-2001	2500	2662	192	5261	10615	23866	4724	28590	37.1
2001-2002	2650	3189	516	5894	12249	31049	5768	36816	33.3
2002-2003	3008	3403	73	6356	12840	30931	5638	36570	35.1

Source: Finance Accounts and *Budget Documents.*

during the same period (Table 4.10). What is disconcerting is the rate at which pension bill has been growing during the 1990s. A growth rate of 26 per cent per annum will put enormous pressure on fiscal balance. The burden may further go up with the possibility that retirement is due on a massive scale from 2006-07 onwards.[6]

The trend for social and economic services under capital outlay is similar to that of revenue expenditure during the same period as the decline in economic services has been compensated by a rise in expenditure on social services to maintain the aggregate at around 20 per cent.[7]

Subsidies: Direct subsidies under the *Sikkim Industrial Promotion and Incentive Act, 2000* (state power subsidy) has steadily increased. The *Act* is now being amended in view of the situation in the other north-eastern states.[8]

With effect from April 1, 2004, the wage bill was supposed to have increased by 70 per cent in order to implement an earlier announcement made by the government that wage rate per day would be raised. Under the mounting pressure of the wage bill, insufficient allocation for maintenance will have a deleterious effect on the assets that are being created under the plan. This tendency of the maintenance expenditure to be residually determined has adverse impact on the delivery of public services including education and health.

4.6 Fiscal Reform Programme and MTFRP

The state entered into a MoU with the Ministry of Finance in May 1999 with the objective of restoring fiscal balance through expenditure management and augmenting revenue collection. MoU between the Government of Sikkim and the Ministry of Finance, Government of India, in pursuance of Medium Term Fiscal Restructuring Policy, Sikkim 2000-05, provide for pegging dearness allowance (DA) at 50 per cent of the rate notified by the central government employees from time to time, and to continue with the debt scheme among other measures. Earlier, the state faced employee unrest owing to non-payment of salaries.

Based on the recommendations of a study sponsored by the state government, a committee has been appointed to implement closure of loss making state level public sector enterprises (SLPSEs) and restructuring of other profit making SLPSEs.

6. The bureaucracy expanded on a large scale when the state became a part of India in 1975.
7. This ratio is generally much higher than that of the non-SCS and also than the majority of the SCS.
8. "Interim memorandum" to the *TFC*, Vol. III, p 56.

TABLE 4.10

Expenditure: 1985-86 to 2003-04 (Select Years) (As a Percentage of GSDP)

	1985-86	*1991-92*	*1993-94*	*1995-96*	*1997-98*	*1999-2000*	*2000-01*	*2001-02*	*2002-03*	*2004-05 R*
Revenue Expenditure	63.54	59.78	50.05	60.10	57.04	63.33	59.25	62.13	66.57	67.85
Interest Payment	4.14	5.73	5.75	6.02	6.70	8.59	9.25	9.26	9.44	9.05
Social Services	18.15	20.19	16.71	21.92	22.03	23.36	21.12	23.19	22.41	23.8
Economic Services	33.07	25.15	19.04	22.82	19.63	20.22	18.09	18.78	22.35	21.85
Capital Expenditure										
	1985-86	*1991-92*	*1993-94*	*1995-96*	*1997-98*	*1999-2000*	*2000-01*	*2001-02*	*2002-03*	*2004-05 R*
Capital Outlay	20.86	26.33	17.83	21.02	16.47	11.23	16.56	21.56	19.62	23.68
Social Services	3.61	6.38	6.10	6.69	5.08	4.31	5.52	7.52	7.85	9.66
Economic Services	15.97	18.42	10.98	13.25	10.38	6.46	10.55	13.22	10.69	12.81

Source: Finance Accounts, various issues and *Budget Documents,* select years.

The fiscal reform programme of the Eleventh Finance Commission, provided incentives for improved fiscal performance subject to the compliance of conditionalities. The state could tap two installments of revenue deficit grants along with the incentives. Delay in the release of the third installment caused liquidity crisis for the state.

The criterion to be fulfilled for the SCS so as to be eligible for release from Incentive Fund is a 2 percentage point improvement in the revenue deficit as a percentage of total revenue receipts from 2002-03 onwards.

The outcome of various measures being initiated by the state government is reflected in the fiscal indicator of revenue account balance over revenue receipts.

TABLE 4.11

Effective Interest Rate on Outstanding Debt

	1986-87	*1990-91*	*1993-94*	*1995-96*	*1997-98*	*2002-03*
Total debt	9.3	13.3	13.2	13.5	14.8	12.3
Debt to the Centre	18.0	16.8	15.1	14.9	16.1	13.5
Internal debt	7.1	11.0	11.1	12.2	13.9	12.8
Small savings & PF	8.8	16.6	16.6	14.3	14.4	9.8

Note: Effective cost of borrowing is defined as the ratio of interest payment in period t and accumulated debt stock at the end of period (t-1) or at the beginning of period t.

Source: Finance Accounts, various issues. GoS.

TABLE 4.12

Fiscal Performance 1999-2000 to 2003-04 (BE)

(in Rs. crore)

	1999-00	*2000-01*	*2001-02*	*2002-03 (RE)*	*2003-04 (BE)*
Revenue Account Balance	-1.86	-99.29	-142.93	-197.90	-199.28
Revenue Receipts	533.87	639.20	750.08	90804	908.04
Rev. Balance as a % of Revenue Receipts	0.35	15.53	19.06	21.79	21.46
Improvement over 1999-2000		15.18	18.71	21.14	21.11
Withheld Grant		25.46	25.61	25.48	24.97
Incentive Funds		0.23	0.40	0.44	0.49

Note: The revised and the budget estimates would change as per Budget for 2004-05. Since revenue receipts include state's share in central taxes, which is exogenous to the state, the indicator has been subject to criticism.

Source: GoS. "Interim Memorandum" to the *Twelfth Finance Commission,* Vol. I, p.25.

4.7 Deficits and Debt

The structural infirmities of the state are reflected in the profile of deficits and debt profile. The resource base is narrow owing to the limited industrial activity and small size of the population. On the other hand, costs of providing public services increase because of the topography and remoteness of the state and sparse density of population. However, as noted earlier, this problem is sought to be overcome by favourable dispensation of plan grants. This explains why the state has a revenue surplus barring one year, i.e., 1998-99 when the state implemented the Pay Commission recommendations.

BOX 4.1

Reform Measures Under MoU and MTFRP

Some of the reform measures are outlined below:

i. A majority of the state taxes have been revised upwards. The taxes are, sales tax, motor vehicles tax, stamps and registration duties, excise duty on liquor and other products, cost of stamp papers, land revenue, and entertainment tax.

ii. User charges for medical tests in government hospitals, and various administrative works, parking fees, have also been revised upward. Charging education fees for secondary and higher levels are under review.

iii. Reining in non-plan revenue expenditure through a ban on creation of new posts and filling up of vacancies, reduction of food subsidy by 10 per cent, reduction of office expenses by 10 per cent and traveling expenses by 25 per cent. Scholarships, stipends and free boarding charges were rationalised. Ban was imposed on purchases of new vehicles unless absolutely necessary.

iv. Some departments have been amalgamated. For example, The Sikkim Nationalised Transport (SNT) and Motor Vehicles Department have been merged together and renamed as the Transport Department. Department of Forests and Department of Fisheries have also been merged furthermore, Welfare Department and the Women and Child Welfare Department have also been amalgamated and renamed as Social Welfare Department.

v. Out of 1252 applications received for VRS, only 138 could be accepted during 2002-03 due to lack of adequate funds. Expenditure incurred to the tune of Rs. 7 crore was financed out of state plan.

vi. The measures in the pipeline are: periodical review of grants, levying tax on professionals, rationalising subsidies by targeting the poor only, discontinuing the policy of conversion of muster roll and daily wage workers to work charged and consequently to regular posts.

vii. Ceiling on Guarantees. The outstanding guarantees given by the state is Rs. 76.7 crore, which is much lower than the prescribed ceiling. Steps are being mooted to create a Guarantee Redemption Fund and Sinking Fund for repayment of market borrowing.

viii. Debt swap schemes: Two outstanding loans of Rs. 10 crore each have been cleared, carrying interest in the range of 13.5 to 15 per cent under the Debt Swap Scheme. The government has resorted to market borrowing through RBI at interest rates of 6.2 per cent and 6.95 per cent in order to repay the previous loans carrying interest of 12.5 and 13.5 per cent respectively.

There has been a surplus in the revenue account except for the year 1998-99 due to the imposition of the additional burden arising out of the implementation of the Pay Commission recommendations. There was a sharp jump in the revenue surplus to 10.9 per cent in 2000-01 from only 0.2 during the previous year due to the rise in non-plan grants to meet the non-plan revenue deficit. Moreover, the revenue surplus has risen further afterwards. This has enabled the state to spend borrowed resources as well as the surplus in the revenue account towards capital formation. Plan grants are linked to the plan size and it is more so for the SCS. With the increase in plan size, an increase in plan grants turns the revenue account into a surplus.

During 1998-99, the fiscal deficit reached its peak at 18.8 per cent of GSDP from 10.4 per cent in the previous year. However, the steady improvement in the fiscal situation till 2002-03 is unlikely to be sustained

TABLE 4.13

Deficits and Debt: 1985-86 to 2003-04 (Select Years) (As a Percentage of GSDP)

	1985-86	*1991-92*	*1993-94*	*1995-96*	*1997-98*	*1999-2000*	*2000-01*	*2001-02*	*2002-03*	*2003-04 R*
Deficits and Debt										
Revenue Deficit	-11.51	-10.54	-9.54	-12.47	-6.34	-0.22	-10.90	-14.63	-18.6	-14.06
Fiscal Deficit	9.14	15.83	8.15	8.33	10.37	11.02	5.54	6.84	0.93	9.55
Primary Deficit	5.00	10.09	2.39	2.30	3.67	2.43	-3.70	-2.42	-8.51	0.50
	1986	*1992*	*1994*	*1996*	*1998*	*2000*	*2001*	*2002*	*2003*	*2004 R*
Outstanding Debts on March 31	32.42	63.29	56.90	57.44	54.76	80.63	80.18	82.61	81.6	81.34

Source: Finance Accounts, various issues and *Budget Documents,* select years.

(Table 4.13). The fiscal deficit is budgeted to shoot up to 16.5 per cent during 2004-05, up from 9.5 per cent in 2003-04 (Revised Estimate).

The primary deficit turned into a primary surplus in 2000-01. This is indicative of a rising interest burden and a falling fiscal deficit in the recent years. With the rise in fiscal deficit, primary surplus turned into a deficit in 2003-04, however small.

In terms of debt sustainability, the evolving fiscal scenario appears to be worrisome. There has been a steady rise in the debt to GSDP ratio from 60 per cent of GSDP in 1990-91 to nearly 81 per cent in the 2002-2003 and it is budgeted to go up to 84 per cent in 2004-05. The sharp jump in the ratio in 1999-2000 by 16 percentage points seems to have remained stable afterwards. There has been a change in the composition of debt. The shares of market borrowing and small savings and provident fund (PF) have risen from 20.8 and 7.5 respectively in 1990-91 to 32.3 and 21.6 respectively in 2002-03 while the debt owed to the centre has declined.

An equally disconcerting fact for the state is the steady increase in debt servicing, i.e., repayment of loans and interest rate combined together, as a percentage of loans. For market loans, there is, in fact, a reverse flow of funds indicating that the state has to keep aside more to service past debts than what the state borrows. There is a clear indication that the situation is worsening for loans from both centre and small savings and provident fund.

TABLE 4.14

Debt Servicing as a Percentage of Loans

Year	*Market*	*Centre*	*Small Savings and PF*
1989-90	23.27	28.67	64.99
1990-91	25.34	65.81	68.29
1991-92	50.05	94.62	63.10
1992-93	57.00	104.36	58.3
1993-94	127.30	101.88	65.22
1994-95	100.80	93.31	86.00
1995-96	98.93	88.55	88.09
1996-97	116.10	89.32	85.07
1997-98	104.83	97.64	84.52
2002-03	130.24	147.99	94.33

Source: Finance Accounts and *Budget Documents*. GoS.

Financing of Fiscal Deficit and Its Composition

Since the state has a surplus in its revenue account in general, capital formation is financed by borrowed resources as indicated by the fiscal deficit as well as by revenue surplus. It has been possible for the government to spend to the tune of 20 per cent of GSDP on capital formation (as measured by capital outlay). However, there is one worrying aspect of financing fiscal deficit apart from its rising magnitude. The use of cash balances to meet the deficit has suddenly gone up. This indicates worsening cash management for the state.

4.8 Fiscal Decentralisation

Based on the recommendations of a cabinet sub-committee, decentralisation of financial powers to the PRIs was implemented from Aug 1, 2003. The objective was to delegate more administrative and financial powers to PRIs at *zilla* and *gram* level in view of the 73rd constitutional amendment.

On account of the geographical imbalances of the districts and the socio-economic living standard of the people, the *Gram Panchayats* are not on the same pedestal. The need is to treat them differently invoking the principles of both horizontal and vertical equity so as to avoid any fiscal imbalances arising out of devolution of grants-in-aid among the rural bodies.

The state government has been providing grants-in-aid to the *Gram Panchayats* at Rs. 10,000 per annum as a lump sum grant to meet their administrative expenditure besides funds under state plan schemes, CSS and central schemes.

The Second State Finance Commission made several recommendations to strengthen the finances of the PRIs. Important among them are listed below:

- To enable the local bodies discharge their responsibilities, steps should be taken to improve the resource base of these institutions.
- Non-plan expenditure and funds for CSS are to be treated as grants to the local bodies.
- One per cent of net proceeds of all taxes collected by the state should be transferred to the local bodies.
- Urban local bodies should impose property tax within urban areas and takeover the urban land tax from the state government.
- Property tax to be imposed and collected by urban local bodies. Urban land tax rate may be enhanced and collection to be entrusted with the urban local bodies.

- Entertainment tax should be raised by 10 per cent and leakages to be plugged.
- Toll tax and parking fees to be charged by the municipal corporations. Among other measures, municipal corporation may also levy professional tax, introduce sanitation tax, increase the advertisement tax and revise the rent of hat shed and rent of super market premises.
- The *Panchayat* units should also impose house tax instead of rupee 1 being collected by the Land Revenue Department. Water tax should be imposed at the rate of Re 1 per tap and water cesses from the user of irrigation facilities.

In view of the detailed recommendations of the SFC, the state should endeavour to enlarge the revenue base of rural local bodies.

4.9 Recommendations and Conclusions

Recommendations to restore fiscal balance and fiscal restructuring are broadly classified into two categories, revenue augmenting measures, and expenditure management.

4.9.1 Revenue Augmenting Measures

The basic objective would be to explore the possibilities of diversifying sources of revenues. Given the narrow revenue base, the state should explore other sources of revenue to reduce state's dependence on central transfers in financing expenditure. Though the growth in revenue has been satisfactory and with the expansion of economic activities at a faster pace as reforms take off, growth in revenue will be insufficient to help reduce state's dependence on centre. As economic activities gain momentum and its coverage widens, the state can devise measures to garner additional resources from these sources. One way to counter falling revenues from lotteries is to curtail explicit subsidies being extended to power and transport through achieving better operational efficiencies and raising user charges.

In fact, revenue from power can reduce state's dependence on centre. This is because power remains the most promising source of revenue for the state in future, given its immense potential, which has largely remained untapped.

Registration fees for vehicles should be raised, for new as well as old. One time registration fee for the new vehicles in line with such practices elsewhere in India can be considered.

The state income tax needs to be revisited to make it more progressive and equitable. The state income tax structure has not been revised since the very beginning. Tax payers with higher incomes pay at a low rate of around 7.5 per cent. An exemption limit as low as Rs. 2400 per annum implies a large tax base, which has grown over the years. However, in order to ensure progressivism, the state may consider raising both the exemption limit as well as the tax rate to be in line with the tax rates prevailing elsewhere.

The state should do the needful to ensure successful implementation of VAT. This entails computerisation of the tax administration and training of staff. In fact the state should be looking forward to computerise the entire tax administration apart from the sales tax department.

The state should take quick decisions on the sick and closed state level public sector enterprises. It may be noted that the state has already initiated measures in this regard. What is required is to expedite the process and not shy away from taking bold measures.

4.9.2 Expenditure Management

In view of a large share of state expenditure in GSDP and limited or narrow resource base, the state stands to gain immensely from focusing primarily on expenditure management, at least in the short run. Public expenditure management would ensure better utilisation of resources for better delivery of services, and achieve both economy and efficiency. Some policy measures are outlined below.

Muster roll and daily wage workers constitute a large share of the state employees. There is pressure on the government to convert these temporary workers to permanent ones. This turns out to be an easy option for the government to create jobs. This is also a measure, which would please almost everybody. Keeping in mind the mounting wage bill and poor work ethics among the permanent employees in general, steps should be taken immediately to ensure that no conversion of muster roll and daily wage workers to regular workers takes place.

The muster roll is, more often than not, inflated, as, some of the workers on roll do not exist. This is one way of siphoning off precious resources. The state government should initiate close scrutiny of the muster roll to eliminate, what we may call 'ghost' workers.

As mentioned earlier, the size of the government is pretty large. The government has also been finding it difficult to downsize because of pressure and limited job opportunities. The first step that the government should take is to stop recruiting people except in highly skill oriented and professional areas. The strategy should be to redeploy people and retrain them whenever possible. If at all necessary, new employment should be offered on a contract basis.

Owing to the hilly terrain and in the absence of public transport within the Gangtok city, the state employees have to depend largely on vehicles provided by the government. This has led to congestion in the city as well as heavy expenditure on fuel and maintenance of vehicles. The state government should explore the possibility of car-pool or replacing cars by small buses for employees of the state secretariat. (See also recommendations in Chapter 13.)

The state government should gradually veer towards outsourcing of select activities. Not only it will ensure efficient delivery of services if steps are taken for proper monitoring, it will also encourage private enterprises without straining the exchequer. More importantly, it will rein in the rising wage and pension bill of the government.

While awarding contract for implementation of various projects and work, parties involved in the process collude, which leads to the inflation of the bill to carve out their shares. A transparent system for awarding public contracts should be evolved to minimise such leakages.

The state government's initiative in distributing powers and resources to the local bodies has been exemplary. Participation of people through active involvement of the local bodies would be a key component of the effective public expenditure management. Transparent budgeting and spending entail participation of the local bodies. Of course, participation of the local bodies may assume expertise, awareness and understanding of the problems or issues involved.

The state has already benefited from debt swaps. The market conditions and debt swaps have contributed to a decline in the effective interest rate on outstanding debt. The state should look for more options to resort to more debt swaps as fast as possible.

In relation to matters with fiscal implications, the Finance Department is often not consulted. Lack of coordination among the departments often put the Finance Department into a difficult situation. Since the Finance Department is entrusted with the responsibility of disbursing resources, all the departments need to seek prior approval of the Finance Department in matters other than those approved ones.

Chapter 5

Education

Education is one of the most important indicators of sociocultural, economic, and human development. Education is essential for enhancing productivity, eradicating poverty, activating demographic transition, and achieving overall human development. On the other hand, lack of education, wisdom and illiteracy leads to low dignity, ignorance and poverty, mental isolation and hampers socio-economic and political maturity. Moreover, education influences other important attributes of human development like fertility, mortality, mobility, occupancy. More importantly, it is a critical instrument for bringing about social, economic and political inclusion and a durable integration of people.[1]

Thus, the process of educational attainment has an impact on all aspects of life and is the best social investment. Therefore, examination of educational attainment across various sub themes of education like literacy ratios, regional spread of educational institutions and associated infrastructure, enrolments and dropouts of the children, higher, professional and technical institutes, becomes imperative while assessing the development paradigm of any particular region.

In Sikkim the scattered settlements across the uneven geography, climatic constraints and limited amount of horizontal interaction have historically hindered the penetration of formal education system in the state. Further, the earlier Sikkimese rulers could hardly think of the importance of the formal and scientific education system. Consequently, while the neighbouring hills of Darjeeling, which historically were a part of the Kingdom of Sikkim, advanced steadily owing to the introduction of formal English education institutions under British India, Sikkim lagged behind educationally.

5.1 Educational Institutions

Traditional education systems of Sikkim were life-centred, practical and experience-based. Growing children, till attainment of adolescence obtained hands-on-knowledge of things, ceremonies, and functions. The family was the focal point of nearly all educational endeavours with key roles being played by women.

Education in Sikkim for the most of the nineteenth century was of the monastic type. Buddhist literature was read both at home and in the monastic schools. They imparted religious education for the preparation of young monks to priesthood. The Tashiding, Thulung, Pemayongtse, and Sangnachaling monasteries were famous as centres of monastic education...[2] Even today the Ecclesiastical Department in the Government of Sikkim has recorded 163 monasteries and temples all over Sikkim excluding the small shrine (Lama, 2001). Monasteries and temples have made a significant contribution to the education in Sikkim.

By the late nineteenth century, there was a gradual advent of the Christian missionary education in Sikkim with some support from the landlords/*kazis*. The Maharaja of Sikkim did not, however, favour the Christian missionary activity. The missionaries were not allowed to live in Gangtok. In 1924, Mary Scott was for the first to be allowed to open a school for girls in Gangtok and the first matriculation class passed the examination (with four candidates) in 1945. The school continued to grow and became a recognised higher secondary school in 1961. One of the main features of the missionary schools for girls was the industrial teaching mainly sewing and knitting. Besides, vocational training was also a part

1. *NHDR: 2001, 2002.*
2. Jangira, 1977 as quoted in Lama, 2001.

of the curriculum. In fact, for many years until the beginning of the twentieth century primary schools set up by the church offered the only means of basic education (Lama, 2001).

The first government school to be established in Sikkim was the Bhutia Boarding School (1906). In 1907, the second government school namely, Nepali Boarding School was started in the present day Lal Bazar area. In 1924 the government merged the Bhutia and Nepali boarding schools into what is today the Sir Tashi Namgyal Academy. In 1920, Sikkim had only 21 schools out of which 6 were government schools, 13 missionary schools and 2 of the schools were under the landlords. The number of schools continued to increase over the years and by 1961, i.e., by the end of the First Plan period the number of schools in Sikkim had risen to 182.

Following the merger of Sikkim in the Indian Union in 1975, the state got tremendous momentum in its educational status in terms of the total number of schools, number of teachers, and quality of education. As on 31.03.05 the total number of government schools in the state including lower primary, primary, junior high school, secondary and senior secondary school was 782. In every government school ranging from lower primary to senior secondary school, pre-primary section is attached.[3] Hence, taking private schools (312) into account, total number of schools in the state is 1094. The state has attained over 70 per cent literacy rate.

5.2 Effective Literacy Rates

The state of Sikkim has seen a marked improvement in its effective literacy (population with age 7 plus years) rates in the past few decades particularly after the merger with India. The total literacy went up from a mere 17 per cent in 1971 to 69.7 per cent in 2001. Preliminary findings of the Economic Census conducted by the Government of Sikkim in 2005 shows that the literacy rate has increased to over 75 per cent in 2005. The increase in literacy has been particularly impressive in the 1990s. Rural literacy has also shown significant improvement from 30 per cent in 1981 to 67.7 per cent in 2001. Female literacy grew from 27 per cent in 1981 to 61 per cent in 2001—an increase of more than 30 per cent and higher than their male counterpart that saw the growth of less than 15 per cent during the same period.

By 2001 the urban areas had an effective literacy rate of over 80 per cent, for males (88.6 per cent) and females (80.2 per cent). However, females are still lagging appreciably behind their male counterparts in the race of educational advancement in the state in both rural and urban areas. The gender gap in this regard is particularly high (16 per cent) in the rural Sikkim. (Figure 5.1)

5.3 Plan Expenditure on Education

The Government of Sikkim has given utmost importance to the education sector during various plan periods. Investment on education during the plan periods in the last 50 years has been much higher than that of the health sector. The allocation to the education sector has shown wide fluctuation during the various plan periods. It started with 7.4 per cent of the total plan outlay during the first plan and rose to 12.4 per cent in the second plan. In the ongoing Tenth Plan, it was 13.2 per cent. (Table 5.1).

5.4 Educational Infrastructure

Although the distribution and density of the population is considered to be a vital indicator of equitable distribution of the infrastructure base across the space for sustainable regional planning exercise in a hill state like Sikkim, physiography including terrain morphology is equally critical factors. Out of the total 1094 schools in the State in 2005, the government runs over 71 per cent and the remaining are under the control of private agencies and the central government (Tables 5.2, 5.3 and Figure 5.2). Among the districts, the east and the north with the highest and lowest shares of population also have the largest and the

FIGURE 5.1

Effective Literacy Rate in Sikkim: 1981-2001

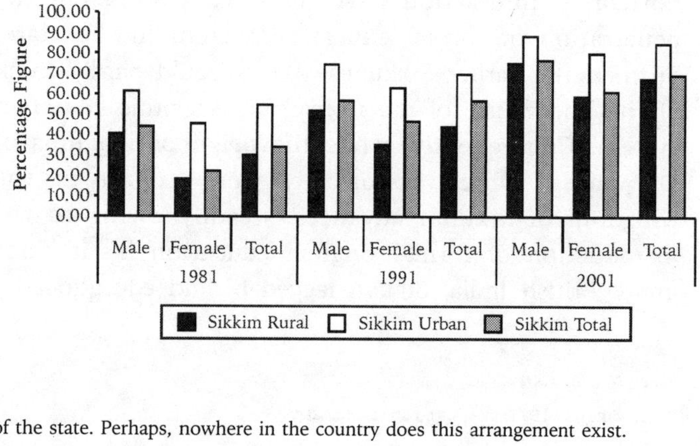

3. Pre-primary section attached to all government schools is the unique feature of the state. Perhaps, nowhere in the country does this arrangement exist.

TABLE 5.1

Plan Investment in the Education Sector

Plan Period	*Total Outlay (Rs. lakh)*	*Outlay for Education (Rs. lakh)*	*% Share to Total Outlay*
First Plan (1954-61)	324	24	7.4
Second Plan (1961-66)	637	79	12.4
Third Plan (1966-71)	971	77	7.9
Fourth Plan (1971-75)	2,036	179	8.8
Fifth Plan (1974-79)	4,010	297	7.4
Sixth Plan (1980-85)	14,780	1,035	7.0
Seventh Plan (1985-90)	28,240	3,719	13.17
Eighth Plan (1992-97)	77,036	8,335	10.82
Ninth Plan (1997-02)	1,09,132	18,770	17.2
Tenth Plan (2002-07)	1,65,574	21,855	13.2

Source: Lama, 2001 and Government of Sikkim. *Tenth Five-Year Plan 2002-07.*

TABLE 5.2

District-wise Govt. Schools: Various Categories 2005

Categories	*East*	*West*	*North*	*South*	*Total*
LPS	35	62	21	48	166
PS	110	95	39	92	336
JHS	48	36	16	47	147
SS	30	23	11	28	92
SSS	19	10	3	9	41
Total	242	226	90	224	782

Note: LPS: Lower Primary School; PS: Primary School; JHS: Junior High School;

SS: Secondary School and SSS: Senior Secondary School.

Source: Data supplied by Human Resource Development Department, Government of Sikkim, 2005.

TABLE 5.3

District-wise Private, Local Body and Government Aided Schools 2005

School Level	*East*	*West*	*North*	*South*	*Grand Total*
LPS	13	20	05	11	49
PS	60	53	07	61	181
JHS	28	15	03	13	59
SS	10	02	03	02	17
SSS	04	01	0	01	06
Grand Total	115	91	18	88	312

Source: Data supplied by Human Resource Development Department, Government of Sikkim, 2005.

FIGURE 5.2

Percentage Share of Government and Private Schools, 2005

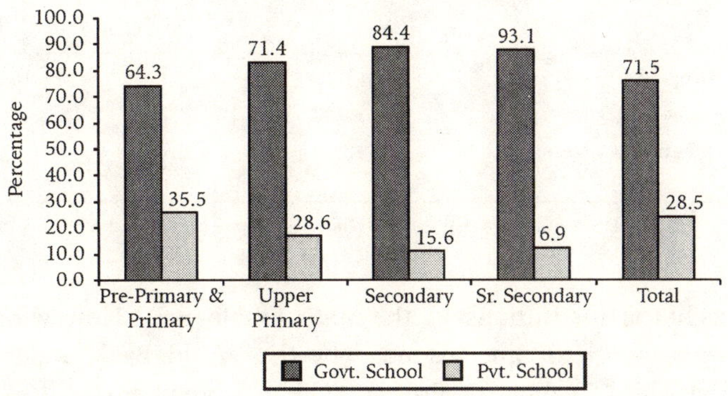

smallest number of schools respectively in all categories.[4]

Interestingly, Sikkim has also successfully promoted over 60 traditional educational institutes like Sanskrit *pathsalas*, monastic schools and *madrasas* spread across the state. (Table 5.4) With the massive expansion of facilities at lower levels, the numbers of those qualifying in the higher secondary examination are rising steadily. Though there has been considerable popular enthusiasm and a growing need for expanding the higher educational institutions, the state has not been able to do much on this.[5] The quota of seats that are available to the Sikkimese in various institutions in some parts of the country has, to a large extent, covered these gaps. These quotas have been very effective. An overwhelming majority of medical doctors, engineers, and lawyers in Sikkim have studied against the quota seats (Table 5.5)

Plan after plan, the Sikkim announced its interest in vocational education and yet, there are few vocational/

TABLE 5.4

Number of Other Schools, 2002

Category of Schools	*Government*				
	East	*West*	*North*	*South*	*Total*
Sanskrit *Pathshala*	8	2	0	2	12
Monastic Schools (*gumpa*)	16	8	14	12	50
Madrasa	1	0	0	0	1

Source: Department of Human Resource Development, Government of Sikkim.

4. There exist a huge difference in the data supplied by the Department of Human Resource Development and that provided by the Department of Statistics, Monitoring and Evaluation. These differences are found in almost all variables ranging from the number of schools to dropout rate and enrolment ratio.

5. Notification to the effect of setting up of colleges at Mangan, Gyalshing, Rhenock, and Soreng (Science college) has been issued. Univers[illegible] [illegible]ted legislation has also been passed in the state assembly in 2003.

TABLE 5.5

Status of Higher Education

Institutions	*Number*	*Location (districts)*	*Affiliations*
Degree College	3 (1 private)	East and South	North Bengal University
Law College	1	East	-do-
Manipal University	1	East	Offers Degrees and Diplomas in Professional Courses like Engineering, Medicine and Information Technology (IT)

Source: Department of Human Resource Development, Government of Sikkim

technical institutions in the state (Table 5.6). However, with the credit line extended by the World Bank under the Third Technician Project (TTP) (September 2001 to December 2005), two polytechnics have been established at Bardang in east and at Chisopani in south district.[6] Of late, a number of independent IT institutes including NIIT, Aptech, and TULEC have set up their centres in the urban areas of east and south districts. Furthermore, since 2003, vocational stream has been introduced in 40 Government Senior Secondary Schools. These are funded by central assistance and include horticulture, dairying, automobile repair technology, IT application, tourism and travel management, hotel management & catering technology and secretarial courses. Recently, some private sector ventures have also been set up including H.M. College of Education at Tadong, Loyola College of Education at Namchi and Carmel Teacher Training Institute at Pakyong.

The east district has the lowest coverage with just 1.52 schools per thousand population. This is followed by south (2.19 schools/1,000 population), west (2.26 schools/1,000 population), and north (2.53 schools/ 1,000 population) (Table 5.7). Similar situation prevails across various categories of education institutes including elementary, secondary and higher secondary. On an average one school in east district handles 121 students followed by south (with 85 students per school), west (with 80 students per school) and north district (with 79 students per school) (Table 5.8).

Thus, the east district has the highest pressure on its educational institutes. This needs to be clearly noted by the education planners in the state. The planners also should be aware that north Sikkim is characterised by some of the formidable physical morphology and the consequent sparse human habitation, as compared to the other three districts.

5.5 Accessibility to Elementary Education

Accessibility to schools is defined as percentage of the population having access to a school within an indicated distance.[7] In 1978, a total of 50.5 per cent (42.35 within the habitation and 8.29 per cent upto 0.5

TABLE 5.6

Technical/Vocational and Professional Institutions (Private and Public)

Institute	*Number*		*Location*	*Discipline*
	1975	*2004*		
Inst. of Industrial Training	None	1	Rangpo	Draftsmanship, plumber and motor mechanic
Advanced Tech. Training Centre	None	1	Bardang	Computer
Centre for Computer and Communications	None	1	Namchi	Electronics & Hardware Maintenance, Computer Science and Tech., Telecommunication Tech.
Himalayan Inst. of Pharmacy	None	1	Majhitar	Pharmacy
Engineering and IT College	None	1	Majhitar	Engineering, IT
Management	None	1	Gangtok	Hotel management

Source: Department of Education, Government of Sikkim

6. Under this project, the total financial assistance for Sikkim is to the tune of Rs. 57.34 crore (90 per cent grant and 10 per cent loan) phased out over the five-year project period. This also includes training of faculty members.

7. *NHDR, 2001.*

TABLE 5.7

Population Density of Schools, 2002-03
(No. of Schools per Thousand People)

Category of Schools	*East*	*West*	*North*	*South*	*Sikkim*
Pre-Primary and Primary	5.10	7.85	8.74	7.49	6.60
Upper Primary	0.52	0.67	0.57	0.71	0.61
Secondary	0.28	0.37	0.62	0.41	0.36
Sr. Secondary	0.18	0.15	0.17	0.14	0.16
Average	1.52	2.26	2.53	2.19	1.93

Source: Sikkim: A Statistical Profile: 2002, 2003. Govt. of Sikkim.

TABLE 5.8

Number of Students per School, 2002

Category	*East*	*West*	*North*	*South*	*State*
Pre-Primary and	103.98	71.60	76.02	78.57	84.07
Upper Primary	263.93	177.79	156.00	151.58	196.98
Secondary	148.21	80.60	48.00	74.54	94.84
Sr. Secondary	105.63	76.33	67.33	91.75	92.03
Average	121.14	80.52	79.31	85.30	94.55

Source: Computed based on *Sikkim: A Statistical Profile: 2002, 2003*. Govt. of Sikkim.

km) of the rural Sikkimese had accessibility to primary schools (Classes I-V) between 0-0.5 km. This was much lower than the national average of 85.13 per cent (78.53 per cent within their habitation and 6.60 per cent up to 0.5 km) of the rural population that prevailed then. By 1993, this figure had drastically improved to 73.88 per cent (65.5 per cent within the habitation and 8.29 per cent up to 0.5 km) as against the national average of 85.50 per cent (77.81 per cent within the habitation and 7.69 per cent up to 0.5 km). In case of the upper primary schools (std. VI-VIII) Sikkim had only 13.22 per cent of rural population with accessibility between 0-1.0 km from the habitation as against national average of 45.57 per cent in 1978.

By 1993, Sikkim's performance improved sharply to 43.26 yet it remained much lower than the national average of 56.91 per cent. The latest data based on 7th All India School Education Survey 2002 show that 87.28 per cent of the rural Sikkimese had access to primary school within 1 km of walking distance and 83.63 per cent to upper primary school within 3 km of walking distance. Another document issued by the state government in 2005 stated that 80.45 per cent of the rural habitation had access to secondary school within 5 km of walking distance and 66.95 per cent of them had access to senior secondary school within 8 km.[8]

5.5.1 Sarva Shiksha Abhiyan (SSA)

The Sarva Shiksha Abhiyan (SSA) a time bound initiative of the central government, in partnership with the state and local governments, and the community aims at providing elementary education to all children in the age group 6-14 years by 2010. It recognises the importance of community owned system, is organised in a mission mode for improving reach and performance of the school system, and seeks to bring about convergence of the existing institutional effort for elementary education at the state and district level. Besides involving the Panchayati Raj institutions/tribal councils in scheduled areas, the states would be encouraged to strengthen the accountability in implementation of the programme by involving NGOs, teachers, activists and women's organisations. The ultimate goal of SSA is to ensure and achieve universal access, universal enrolment, universal retention and universal achievement.

The SSA Project has been implemented in all the four districts of Sikkim. The NGOs including Multanchi Lom Aaal Schizom (North District); Himalayan Education Society (South District); Vidhya Bharati (East District); Teesta Tendong (South District) and Milan Sewa Samaj (South District) have been entrusted with the work of establishing and running alternative schools in the schoolless habitations as per the norms prescribed by the Ministry of HRD, Government of India. The achievements made under the SSA till mid 2005 are:

- Construction of 21 new buildings for primary schools have been completed.
- 104 additional rooms have been constructed.
- 433 toilets for schools have been constructed.
- Drinking water facilities in 274 schools have been made available.
- Construction of one BRC has been completed.
- 6 CRC have been constructed.
- 90 schools have been provided with electricity facility.
- Boundary walls to 27 schools have been provided.
- 40 new primary schools have been opened in habitations where there is no school.

8. Data supplied by the Department of Human Resource Development, Government of Sikkim, Department. *Education Information: Sikkim*, July 2005.

- 37 primary schools have been upgraded to upper primary schools on need basis.
- 22 alternative schools are functioning in the schoolless habitation where establishment of primary schools does not meet the norms.

Since it is a very new programme its impact is yet to be assessed. However, a quick visit to some of the project sites presented us with the following views:

- Not much of dissemination and awareness about the mission of the programmes has been made. As a result, it is also considered as any regular development intervention by both the implementing agencies and the beneficiaries. Contrary to the claims, not much involvement of agencies other than the governments could be seen in its implementation. As a result, the accountability and transparency elements are conspicuously missing
- The monitoring and evaluation mechanisms are yet to be put in place and hence the chances of efficacy of programme distribution being highly imbalanced both in terms of geographical and demographic reach are quite high. However, some initiatives like the concurrent evaluation by the North Bengal University (NBU) as the external monitoring agency and monitoring and evaluation by the Joint Review Mission (JRM) belonging to the international funding agencies, are being initiated in recent months.

5.5.2 *Enrolment Rate in Sikkim*

Age specific enrolment ratio refers to percentage of children enrolled/attending schools in a particular age group, irrespective of the level/class of enrolment to the total population of children in that age group. A higher ratio on this measure implies a higher educational participation. This measure, however, suffers from a limitation that it does not give the schooling level/class at which the students are enrolled.

The enrolment ratio in Sikkim, according to census reports increased from 51.7 per cent in 1981 to 58.2 per cent in 1991 for the age group 6-10 years as against the national average of 47.2 and 51.2 per cent respectively. Similarly, for the age group 11-14 years the increase in the ratio was by almost 14 percentage points from 61.0 per cent in 1981 to 74.9 per cent in 1991. The comparable figures for the country in 1981 and 1991 were 50 per cent and 62.1 per cent respectively. The age specific enrolment ratio is significantly lower in age group 6-10 years than in age group 11-14 years in 1981 as well as 1991. Much of this difference in age specific enrolment between the two age groups disappears if one drops enrolment ratio of children at age 6 years which is considerably lower, *vis-a-vis* other age groups in both rural and urban areas.[9]

A gender segregation of the enrolment rates in the state would give us a clearer picture in this regard. As against the enrolment ratio of 57 per cent for boys the same was 46.1 per cent for girls in 1981 in the age group 6-10 years reflecting the gender gap of more than 10 per cent. This improved to 61.1 per cent for boys and 55.3 for girls in 1991 reducing the gender gap to less than 6 per cent in a decade. For 11-14 years age group, the enrolment rate for boys was 70.3 per cent and 51 per cent for girls in 1981 highlighting a massive gender gap of about 20 per cent. It is, however, encouraging to note that the same figure increased to 78.4 per cent in case of boys and a tremendous 71.3 per cent with respect to girls in 1991 bringing down the gender gap to about 8 per cent in 10 years.

The state government has taken initiatives to enhance the efficiency of elementary education over the years. The reduction in gender gap in the children's enrolment rates between 1981-1991 has been noteworthy. Sikkim, in fact, has performed much better than most of the states in the northeast region.

A survey conducted by NFHS-2 during 1998-99 found that in Sikkim the total age specific enrolment rate for the age group 6-10 years was over 91 per cent and there was less than 1 per cent rural-urban difference. For the age group 11-14 years the enrolment ratio was about 86 per cent. And interestingly, the rural areas have registered higher enrolment rate of 86.4 per cent as against the 79.7 per cent in the urban areas. Across the sexes, there is hardly any gender gap observed. The enrolment ratio is over 90 per cent for both boys and girls in the age group 6-10 years. Surprisingly, for the age group 11-14 years the enrolment ratio of girls is higher with 88 per cent than boys with 85 per cent (Table 5.9).

The latest data show that at the aggregate level enrolment of girls in 2004 is more than that of boys. Though at the I-V and XI-XII levels the enrolment of girls have been marginally lower than that of boys, at the VI-VIII and IX-X levels, it is much higher. (Table 5.10)

9. *NHDR, 2001.*

TABLE 5.9

Children Aged 6-17 Attending School, 1998-99 (%)

Age Group (yrs)	*Male*			*Female*			*Total*		
	Urban	*Rural*	*Total*	*Urban*	*Rural*	*Total*	*Urban*	*Rural*	*Total*
6-10	98.6	90.9	91.4	88.0	91.2	90.9	92.6	91.0	91.2
11-14	90.9	84.7	85.3	70.7	88.2	85.9	79.7	86.4	85.6
15-17	76.7	65.4	66.9	64.3	64.9	64.8	70.7	65.2	65.9
6-14	93.5	88.0	88.5	77.3	89.8	88.5	85.2	88.9	88.5
6-17	88.0	82.7	83.2	73.4	83.6	82.6	80.2	83.2	82.9

Source: NFHS-2: 1998-99, 2001. Sikkim.

TABLE 5.10

Year-wise and Class-wise Enrolment of Students 2001-2004

Class	*2001*			*2004*		
	Boys	*Girls*	*Total*	*Boys*	*Girls*	*Total*
I-V	38837	38166	77003	39502	39083	78585
VI-VIII	11779	12843	24822	12585	14964	27549
IX-X	4236	4014	8246	4489	4658	9147
XI-XII	2520	2057	4577	3253	2878	6131
Grand Total	69577	68079	137656	70093	70993	141086

Source: Government of Sikkim (2005). *Education Information: Sikkim,* July, Department of Human Resource Development.

5.5.3 Dropout Rate in Sikkim

Dropout refers to those students dropping out of the class/classes. The dropout rate is the percentage share of the same. The concept of dropout reflects the internal inefficiency of the education system and roughly indicates the wastage involved in the school education. Various factors coexist and interact including economic compulsions and social pressures in the entire process of dropping out of the school-going children.

Sikkim has witnessed a notable decline in the dropout rates of the children from the schools over the years. 63.6 per cent of the children in classes I-V dropped out in 1981-82. This figure declined to 48 per cent in 1992-93 and 41.3 per cent 1997-98 as against the national averages of 53.5 per cent, 45.01 per cent and 39.58 per cent respectively. For the boys, the dropout rate declined from 61.5 per cent in 1981-82 to 45 per cent in 1997-98 and for girls from 66.5 per cent to 45.22 per cent during the same time period. The girls have done relatively better.

In the category of classes I-VIII, the dropout rate was 99.1 per cent (highest in the country) in 1981-82. This means over 99 per cent of the school-going children dropped out without going beyond class VIII. The same figure declined to 80.3 per cent in 1992-93 and 67.4 per cent in 1998-99. These figures are much higher than the national average for the same period, which stand at 72.1 per cent, 61.1 per cent and 56.8 per cent respectively. Among boys and girls the dropout rates were 99 per cent for both the sexes in 1981-82; by 1998-99 it declined to 70.8 per cent for boys and 63.3 per cent for girls.

Surprisingly the latest data provided by the Department of Human Resource Development in the state show a very drastic improvement in the dropout rates (Table 5.11). On the other hand, available data also indicate that as the students climbed the education ladder the number of children enrolled steadily fell indicating that the drop out phenomenon persists in a much more remarkable manner. For instance, out of the total number of students enrolled (1,36,273) in 1998-1999, the percentage share of pre-primary[10] and primary was 75 per cent, upper-primary 17.6 per cent, secondary

TABLE 5.11

Stage-wise Drop Out Rates

Stage/Classes	*Boys*	*Girls*	*Total*	*Remarks*
I to V	15.37	15.06	15.22	Primary Stage
VI to VIII	14.44	11.19	12.64	Upper Primary Stage
I to VIII	23.02	21.70	22.39	Up to Elementary Stage
IX to X	12.00	16.66	11.35	Secondary Stage
I to X	27.13	25.39	26.29	Up to Secondary Stage

Source: Government of Sikkim (2005). *Education Information: Sikkim,* July, Department of Human Resource Development.

10. The State Government however, does not feel inclined to include pre-primary enrolment as it is a preparatory stage for entering into the school system.

4.46 and senior secondary was 2.54 per cent. Out of the total number of students enrolled (1,37,673) in 2002-2003, the figures for the same categories were 71, 18, 6.7 and 4.17 per cents respectively.[11] (Table 5.12 and Annexure A-20)

Though this indicates some positive changes in the higher ladder of education in recent years, the situation remains as grim. The National Family Health Survey-2 attributed the following reasons for non-attendance of the school children in the age group 6-17 years (Table 5.13).

5.5.4 Teacher-Student Ratio

The state has one of the lowest teacher-pupil ratios in the country. In other words, Sikkim has a very high number of teachers per school across all categories. In the last 24 years the state has maintained an average teacher-pupil ratio of 17 at the primary level, 19 at upper primary level, and 17 at the secondary level.

At the same time it should be highlighted that the distribution of the teachers in the government schools at all levels in general and primary level in particular has not been balanced across the districts and the corresponding villages. Schools in the east district, particularly in and around Gangtok are observed to have more teachers than required. The situation is reverse in case of the schools situated in the interior villages of the state particularly in north and west district. Enquiry in the Department of Education and with concerned citizens at various locales did reveal that the local politicians many a times influence the appointments in the schools. This facilitates the candidates of the influential politicians to be inducted in the schools with easy

TABLE 5.12

District-wise Enrolment in Government Schools, 1998-2003 (No.)

Category	*District*	*1998-99*	*1999-00*	*2000-01*	*2001-02*	*2002-03*
Pre-primary and Primary						
	North	7,479	7,718	9,654	7,585	7,233
	East	41,686	40,964	39,615	38,446	36,457
	South	27,754	27,997	28,285	28,410	28,107
	West	25,756	24,869	26,278	25,770	26,042
	State	1,02,675	1,01,548	1,03,832	1,00,211	97,839
Upper-Primary						
	North	1,399	1,414	1,560	1,512	1,531
	East	11,083	10,703	11,349	11,120	11,269
	South	5,739	5,803	6,063	6,071	5,914
	West	5,825	5,804	6,045	5,919	6,088
	State	24,046	23,724	25,017	24,622	24,802
Secondary						
	North	332	474	480	531	535
	East	2,942	4,017	3,557	3,934	4,308
	South	1,539	2,117	1,938	1,866	2,247
	West	1,265	1,543	1,612	1,915	2,198
	State	6,078	8,151	7,587	8,246	9,288
Sr. Secondary						
	North	210	173	202	254	341
	East	1,810	1,874	1,690	2,442	2,893
	South	618	644	734	943	1,261
	West	836	666	687	938	1,249
	State	3,474	3,357	3,313	4,577	5,744

Source: Sikkim: A Statistical Profile: 2002, 2003. Govt. of Sikkim.

11. In 2004, it further improved with the share of enrolment of upper primary rising to 22.69 per cent, secondary level to 7.53 per cent and senior secondary level to 5.02 per cent as per the data supplied by the Department of Human Resource Development, Government of Sikkim, in August 2005.

TABLE 5.13

Reasons for Not Attending the School for Children between 6-17 Years

*Main Reason for Never Attending School (%)**	*Male*	*Female*
School too far away	9.8	9.9
Education not considered necessary	0.0	4.9
Required for household work	21.9	20.0
Required for farm/family business	1.4	2.4
Required for outside work for payment in cash or kind	13.3	20.8
Costs too much	8.7	7.6
Required for care of siblings	1.4	6.2
Not interested in studies	12.9	9.7
Other	27.9	18.6
Don't know/missing	2.7	0.0
*Main Reason for Not Currently Attending School (%)***	*Male*	*Female*
School too far away @	1.2	2.5
Further education not considered necessary	1.1	1.3
Required for household work	3.6	14.3
Required for farm/family business	3.5	2.5
Required for outside work for payment in cash or kind	8.8	2.5
Costs too much@@	4.8	5.5
Required for care of siblings	0.0	2.6
Not interested in studies	56.2	32.7
Repeated failure	9.8	9.5
Got married	1.2	6.5
Other	7.4	9.7
Don't know/missing	2.4	10.3

Note: * For children who never attended school; ** For children who have dropped out of school; @ The Department of Human Resource Development of the state would like to call it topographical hindrances; and @@ The Department of Human Resource Development of the state would like to call it first generation learners.

Source: *NFHS-2: 1998-99, 2001.*

access to the urban areas like Gangtok, Namchi, and Jorethang.

5.6 Quality of Education

Sikkim has been awarded the best performing state status in the field of education among smaller States for the last two consecutives years 2004 and 2005 by *India Today* magazine. However, the quality of education particularly government schools is a matter for concern. This has been debated in many fora in the state including the State Planning Commission primarily focusing on: (i) relatively lower pass percentage in the high and secondary final examinations; (ii) increasing diversion between overall orientations of the education system and the changing needs of the economy and society; and (iii) overall orientation and capability of the students. The state has tried to grapple with it by making the education system more accessible through subsidies and other facilities, by encouraging the private sector to participate in the development of educational institutions and by introducing a number of professional institutions in the state.

The main problems however, continue to defy any solutions. For instance, the quality of teachers has been a serious issue. Because of the very nature of political history the entire recruitment process of the teachers at all levels had to be carried out in specific and unusual situations. The time demanded a quick recruitment to match the needs and requirements. There were not many qualified people within Sikkim for such recruitment both because of the poor level of educational development in the pre-1975 period, and also the availability of other attractive avenues across the state.

There are several examples of under-qualified teachers engaged in teaching, teachers remaining absent for months together without any alternative arrangements, teachers remaining untrained for several years, teachers getting transferred according to the whims and fancies of politicians and crucial vacancies remaining unfilled for several years. All these happen despite of the most attractive salary and promotion package and other incentives in the country. The state has a huge Education Department (renamed since 2004 as Department of Human Resource Development) to manage, regulate, and evaluate the performance of various schools.

As a result of the enlivened debate on the quality of education, the state has started showing strong commitment to quality education. Vide a minute of the Sikkim State Planning Commission meeting held in July 2002, it was clearly pointed out that:

> The Education Department has still no definite plan to train their teachers despite existing training institutions and manpower. At today's rate, it may take 10-15 years to complete the process of training the untrained teachers, which should be done more rapidly.....It should draw immediately a plan incorporating a timetable for training, selection of institutions, numbers to be trained per year and the level of assistance to be provided by the government. Steps should be taken to upgrade the State's training institutions for full capacity utilisation.

Efforts are being made for improving the quality of teachers through various teachers training programmes. District Institute of Education and Training (DIET),

Gangtok is being revamped to make it more effective and dynamic in the training programme for all categories of teachers of both government and private schools.

Since October 2002, a 6-month course called Certification in Primary Education (CPE) has been introduced with the help of Indira Gandhi National Open University (IGNOU) in the Distance Education Mode. It has opened 10 study centres all over the state for CPE and three centres for B.Ed programmes for secondary school teachers. Out of 4919 primary teachers (as on 31.12.04), 3023 have been trained under CPE. Similarly, District Institute of Education and Training (DIET) Gangtok, has started a 2-year Pre-Service Primary Teachers Training Programme from the academic session 2003. Similarly, 982 out of 3031 graduate and post graduate teachers (as on 31.12.05) remain trained. All expenditure pertaining to teacher training through IGNOU is borne by the state government. Besides, there are three private TTIs located in south and east districts that impart training to the qualified persons both in service and outside service. These institutes are also open to the candidates from outside Sikkim.

For the in-service science graduate teachers the facilities for their post graduate programmes have been provided at Sikkim Manipal University at Gangtok since 2003. Under this 19 teachers are now pursuing the course.

5.7 Teacher Recruitment Policy

Sikkim follows a 'son of the soil' policy in recruiting the workforce for employment in all the departments of the state, including education. This has been a practice more so after the merger of Sikkim with India. For the recruitment of the teachers, advertisements are brought out in the state gazetteer from time to time. Only Sikkimese subjects are recruited on a regular basis. Under the exceptional cases when the subjects of Sikkim do not possess the required qualification for an essential vacancy like postgraduate science teachers or for faculty positions in colleges or technical institutes, outsiders are recruited generally on contract basis.

Such policy in the state has impacted upon the society and economy both positively and negatively. On the positive side, the state has been, to some extent, successful in reserving jobs to the ethnic Sikkimese and check in-migration. On the other hand, 100 per cent reservation of jobs to the state subjects has impacted on the quality, efficiency and effectiveness in all the sectors of the economy including education. This has led to continuous recruitment of unsuitable and under qualified local people in positions that have serious long-term socio-economic and other development implications. At the same time, because of job surety, even the best qualified Sikkimese studying outside the state who could have otherwise significantly contributed in other spheres, have tended to come back to join a post that clearly underutilises their skills and capacities. This has also discouraged many talented Sikkimese to go out of the state for greener pastures.

Against the backdrop of the reform process that the state has steadily injected into its economic and political system, Sikkim cannot afford to block the unhindered horizontal exchange and mobility of goods, knowledge, skills, and institutions from other parts of India and abroad. Given the development needs, planning orientations and targeted high growth regimes, this state cannot restrict the inward movement of global talents—in the form of dynamic development managers, efficient and quality teachers, trained development professionals, and private sector institutions and non-governmental agencies. To what extent these inductions and mobilisations should be regulated is only a question of clear policy framework and institutional arrangement.

5.8 Higher and Technical/ Professional Education

Sikkim does not have its own University, as of now. The colleges of Sikkim are affiliated to the North Bengal University (NBU) located in the district of Darjeeling, West Bengal. However, the state has passed Sikkim University Bill, 2003 with a view to establishing academic and research intensive university in the state. The Union Government has just passed a bill in the parliament providing a Central University to Sikkim.

Even after 30 years of merger with India, there are no facilities for any post-graduate studies in the state. The establishment of a Central University will impart certain 'completeness' to the state's educational system. This will also give a new thrust on the state of research and academic activities in the state which has been at low ebb. In the absence of any institution of higher learning, no government action particularly in the field of economic development is subject to independent assessment. This type of indigenous critical assessment is highly required in a resource scarce and environment-sensitive state like Sikkim. Till now most of such studies and assessments have been carried out by outside agencies. The University is required mainly on the following grounds:

- It can introduce a range of courses that are specific to hill and mountain regions including those on biotechnology, eco-tourism, mountain ecology, hill farming, border trade and natural resource management.
- It will cater not only to the local population but to the population in the adjoining countries including Bhutan, Nepal, Bangladesh and Myanmar.
- It will facilitate a better documentation of Sikkim-specific subject/areas through research as absence of documented, authentic records is currently the greatest drawback.
- A university's presence could enhance the academic environment, build capacity, and induct outward looking values so necessary to the hill students.
- The need to open new colleges in future will be inevitable. It would be worthwhile to have Sikkim colleges affiliated to a Sikkimese University rather than to a university which is Apathetic to the Sikkimese needs and sentiment.

The establishment of Sikkim Manipal University in 1998 in the state with two technical colleges under it, *viz.*, Sikkim Manipal Institute of Technology (SMIT) and Sikkim Manipal Institute of Medical Sciences (SMIMS) have given a new dynamism to the state's education system. Besides introducing courses in the fields like engineering, information technology and medicine, the university could solidly impact upon the following:

- orientation of Sikkimese students as they have access to these courses and exposure to a more diverse group of teachers and students from across the country;
- besides enhancing the importance of modern technology and its practice in the state, this new intervention is changing the outlook of the young Sikkimese students both in terms of career pursuits and in handling the affairs in the state. The advent of the computer age has begun to equip the Sikkimese students with adequate knowledge and exposure in the area;
- tourism and all related activities got a big boost as both the people attached to this institution and the advertisements put up by this University instantly made people aware of the beauty and importance of Sikkim; and
- state education and other related administrative departments could create a healthy competitive atmosphere in the education system which could further lead to more and more private sector participation in the field of education.

Despite the various incentives provided by the state government, the Industrial Training Institute (ITI)[12] has not been able to attract young Sikkimese. This is both because of easy availability of other non-technical, unskilled, better paid and secure jobs provided by various departments in the state so far, and also an altogether different orientation of the state. On the other hand, students do question about the very quality of education and training imparted by the Institute.

However, the situation is fast changing. Government jobs have begun to saturate now. At the national level, the skills and technical knowledge are getting more importance. More importantly, opportunities for the skilled people are growing by leaps and bounds both in terms of steady career pursuits and diversity. The growing unemployment in the state makes it imperative for the Sikkimese youth to engage in technical skills and other capacities.

The two polytechnics established in 1999 under the World Bank funded initiative are doing relatively very well in the state. The state government intends to develop these institutes as models and centres of excellence with the latest technologies and facilities. The two graduated batches of students from the institutes have been successfully placed in industry both within and outside the state. This is definitely a new trend for the Sikkimese. (Directorate of Technical Education, Govt. of Sikkim).

5.9 Smart School Concept

To create the prospective labour forces of Sikkim, suitable, useful and in consonance with the new age, the state has decided to start 'smart schools' in the state. The concept of smart school is based on modern curriculum including science and technology, computer and environmental subjects. It would change the conventional educational pattern and bring about a

12. Set up in 1976, at Singtam, this Institute conducts technical courses like draughtsman, electronics mechanical, electrician, fitter, mechanic (motor vehicle), welder, and plumber at the diploma level.

more holistic educational approach in the state. The state government has taken a conscious decision to embark on a computer literacy programme at the senior and senior secondary levels. With the introduction of computer education in 29 senior secondary schools by 2003 the first batch is already out.

5.10 Subsidies and Privatisation

Subsidy in the education sector has been there since long. The Veda Prakash Report of 1976 mentioned that "recognising that the single most serious obstacle to the spread of education in the state is the poverty of its people, the state government has also taken a number of measures to make schooling less expensive and also extend financial support to the weaker sections of the society."[13] Over the years the subsidies have started taking more political tones and increasingly moved away from the social principles and economic justifications. The following provisions are made by the State Government in the education sector.

- free textbooks, exercise books, uniforms. (free textbooks and tuition started in the 1980s; free exercise books after 1994);
- free textbooks from pre-primary/I to Class XII;
- free exercise books from pre-primary/I to Class XII;
- free uniforms from pre-primary to V;
- no tuition fees from pre-primary to XII;
- mid day meal in the form of rice from pre-primary to Class V; and
- though central government norms do not have provisions for pre-primary schools, in Sikkim it is distributed from pre-primary to Class V. This is a central programme.

BOX 5.1

Education in Sikkim—A Teacher's Perspective

Subsidisation of elementary education in the state has led to irresponsibility on the part of the students and parents. It has, moreover, led to incompetence among the students.

Reorientation of our education system is needed in such a way that our students become more competent and dynamic, which will help them to come at par with the mainstream Indian students.

Sikkim needs its own university; the University of North Bengal does not understand the need, demand, and aspirations of the Sikkimese students.

A strong political will is required to upgrade and update the status of higher education in Sikkim and make higher education more relevant to the present development scenario and market opportunities.

Vocational, technical, and professional courses including information technology, management, media, advertisement, bio-technology, development studies/planning including rural development, engineering etc that are concerned with the present development dynamics need to be strongly emphasised upon rather than the traditional BAs/BScs and MAs/MScs.

Source: Based on the discussion with M. P. Thapa, Head, Dept. of Zoology, Government College, Sikkim.

People are naturally happy with all these subsidies. Parents even if they could afford, do not have to spend anything on their children's education. More adversely, students do not have to fear the risk of discontinuation of the facilities even if they fail in the annual examination and are detained in the same class. However, the biggest question is that of the target group and the sustainability of the entire subsidised education in the state.

The perceived advantage of the entire subsidies education was to bring maximum people under the ambit of educated lot so that the state attains a higher status in one of the critical areas of human development. However, these subsidies without any target groups and achievement records have started becoming counter productive. All the people regardless of their socio-economic backgrounds are given these subsidies. The absence of monitoring and evaluation of the impact of subsidies has, in fact, made the entire process directionless, as no one knows where and when they should call it a stop.

Despite certain positive indicators including the improvement in pass percentage of Class XII student from 57 per cent in 1996 to 70 per cent in the last few

14. Prakasha, Veda (1976). *Extending Educational Opportunity in Sikkim: A Report on the State's School System with Special Reference to its Administration*. New Delhi: National Staff College for Educational Planners and Administrators.

years and increased competitions for scholarships, a general impression is that the standard of education has gone down. This is mainly because education has become a free public good. Students have become docile and disinclined as there is no competitive atmosphere. There is no cost involved in their bad performance in the school.

Interestingly, despite these provisioning of subsidies a large number of private schools have come up in the last decade or so. Almost 45 per cent of these are located in the east district, 25 per cent in south and 22 per cent in west. Most of these schools charge a much higher fees and no trace of subsidies are found in any categories and classes. This indicates: a) the quality and standard of education in the public sector may not be commensurate to the expectations of the parents, b) the parents would like their children to speak English right from the school level so that they can face more competitive atmosphere in future, c) equally large number of people are willing to pay for education of their children, d) the private schools have better infrastructure bases, and e) the private schools are more accountable as far as the students' performance is concerned. Unlike government aided schools, the performance of these schools is judged by its final results which if not found to be consistently satisfactory, may ultimately lead to withdrawal of the children from the school.

5.11 Library Facilities

Despite the mushrooming of schools both in the public and the private sector, the library facilities in the state, both public and attached to the school are very poor. This has adversely affected the reading habit of the young children. Interestingly one can find budget provisions for library facilities in a number of departments including rural development and education. The consequential impact on creativity and other academic activities is quite visible. Rural Functional Literacy Programme (RFLP) which aimed at equipping the rural illiterate adults with literacy and practical knowledge about farming, health and hygiene and civic matters was only briefly inducted into the library system in the state. It would have otherwise served a major purpose in creating a parallel process of education at all levels. However, this project has also come to a standstill for the last few years mainly on the grounds of lack of funds. The *Jan Shiksha Nilayam* one of the several missions started by the central government, pertaining to adult literary programme has also not taken off mainly due to non-availability of funds.

5.12 Investment in Education and Employment Prospects

The education sector remains one of the most potential tertiary areas for the purpose of investment and employment generation in Sikkim. The state has a distinct comparative advantage with regard to its climatic set up, geographical location and overall environmental quality. The state can open several good residential schools–private and semi-private with strong emphasis on the quality of education, new courses, and modern innovative teaching, particularly in South Sikkim. Because of the political instability and Gorkhaland agitation, Darjeeling, the traditional bastion of education in the eastern Himalayas has almost lost its importance as a place for quality school education. For long, three hill subdivisions of Darjeeling, Kurseong, and Kalimpong used to provide the best schools for the entire eastern Himalayan region. Thousands of students from north east, Bengal, Bihar, Nepal, Bhutan, Bangladesh, Myanmar and many other foreign countries studied there.

However, due to the political disturbances in the hills in the last 20 years, the once qualitative functioning of the schools has sharply deteriorated. This has led to a serious dislocation among the parents across the region. At the same time because of the Maoist problem in Nepal, terrorism in Bhutan, instability in Bangladesh and north-east India, there has been a huge vacuum at the moment with people trying to locate better schools broadly in the same vicinity. This is where a major opportunity lies for Sikkim, which has some of the best locations for boarding schools and institutions.

Therefore, education as an enterprise will be very vital in Sikkim. This state can be a major destination for the educational and professional institutions as it can attract students from all the neighbouring states, countries, and NRIs abroad. For many years now, the Sikkimese have also been going to other cities for both regular and professional education. This has been facilitated by the special quota for admission to these courses extended to Sikkim for its late entry into the Indian system of education.

There remains a great scope for the private institutes imparting education on technical—traditional and modern—areas to work in Sikkim. There are no private institutes worth the name in Sikkim, which can provide training in skills and other professional areas. Therefore, the emphasis must be added to disciplines like computer software and information technology, accountancy, chemistry, physics, medicines, and in management areas like business, rural, and tourism. The demand for specialised management personnel will increase with the growing complexity and size of industrial establishment and other tertiary sector activities like tourism and trade. Equally vital will be apprenticeship programme as several new collaborative ventures are likely to be set up.

However, parties interested in joint ventures in Sikkim in the educational fields have very often come across issues of strong regionalism, difficulty in getting qualitative local resource persons for teaching, higher costs of hiring people and teachers from outside and the rigidity in laws including land acquisition, administering the setting up of schools and institutions for higher professional learning.

In fact, educational institutions triggered by private initiatives can reduce a tremendous outflow of Sikkimese resources that go on to educate the Sikkimese children outside Sikkim. On the other hand, these institutions can attract a whole lot of students from the neighbouring countries also, thereby internalising a whole range of benefits including tourism.

In order to encourage these activities, the Sikkim Government must make necessary changes in its laws and policies. This ranges from the issues related to land acquisition to investment regime and from reservation of seats for the Sikkimese to permitting students from other countries and affiliating these schools with the best secondary boards. The subsequent multicultural character of students will have sharp positive impact on the academic ability of the local students both in terms of enhancing their competitive edge and the acceleration of the tourism industry in and around the institutions.

5.12.1 Potential Areas

- Schools at all levels, primary, secondary, and higher secondary in different districts.
- Colleges with traditional courses like social science, commerce, and science.
- Technical universities like engineering, medicine, architecture, computer science, biotechnology and environmental sciences.
- Professional institutes like mass media, accountancy, corporate and environmental law, fashion technology, and tourism.
- Management schools like rural management, hotel, business, and personnel.
- Industrial training institutes including apprentice programmes.

BOX 5.2

Pakshep Upper Primary School: A Status Report

This school is located at the periphery of Kazor Busty about three km away from Mangan. It has total students of 274 out of which 239 are in pre-primary and primary and 35 in upper primary levels. The upper primary level was appended only a year ago under the centrally sponsored scheme *Sarva Shiksha Abhiyan (SSA)*. There are eight primary teachers and three graduate teachers. There is a provision of mid-day meals thrice a week for class I to V. Officially there is no provision of mid-day meal for the pre-primary children but the school has made its own arrangement in this respect. The mid-day meals generally consist of *khichdi* made of rice, pulses and vegetables.

Observations based on the discussions with the staff and principal of the School and our own assessments are noted as follows:

- Most of the classrooms are in bad condition. Walls have developed cracks wide enough to permit the sunlight to pass in and most of the doors and windows of the schools are broken.
- There are lesser number of desks and benches than required for the total students.
- There are no adequate sanitation facilities: the water tank has been empty since several days, and the toilet is in a pathetic shape.
- There is no playground for children.
- There is no electricity connection in the school.
- The dropout rate is high. The reasons as cited by the teachers of the school are poor economic conditions of the parents, illness of the parents, other family problems, migration etc. The rate of enrolment is fairly high but as the students go to the higher classes, the number decreses. Most parents, whenever they find on opportunity to get temporary employment, that fetch daily wages take their children out of the school.

Source: Based on a visit to the school in July 2004.

The new thinking provided by the present political leadership and dispensation in the state with regard to diversification of development agencies and institutions have brought in a range of national and international NGOs and development organisations and donor agencies including the Asian Development Bank, the World Bank, United Nations Development Programme, United Nations Conference on Trade and Development,

Ford Foundation, UNIDO, US-AID and Swiss Aid. They all have joined hands in the cause of promoting sustainable development in the state.

There is no study carried out to show the exact nature of manpower availability in Sikkim in terms of technical, skilled, and semi-skilled and professionals. There is a strong need to sensitise the policymakers and the parents alike about the changing nature of employment opportunities both at the state and the national level.

5.13 Recommendations

The state needs to thoroughly streamline the existing education system in the following areas:

- *Ad hocism* must give way to a more systematic and better planned approach
- Rationalisation of the functional composition of Human Resources Development Department must be carried out, as there exists excessive centralisation in administration, curriculum formulation, teacher's amenities, school planning and other mundane matters in the department located in Gangtok. This should involve increasing devolution in all these areas to districts, sub-divisions, and *panchayats*.
- The Human Resources Development Department located in Gangtok is over staffed. There is no linkage between the huge staff members in the department and the performance of the education system in the state. Human resources are under utilised at the Gangtok level, whereas there is a serious dearth of human resources at the districts and *panchayat* levels. The redeployment of these human resources should be urgently taken up by deputing at least 60 per cent of them located in Gangtok to districts and the *panchayats*.
- The state must rethink on and drastically change its policy of recruitment based on only emotive criteria like Sikkimese subject. This has adversely affected the quality and efficiency of the education sector in the state. Unless the state government makes its recruitment based on merit, qualifications, and skill and makes it attractive for the talents outside the state, the investment and progress claims it has been making will all go in vain. The short term political gain should not be at the cost of compromising quality, competitiveness and opportunities of the entire upcoming and future generation of Sikkimese.
- Government should immediately stop aiding private schools.
- The mushrooming of private schools need to be monitored in terms of intake policy, teacher recruitment, locational issues, infrastructure, fee structure and quality.
- Although, in Sikkim the level of literacy both of male and female is higher than the national average, there is a notable gap of over 15 per cent between male and female literacy rates in the state. A major task ahead therefore, is to reduce this gap and make it balanced in the next 10 years. Over 40 per cent of the women in Sikkim are still illiterate.
- Planning, monitoring, and evaluation should be a key element in the education system particularly in areas like school performance, school building maintenance, teaching quality, curriculum review, and teacher training.
- At State level a semi-government Education Regulatory Committee consisting of officials, private sector, civil society members, professionals and experts may be set up to monitor the quality of education, supervise the maintenance of all the education related institutions in the State and oversee the broad orientation of higher education policy and system in the State.
- Massive institutional revamping is required which should include the setting up of Board of Secondary Education, University Management Board, and Private Institutions Regulatory Board.
- Teachers training should be made compulsory after every five year cycle, at all levels in both government and private schools. Exposure to other schools and institutions of all the teachers within and outside the state must be encouraged and tagged with scale upgradation.
- Teachers' training facilities must be expanded drastically by identifying the outsourcing points both private and existing facilities in other states and also steadily developing its own capacity.
- Capacity building of *panchayat* members for effective management of primary schools should be steadily carried out.
- Primary schools with thin enrolment should be closed down. Students could be brought to nearby boarding schools. Teachers released should be redeployed.

- School maintenance rather than expansion in numbers and upgradation should be a major thrust. At least 25 per cent of the education outlay should be devoted to maintenance of schools for at least the next 8-10 years.
- The state should have a very clear higher education policy. The Union Government's decision to set up a Central University should be implemented urgently. A high level team drawn from both public and private sector educational services may be set up to provide a blueprint of the University in terms of physical structures, curriculum, recruitment, teaching faculty, research components and other aspects so that the University can harness some of its comparative advantages and also could have some unique features.
- The State Board of Investment should declare education as one of the key opportunities for private investment and also make enabling laws particularly in terms of land acquisition and other physical infrastructure for setting up of private ventures in the education sector. The idea should be to make Sikkim the most sought-after educational destination in the next one decade for the entire eastern Himalayan region and also the neighbouring countries. The North East Industrial Policy should be amended so as to include the educational services in its coverage. Make the subsidies highly merit-based and target-oriented and divert the funds thus released to the maintenance of schools across the state.
- Database and information network on the education system is still at a nascent stage. Many of the critical data are still not available at all or on a regular and reliable basis. This must be corrected urgently.
- The state should set up a range of both publicly and privately funded research institutes on major areas like biodiversity management, medicinal plants and herbs, eco-tourism, mountain ecology, intellectual property resources, and cultural anthropology. Sikkim requires an array of technical and professional institutions rather than a University. Institutions related to IT, tea, tourism, health, horticulture-floriculture, biotechnology, engineering, mountain ecology, mass media, management and fashion technology are very vital.

References

Banerjee, R. (1997). "Why Don't Children Complete Primary School? A Case Study of a Low-Income Neighbourhood in Delhi", *Economic and Political Weekly*, Vol. XXXII(32): 2053.

Chandna, R.C. (2000). *Geography of Population: Concepts, Determinants and Pattern.*, New Delhi: Kalyani Publishers. pp. 254-55.

Department of Education (2003). *Annual Report, 2002-03*, Government of Sikkim.

Jangira, N.K. (1977). "Educational Change in Sikkim", *Sikkim Education Newsletter*, Annual Number. Gangtok: Directorate of Education, Government of Sikkim.

Lama, Mahendra P. (2001). *Sikkim Human Development Report 2001*, New Delhi: Social Science Press.

Lama, Mahendra P. (*ed.*) (2003). *Glory of New Sikkim*. Gangtok: Department of Information and Public Relations, Government of Sikkim.

International Institute of Population Studies (IIPS) and ORC Macro. *National Family Health Survey (NFHS-2), 2001 India, 1998-99, Sikkim*. Mumbai.

Prakasha, Veda (1976). "Extending Educational Opportunity in Sikkim", A Report on the *State's School System with special reference to its Administration*. New Delhi: National Staff Educational Planners and Administrators.

Chapter 6

Health

The endeavour of the state government has been to reach the basic health needs at the doorsteps of the rural mass that forms the overwhelming component of the population. From 1975 onwards the emphasis has been on providing preventive and curative services to the rural areas. With this effort, the state strives to reduce the infant and maternal mortality in the state. As the health facilities were made more and more accessible to the remotest villages and *bustees* of various revenue blocks and districts, healthcare as a means of social upliftment acquired rapid momentum.

TABLE 6.1

Macro-Health Indicators: Sikkim and India

Indicators	*Sikkim*	*India*
Sex Ratio (2001)	875	933
Crude Birth Rate SRS 2003	21.9	24.8
Crude Death Rate SRS 2003	5.0	8.0
Natural Growth Rate SRS 2003	16.9	16.8
Maternal Mortality Rate (2000) per 10,000	-	407
Life Expectancy at Birth (2001-2006)		
Male	N.A.	64.1
Female	N.A.	65.8
Neo-natal Mortality Rate (1998-99)	26.3	43.4
Post-neonatal Mortality Rate (1998-99)	17.6	24.2
Infant Mortality Rate SRS 2003	33	60
Under-five Mortality Rate (1998-99)	71.0	94.9
Child Mortality (1998-99)	28.4	29.3
Total Fertility Rate (1998-99)	2.75	2.85

Sources: Health Information Bulletin: Sikkim 2003, Department of Health Care Human Services and Family Welfare, Government of Sikkim; For 1998-99: *NFHS-2: 1998-99, 2001*; For 2001: *Census of India*.

The results of improved healthcare are partially manifested in the differential between birth and death rates. By 2003, the crude birth rate in the state has gone down to 21.9 as against the national average of 24.8. In case of the death rate also, Sikkim's figure of 5.0 stood much lower than the national average figure of 8.0 per thousand population. The falling mortality rate in the state is another crucial feature indicating better delivery of both healthcare services and improved nutrition and improved literacy of women. Though the life expectancy rate is not available for Sikkim, it is stated that not even one per cent (0.54 per cent) of the total population is expected to die before the age of 50 yrs. Except the sex ratio, Sikkim did relatively well in achieving most of the national norms set under the "Health for all by 2000" of the Central Govt after it signed the *Alma Ata Declaration of 1978*. Polio has been eradicated from the state. There are negligible cases of under weight births, infant mortality rate (IMR) is 33, and under 5 mortality rate is also better than the national average. The state had a lower natural growth (16.2) than the national average (17.2) (Table 6.1).

6.1 Sex Ratio Intrigues

The issue of sex ratio has been quite intriguing in Sikkim. According to the 1991 census, the male constitute 53 per cent and female 47 per cent of the total population in the State. Like general trend of sex-ratio in India, the town (urban) sex-ratio in Sikkim stand to be 750 as against 892 in the rural areas. Numerically, Sikkim is decidedly a male dominated society i.e. 878 female for 1000 male (875 in 2001). This means a shortfall of 122 females to reach the equilibrium point (Table 6.2).

TABLE 6.2

Sex Ratio in Rural and Town Areas of Sikkim-1991 (Number of Females per 1000 Males)

Districts	*Rural*	*Town*
North	836	581
Chungthang	782	
Mangan (HQ)	852	581
East	883	759
Gangtok (HQ)	875	764
Pakyong	901	
Rangpo		778
Singtam		712
South	898	693
Namchi (HQ)	914	620
Ravoong	872	
Jorethang		719
West	919	760
Gyalshing	910	626
Soreng (HQ)	928	
Nayabazar		866
Sikkim	**892**	**750**

Note: HQ: District Headquarter.

Source: Sikkim: District Census Handbook, Part XII-A & B, Series-22, Census of India, 1991, pp 42-43, Directorate of Census Operations, Sikkim.

On the other hand, the sex ratio at the national level has more or less consistently declined from 972 in 1901 to 927 in 1991. In case of Sikkim, though it started declining in 1941, a sharp decline has actually been witnessed only since 1971 (Table 6.3). The sex ratio is seen to be generally low in the town areas with as low as 581 in Mangan in the north and 620 in Namchi in the south. Whereas in the rural areas it is found to be generally high as indicated by the highest ratio of 928:1000 in Soreng in the west (Table 6.3). Among the districts, the north with 836 in the rural areas, and 581 in the towns, has the lowest female-male ratio in the state. Since the north is predominantly a tribal dominated area, it can roughly be said that this low ratio is more noteworthy among the tribals of the state.

Unlike many other Indian states, particularly in the northern India, the sex ratio in the age group of 0-4 is relatively very high (964 females per 1000 males) in Sikkim. This is a very strong indicator of respect for girl children in the state. It confirms that the people in the State do not practise ills like female foeticide. This ratio for most of the Indian states will be rather much lower. Even in the age group belonging to 0-29 years for the state as a whole, the female population remains

TABLE 6.3

Sikkim and India: Decennial Sex Ratio 1901-1991 (Number of Females per 1000 Males)

Year	*Sikkim*	*India*
1901	916	972
1911	951	964
1921	970	955
1931	967	950
1941	920	945
1951	907	946
1961	904	941
1971	863	930
1981	835	934
1991	878	927
2001	875	933

Source: Census of India.

relatively higher thereby leading to a much higher sex ratio of over 90 per cent. One finds a drastic fall in the sex ratio after the 0-29 years of age group and steadily goes down to as low as 65.5 per cent (i.e. 655 females per 1000 males) by the time they attain 55-59 age group. It again starts improving steadily after the 60-64 age group and reaches a better ratio of 86 per cent in the 80+ age group (Table 6.4).

TABLE 6.4

Distribution of Sex Ratio by Age Group

(per cent)

Age Group	*F/M Ratio*
0-4	96.45
5-9	98.34
10-14	95.03
15-19	92.23
20-24	90.14
25-29	91.06
30-34	83.74
35-39	75.46
40-44	72.63
45-49	70.21
50-54	66.23
55-59	65.45
60-64	72.41
65-69	74.70
70-74	72.47
75-79	77.89
80+	85.65
Age not stated	83.78
Total	87.80

Source: Census 1991.

One possible but a strong reason for such a behaviour of sex ratio, *vis-a-vis* the different age groups could be that the mortality rate among the females in the age group of 30-59 is relatively much higher than in the age group of 0-29 and 60 year onwards. In fact, the mortality rate among the females becomes much sharper as they climb the age ladder between 30 to 59 years. The government officials in Sikkim are also of the opinion that adverse sex ratio is due to high maternal mortality though no consistent data are available in this aspect. This could be to a certain extent explained by the fact that over 66 per cent of the girls get married in Sikkim by the time they attain 20 years of their age.

The steady improvement of sex ratio after 60 years of age shows that females having good health have a much higher longevity. In other words, females who survive the 30-59 age groups tend to live a life span as enjoyed by their male counter-parts.

Death rates in girl child is in no way different from the boys. In other words, there has been no sex differences in mortality among children. However, the adverse impact of early marriage is largely reflected in the female deaths in the 15-50 year age group which is twice as high as in males in the same age.

This is a very serious phenomenon. The related issues need to be looked into and analysed from various angles. In fact, this may ultimately give a clue to the female children and women health issues on a more specific area and for a more precise target group. Immediate interventions are needed in the areas of nutritional deficiency diseases like anaemia and also infection, haemorrhage, obstructed labour, abortion and other proper maternity care.

Some demographers attribute this low female-male sex ratio to the immigration of large number of male labour force into the state. This is reflected by the fact that the maximum decline in the ratio took place in the decade of 1971-81 which also brought the maximum number of people from outside Sikkim. The overwhelming proportion of male population among the migrants is also corroborated by the fact that it constituted as high as 61.54 per cent, 60.88 per cent, and 56.88 per cent of the total migrants in 1971, 1981, and 1991 respectively. It is also noteworthy that this was the decade (1971-81) which recorded the highest decadal growth rate of over 50 per cent. This is further corroborated by the fact that the lowest sex ratio of 564 females per 1000 men was obtained among the in-migrant population who have migrated to the state from other states of India and also from countries outside India.

There are other arguments extended by some experts to explain the low sex ratio. They attribute it to the very low female-male ratio that are found in the urban areas of Sikkim. However, this argument also cannot be carried forward because the weight of the urban population in the total state population has been hardly 21 per cent.

6.2 Plan Expenditure on Health

In Sikkim, the share of health sector in the total plan expenditure has witnessed a fluctuating trend across the plan periods. During the First Plan period (1951-56) a total of Rs. 23 lakh constituting over 7 per cent of the total plan outlay was allocated to the health sector. This figure rose to 9.4 per cent comprising Rs. 91 lakh during the Third Plan period. Since then there has been a steady decline in the share of health sector to the total plan outlay and reached its *nadir* during the Seventh Plan period with hardly 2 per cent of the total plan outlay under the fold of the health sector. In absolute terms however, the share has been steadily going up from Rs. 23 lakh in the First Plan to Rs. 80 crore in the Tenth Plan (Table 6.5).

6.3 Poverty and Malnutrition

Though the percentage share of people living below the poverty line has steadily gone down from 50.86 per cent in 1973-74 to 36.55 in 2000-01,[1] Sikkim has not been able to escape from the vicious cycle of poverty and malnutrition. Sikkim, with one of the highest per capita incomes in the country, also had the fifth largest population (at least till 2001) in terms of percentage

TABLE 6.5

Sectoral Allocations of Actual Expenditure during the Plan Periods

Sectors	*Seventh Plan*	*Eighth Plan*	*Ninth Plan*	*Tenth Plan*
Medical and Public Health (%)	1.93	9.2	5.6	4.84
Total (Rs. crore)	216.67	770.36	1091.32	1,655.74

Source: Various *Plan Documents*, Planning and Development Department, Government of Sikkim.

1. National Planning Commission, *Tenth Five Year Plan 2002-07*. However, as per the preliminary findings in the *Economic Census* conducted in Sikkim in 2005 by the State Government, the ratio of people living below poverty line has gone to 19.2 per cent.

figure living below the poverty line depicting highly uneven distribution of income. Correspondingly, malnutrition continues to be a major cause of concern in the state. This is despite a range of interventions by the state including more effective reach of food distribution under PDS and other food related schemes aimed at the lower echelons of the society.

Though the study done by the state Health Department mentions less than one per cent of the undernourished people in rural Sikkim (Table 6.6), data provided by the National Family Health Survey, 1998-99 (NFHS) indicates that there are still a large number of children that are undernourished (Table 6.7).

6.4 Reproductive Health Related Issues

A majority of the women's health problems are in one way or other related to their reproductive health and is broadly affected by two factors–biological (natural including unsafe abortion, pregnancy related complications and reproductive tract infections) and sociocultural (man made including discriminatory childcare, sexual abuse, environmental and occupational health problems), apart from the availability of health and nutritional facilities. The above factors influence and counter influence women's health in varied proportion during her entire life cycle. Despite considerable efforts made by the state Health Department, some of the indicators of reproductive health status are rather dismal (Table 6.8). For instance, births whose mothers were assisted at delivery by doctors and ANM/nurse/LHV are still hardly 40 per cent. This has to be drastically improved.

TABLE 6.6

Percentage Share of Malnourished in Rural Sikkim

	Total			*0-15 years*		
	Male	*Female*	*Person*	*Male*	*Female*	*Person*
State	0.41	0.36	0.39	0.35	0.34	0.35
East	0.55	0.43	0.46	0.45	0.30	0.38
West	0.00	0.00	0.00	0.00	0.00	0.00
South	0.67	0.75	0.71	0.63	0.90	0.76
North	0.31	0.10	0.21	0.23	0.00	0.12

Source: Gyatso and Bagdass, 1998.

TABLE 6.7

Nutritional Status (%)

Women with Anaemia*	61.1
Women with Moderate/Severe Anaemia*	23.8
Children Age 6-35 months with Anaemia*	76.5
Children Age 6-35 with Moderate/Severe Anaemia*	48.1
Children Chronically Undernourished (stunted)**	31.7
Children Acutely Undernourished (wasted)**	.48
Children Underweight**	20.6

Note: *–Anaemia-hemoglobin levels <11.0 grams/deciliter (g/dl) for children and pregnant women and <12.0 g/dl for non-pregnant women. Moderate/severe anemia hemoglobin level <10.0 g/dl.
**–Stunting assessed by height for age, wasting assessed by weight for height, underweight assessed by weight for age.

Source: NFHS: 1998-99, 2001.

TABLE 6.8

Safe Motherhood and Reproductive Health Status (%)

Birth within 24 months of previous birth	29.7
Births whose mothers received:	
Antenatal check up from a health professional	69.9
Antenatal check up in first trimester	30.2
Two or more tetanus toxoid injections	52.7
Iron and folic acid tablets or syrup	62.4
Births whose mothers were assisted at delivery by:	
Doctor	19.2
ANM/nurse/midwife/LHV	15.9
Traditional birth attendant	0.6
Women reporting at least one reproductive health problem	48.6

Source: NFHS: 1998-99, 2001

6.5 Status of Immunisation

The vaccination of children against six serious but preventable diseases namely tuberculosis, diphtheria, pertussis, tetanus, poliomyelitis and measles has been an important task for the child healthcare system in Sikkim. Hardly 30 per cent of infants were immunised against the six killer diseases, tuberculosis, diphtheria, tetanus, polio, whooping cough and measles in 1976-1977. This steadily increased to over 90 per cent by 2002 (Table 6.9).

In the last five years there has been a fluctuating trend in the immunisation achievements of various vaccine preventable diseases in the state. However, there have been cases when the achievements of the immunisation performance were higher than the target. This has, particularly, been the case with respect to the BCG among the children. By 2001-02, the achievement levels were over 90 per cent in almost all of the immunisation programmes. Across the districts, the immunisation performance has been over 85 per cent in all the categories of vaccine in most of the districts. (Table 6.10).

TABLE 6.9

Progress on Immunisation (1997/98–2004/05)

Particulars	*1997-98*	*1998-99*	*1999-00*	*2000-01*	*2001-02*	*2004-05*
TT for Women	53.3	60.1	69.3	67.3	71.4	78.8
DPT	88.9	100.3	95.6	86.1	90.9	89.5
Polio	89.7	99.8	95.2	86.1	92.0	94.3
BCG	100.0	100.4	102.4	101.6	92.5	95.5
Measles	76.1	89.1	87.7	81.8	84.8	97.1
DT for 5-yr. Children	89.7	109.2	94.9	87.2	99.5	NA
TT for 10-yr. Children	94.9	122.5	86.1	103.1	105.3	NA
TT for 16-yr. Children	39.0	52.5	35.6	56.2	44.8	NA

Note: Figures refer to percentage achievements of the targeted population. NA – Not available.

Source: Health Information Bulletin, Sikkim: 2003, and latest data supplied by Department of Health Care, Human Services and Family Welfare, Government of Sikkim.

TABLE 6.10

District-wise Immunisation, 2004-05

Particulars	*East*	*West*	*North*	*South*	*State*
TT for Pregnant Women	83.9	84.9	76.7	86.8	78.8
DPT	89.6	101.7	97.4	84.5	89.5
Polio	98.2	101.3	101.2	89.4	94.3
BCG	89.4	94.9	97.7	87.6	95.5
Measles*	89.0	97.1	93.9	82.2	97.1
DT for 5-yr Children*	88.3	140.8	41.9	108.7	99.5
TT for 10-yr Children*	97.3	144.1	47.3	102.8	105.3
TT for 16-yr Children*	46.2	42.5	14.3	47.7	44.8

Note: The figures refer to the percentage achievements of the targeted population; *-are 2001-02 figures. TT-Tetanus Toxide, DPT-Diphtheria Pertussis Tetanus, BCG-Bacillus Calmeti Guerin, DT-Diphtheria Tetanus.

Source: Health Information Bulletin, Sikkim: 2003, and latest data supplied by Department of Health Care, Human Services and Family Welfare, Government of Sikkim.

6.6 Environmental Sanitation

Environmental sanitation has important implication on the health status of a population and is emerging as a new area of concern. Environmental sanitation in terms of housing, water supply, and personal hygiene of the population form an important indicator for judging the health status. In Sikkim, the diseases related to inadequate health awareness and education like worm infestation, coughing, goitre is most common. They all arise out of improper environmental sanitation.

6.6.1 Housing

Available data reveal that only about 27 per cent of the houses are *pucca* in rural Sikkim with highest share of 32.7 per cent in north Sikkim.[2] The figure comes to over 61 per cent in case of urban Sikkim. Sikkim has only 11 per cent of the total population living in urban settlements. Thus, there should be a major concern among the development planner that about 90 per cent of the Sikkimese live in rural Sikkim out of which over 53 per cent live in *kutcha* houses prone to various forms of health hazards both natural and man made. However, we expect the situation to have improved very steadily after this survey was conducted in 1998. This is because over the last almost ten years the government has extensively distributed housing grants of Rs. 20,000 each and free CGI sheets for needy families for house construction. In 1998-99 alone over 6,000 households got such supports.

6.6.2 Fuel

Rural areas across the districts of Sikkim mainly depend on biomass like firewood (including fodder remains), cattle dung, coal, followed by kerosene for cooking. Even in urban areas except for the east district, the main fuel for cooking is wood. In case of the east district the main fuel for cooking is kerosene followed by LPG. Since rural people are found to be spending on an average 74 per cent of their time indoor, the use of biomass especially for cooking and heating purposes could have led to appreciable indoor pollution (carbon monoxide, nitrogen oxides and

2. As per the preliminary findings in the *Economic Census* conducted in Sikkim in 2005 out of the total 1,01,607 houses, 29 per cent live in *pucca* houses, 45 per cent live in semi-*pucca* houses and over 26 per cent live in *kutcha* houses.

suspended particulate matter), which negatively impact upon the human health (including acute respiratory problems, chronic lung diseases, cancer, adverse pregnancy outcomes, like stillbirths) particularly among the females and children.

6.6.3 Drinking Water

In both the rural and urban areas of Sikkim, the main source of drinking water is tap water with over 77 per cent in rural areas and 84 per cent depending exclusively on the tap water. Remaining 17 and 12 per cent in the rural and urban areas use natural springs, respectively. Nonetheless, all the tap waters have their source in natural springs and small *jhoras*. They have been connected to the households both at individual and community levels either through rubber pipelines or the traditional bamboo poles.

Traditionally the waters of the mountains were so clean that there was no need for any purification. Even today the status of water quality in the mountains remains better than that available in the plain areas. Over 70 per cent of the households purify water for drinking by boiling it, while about 8 per cent use water filter for the same. At the same time over 26 per cent of the Sikkimese drink water without purifying it. This figure is higher for the rural areas (30 per cent) (Tables 6.11 and 6.12).

6.6.4 Sanitation Facility

A study conducted in the state[3] found out that open field defecation although declining, has still been the major method of excreta disposal in the rural Sikkim with 46.42 per cent. There was also a declining trend in the use of service type of latrines both in the rural (26 per cent) and urban areas (58.27 per cent). Across the districts the study found out that open field defecation was maximum in the north district (53.10 per cent) followed by west (51.56 per cent), south (46.95 per cent) and east districts (34.56 per cent).

Another study[4] found that only 55 per cent of the households have a flush toilet (using either piped water or bucket water for flushing) while 18 per cent had a pit toilet or latrine and 27 per cent had no sanitation facility at all in Sikkim. It found a large rural urban gap with respect to sanitation facilities as 83 per cent of the urban households had a flush toilet compared to only 50 per cent of rural households (Table 6.13).

TABLE 6.12

Methods of Drinking Water Purification in Sikkim*

Methods	*Urban*	*Rural*	*Total*
Straining through Cloth	1.2	2.0	1.9
With Alum	0.0	0.3	0.2
With Water Filter	25.0	4.9	7.8
Boils Water	86.6	67.5	70.3
Electronic Purifier	0.0	0.5	0.5
Other Methods	0.0	0.4	0.3
Does not Purify	9.1	29.5	26.5

Note: *–Total adds to more than 100 per cent because households may use more than one method of purification.

Source: NFHS-2: 1998-99, 2001.

6.7 Health Infrastructure

Although 2 PHCs and 2 PHSCs were functioning in 1975-76, substantial additions have been made in the last 30 yrs. The east district has the highest pressure of population per health facility while the north has the lowest. District Hospital/CHC of east district handles over 2.45 lakh population while that of south, west and

TABLE 6.11

Sources of Drinking Water

Sources	*East*		*West*		*South*		*North*		*Total*	
	R	*U*	*R*	*U*	*R*	*U*	*R*	*U*	*R*	*U*
Tap	74.8	89.9	85.7	76.4	78	61.6	63.6	91.4	77.8	84.5
Natural Spring	20.0	8.1	10.4	15.1	15.5	31.1	33.1	6.9	17.1	12.3
Others	5.2	1.9	3.9	8.5	6.5	7.3	3.2	1.6	5.1	3.2

Note: R-Rural; U-Urban.

Source: Gyatso and Bagdass, 1998.

3. Gyatso and Bagdass, 1998.
4. *NFHS-2: 1998-99* (2001).

TABLE 6.13

Households with Sanitation Facilities (%)

Amenity	*Urban*	*Rural*	*Total*
Flush Toilet	82.9	50.2	55.0
Pit toilet/Latrine	7.9	19.4	17.7
No Facility	9.1	30.5	27.3

Source: NFHS-2: 1998-99, 2001.

north districts handle 1.31 lakh, 1.23 lakh and 0.41 lakh respectively. The average for the state in this respect is over 1.35 lakh. The average population per PHC counts out to be 30630 in the east district, 21921 for south, 17608 for west and 13677 for north district and the average state figure is over 22500. The average population per PHC is 5105 in the east district while for that of south west and north districts are 3372, 3006 and 2159 respectively. On average, Sikkim handles 3600 people per PHC. Except the north district, the population per CHC in all the districts are more than the national norms of 1 lakh per people per CHC. For PHC also the east and the south districts serve more population than the national norm of 20,000 people per PHC (Tables 6.14 and 6.15).

6.7.1 Regional Pattern of Health Facilities in Sikkim

Across the regions of the state there is a state level hospital located at Gangtok in the East district. There are four CHCs distributed one each in the four districts of the state. There are 24 PHCs in the state. The east district with the highest concentration of the population has 8 PHCs followed by west with 7 PHCs, south with 6 PHCs and north district with 3 PHCs. The state has a total of 147 Primary Health Sub-Centres out of which 33 per cent of the PHS are located in the east district, 28 per cent in the west, 27 per cent in the south and 13 per cent in the north district. The State Referral Hospital located in Gangtok has a total of 300 beds and serves as a nodal health centre for the whole state.

Sikkim has more doctors than the suggested national norm of 1 doctor per 3500 people. The average figure for the state in this regard is 3106. Similarly as against the national norm of 5000 the average number of population per nurse at the state level is over 3300. Across the districts, however, the distribution is not on an equitable basis. The east district has only 1958 population per nurse as against 12,000 in the west district. Sikkim is in a better position both at the state level and across the districts in case of the health assistants, health workers, and lab technicians than the suggested national norms.

The health centres have been fairly well planned across the space and the remotest of the villages are provided with the health centres. Some inadequacies and lack of appropriate planning are, nevertheless, observed in terms of necessary infrastructures including the number and quality of health staff, availability of medicines, etc., that the state needs to address.

6.8 Utilisation of Health Services

In Sikkim, public sector continues to dominate the health utilisation pattern. Over 75 per cent of the health delivery in 1997 was shared by the public sector both in rural and urban areas and the trend is increasing in nature. Although the private sector is gradually creating their niche in urban areas, they are yet to make any distinct progress (Table 6.16).

TABLE 6.14

District-wise Distribution of Health Facilities

	Number					*Percentage Share*				
Particulars	*East*	*West*	*North*	*South*	*State*	*East*	*West*	*North*	*South*	*State*
Health Institutions										
State Referral Hospital	1	0	0	0	1	100	0	0	0	100
Community Health Centres	1	1	1	1	4	25	25	25	25	100
Primary Health Centres	8	7	3	6	24	33	29	13	25	100
Primary Health Sub-Centres	48	41	19	39	147	33	28	13	27	100
Beds										
State Referral Hospital	300				300	100	0	0	0	100
Community Health Centres	100	50	50	100	300	33	17	17	33	100
Primary Health Centres	80	70	30	60	240	33	29	13	25	100

Source: Health Information Bulletin: Sikkim, 2003 and latest data supplied by Department of Health Care, Human Services and Family Welfare, Government of Sikkim.

TABLE 6.15

Health Infrastructure in Sikkim, District-wise

Particulars	*East*	*West*	*North*	*South*	*Sikkim*
		Population per Health Institution			
State Referral Hospital	540851	0	0	0	5,40,851
Community Health Centres	2,45,040	1,23,526	41,030	1,31,525	1,35,213
Primary Health Centres	30,630	17,608	13,677	21,921	22,535
Primary Health Sub-Centres	5,105	3,006	2,159	3,372	3,679
		Population per Bed			
State Referral Hospital	1802	0	0	0	1,802
Community Health Centres	2450	1232	820	1,315	1545
Primary Health Centres	3,063	1,761	1,368	2,192	2,254
Primary Health Sub-Centres	0	0	0	0	0
Population per Doctor	1738	5136 9	2,735	3,653	2,504
Population per Nurse	1,929	12,326	5,861	7,737	3,359
Population per ANMs	1,360	1,866	1,641	1,144	1,445
Population per Health Assistants	18,830	24,635	13,674	16,438	18,638
Population per Health Worker	1,990	1,642	1,109	1,906	1,778
Population per Lab Tech	7,896	12,317	8,205	10,116	9,319

Source: Health Information Bulletin: Sikkim, 2003 and latest data supplied by Department of Health Care, Human Services and Family Welfare, Government of Sikkim.

TABLE 6.16

Health Services in Rural Sikkim: Utilisation Pattern (%)

	East		*West*		*North*		*South*		*Urban*	
	1989	*1997*	*1989*	*1997*	*1989*	*1997*	*1989*	*1997*	*1989*	*1997*
Hospital	14.9	42.5	4.7	45.3	5.1	18.9	20.5	25.0	35.8	51.8
PHC/PHSC	35.8	49.2	50.2	47.2	38.3	52.8	46.5	72.0	34.4	25.9
Independent Practitioners	2.5	0.0	4.2	0.0	9.8	3.8	2.4	2.3	0.0	1.8
Private	1.0	8.3	4.7	5.7	8.5	22.6	1.8	0.8	5.3	17.7
Others	0.7	0.0	0.9	1.9	6.1	1.9	0.5	0.0	0.7	4.7

Source: Lama, 2001.

TABLE 6.17

Status of Health Delivery Services in Sikkim (%)

	1991-92	*1995-96*	*2000-01*
In-Patients	4.63	4.56	5.36
Out-patients	95.37	95.44	94.64
Total Patients Treated *(No)*	3,05,142	3,70,770	5,26,580

Source: Health Information Bulletin: Sikkim, 2003, Department of Health Care Human Services and Family Welfare, Government of Sikkim.

Such pattern highlights two important points. Firstly the public health sector is doing well in Sikkim in that the quality, efficiency and effectiveness has been maintained and secondly, majority of the people cannot afford to use private health facilities. Though the emphasis of the public health has been on providing preventive, promotive and curative services across the districts, the steady increase in the number of people seeking treatment in the state does indicate that the pressure on the public facilities is going to be enormous. (Table 6.17). Therefore, private participation as a parallel service provider is to be consciously promoted.

6.9 Traditional Medicines

Sikkim is the land of faith healers. For every disease there is a medicine indigenously developed and totally dependent on its own natural resources and strong spirituality. There are *dhami, jhankri, phendongba* and *bonbo* in Nepali community, *pow* and *nejum* in Bhutia community and *bumthing* in Lepcha community. For these powerful faith healers, *jhar phuk* is the key word and the first step in an interestingly interspersed and inexpensive treatment.

There has been a long felt need to record traditional systems of medicine (TSM)—related knowledge and to know whether natural biodiversity components are being used effectively for healthcare. There are attempts by Sikkim Voluntary Health Association (SVHA) to the documentation of this knowledge. It is very important for the local people to help and cooperate with this Association's effort so that a dependable database on TSM healthcare system could be documented. Local peoples' knowledge on traditional system of healthcare, its scientific analysis and correct interpretation of the mystic beliefs are some of the areas, which need documentation. This will help in identifying death caused by various diseases prevalent in remote villages.

Even ten years back, the most prevalent and first resort treatment for a villager used to be a traditional faith healer. In some cases these faith healers are very useful as they understand both the nature of disease in a more practical way and also have some long experimented treatment with indigenously prepared medicinal provisions. However, they have limitations to their treatment practices. As the literacy rate, awareness, and social mobilisation have undergone strong fillip through modern communications and other physical exposures, the allopathic treatment started getting increasingly accepted by the same village folks. This is very easily reflected in the increasing pressure on the PHCs and PHSCs.

The faith healers are vital pillars of Sikkimese folk traditions. One never knows whether some of their practices and knowledge have already been taken by the educated practitioners and the laboratories owned by the multinationals only to convert the traditional faith healing practice into full fledged commercial ventures. No one has done anything in this regard in the entire eastern Himalayas as only a microscopic minority has heard about the humdrum of intellectual property rights at the global level. In the absence of any systematic study of the faith healers and their impact on the Sikkimese society, it is very difficult to assess their vanishing traits and population.

There are no cross-purposes in the existence of faith healers and the modern day medical practices. They are never at loggerheads even if they are treating the same patient, moreover, with different interpretation. They coexist and complement each other to a large extent as the former stresses on psychotherapy and the latter, on medical therapy.

Interestingly, many of the modern day health workers including the crucial compounder in the PHCs are very often traditional faith healers as well. Throughout the day they fiddle with allopathy and the computer, but in the evening, they do the traditional chores of a faith healer. This is a magnificent blend of tradition and modernity, a continuity amidst change.

There are no conscious efforts to conserve these much sought after but neglected village folks. These faith healers are being given health education training for assisting the Health Department. They can always be a major complement to the entire chain of activities of the Health Department, as they continue to rule the roost among the simple village folks.

6.10 Major Morbidity Cases

'Tuberculosis' has been one of the major heath problems in the state of Sikkim. The *Gangtok Times* (24 January, 2000) reported the detection of 170 tuberculosis cases every month in Sikkim which is over 2,000 per annum. Against a national average of just over 40 TB cases per lakh people, the figure for Sikkim stands at 87 cases.[5] With an average cure rate less than one-third half a decade ago and 77 per cent most recently, the progress in combating this disease has been commendable in Sikkim. However, still the mortality resulting from this disease is fairly high. Steady growth of drug resistant strains due to irregular medication, discontinuation of treatment and reluctance to go for treatment often exasperate the situation. Some of the major causes behind the widespread prevalence of this disease may also be the hostile geographical location of the state, low level of awareness, poor living conditions including malnutrition and improper housing & sanitation, bad habits of the people (more of liquor and less of nutritious food), eating of half cooked or uncooked meat by the tribals especially in higher elevations, and lack of commitment on the part of the medical practitioners. Such situation highlights that TB in Sikkim need to be addressed on a priority basis through awareness, literacy, proper manpower planning and greater resource allocation.

Under the Revised National Tuberculosis Control Programme (RNTCP) there is a 60-bed district

5. Lama, 2001.

tuberculosis centre (DTC), in Namchi and 10-bed mini DTC in the other three districts; five tuberculosis units (TU); 18 microscopic centres (MC) and 561 directly observed treatment (DOT) centres. The main objectives of RNTCP are to achieve a cure rate of 85 per cent and detection rate of 70 per cent cases. Case detection is primarily done by sputum microscopy and treatment of cases by DOT. To facilitate the proper implementation of programme TB Control Societies (both at the state and district levels) have been formed.

Since the last few years, focus has been retained on information, education and communication (IEC) activities for creating better awareness among the patients and the public on curability of the disease, and also on the danger of not getting timely treatment. The message of the availability for free services for detection and treatment has been widely published. As a consequence, 77 per cent cure rate was achieved in 2002-03

This leads to the larger issue of quality of life which is intimately related to income and the level of education. Poor families without education are prone to malnutrition and hence various disease vectors. A disease like tuberculosis is mainly a result of malnutrition. The emphasis should be on improving the quality of life through income and education improves.

6.10.1 Iodine Deficiency Disorders

The state of Sikkim had been identified as the hyper endemic region of iodine deficiency disorders (IDD) by the central government, Indian Council of Medical Research (ICMR) and by the state government itself on the basis of the sample survey conducted at various points of time. A central government survey (1976) showed goitre prevalence to be 37 per cent in Sikkim. While cretinism (extreme iodine deficiency leading to mental retardation was prevalent among people who were more than 51 years old, goitre was three times higher among women as compared to men with the east district recording highest prevalence of both goitre (60.92 per cent) and cretinism (4.93 per cent) and north district the lowest (45.84 per cent and 1.67 per cent, respectively).

Various combating measures were devised by the state realising the alarming situation in this respect. A recent follow up survey undertaken in 1998 by the state government has shown a decline in the goiter prevalence to 16.8 per cent and cretinism to 1.8 per cent. Unlike many other parts of the country, Sikkim, does not lack awareness about the importance of iodised salt. The key issue, however, is the retention of adequate iodine content, particularly in the rural conditions, which limit the effectiveness of IDD interventions.

6.11 Geography and Environment

The geographical location of Sikkim has been an important physical attribute that has a bearing on the health status of the state. The varying hilly terrain across the region, often inaccessible to many cases, prevents the efficient delivery of the health services to the most needy in the interior. Unlike in the plains, the geomorphology of the hills does not permit motorable road networks across the interior of the villages. The health staffs have to trek for a considerable distance from the main road into the villages with scattered and sparse settlements along the slopes. Another critical dimension is the fact that traditionally women have been the main collectors of drinking water, fuel wood, fodder, fruits, wild roots etc from the nearest available sources. As these sources are now on the way to depletion, they are forced to do their daily journey farther away. Such situations have not only prolonged their working hours, but have also deprived them of leisure and given rise to complexities of health problems.

A major option available and now being increasingly followed is to train the *Panchayat* members in the basic heath care systems and hand over the running of the PHCs to them.

Environment along with geography has been instrumental in directing the health of the people across the regions of Sikkim. The state exhibits various types of climates from subtropical in the lower altitudes to alpine in higher elevations representing a strong vertical zonation of climate. The lower altitudes with moist subtropical climate has been a breeding ground for many disease vectors like mosquitoes, flies, bacteria and viruses, often threatening the health of the Sikkimese. In the higher elevations, the harsh climatic conditions prevent the efficient functioning of the health services where the settlements are extremely sparse and scattered across the steep slopes. Such environmental externalities require proper spatial and vertical planning of health services with special emphasis on the quality of the services and horizontal network.

BOX 6.1

Health Subcentre, Shakyong Village, West District

Shakyong village is located 6 km. from Gyalsing in the West district of Sikkim. The village has 400 households with the population of 2493 as in April 2004. It has 14 small hamlets with 6 *panchayat* wards.

This village has a health subcentre with three staffs: one compounder, a sister, and an attendant. The village is almost free from the problems of goiter, malaria, TB, polio and leprosy. The village sometimes witnesses viral hepatitis/jaundice but it is highly seasonal. In recent times some cases of hypertension have been observed across the village. According to the compounder of the health centre this is mainly because of the unemployment and high degree of alcoholism in the village. Further, the villagers argue that the degradation of natural resources majorly drinking water sources (natural spring), domestic fuel, fodder and declining agriculture production often have played role in this regard.

The subcentre has no problem of medicine supply and availability. Most of the health related programmes are organised. One outreach programme is organised every month. However, the health staffs often face difficulties in delivering the health services as the hamlets are scattered across the terrain of the village spread over 4 km. During the time of emergency like delivery cases, they have to walk across the terrain, as there is no motorable network in the interior. During other problems like snakebite (which is quite often), dog bite etc the health centre is not quipped to handle the situation, as there is no refrigerator to store the medicine needed for the purpose. Sometimes it so happens that while the staffs are in the interior of the hamlets attending the multiple emergency cases some villagers may visit the health centre only to find the centre locked. This makes the people think that the health staffs do not deliver their service regularly and efficiently. Further, the health centre has no computer. This has led to poor management of the database pertaining to the health issues in the area.

Source: Based on focus group discussions and inputs from the Compounder, Primary Health Subcentre, Shakyong Village in July 2004.

6.12 Urban Environment and Sanitation: AusAid Intervention

Sikkim became one of the strategic partner states for AUSaid in 1998. The Gangtok Urban Water Supply and Environmental Sanitation Project funded by AUSaid added a new dimension to the entire question of total health management in the state. This project mainly focuses on:

- improvement in urban water supply;
- sanitation extension and improvement;
- integrated drainage system;
- overhaul of solid water management;
- institutional reform and restructuring;
- review of tariff;
- billing and revenue collection;
- environmental health improvement;
- service delivery to the poor and vulnerable; and
- implementation of development control

This is one of the first projects that brings in a strong element of people's participation in the functioning of public utilities in terms of meeting of health and sanitation needs, management, revenue collection and sustainability. This project is looked forward to by the people as an alternative to pure government project. Depending upon the success of this project, a range of such interventions could inject a new tenor and system of more efficient and sustainable health management in the state.

6.13 Sikkim Manipal University: Changing Face of the Health Sector

Sikkim Manipal Institute of Technology is a University College of "Sikkim Manipal University of Health Medical and Technological Sciences (UGC code 130/22)" which has been set up by an Act of Sikkim Legislature. It primarily proposed to set up medical and engineering degree colleges under the auspices of the Sikkim-Manipal University and to augment medical facilities with the establishment of a central referral hospital. This is the first institution of its kind in Sikkim to provide basic education in health and engineering. However, there is still rather small presence of Sikkimese students.

In the medical college, 20 per cent of the total seats are reserved for the locals. The permanent campus at Majhitar is ready for take off. The 500-bed referral hospital, a vital part of this institute, treats patients referred to the hospital by the Sikkim government and from outside the state. Patients referred by STNM Hospital are treated free. The Institute also offers courses on electrical & electronics, computer and civil engineering.

The setting up this first-ever joint sector initiative in the health sector is likely to generate plenty of employment opportunities for the Sikkimese. The employment policy which is agreed upon ensures this prospect.

- 100 per cent locals absorbed in Class IV category both skilled, and semiskilled manpower
- Five local lecturers as part of the engineering faculty
- A number of local doctors are already practising in departments like gynaecology, ENT, and paediatrics.

This initiative has shown that there is a huge scope for opening such instates in Sikkim, which can draw students, patients, and health experts from across the country. The fragile political situation in other parts of the north east region and the neighbouring countries will further make this type of venture in Sikkim more and more attractive. Therefore, health should be included as an exclusive investment opportunity in the development dynamics of tertiary sector in Sikkim.

6.14 Health Insurance

Sikkim incurs large-scale expenditure on sending people out of Sikkim for health treatment. The state government literally bears the treatment cost of a large section of patients who cannot be treated in the state and are referred to outside. This takes place both in official and unofficial manner. This is besides the fact that the state provides free medicines and free diets in most of its hospitals.

This has led to a huge drain in the state exchequer. The most serious question is that of sustainability. This issue needs to be addressed in a multipronged manner:

- create and disperse the facilities in the rural areas by bringing all the basic equipment, diagnosis, and testing facilities in the rural areas;
- deconcentrate the facilities in the urban areas;
- link the major hospitals in other cities through telemedicines and other swift techniques;
- health insurance for the people; and
- raise resources through health taxes.

6.15 Recommendations

- The major concerns in the health sector today are related to both the changing nature of health requirements and the pressure on the existing health amenities. Health problems related to environmental pollution, improper sanitation and potable water supply continue to remain alive in the rural areas of Sikkim, whereas the gradual emergence of diseases like coronary, AIDS, diabetes in the urban areas and re-emergence of once dreaded disease like tuberculosis are a major challenge.
- The emphasis naturally should be more on preventive aspects for which the most vital instrument will be the health awareness related activities. Therefore, extra efforts need to be made to organise health-related education activities, camps, orientation programmes, through mass media like films, literature, exhibitions, etc. These efforts should be comprehensive both in terms of target groups and agencies who carry out these tasks. There should be strong components of NGOs and other social welfare private agencies in these initiatives.
- All the medical officers posted at rural areas are given a minimum of six months orientation training at the district hospitals regarding medical problems in the villages. However, the villagers find many of them naive about the basic health issues, as they were never exposed to village situation. This needs to be urgently looked into as this has implications on future research and newer interventions as well. At the same time reorientation of medical education is required because the realities in *bustees* and villages are different. A compulsory posting policy of all government doctors in the sub-divisional and lower level hospitals with strong rural 'bias' for at least a period of 5 years needs to be implemented.
- Primary healthcare is increasingly neglected as indicated by the poor state of some of the sub-primary and primary health centres. Whereas the situation demands a solid emphasis on primary. These primary heath centres need to be rejuvenated by inducting better provisions including medicines, basic healthcare instruments, technical manpower and management. The management of at least 70 per cent of these centres directly by the qualified villagers, *Panchayats*, NGOs and even welfare oriented private agencies and trusts should be encouraged. This should also include organisations like Sikkim Voluntary Health Association of India, Red Cross Society, Association of Social Health in India and Sikkim Women's Welfare Organisation. Some of these NGOs are already involved in providing health

education awareness in hygiene and other communicable diseases.

The immediate targets should be to achieve comprehensive immunisations 100 per cent of the rural children, at least 90 per cent coverage of mothers during delivery by doctors and ANM/ nurse/LHV assistance, 50 per cent outsourcing of services particularly medical/lab tests both in the rural and urban areas, 15 per cent of the health budget to be used by primary health centres for educating people about preventive healthcare. Provision of a computer and refrigerator is essential in all the PHCs and subcenters

- Nutrition is increasingly becoming a serious issue. The real challenge is to make food easily affordable and accessible. This should include 20 per cent of the health budget to be allocated for the strengthening and wider role of *Anganwadi* centres and ICDS particularly on nutrition reach and management. A coordinated approach by Health-Rural Development-Social Welfare and Food Security Departments to reach the rural and urban population with a view to eliminate malnourishment by 2012.
- There are concerns regarding the non-availability of specialist and trained technicians particularly even in the district level hospitals. This has led to outflow of even general patients to plain areas including Siliguri, Calcutta, Delhi and Madras. This is likely to be more acute in the days ahead as hospitals are getting increasingly choked with increase in population. This could be to a large extent minimised if a well thought out manpower planning in this sector can be done. There should be adequate provisions for telemedicines with interconnection for exchange of opinions with major health institutes both within and outside the country. An array of services including lab test, X-rays and scanning could be outsourced by inviting reputed health service providers in the State. The state has to undertake a first-hand survey of manpower available in the health sector in the state in both technical and non-technical categories. This data bank will go a long way in consolidating the effort made by the state in creating health amenities. Upgradation and updating of the existing knowledge of the professionals and health workers through periodic training facilities on the new technological advancement must be made compulsory.
- Another critical concern has been the poor coordination among the health-related departments like Rural Development mainly for water, salt, and education for health awareness. Health being a relatively low priority area, not much importance is given by other departments for inter-departmental coordination. As a result, they are sometimes found to be working at cross-purposes leading to both wastage of resources and erosion in peoples' confidence in the delivery mechanism of the governmental agencies. To improve inter-departmental coordination besides regular meeting of the officials, the involvement of village *panchayats* and the target groups are very vital. This can be done by garnering support of the elected individuals and bodies at all levels.
- The Health Department located in Gangtok is over staffed. Human resources are under utilised at the Gangtok level, whereas there is a serious dearth of health related human resources at the districts and *panchayat* levels. The redeployment of these human resources should be urgently taken up by deputing at least 60 per cent of them located in Gangtok to districts and the *panchayats*. The location and distribution of health centres and health staff need to be carried out not only in terms of population but also on the basis of the climatic conditions, micro-topography and geomorphic complexities.
- A rather neglected area has been the management and maintenance of the massive infrastructures created. The question of resource crunch and the subsequent issues of manpower deployment may in fact be a major stumbling block in the management of health sector. This will be heightened by the increase in the incidence of diseases arising out of both poverty and stress factors. A State level semi-government Education Regulatory Committee consisting of officials, private sector, civil society members, professionals and experts may be set up to monitor the quality of health, supervise the maintenance of all health related institutions in the State and oversee the broad orientation of health policy and system in the State.
- Though the data and information base on health sector is relatively more developed in the state, there is no information to verify many of the health standards like life expectancy at birth, net reproduction rate, and family size. The state

needs to upgrade and rationalise the health information system and database urgently. All these data at various levels should be easily accessible to all.

- The health insurance, as a second-generation reform measure must be encouraged both to make the health amenities more sustainable, and efficient use of health and financial resources.
- There are no institutionalised monitoring and evaluation mechanisms on any of the health related projects. This has made the system slow, tardy, insensitive, and inefficient. Each project will have to have a very strong content of monitoring and evaluation both in house and independently from outside.
- Health sector as a potential investment avenue, if promoted could bring about a large and diverse revenue and employment generation opportunities. A large number of people from the neighbouring states and even the countries including Nepal, Bhutan, China, and Bangladesh could use these facilities. This would also cater to the increasing needs of the state of hospitals with modern facilities. The North East Industrial Policy should be amended so as to include the health services in its coverage. The state's private investment policies should directly promote health sector as investment options in the following areas:

- setting up modern health facilities;
- commercial use of medicinal plants and herbs;
- intellectual property rights in the practices of folk medicines;
- development of exclusive health resorts, and
- building tourism related health facilities.

References

Department of Health Care, Human Services and Family Welfare (2003). *Annual Administrative Report, 2002-03*. Government of Sikkim.

Gyatso, T.R. and B.B. Bagdass (1998). *Health Status in Sikkim*. Gangtok: Department of Health & Family Welfare, Government of Sikkim.

Hazara, Jayanti (1998). "Women and Health", *Geographical Review of India*, 60(4): 518-33.

International Institute of Population Studies (IIPS) and ORC Macro (2001). *National Family Health Survey (NFHS-2), 1998-99*. Mumbai.

Lama, Mahendra P. (2001). *Sikkim Human Development Report 2001*. New Delhi: Social Science Press.

PMED (2004). *Health Information Bulletin—Sikkim: 2003*. Department of Health and Family Welfare, Government of Sikkim.

WHO and UNCF (1978). *Primary Health Care—A Joint Report*. Geneva.

Chapter 7

Infrastructure: Roads, Telecommunications and Power

7.1 Importance of Basic Infrastructure

Economic progress is intrinsically linked to the physical infrastructure of a state. For Sikkim, which is landlocked and has an international border along almost three-quarters of its boundary, infrastructure that enhances its connectivity and increases communication is vital to any strategy aimed at expanding employment and income-generating opportunities in the state. In the absence of rail or air services, roads are the only means of transporting people and goods. The road network can thus be considered essential state infrastructure, but its slow pace of expansion and poor maintenance has, over the years, directly impacted overall development. Almost every sector—agriculture/animal husbandry, rural development, health, education, social welfare, etc.—has been handicapped by the lack of good roads. An example is the almost exclusive dependence on middlemen for marketing agricultural and horticultural surpluses, because of poor road linkages and high transport costs.

A good telecommunications system can help overcome some of the geographical and locational disadvantages of the mountainous state, in the absence of a good road network. The expansion of fixed line telephone network across the state, the successful proliferation of mobile phones in the Gangtok area, and the spread of internet connectivity to even remote parts of the state have increased connectivity among people once living in isolation.

Rapid development in recent years, and the expected expansion in industrial activity has put pressure on power supply in the state, prompting the government to begin exploiting the state's vast hydel potential. As much as roads and telecommunications, good power supply is essential to realise the full potential of almost all other sectors, and indispensable for development aimed at improving living conditions and increasing access to employment. Good quality power supply can play an important part in inducing industry and businesses to move to the region; exports of power can also be an invaluable source of revenue, especially for a state with limited options for revenue generation.

7.2 The Road Network

The road network in the state can be broadly classified into roads constructed and maintained by the state government (1,906 km) and by the Border Roads Organisation (BRO) (718 km).

7.2.1 State and District Roads

When the planning process began in Sikkim in the mid-1950s, there was no road network, apart from a very narrow road linking Gangtok to Rangpo, and a few kilometres of road around Gangtok. The major townships were connected by mule-tracks, which jeeps traversed with extreme difficulty. With the initiation of planning, a natural priority was given to connecting as many places as possible with good roads, using whatever modest finances were available at the time. This led to the construction of low-cost, narrow roads with steep gradients and low-tonnage bridges.

The roads and bridges built in the state prior to the merger were also narrow, in line with the transport needs and vehicles of the time. However, rapid increases in technology and improvements in overall development has meant a tremendous growth in the number of passenger vehicles, and a need for higher-load carrying goods vehicles, to transport goods in and out of different parts of the state.

Thus in addition to addressing the need for constructing new roads and bridges that would increase access to once-inaccessible villages and areas, since the Fifth Plan on, much of the road expenditure has been on widening and upgrading the original roads, culverts, bridges and drainage systems. The construction or widening of roads in the mountains requires several stages of work. During the Ninth Plan much of the work was consolidation—upgrading earth roads, improving drainage and widening and resurfacing others to basically make road transport more economically efficient and give a boost to tourism. Earthen roads were upgraded to water-bound macadam (WBM), and the latter to black-topped roads. Proper and efficient drainage systems had to be introduced, to guard against potholes and wear and tear. New roads were constructed based on the specifications for hill roads in other parts of the country. Roads were thus wider, with easier gradients, and bridges had higher load-carrying capacities.

State government roads are categorised by quality into state highways, major district roads, other district roads, and rural roads. As Table 7.1 shows, expansion of road length has been slow, and much of the Plan funds have been used to upgrade the road and bridges network. Road density (length of road per 1,000 sq. km.) has been increasing in Sikkim since 1981-82, but the state still ranks a low 27 (of 31 states) in 1996-97, with less than half the road density of similarly mountainous states, such as Himachal Pradesh.

7.2.2 Rural Roads

Rural roads are especially important, even to improve villagers' access to basic services such as education and health, markets, and so on. So far, about 93 per cent of the villages have been connected by road.[1] Since 2001-02, rural roads are being upgraded and repaired under the *Pradhan Mantri Gramodaya Sadak Yojana.* However, the pace of work has been slow, and will need to be accelerated if development is to spread to the rural economy in general.

TABLE 7.1

Expansion in the Sikkim State Road Network (March 31, 2004) (km)

	1998	*1999*	*2000*	*2001*	*2002*	*2003*
B.T	849	837	849	930	972	1,005
WBM	592	574	566	517	475	453
Earthen	306	321	333	382	409	420
Bridle	28	28	28	28	28	28
Total	1,775	1,760	1,776	1,857	1,884	1,906

Source: Mid-Term Appraisal Report for Tenth Plan Roads and Bridges Department, Government of Sikkim, January 2004.

7.2.3 National Highway 31A—The State's Lifeline

Sikkim's only road link with the rest of the country is the National Highway 31A. The highway is 92.6 km. long, of which 51.3 km. is in West Bengal and the remaining 41.3 km. is in Sikkim, connecting Rangpo to Gangtok. Maintenance is carried out by Project *Swastik* of the BRO, which also looks after the North Sikkim Highway (NSH), the 96-km. road connecting Gangtok to Chungthang in the north district. Heavy rainfall for several months of the year, and frequent landslides mean that the state's road-link is often disrupted, despite continuous maintenance work by the BRO. The initial proposal to widen NH 31A to a four-lane highway has been rejected by the BRO for security reasons. A second option, the construction of an alternate highway linking Sikkim with the rest of the country, is under serious consideration.

7.2.4 Highway Links to Nathu La Pass

Nathu La is the shortest possible (500-590 kms between Gangtok and Lhasa) and most viable route to the whole of western China region. The other routes including the Shipki la pass in Himachal Pradesh and Lipulekh in Uttarakhand opened in early 1990s are comparatively very hostile and rugged. Nathu La reopening very much coincides with 'develop-the-west' campaign launched by the Chinese government since 2000. China's western region covers two-thirds of the nation's territory, with a population making up nearly 23 per cent of the national total. It comprises of nine provinces and autonomous regions with plenty of land and natural resource including Gansu, Guizhou, Ningxia, Qinghai, Shaanxi, Sichuan, Tibet, Xinjiang and Yunnan. After Eastern China's 14000 km long coastlines brought fortunes to China in the last two decades, it is now western China with 3500 km land frontier lines that will become second golden area of reopening. The completion of 1142 km long railway line—an engineering feat—connecting Lhasa with mainland China through Golmud city in Qinghai brings a much larger dimension to this reopening.[2]

1. Background Note for the State Planning Commission.
2. Lama, 2006a.

The successful conduct of the business through this route could generate scope for a range of such openings between the neighbour-locked North Bengal and whole of North East region and the neighbouring countries. This includes Stilwell Road built during the Second World War that connects Assam with Kunming (China) *via* Myanmar. The ports of Calcutta and Haldia could be used more elaborately. This more scientific openings of borders for economic and commercial purposes could in fact steadily replace the dominant security debate by the development discourse and gains in this conflict torn North East region. This is the way to realise the larger goals of India's Look East policy and consolidate sub-regional groupings like South Asia Growth Quadrangle (SAGQ) and Bay of Bengal Initiative for Multi-Sectoral Techno-Economic Cooperation (BIMSTEC).[3]

The most crucial 143 kms road link between Siliguri—Nathu La road *via* Gangtok town requires very drastic upgradation. All the major segments are found to have deficiencies in areas of operation, safety, and road conditions. These include congestion and delays through built-up areas, deficient road surface conditions, deficient geometric features, no pavement edge markings and uncontrolled roadside developments and encroachments, bridges, and culverts requiring rehabilitation and reconstruction and widening.[4]

The highway is also expected to act as a vital link to the old trade route between India and Tibet/China through the Nathu La pass. Efforts to improve the highway and link it with the pass are being looked after by Sikkim Industrial Development and Investment Corporation Limited (SIDICO); Infrastructure Leasing and Financial Services Limited (IL&FS) is currently carrying out a feasibility study on this. Future plans for the highway include linking it with the east-west corridor and with the golden quadrilateral, so that the state becomes better integrated with the other parts of the country.[5]

For operational and phased development purposes the entire existing 143 km length highway has been divided into three segments:

Segment A: Sevoke to Rangpo	52 km
Segment B: Rangpo to Gangtok	40 km
Segment C: Gangtok to Nathu La	51 km
Total	143 km

In addition, new construction for 2 bypasses needs to be undertaken:

Segment D: Melli to Singtam (approx. 53 km)

Segment E: Ranipul to Kyangnosla (approx. 45.5 km)

Given a higher level of expectation, the nature and composition of trade through Nathu La and the topographical constraints on the existing Jawaharlal Nehru Road from Gangtok to Nathu La, the search for alternative roads to reach this pass is already on. The multiple routing to reach Nathu La should be explored both to avoid congestion and minimise the uncertainties brought about by weather/climatic conditions in the region. This would also reduce environmental degradations caused by single road dependence.[6]

The Sikkim government submitted a memorandum to the Ministry of Surface Transport, demanding a national highway from Nathu La to Gangtok and the upgradation of the state highways. It mentioned that "trade will come to a standstill if the infrastructure is not upgraded and dependence on the present highway not ended. Highway 31A, which extends from Siliguri to Gangtok, is only around 5 metres wide when the specifications are for 7 metres. The road that extends from Gangtok to Nathu La is even worse, in the width of only 4 metres. The highway was often 'affected by landslides'.

In the wake of the reopening of Nathu La trade route on July 6, 2006, the Union Government announced that a new 2 lane highway will be built between Sevoke in Siliguri to Nathu La by the BRO. This road will be completed by 2009.

There are, however, alternatives to the existing highway which include the existing border road from Damdim to Nathu La which follows the direction from Dam Dim *via* Lava to Pedong to Kupup to Nathu La Pass.

Another study conducted by Sur Technical Services[7] along with their collaborators Geo Consult ZT—Gmbh of Salzburg—the world leaders in Tunneling technology—has recommended a new tolled 4-lane

3. Lama, 2006b.
4. Lama, 2005.
5. Chief Minister's speeches, in the Background Note for the State, Planning Commission.
6. Lama, 2006b.
7. The same Kolkata based company has been a consultant for a stretch of 4-lane toll highway including tunnels and bridges of the Asian Highway from Thailand border town of Myawaddi to Indian border town of Tamu (1411 km).

expressway to be built linking Sevoke (other side of Jubilee Bridge) to Gangtok by tunneling and bridges, whereby the distance could be reduced from 93 kms. at present to only 47 kms. This expressway will be all weather unlike the present existing NH 31A which has a number of faults, resulting in landslides during the monsoons. This expressway will be designed for an optimum speed of 80 kms/hour as per IRC guidelines and shall be of international standards. The consultants have proposed a pre-feasibility study and have made a rough estimate of the cost and time taken to complete the project. They have found out that the cost will not be very much higher than the construction of the 4-lane NH 31A along its present alignment of 93 kms.

The total cost of the project can be recovered in 7½ years time, keeping in mind the additional traffic likely to be generated by opening international trade with China through Nathu La. This project will be ideally based Built Operate and Transfer (BOT) basis. The time taken for coming from Gangtok to Siliguri will be reduced to 60-75 minutes only, for a toll payment of Rs. 50 only. This expressway offers a distinct possibility of having a rail connection between Nathu La and Sevoke.[8]

7.2.5 Constraints and Options

Construction costs are high, because of the mountainous terrain crisscrossed by several streams and rivulets, which require the construction of cross-drainage structures, such as culverts and bridges. Well-constructed gutters are essential to ensure that drainage takes place properly, to prevent water logging and degeneration of the surfaces through erosion. New roads have to be carefully planned, especially as the threat of landslides becomes exacerbated as more roads are built. Road construction should be sanctioned only after a rigorous environmental impact analysis has been conducted.

Given the difficulty of construction and upgradation work in a state such as Sikkim it is important that the extension of the road network and upgrading and widening is done with a long-term perspective. For this, construction work needs to be based on up-to-date technology for mountain roads, and incorporate long-term solutions for erosion and landslides, after appropriate surveys of the area have been conducted.

So far, most of the road planning, design and construction in the state have been provided by the Department of Roads and Bridges and small labour-intensive road constructors. However, they do not have the capacity to upgrade and extend the road network in line with future requirements. As the *Vision Document* suggests, "The importance of roads to the state's development means that they cannot be built based on short-term goals, such as employment generation or saving funds. Such an approach could prove more expensive in the long run as poorly built roads get washed away and have to be entirely replaced. It would be far more cost effective in the long run, if the roads are built with the best available material and with all the appropriate supporting structures—retaining walls, drains and parapets—to allow them to withstand landslides, heavy monsoon rain—and even earthquakes." Well-built roads also have lower maintenance expenses.

To overcome the capacity constraints and increase the pace of road and bridge construction, private professional engineering firms could be contracted to design larger and costly sections of the road suitable for mechanised construction. The department's role will shift to that of planner, administrator and maintainer of roads; the private construction firms can be supervised by private professional engineers representing the department.

High rainfall and the fragility of the terrain mean that roads need constant repair. Road surfaces, the lining gutters and cross-drainage channels are constantly being worn away because of landslides and erosion. Roads often sink or get covered with debris which cause breaches in the network. Repairs have to be carried out as soon as possible to ensure that transport and communication does not get blocked. The Eleventh Finance Commission has recommended that the maintenance of the assets created during the Eighth and Ninth Plans have to be provided for in the plan. The state meets only 20 per cent of the maintenance expenses for state roads.

7.3 Transport

7.3.1 Road Transport

Sikkim Nationalised Transport (SNT) has been in continuous service since 1946 when it was started as a

8. Excerpted from the letter written by Somenath Sur, proprietor, Sur Technical Services, Kolkata to Managing Director, SIDICO, Government of Sikkim on December 21, 2003.

trucking service. In 2003-04, it had a fleet of 106 buses and 106 tankers/trucks,[9] with services on 43 passenger and goods routes. It has a monopoly on transport services in the state

Table 7.2 gives the age profile of SNT's fleet of trucks and buses in 2003. Of these, 6 buses and 14 trucks were scrapped during the year, but even so, 69 buses and 59 trucks were declared 'overaged.'[10] This means that the vast majority of SNT's fleet (69 per cent of its buses and 63 per cent of its trucks) are past productive age and need to be replaced, as they add to environmental degradation, and also violate national policy on pollution.

SNT's net losses have been increasing, from Rs. 4.97 crore in 2002-03 to an estimated Rs. 6.21 crore in 2003-2004. Of the 43 routes allotted to the enterprise, only 17 are profit-earning, and of the remaining, only 14 cover their variable costs. While SNT has managed to reduce its staff strength from 553 in 2000-01 to an estimated 462 in 2004-05, staff productivity measured in km per worker per day has fallen in the same period from 22.3 to an estimated 18.04.[11]

Bus services even between two busy urban centres such as Gangtok and Namchi are infrequent, and this adds to transaction time and costs. Some of the more economic routes are serviced by shared private jeeps, however, this is a relatively expensive form of transport.

TABLE 7.2

Age Profile of SNT's Fleet (March 31, 2003) (Number)

Age	*Buses*	*Trucks*
0-1	2	11
1-2	7	5
2-3	6	5
3-4	3	0
4-5	1	3
5-6	2	2
6-7	3	7
7-8	7	0
8-9	0	5
9-10	3	8
10+	72	60
Total	106	106

Source: Transport Department. *Financial Resources for Annual Plan 2004-05*, SNT Division, Government of Sikkim.

Given SNT's increasing operating losses, despite reduced staff strength, a strong case can be made to invite well-regulated private bus companies to operate on some routes. The shifting dynamics of urbanisation and rapid growth of some rural marketing centres (see chapter on urban development), calls for a re-assessment of the bus transport network and frequency in the state.

A high-capacity public transport system needs to replace the army of taxis operating in Gangtok, which will also help decongest the major arterial roads. More frequent services by smaller buses on the more popular routes should be introduced immediately. Smaller private buses can also be employed to charter workers to and from office complexes, such as Tashiling in Gangtok, which is impossible for the full-sized buses to negotiate, which would greatly ease the traffic jams, noise, and air pollution around this complex.

7.3.2 *Air Transport*

At present the only air services in the state are a four-seater helicopter service from Gangtok to Bagdogra, but this caters to an almost insignificant proportion of transport activity. The closest air-link with the state is through Bagdogra airport, which is around four hours by car from Gangtok. Helicopter links exist between Bagdogra and Gangtok, but the fare is prohibitive, and the number of seats limited. From the long-term development perspective, to establish better links with the rest of the country, a good airport and efficient air services have become imperative for the state.

The central government has sanctioned an airport for Sikkim, and the state government recently signed a memorandum of understanding with the Airport Authority of India (AAI) for construction at Pakyong. Of the estimated construction costs of Rs. 263 crore, the central government has given a special grant of Rs. 110 crore, and the Eleventh Finance Commission a grant of Rs. 50 crore.[12] Land has been acquired for construction of the airport and the forest department has begun the environment impact assessment.[13] Construction, however, has been stalled because the detailed project report of the AAI indicates that additional land is needed, for which finances have to come from the state government.

9. Transport Department, *Financial Resources for Annual Plan 2004-05*, SNT Division, Government of Sikkim.
10. Ibid., Statement II.
11. Ibid.
12. "Roads and Bridges", *Mid-term Appraisal: Tenth Five Year Plan.*
13. *Economic Survey 2003-04.*

7.3.3 Rail Transport

The State government has been making representations to the Central Government for a rail link. A feasibility report on linking the New Jalpaiguri in West Bengal with Rorethang in the East District of Sikkim by a 75-km. broad-gauge Trans-Himalayan railway line is under active consideration by the central and state governments.[14]

7.4 Telecommunications and Information Technology

7.4.1 Telecommunications

The telecommunications network in the state was very limited prior to the setting up of the Sikkim Telecom Department under the West Bengal circle of Bharat Sanchar Nigam Limited (BSNL) in 2000. The expansion in the number of exchanges capable of handling many more lines, has increased the number of landlines from 3,000 in 1999 to 49,350 in 2004. Many of these have been supplied under the PCO-booth scheme to unemployed people, to increase self-employment opportunities in the state. The department has set up village public telephones (VPTs) in 374 of the 427 revenue villages. The remaining villages are too remote for cable or WLL systems, but the department plans to link them through satellite.

Mobile telephone services have also grown rapidly from their introduction in 2004 (Table 7.3). An earlier monopoly of Reliance, mobile services have now been practically taken over by BSNL, which has 98 per cent of the market. At present mobile services are only available as far as Mangan in the north district, but a long-range switch is planned to extend services beyond this.

Good telecommunications can help the state overcome some of the handicaps imposed by the mountainous terrain by increasing access, especially for those living in remote areas, to information, goods, and social and economic services. If managed effectively, it could deal with one of the major problems of the state—increasing urban migration, by improving self-employment prospects and giving industries some incentive to locate away from urban areas. The proliferation of community information centres (CICs), enabled by the expansion of the telecommunications network, could give a boost to other sectors such as tourism, horticulture, and agriculture. On the macro-level, improved telecommunications helps the state integrate more closely with the rest of the country.

TABLE 7.3

Telephone Connections, 2004

Connections	*North*	*East*	*West*	*South*	*Total*
Landline	1,792	33,340	7,408	6,800	49,340
Mobile	1,000*	9,700	2,000*	2,000*	14,700*

Note: *–is approximate figures.

Source: Telecom Department, Sikkim.

However, the Telecom department has established this network at a cost. Its losses have been rising because of high arrears from post-paid connections. It also faces a resource crunch because of the high cost of laying landlines in a mountainous terrain, prone to heavy rains, frequent landslides and natural hazards, factors which also contribute to disruption in services, and raise maintenance costs. The national norms for setting up telecom services are based on conditions in plains and are inappropriate for hilly regions; these need to be amended to allow an appropriate increase in funds. The Telecom department could shift its focus from expanding its mobile network to providing universal access to telecom services.

7.4.2 Information Technology

Information technology is high on the government's agenda, and the Department of IT was created in August 2000. Its mandate was to expand the electronic networks and to incorporate IT in the daily functioning of the government. The department has been training officials on software use, maintaining official documents on the internet and establishing CICs across the state.

E-governance has been slow to take off, even though computers have been made available to a large number of government officials, and several have received training in their use. Official communication is still carried on in the traditional fashion, through hard copy, and meetings are conducted in person. Much of the delay in sending and receiving information can be cut down and the process of decision making within government will be reduced if a more effective use is made of the computer network. In fact, in a mountainous state such as Sikkim, a

14. Website of the Sikkim Government, Department of Mines and Geology; and *Tenth Plan for Sikkim, Vol 1*, p.196.

well-maintained widespread computer network can be especially effective in saving time and money. Ultimately e-governance can be used to make the functioning of government more transparent, and reduce corruption. Projects can be given clearances on line, progress can be monitored, all of which will help minimise the misuse of funds.

The establishment of 40 CICs across the state, even in areas as remote as Dzongo, have exposed a large section of the population to the use of computers in daily life. This has greatly increased the government's interface with the public and enhanced the quality of some state services. For example, with the help of CIC operators, users can download forms such as old-age pension applications (which at one time involved a trip to Gangtok), and access records, and farmers can check prices of products, such as large cardamom, or the updated weekly by the Spices Board. The success of this depends on the supply of accurate, timely data from each department to the Department of IT, which has not always been forthcoming. The nomination of a nodal officer in each department who can interface with the IT Department will ensure a more smooth and timely transfer of information. Alternately, maintaining government websites, may be contracted out to private software companies.

7.4.3 Recommendations: Infrastructure Development Package[15]

Given the extent of infrastructure required and the likely gains in the long run it would be prudent to put in place a one time Infrastructure Development Package. This would greatly facilitate the development of Nathu La trade route both within Sikkim and its periphery areas in Darjeeling district. It is recommended that a sum of Rs. 1650-1700 crore may be allocated for this purpose to be used in a phased manner by 2012. (Table 7.4).

TABLE 7.4

Allocations of Infrastructure Development Package

Sectors	*Investment (Rs. crore)*
Roads: National Highway and Jawaharlal Nehru Marg – 2 lane construction	
Sevoke to Rangpo	299-320
Rangpo to Gangtok	205-216
Gangtok to Nathu La	405-430
Airport at Pakyong	339
Trade mart along with customs, security, terminals and parking lot, electricity etc.	230
Warehousing facilities	70
Rest and recreations	88
Total	1636-1693

These investment requirements are arrived at from a number of studies and discussions with institutions, governmental agencies, experts, and professionals.

This pool of fund could be contributed by the Union Government, North Eastern Council or could be mobilised within and outside the country from sources like the World Bank, Asian Development Bank, UNDP and other donor/funding/credit agencies.

7.5 Power Development: Structure, Potentials and Challenges

Prior to 1975, the power requirements of Gangtok and a few townships along the National Highway were met from the Jali Power House commissioned in 1964. There were only 8 declared towns in Sikkim which availed electricity till the end of 1975. The rest of the areas throughout Sikkim were spelled with black mask. By the end of 1978, the state had a generation capacity of 3 MW from three of its small hydel stations, i.e., Jali Power House, Rimbi Micro Hydel, and Rothak Micro Hydel. The state decided to undertake the extension of electrification to the small townships and villages at a faster pace. Since then several projects have been commissioned (Table 7.5). Besides this the state has a central share of power (Table 7.6).

However, the experience with these drawals has been rather disappointing as they are marred by frequent interruptions owing to tripping etc. Even otherwise, the existing transmission system of West Bengal is weak and dependence on such a network for drawal of the state's share of central sector power would always be subject to disruption.

Though it is overwhelmingly the domestic consumers (almost 85 per cent) that are users of electricity in Sikkim, the share of domestic consumption is 32 per cent lower than that of the commercial consumption (34 per cent) (Table 7.7).

15. Lama, 2005.

TABLE 7.5

Power: Installed Capacities (31st March 2003)

Power House	*Installed Capacity at Year-end (kW)*
Lower Lagyap (H)	12,000
Jali Power House (H)	2,100
Rimbi-I (H)	600
Rongnichu-II (H)	2,500
Chaten (Lachen) (H)	100
Rimbi-II (H)	1,000
Lachung (H)	200
Mayongchu (H)	4,000
Upper Rongnichu (H)	8,000
Kalez K.H.E.P (H)	2,000
Rothak (H)	200
Rabomchu (H)	3,000
Diesel (D)	500

Note: H: hydel; D: diesel.

Source: Department of Power, Government of Sikkim.

TABLE 7.6

Sikkim's Share in Central Power Supplies

Farakka STP	26 MW
Talcher STP	24 MW
Kehlgaon STP	10 MW
Chukha HP (Bhutan)	6 MW
Rangit – III H.P.	8 MW
Total	74 MW

Source: Department of Power, Government of Sikkim.

TABLE 7.7

Consumer Categories and Consumption Profile (March 31, 2002)

Consumers Category	*% of Total No. of Consumers*	*% of Total Energy Sales*
Domestic	84.8	32.2
Commercial	10.5	34.3
Industries	0.4	16.0
Public lighting	0.2	17.8
Others	4.1	
Total	59,029 (no.)	78.70 MU

Source: Department of Power, Government of Sikkim.

7.5.1 Power Scenario

Though the power sector has consistently received relatively much higher share in the plan outlay (9.2 per cent in the First Plan (1954-1961), 10 per cent in the Fifth Plan (1974-1979) and 19.4 per cent in the Ninth Plan, amounting to Rs. 284.09 crore in the last 24 years), the rate of increase in the power output has not kept pace with the rapidly increasing demand which at present is of the order of 15-20 per cent per year. The estimated peak shortfall has increased almost three-fold from 5.7 MW in 1988-89 to 14.03 MW in 1997-98. The annual growth rate of this shortfall (12.32 per cent) has been almost double (6.85 per cent) than that of the installed capacity. This is likely to be more serious in the absence of Rathong Chu project.

However, the installed and firm capacity of the operational units in the last 29 years since 1975 works out to about 1.4 MW installed capacity (0.8 MW firm) per year. The state needs to add at least 4-5 MW firm capacity every year to cater to the increasing load demand. Had it not been the ongoing Teesta V project, this gap is going to be glaring within a few years as number of power intensive industries like calcium carbide and ferro-alloys have come up in the state. The requirement, both household and institutional, in the urban and rural areas is also growing rapidly. In fact, the unreliable and inadequate power supply has been attributed as a major reason for the state's inability to attract private investors in industrial activities. Without any major industrial activity also, the peak load demand of the state by 2011 is expected to reach 80 MW.

BOX 7.1

The Increasing Demand for Power

The demand for power will increase drastically in the next couple of years because of:

- burgeoning domestic demand triggered by changing consumption pattern of the consumers;
- intensification of rural electrification projects;
- power-driven industrialisation arising out of the liberalised investment scenario in the state;
- likely expansion of tertiary sector activities including tourism, education, health and communications;
- infrastructure required to conduct cross-border trade with the Tibet Autonomous Region of China *via* Nathu La; and
- attractiveness of power trading both within and outside the country.

Rural Electrification

Rural electrification has been the most daunting task in Sikkim both because of the extreme and unfriendly topographical conditions and the huge technological and financial resources involved. Unlike the villages in the plains which comprise clusters of habitations, the configuration in the hills of Sikkim is highly scattered sometimes making any community project pretty much uneconomic. They are all scattered and the distribution becomes very difficult. The state has declared that it has achieved 100 per cent rural electrification.[16] However, this definition has now been changed by the Ministry of Power according to which a minimum of 10 per cent of the households in a village have to be electrified and school buildings, PHC and community centres in the village should be electrified before declaring the village electrified. As per this modified definition, the state has electrified 70 per cent of its villages.

The state has realised that the availability of power in rural areas will lead to economic development and its attendant spin-off benefits like food security, better health, and literacy. However, the use of electricity in villages for productive and subsistence needs is still very limited. The actual benefits of the investments made in the rural electrification programme can only be realised if the people are in a position to use electricity for their day-to-day activities as well as for industrial and commercial activities. Therefore, both 100 per cent rural electrification programmes and widespread use of electricity by the rural people would mean a major upward shift in the demand for electricity.

Subsequently, after reaching the target of 100 per cent electrification, the department took to intensification schemes, i.e., extension of electrification to the uncovered households along with providing two-point free connections to the households under poverty line in accordance with the National 20-Point Programme. All the 405 habitable revenue blocks in the state had access to electricity by March, 1991 thereby making it the first state in the entire eastern region to have cent per cent coverage of electricity. This is despite the fact that Sikkim was 25 years behind other states in the central planning process. With the completion of Lachen Micro Hydel Scheme, which harnesses Lachen Chu to generate 2x50 kW at a drop of 150 feet, the tribals of Lachen have also got access to electricity.

Hydel-Power Potential

In Sikkim, its hydel-power potential of 8,000 MW remain highly unharnessed. As a result, in the total hydel-power installed capacity in the country, Sikkim hardly contributes 0.2 per cent.[17] The state government has always been perturbed by the fact that the central government has paid very little attention to harnessing these great potentials in the state. This attitude becomes more blatant, when the central government participates more aggressively in the development of hydel power potentials in the neighbouring countries like Bhutan and Nepal with massive grant elements in the investment made.

In order to commercialise the hydel potential of the state, the government has constituted Sikkim Power Development Corporation Ltd. (SPDC) to implement both hydel-power projects and to lay the associated transmission lines. Though a number of hydel-power projects were to be undertaken during the Ninth Plan and the Tenth Plan including Rolep I (9 MW), Rolep II (12 MW), Bagchachu (6 MW), Lachungvhu II (3 MW), Lachenchu II (0.45 MW), Rangpuchu (1 MW) and Lower Kalez Khola (3 MW), at the moment the following projects are under construction:

(a) 510 MW Teesta–V	-	NHPC
(b) 3 MW Lachung Hydel Project		Under State Government
(c) 6 MW Relli Hydel Project		
(d) 5 MW Rongli Hydel Project	-	
(e) 2 MW Mangley Hydel Project		

BOX 7.2

The Teesta Hydel-Electric Project Stage V

This (510 MW) project is estimated to cost Rs. 3,000 crore and is being built by National Hydro-Electric Power Corporation. This project will largely cover the axiomatic gap between the power requirement and its generation in the state which was being met through drawing central sector power and could also make Sikkim a major power exporter in the country.

16. The existing definition of an electrified village is: "a village will be deemed to be electrified if electricity is used in the inhabited locality within the revenue boundary of the village for any purpose whatsoever." *The Tenth Plan 2002-2007* (Planning Commission, Government of India) summarily mentions that 'there is need to change this definition so as to declare a village as electrified only if a minimum number of households in that village are provided with electricity connections.'

17. Central Statistical Organisation. *Statistical Abstract India, 1997.* New Delhi: Department of Statistics, Ministry of Planning and Programme Implementation. p.170.

Micro-Hydel Potential

Equally potential areas have been the micro-hydel projects which could be developed on the Chinese pattern of feeding to a common grid all over the small tributaries of the rivers which may add a lot million kW. There are quite a few projects which have been identified in this category on the recommendations of the Geological Survey of India. The parameters like hydrological and meteorological data have been established. These projects should be developed keeping in view the end users. This implies a pre-linkage of domestic and industrial users to the projects. If finance remains the constraint for its exploitation, each site should be leased out to local entrepreneur for development and sale of power on lease. For all these, an exclusive technical and highly professional apex institution needs to be created.[18]

BOX 7.3

Importance of Small Hydel Projects for Sikkim

The state has sizeable potential in all its higher ranges:

- plants are comparatively more viable for remote and inaccessible areas than other commercial fuel systems;
- easier to design and manufacture locally;
- sophisticated and expensive instrumentation and control system can mostly be avoided;
- the operation and maintenance costs of privately owned and operated plants are much lower;
- indigenous design and manufacture of such plants contributes towards development of local industrial base including technical expertise which is useful for other development work;
- surplus power can be supplied to the national grid; and
- local people can build, operate, and own.

More importantly, all these have led to huge cumulative outstanding for Sikkim towards power generating public sector units like NTPC. This has exposed the gravity of power mismanagement. The NTPC and PGCI Ltd., have already started regulating power supply to many of the states including Sikkim mainly on the ground of default in outstanding payments for the use of power supplied by these two corporations.

Environmental Concerns

Sikkim is geologically a fragile region. The power situation in the state also got a major setback when the run-of-the-river 30 MW Rathongchu project (total cost of Rs. 71.19 crore) was withdrawn full three years after its implementation mainly on grounds of disturbing the cultural ecology of the project area. This project was aimed at meeting a demand-supply gap in the late 1990s. This project had already incurred the expenditure of Rs. 14.89 crore by March, 1997, in the construction of 5.5 km approach roads, 4.5 km water conductor system, residential and non-residential buildings and erection of 11 kV lines. This project was also techno-economically cleared by the Central Electricity Authority. One of the very vocal non-governmental organisations, Concern Citizens, in fact, took the case to both High Court and the Supreme Court following which the project was withdrawn by the state government.

Even in the case of the ongoing Teesta Hydel Project V, there are apprehensions about its ecological sustainability and rumblings particularly with regard to displacement, rehabilitation and resettlement. Though this project is likely to generate ample employment opportunities and a direct annual benefit of Rs. 125 crore per annum, before launching this project, a large scale consultation had to be undertaken to make it acceptable to maximum number of people. This process of consultation should be initiated in at least other major projects in the state in order to avoid the protracted controversies and the resulting spiraling costs that the Tehri and Narmada in India, Kalabagh in Pakistan, and Arun III and Mahakali in Nepal have faced.

7.5.2 Reforms and the Power Sector

The absence of a clear-cut, comprehensive state-level hydel power policy aimed at attracting the private sector had been a major stumbling block in any efforts to invite the private developers in power sector. This was also attributed to the underdeveloped state of manpower and the management capacities, limited knowledge of the technicalities involved in both inviting the IPPs and also working with them. These issues have now been widely discussed in the state. The Sikkim State Planning Commission in one of its meetings emphatically 'expressed its concern over the sluggish performance and piling up of liabilities of the Power Department. The Commission saw no reason why the government should not run the sector on purely commercial lines. In that case it would be necessary to set up a regulatory body. The maintenance of the *status*

18. Junejo, 1994.

quo to produce and sell power by the department would cause more loss in the sector. The Commission also asked the department to do serious groundwork with the help of experts and professionals before any negotiation on the private sector participation in the power sector is initiated.[19]

Against this background a definite move was made in the recent months when the state decided to invite the independent power producers and signed a number of project deals with them. As a result, the following projects have been allotted to different private developers under joint venture and projects have been awarded to the developers. (Table 7.8)

Letters of Intent have already been issued to all the developers. In case of Teesta-III, an Agreement has already been drawn with M/s Teesta Urja Ltd. Cases of other developers for signing firm agreement are under process.

The salient features of the agreement will be:

(i) The developer shall earmark/allocate 12 per cent free power to the state for the first 15 years. From the 16th year to the end of the 35th year, the developers shall give 15 per cent of the generation to the state.

(ii) After 35 years the project will be handed back to the state free of cost.

(iii) State will be allowed to put 26 per cent of equity share. Fund for this equity shall be arranged by the developer against securitisation of the 12 per cent free power.

(iv) To the extent available, all the Class III and Class IV employees will be sourced locally.

TABLE 7.8

Sikkim: Private Participation in the Power Projects

Lachen	NHPC	210
Rangyong	GVK Industries Ltd., Hyderabad	141
Panam	Nagarjuna Holdings Pvt. Ltd., Hyderabad	200
Lingza	Punj Lloyd Ltd. New Delhi	120
Rongnichu Storage	Chhattisgarh Elect. Company	95
Talem	Shyam Energy Ltd. Kolkata	75

Source: Department of Energy and Power, Government of Sikkim, Gangtok.

(v) Other than the major works like construction of dam, HRT, penstock, power house, etc. all miscellaneous works will be tendered amongst the local contractors.

Besides above, the following projects (Table 7.9) have been awarded to NHPC which will be developing the projects as per the guidelines of the Government of India.

TABLE 7.9

Projects to be undertaken by NHPC

Projects	*Name of Developers*	*Capacity (MW)*
Teesta IV	NHPC	495
Lachen	NHPC	210

7.5.3 Restructuring the State Monopoly

Like in other states the power generation and its supply continues to remain a state monopoly in Sikkim as well. The government owns, operates, and regulates the power entities. This has resulted in overlapping and to a large extent undemarcated responsibilities with lack of accountability in terms of sector entities, operational performance and service standards and codes. The performance, of these utilities therefore, remained far from satisfactory. More significantly, most of the power generating units remained highly dependent on the subsidies inputs provided by the state and remained thoroughly unexposed to any competitive and efficient atmosphere. Consequently they started becoming sick.

The power distributing units lacked commercial independence, suffered from unclear definition of the corporate structure and responsibilities. On top of the low tariff rate in relation to the financial requirements of the operating entities, high system loss and low collection from the consumers ultimately made these entities both defaulters and sick. This was heightened by the falling level of domestic public investment as well as the development partners.

The revenue-expenditure gap in the state is a staggering amount of Rs. 141.36 crore for the 24-year period of 1979-2003. The gross operating deficit (i.e., revenue receipt minus revenue expenditure) for 2002-03 alone was Rs. 30 crore. This can be improved only if there is a drastic upward revision in the tariff and

19. Minutes of the Sikkim State Planning Commission meeting held in Gangtok July 5-6, 2002.

effective utilisation of plant through improvement in plant load factor (PLF) particularly in non-peak hours. The level of PLF is a dismal 30-40 per cent in the state (*see* Annexure Table A-21)

The total energy sold during 2002-03 was 73.27 million units and the revenue realised was Rs. 13.31 crore. The average revenue per unit (kWh) sold is Rs. 1.82/kWh and the average cost of energy delivered works out to Rs. 3.34/kWh. The average cost of supply is almost twice more than average realisation. This is due to very high T and D losses, high operational costs (mainly due to unproductive and excess manpower) and low revenue realisation (mainly due to unmetered supply and inefficient manpower for its reading and collection). On the other hand the low realisation is due to poor metering, billing, and poor revenue collection (Annexure Table A-21)

As against this, the average tariff in the state has sharply increased to 290 paisa per unit in 2005 from an average of 70 paise per unit in 2000 (Table 7.10 and Table 7.11). Surprisingly the commercial tariff is not much higher (hardly 16 per cent) than the domestic tariff (Table 7.12). This could be because of the conscious policy of the Government to make the investment opportunities more attractive in the state. Revenue collection and revenue expenditure gap is ever expanding. In a major policy change, the government exempted the defaulter rural consumers of all their electricity rent payments up to February 1999. This costs the exchequer almost Rs. 2 crore. This has benefited 55,000 to 60,000 households. Others who paid the rent regularly have been crying foul as they find that they are discriminated against. They are all asking for the return of the rents that they have paid. Now the situation is that many people are not in a mood to pay their electricity bills, as they think, that they may be exempted again in future. This is what has happened in many other states, including Punjab.

As of now, it looks that the Power department is spending more money to collect much lesser money. However, a majority of people are willing to pay a higher tariff if the quality and regularity of supply of power is ensured. So it is a question of what comes first, hike in tariff or improved quality in supply.

The reduction in energy sales during 2001-02 onwards is because of the fact that this was for the first time a more realistic presentation of T&D losses were shown. In the past, a suppressed and estimated T&D losses were presented. A quantum jump in the deficit of 2002-03 is due to additional expenditure in the settlement of outstanding dues to central power sector against import of power from the central sector generating stations (Table 7.13).

It is a great dichotomy. The Power department has become bulky, unwieldy and are not at all

TABLE 7.10

Domestic Electricity Tariff in the State in 2000 (paisa per unit)

Consumption Levels	*Rural Tariff*	*Urban Tariff*
Up to 50 units	70	100
Between 50 and 100 units	100	130
Over 100 units	125	155

Source: Department of Power, Government of Sikkim.

TABLE 7.11

Domestic Electricity Tariff in the State in 2005 (paisa per unit)

Consumption Levels	*Rural Tariff*	*Urban Tariff*
Up to 50 units	100	150
Between 50 and 100 units	150	200
Between 100 and 400 units	200	250
Over 400 units	300	350

Source: Department of Energy and Power, Government of Sikkim.

TABLE 7.12

Commercial Electricity Tariff in the State in 2005

Rate (Tariff)	*(paisa per unit)*
Consumption Levels	
Consumption upto 200 units	300
In excess 200 to 400 units	350
Exceeding 400 units	400

TABLE 7.13

Operational Performance 2002-03 (MU)

Energy generated	42.48
Energy purchased	125.00
Total energy available	167.48
Energy sold	78.70
Energy loss in the system	88.78
Loss (%)	53.00

Note: Loss per cent is excessive.

Source: Department of Power, Government of Sikkim.

commensurate to what they are contributing. This department alone has a total of 128 gazetted officers, 893 non-gazetted officers, technical staff, ministerial staff, and 1652 muster roll staff (Table 7.14). These figures given by the department in 2005 are much lower than the figures given in the ASCI report in 2004. As per the ASCI figures the Department had a total of 105 gazetted officers, 106 non-gazetted officers, 1,090 technical staff, 655 ministerial staff, 67 accounts staff and 2,447 muster roll staff.[20] All they have to do is to generate 45 MW of power and distribute another 50 MW imported from other regions.

The per-unit cost of generation, transmission and distribution is also increasing steadily. In both the rural and urban areas combined (Table 7.15).

The privatisation of the power sector is likely to trigger a major controversy on the issue of withdrawal of subsidies given by the state to various categories of activities and groups. Though it is well known that a significant portion of these subsidies go to rich people, to work towards its removal, is a great political risk. However, this loss to the state exchequer caused by protracted subsidies cannot remain unaddressed. It is ironical that the sector which the state always boasted of having the most serious development potential has become the biggest drain of public resources. This just cannot sustain. Therefore, the state has to take remedial steps to make the power sector an efficient, vibrant and a major revenue earning sector in the state.

The state has undertaken a series of reform initiatives which included appointment of a cabinet sub-committee on power sector. It has set up a State Electricity Regulatory Commission with a view to restructuring of power sector and also to making it a development driver by revenue generation. The state is now working on restructuring.

7.5.4 Approaches and Strategies

There has been a detailed study done on different phases of power projects on the Teesta river. The Teesta and Rangit valleys can offer a magnificent model to develop all resources under one comprehensive programme. The entire basins of the Teesta, Rangit, and their tributaries can be designed for proper use, conservation, and development of the natural resources

TABLE 7.14

Power Department: Number of Employees

S.N.	*Name*	*Nos.*
1.	Gazetted Officers	128
2.	Non-Gazetted Officers	893
3.	Technical Staff	
4.	Ministerial Staff	
5.	Muster Roll Staff	1652

TABLE 7.15

Cost of Generation, Transmission and Distribution

Year	*P/U Cost (paisa)*
1995-96	112
1996-97	127
1997-98	140
1998-99	145
2002-03	334

Note: The per-unit cost is the ratio of revenue expenditure to the sum total of kWh generated within Sikkim and power purchased from the central sector power stations.

Source: Department of Power, Government of Sikkim.

BOX 7.4

Long- and Short-Term Approaches to Power Projects

Long-Run Objectives

- taking up of larger hydel power stations in the Teesta basin through independent power producers (IPPs) aimed at long term prosperity of the state and the country at large.
- efficient management of the Teesta river system together with evacuation and marketing of energy from all the stages of Teesta cascade.

Short-term Objectives

- quicker implementation of small and mini-micro hydel schemes to attain self-sufficiency in power requirement of the state.
- extending the 132 kV line from the Eastern Region to the state for import and export of energy.
- remodelling and re-strengthening including refurbishment of existing electrical installations at all hierarchical levels of operating system by employing the latest available technology and scientifically organising the distribution system. Further, it is required to install bulk and TOD metres at each transmission and distribution point for energy auditing and providing temper proof electronic metres at the premises of potential consumers.

20. A study on restructuring the power sector in the state was conducted by the Centre for Infrastructure Management & Regulatory Studies, Administrative Staff College of India (ASCI), Hyderabad in 2004.

for general welfare in terms of physical, social, and economic development. This means construction of moderate-sized dams at convenient locations to suit and blend the topographic conditions of the terrain. This would enable to develop various facilities i.e., power production, flood control, navigation, water life and fisheries, recreation and water sports, water supply, industrialisation, erosion control, agricultural production, job skills, tourism, and ultimately economic growth.

Table 7.16 gives us a glimpse of the projects that are likely to be completed by 2011. This clearly indicates that Sikkim will have a net share of over 500 MW from all these projects. This 500 MW is from royalty alone. The share that will be receivable from the equity will be separate, thereby giving it a clear option for effective use in the domestic sector and for trading with others.

Among these projects, Teesta Hydroelectric Project Stage V is going to be completed within the next couple of years. One of the six hydel-power schemes in the cascade identified on the Teesta basin, this project is under construction by National Hydro-Power Construction (NHPC) and is a run of the river scheme located in the East District. It is connected by an all-weather road. The project envisages construction of a 95-metre high concrete dam across the Teesta near Dikchu and 15 km long tunnel up to Dhupidara near Sirwani and an underground power house there.

Considering that the project generates 2,172 million units annually, the sale rate of energy has been worked out to 295 paise per unit after considering 12 per cent free power to Sikkim. Some important benefits that the state can derive out of this project are as under:[21]

A minimum of 12 per cent free share of energy to the state or compensation at an agreed terms, in lieu of it, in case the state cannot utilise its share partly or fully. This share can yield a revenue of about Rs.75 crore per annum to the state.

- Employment opportunity for the local people during the period of construction and
- operation and maintenance thereafter.
- Business opportunity for the local contractors based on their financial capability,
- experience and managerial capacity.
- Training opportunity to the local youths for the jobs required during and after the construction period.
- Social facilities like hospitals, school, community centre, bank, post office, shopping centre and any other institution that will provide social benefit to the local people.

The ongoing Teesta V project generates direct employment of 976 persons. It also generates a large number of employment opportunities indirectly, including in Sikkim National Transport for transporting goods from Siliguri to project site in Singtam, compensatory afforestation adoption of villages, landslides stabilisation, muck deposit sites, fruit and fodder plantation, green-belt development, catchment area treatment, project hospital, Ladies Welfare Association, etc. The welfare side of the project is also very interesting. Between 2001 and July 2004, the project site hospital provided treatment for 56,171

TABLE 7.16

Projects Scheduled Under the Central/Private/Joint Sector during Tenth Plan

Projects	*Name of Developers*	*Capacity (MW)*
Teesta I	SMEC Pvt. Ltd. N Delhi	320
Teesta II	Him Urja Pvt. Ltd. N Delhi	330
Teesta III	Athena Projects Pvt. Ltd	1,200
Teesta IV	NHPC	495
Teesta VI	LANCO Energy Pvt. Ltd. N Delhi	360
Rolep	Amalgamated Trans India Ltd. N Delhi	36
Ralong	Amalgamated Trans India Ltd. N Delhi	40
Chakungchu	Amalgamated Trans India Ltd. N Delhi	50
Sada-Mangder	Gati Ltd, Hyderabad	71
Chuchachen	Gati Ltd, Hyderabad	99
Bhasmay	Gati Ltd, Hyderabad	32
Rangit II	Gammon India Pvt., Mumbai	60
Rangit IV	Jal Power Co. Ltd. Hyderabad	90
Dikchu	Sneha Kinetic Power Project Ltd.	105
Lachen	NHPC	210
Rangyong	GVK Industries Ltd., Hyderabad	141
Panam	Nagarjuna Holdings Pvt. Ltd., Hyderabad	200
Rukel	TCI Finance Ltd. Secunderabad	33
Lingza	Punj Lloyd Ltd. New Delhi	120
Rongnichu Storage	Chhattisgarh Elect. Company	95
Talem	Shyam Energy Ltd. Kolkata	75
	Total	4162

21. *Annual Reports, 1996-97and 1997-98,* Power Department, Govt. of Sikkim.

patients. About Rs. 30 million per month is being spent in the local markets by the project workforce to meet their basic needs and this provides many opportunities for local business community. All these levels of employment are likely to go up once the transmission and distribution network are laid.[22]

7.5.5 The Possibility of Power Exports

There is a tremendous scope for Sikkim to undertake power trading both inside and outside the country. Annexure tables A-23–A-26 give the power demand projections under various scenarios by different agencies. It varies from 60 MW to 163 MW during the period 2004-2011. Given the power demand growth pattern in the state, Sikkim would hardly be able to effectively use even one-fourth of what it is likely to generate from Teesta V project alone. The other Teesta basin projects which are on the pipeline could all be well meant for export purpose only. Besides the direct revenues fetched by power exports from Sikkim, it will save a hefty sum of financial resources which it has been otherwise expending on importing power from Bhutan and other central sector units. At the same time there are huge demand for power in various regions of India and also the neighbouring countries like Bangladesh, Myanmar, Pakistan, Sri Lanka, China and certain parts of Nepal.[23]

The pace of development that is catching up in the western regions of China under its "develop-the-west" campaign launched in 2000 would require hefty and constant doses of energy supplies. The supplies from the mainland China may not be feasible on the long term basis. The possible feasible options are importing electricity from the neighbouring countries including from India and Bhutan and also extending gas pipelines that are being negotiated among India-Pakistan and Iran. "China's electricity demand has more than doubled in the last decade and will probably almost quadruple by 2020.....Moreover, only 80 per cent of the population is now connected to China's electrical grid; continued rural electrification will add still another force for higher electricity demand growth.[24]

The power map of India has five different regions, *viz.*, northern, southern, western, eastern and north eastern. The northern and the southern regions faced maximum demand-supply gaps. Except the eastern region all the regional grids face perennial energy shortage. In other regions, seasonal surpluses occur mostly during off-peak hours in the periods of lean demand of weather-beating and agricultural pumping loads.

The eastern and the north-eastern regions are expected to have surplus electricity by 2006-07. Given the fact that significant interregional transfer of electricity already takes place in the country, this power is likely to be evacuated to other regions facing deficit, primarily southern and western regions

Region-wise projection of power demand and supply for 2012 indicates a serious shortfall in all the major regional power markets, *viz.*, northern, southern and western. Since the projected surplus power in the east and northeast regions would not be adequate to meet the gap in demand, the import of additional power from the neighboring countries particularly Bhutan also remains as the least cost viable option.

The power export could be realised easily because of both the existing and future transmission network. For instance, in India, there are two varieties of exchanges taking place within the country, *viz.*, the interstate and interregional exchanges. Scheduled interstate exchanges within the same region take place in limited quantity. The unscheduled interstate exchanges take place due to diversity in demand and over drawls by the states. Bilateral exchanges, mostly seasonal, also take place between the states in the same region and in different regions based on mutually agreed rates from time to time.

Interregional exchanges take place mainly from the surplus eastern region to the northern, western, southern and north-eastern regions. The present inter-regional transfer is of the order of 900-1,200 MW from eastern region to the neighbouring regions and is firm in nature. Currently, the eastern region accounts for 78 per cent of total power exchange taking place among the regions. The total power transfer capacity for the inter-regional transmission system is about 5500 MW at 220 kV and above level and in HVDC back-to-back systems.

The regional power systems are proposed to be operated in two clusters by 2007-08, one comprising

22. Based on the visit by the research team at the Teesta hydel project Stage V site at Singtam in August 2004.

23. Lama, Sainju and Ahmad, 2005.

24. In the Chinese energy system the share of solid fuels was over 76 per cent, followed by oil with 19 per cent, gas 2 per cent and hydel power 1.8 per cent in 1995. This is projected to be 70.6 per cent, 32.8 per cent, 5.26 per cent and 2.53 per cent respectively by 2010. *China's Worldwide Quest for Energy Security*, International Energy Association and OECD, Paris, 2000, p. 21 For details see Lama, Sainju and Ahmad, 2005.

northern, eastern and north-eastern regions and the other western and southern regions, each cluster operating in a synchronous mode. Synchronous operation of both clusters is expected by 2012-13. On the other hand, there already exists a considerable network of inter-connections among the South Asian countries. India's Power Grid Corporation has worked out the inter-connections required, their feasibility and the cost and benefits to the participating countries in the South Asia Growth Quadrangle (SAGQ) region consisting of Bangladesh, Bhutan, the North-East region of India and Nepal.[25] All these inter-connecting channels will very well match the Indian effort to have integration of all regions to form a National Grid in near future. In case of likely exports of power from Sikkim to TAR in China, this transmission network has to be expanded to the Nathu La trading point and be interconnected with the lines across the border.

Nearby Bhutan is an apt example of how the hydel power potential could transform the entire economic system and development orientation. Bhutan's revenue from the power exports to India (1,472 GWh) from the 336 MW Chukha project on river Wanchu was Nu 2,367 million ($52 million) in 2002-03. This constituted almost 45 per cent of Bhutan's exports to India and 11 per cent of the Kingdom's GDP.[26] The Chukha model of power trading between India and Bhutan has worked very well with the latter exporting as much as 76 per cent of its generation.[27]

7.6 Recommendations

The Nathu La trade route will change the basic structure of the Sikkimese economy by refocusing on its comparative advantages like scientific harnessing of natural resources, emphasis on eco-tourism and other service related activities. Sikkim could be a major trading zone like Singapore. Therefore the following steps may be undertaken expeditiously.

i) Implementation of all the major recommendations of the Nathu La trade study Group including the promotion of trade in services like tourism, education, energy and software and information technology through this trade route and gradual opening of this trade route to countries like Bangladesh, Bhutan and Nepal.

ii) Infrastructures development as suggested in section 7.4.3 above

iii) The Sherathang mart urgently requires permanent structures that could match the projected volume of trade and infrastructure development like construction of amenities like Guest House, Hotel, parking places, expansion of roads, electricity, communications, drinking water etc.

- Despite the serious conservation efforts made by the state, the traditional pattern of energy consumption has put tremendous pressure on the forest resources of Sikkim, thereby entailing natural disasters, threatening mountain ecology and damaging biodiversity resources. On top of this, the changing pattern of power supply and consumption with a particular bias on petroleum, gas, and coal has led to outflow of precious state resources. There has been a remarkable increase in the demand for power in Sikkim. Power sector which should have been the most potential revenue earning source for the state has been in fact the single most vital drain in state's resources. Therefore, the thrust should be on harnessing the hydel power potentials of the state as a means to energy security in the state.
- An equally critical issue has been that of inefficient and imprudent use of energy sources. In the commercial energy front energy prices have often been too low, revenue collection unsatisfactory and the system losses enormous, particularly in both transmission and distribution. The inadequate revenue flows therefore, could not cover even a reasonable share of investment costs. All these adversely affected investments in new capacity additions. These are doubly enhanced by inefficient and technically unsound distribution network, poor management, weak administration, overstaffing with untrained and undisciplined employees and corruption both at utility and consumers levels. A high proportion of losses at T&D level includes non-technical losses like theft and pilferage.

The restructuring of power sector in a time-bound manner is therefore essential. In this regard, the road map provided by the ASCI report

25. Singh, 1998.
26. *Selected Economic Indicators 2000*, Thimphu and Kuensel, 2004, Thimphu.
27. Agreement between Power Trading Corporation of India Ltd and Department of Power of the Royal Government of Bhutan (DOP) on Chukha Power Trading, 2000.

of 2004 needs to be thoroughly discussed with all the stakeholders and implemented by mid-2005.

- How would the poor people be affected by the power sector reforms? Can they afford to get electricity ? Overwhelming majority of them are still dependent on locally produced biomass fuels. These fuels are increasingly becoming over stressed and unsustainable. A viable alternative is to provide them with electricity both for subsistence and production requirements (agriculture, industries and social actions). Therefore, power generation should also aim at directly benefiting the rural masses and provide them with new opportunities for their livelihood.

  If this happens their dependence on fuel wood and agriculture residues would go down and a halt to deforestation would reduce the problems of landslides, flash-flooding, soil erosion and siltation in many areas. Electricity can increase the efficiency of the people both on and off fields in the rural and urban areas. It is a well established fact that wherever electricity is available, the agricultural productivity tends to be considerably high.

- The investment in the power sector in the state must be made more broad-based and competitive. This can only be done by pooling the best power sector players and agencies from across the world. For this the state has to make its investment policies and enabling laws both attractive and friendly. The present mode of relying on just one or two power development agencies will be detrimental to the long run interest of the state both in terms of efficient harnessing of power potentials and also technology, cost of production and other forward and backward linkages.

- The thrust of power development in the state should be in power trading and export. A serious and institutionalised machinery should be set up. This should urgently conduct a preparatory mission in areas like generation, assessing demand compositions in various regional and neighbouring countries, putting in place transmissions lines and drawing modalities and mechanisms of power trading. The possibilities of power trading with other states and the neighbouring countries should be explored urgently.

- The environmental impact assessment studies for the power projects should be carried out in a more transparent, open and all encompassing manner, particularly in terms of involving the local stakeholders. All these studies should be easily accessible to the public. A statewide public hearing forum should be set up to discuss the EIA report of any project before it is implemented.

References

Administrative Staff College of India (2004). *Restructuring the Power Sector in Sikkim,* A report prepared by the Centre for Infrastructure Management & Regulatory Studies, ASCI, Hyderabad.

Central Electricity Authority (2000). *16th Electric Power Survey.* New Delhi.

Central Statistical Organisation. *Statistical Abstract India, 1997.* New Delhi: Department of Statistics, Ministry of Planning and Programme Implementation. p.170.

Junejo, A.A. (1994). *Mini- and Micro-Hydropower Development in the Hindu Kush-Himalayan Region: A Synthesis Report based on Five Country Reports from Bhutan, China, India, Nepal and Pakistan,* International Centre for Integrated Mountain Development (ICIMOD).

Lama, Mahendra P. (1999). *Energy Cooperation in South Asia: Issues, Challenges and Potentials,* South-South Solidarity, Delhi.

———. (2005). *Sikkim-Tibet Trade via Nathu La: A Policy Study on Prospects, Opportunities and Requisite Preparedness.* Prepared by Nathu La Trade Study Group for the Government of Sikkim.

———. (2006a). "Trade is only the Beginning of the Story", *Indian Express,* June 18.

———. (2006b). "Beyond Nathu La: Sikkim Shows the Way", *Statesman,* June 26.

———. (2006c). "Passing the Yuan", *Hindustan Times,* July 4.

———. (2006d). "The Forward Policy and Southasia", Himal Southasian. September. Kathmandu

———. (2006e). "Decentralised trade: Nathu La and China's Local Integration Strategy", Tribune, October 17. Chandigarh.

———. (2006f). "The Dragon's Local Turn: Hu's South Asia Visit Fits in with China's South Asia Plans", DNA (Daily News and Analysis), 20 November. Bombay.

Lama, Mahendra P., Man Mohan Sainju & Q.K. Ahmad (2005). "Reforms and Power Sector in South Asia: Scope and Challenges for Cross Border Trade", in Mohsin S. Khan (*ed.*) *Economic Development in South Asia.* New Delhi: Tata McGRaw–Hill.

Power Department (various years). *Annual Reports (1996-97 & 1997-98).* Government of Sikkim.

Power Trading Corporation of India 2000 and CEA. Executive Summary, January 2003.

Royal Monetary Authority of Bhutan (2004). *Selected Economic Indicators,* September 2000. Thimphu and Kuensel. Thimphu.

Shangle A.K., S.P. Kakran and Navin Kumar (2000). "Hydropower Development Scenario in SAARC Countries: An Overview of Indo-Bhutan and Indo-Nepal Projects", in R.S. Goel and R.N. Srivastava (eds.) *Hydropower and River Valley Development: Environmental Management, Case Studies and Policy Issues.* New Delhi: Oxford & IBH Publishing Co. pp.378.

Singh, R.P. (1998). *Report on the visit of the Chairman-cum-Managing Director POWERGRID to Bangladesh.* Delhi: Power Grid Corporation of India Limited.

USAID-SARI (2001). *The Four Borders Project: Reliability Improvement and Power Transfer in South Asia: A Pre-feasibility Study.* E Program by Nexant. November. pp.2-11.

Chapter 8

Agriculture, Horticulture and Animal Husbandry

Land plays an important role in Sikkim's economy. More than 64 per cent of the population depends on agriculture for its livelihood, and 89 per cent of the people are rural-based and involved in land-based activities. However, the share of the primary sector (comprising mainly of agriculture and allied activities) has been gradually declining over the last decade: from 38.36 per cent in 1993-94 it fell to an estimated 29.78 per cent in 1999-2000 (to the gain of the tertiary sector share which increased from 44 per cent to 48.37 per cent in the same period, and the secondary sector which increased from 17.56 per cent to 21.86 per cent).[1] The real agricultural growth rate has also declined from 8.37 per cent between 1980-81 and 1992-93 to negative 0.2 per cent between 1993-94 and 1999-2000 (Table 8.1).

Given the importance of land-based activity in Sikkim's economy, and limited opportunity for any large-scale employment in other sectors, development strategy will have to address the constraints on increasing productivity in agriculture, horticulture, and animal husbandry. The Tenth Five-Year Plan for Sikkim also identifies agriculture and allied activities as a major area that can help deal with issues related to poverty and unemployment in the state. Expanding income-generating opportunities in these sectors will also help to stem the drift to urban centres and ease the growing pressure on urban environments. This will further increase state revenues, as the main horticultural crop production becomes increasingly commercial. However, if this is to happen, several policy initiatives will have to be seriously followed through. The following section analyses the nature of farm-based activity in Sikkim, and the underlying causes of low productivity in these sectors.

TABLE 8.1

Primary Sector Growth Rates

	1980-81 to 1992-93		*1993-94 to 1999-2000*	
	Nominal	*Real*	*Nominal*	*Real*
Gross State Domestic Product	15.6	11.05	15.5	9.3
Agriculture and Allied Activities	13.3	8.26	8.7	0.14
Agriculture	13.38	8.37	8.6	-0.2
Forestry & Logging	12.3	-1.00	11.6	4.8
Fishing	23.4	8.01	4.3	3.1
Mining & Quarrying	20.1	8.65	-6.5	-9.3

Source: Table 3.1 in Chapter 3 of the Present Report.

8.1 The Nature of Agriculture and Related Sectors in the State

Agro-climatic conditions in the state range from sub-tropical in the lower valleys to alpine in the higher altitudes, and support the cultivation of a wide variety of crops, fruits, and vegetables and commercial crops, and breeding of a variety of animals from chicken, cows, and pigs to yaks, and ponies. The diverse ecological conditions give farm-based activities the advantages of a high degree of variety, but the disadvantages of small scale production.

Mixed farming is practised by most farmers, who cultivate crops mostly for home consumption, and some fruit and vegetables for consumption and sale, in conjunction with breeding a few farm animals and poultry. While a large proportion of farmers cultivate maize, rice, and large cardamom, intercropping is common; maize is frequently grown in fruit orchards,

1. *Tenth Five-Year Plan*, Volume I, Government of Sikkim, p.2.

and fodder trees grow on the boundaries of terraces, which serve as a ready source of green fodder. The crop and livestock production system in the state can be characterised as low input, low risk, and low yield, as farmers, whether of crops or livestock, typically follow traditional farming methods.

8.1.1 Agriculture

The principal food crops cultivated are maize and rice. Wheat, mustard, and buckwheat are also major crops. Till around 1980, very little wheat was grown in the state, and farmers used to cultivate maize and rice through mono-cropping. After its introduction, wheat is cultivated in rotation with rice in the fallows in winter. The re-estimation of agricultural output in 2001-02 using the *gram panchayat* as the unit instead of the district, resulted in a revision downward of almost all the data on area, output, and productivity (*see* Annexure Tables A-28 and A-29); the break in time series, however, makes trend analysis difficult. However, in the subsequent two years for which data is available (2001-02 and 2002-03), yields for rice, maize and pulses and, in fact, for all food grain has fallen. Area under cultivation for almost all food grains has also decreased, as farmers are increasingly shifting to cultivating oilseeds or more commercial horticultural crops, such as ginger (Tables A-28 and A-29).

8.1.2 Horticulture

Large cardamom and ginger are the main horticultural spice crops, grown mainly for sale to outside markets. The wide range of agri-climatic zones allow the cultivation of a variety of fruit (mainly mandarin oranges, guavas, mangoes and bananas), vegetables (notably potatoes) and flowers (varieties of orchids, gladiola, anthuriums, and rhododendrons). Revised data since 2001-02 and 2002-03 shows that in these two years, even though there has been an expansion in the area under citrus fruit, large cardamom and ginger cultivation, yields have fallen in all cases (Annexure Table A-29).

Large Cardamom

With 59.9 per cent of the global market for large cardamom, India is the largest producer in the world, followed by Nepal with 33 per cent of the market and Bhutan with 13 per cent (Figure 8.1). Of the Indian output, almost 88 per cent comes from Sikkim, which can safely be presumed to be the largest producer of large cardamom in the world. Most of Sikkim's large cardamom output is sold outside the state: of the 4,700 MT produced in 2000-01, 4,550 MTs (97 per cent) was sent out of the state, mostly to the markets of Delhi (52 per cent), Amritsar and Mumbai, to be exported to other countries, mainly Pakistan.

FIGURE 8.1

Large Cardamom Production: World and India

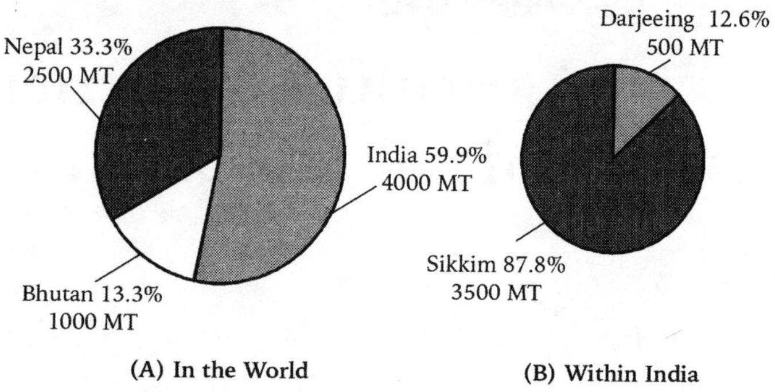

Source: Lata *et al.*, 1999.

Ginger

Ginger is the second most important cash crop in Sikkim and the main agricultural export of the state. Sikkim is among the top ginger-producing states in the country. Most of the ginger output is sold outside the state: in 2000-01, of the 24,000 tonnes produced, 17,600 tonnes (73 per cent) was exported, mostly (70 per cent) to the Delhi markets.

Other Horticultural Produce

Floriculture: The vast agro-climatic sweep across three major zones allows the production of more than 4,000 varieties of plants and shrubs, and 450 species of orchids.

Fruit: Sikkim oranges have been the main fruit grown in terms of area and output, but diseases and aging trees have adversely affected production in recent years. The government has initiated a rejuvenation programme, involving replantation, which farmers have been slow to implement because of the interim loss in income. The poor storage quality of Sikkim oranges has affected its marketability. Other fruit include apples, bananas, and more recently efforts to introduce passion fruit and kiwi fruit.

Vegetables: A variety of vegetables are grown, depending on climate and terrain, of which potatoes are the major root crop. Also grown is a special red Sikkim chilli locally known as *dalle khorsani*, which has recently begun being processed into a chilli paste and pickles. However, despite local production, imports of vegetables into the state are high in proportion to its 'exports' to outside markets. Marketing and transport constraints have hampered the state from exploring its potential as a supplier of off-season fresh vegetables to markets in the plains.

8.1.3 Animal Husbandry

Animal husbandry is an integral part of the rural household economy of the state. Livestock or poultry-rearing is the main occupation or major supplementary activity of an estimated 89 per cent of the population. There are broadly two forms of animal husbandry practice in the state depending on regional and climatic factors. For people living in higher altitudes (in the north, west, and east districts), such as the Lachungpas, Lachenpas, Gurungs and Sherpas, livestock rearing is the main occupation, and has been so for decades. They rear yaks, sheep, upland cattle and equines, which are mainly fed by grazing.

The second and more dominant form of animal husbandry practice is as part of a mixed farming system of the lower and mid-altitudes. The main occupation is the cultivation of field and horticultural crops, and animals are reared mainly to sustain these activities by acting as a source of farm manure and bullock power (especially as mechanisation is infeasible given the small size of tracts).

Increases in the output of livestock products have not kept pace with demand. The Department of Animal Husbandry has made attempts to tackle one of the main problems, the poor quality of animal stock, but as table 8.2 shows, while crossbred numbers are increasing, so are the poor quality indigenous varieties.

TABLE 8.2

Trends in Livestock Population: Crossbred and Indigenous (Number)

		1997 #	*2002**	*Per cent Change*
Cattle	Crossbred	51,542	81,629	(+) 58.37
	Indigenous	90,961	1,10,560	(+) 21.55
Sheep	Crossbred	730	216	(-) 70.41
	Indigenous	4,293	5,530	(+) 28.81
Pigs	Crossbred	12,000	19,118	(+) 59.31
	Indigenous	14,975	21,820	(+) 45.70

Note: #–16th Livestock Census; *–Provisional data, 17th Livestock Census.

Source: Department of Animal Husbandry and Veterinary Science, Government of Sikkim.

BOX 8.1

Livestock Farming: Appropriate for the Terrain and Environment of Sikkim

Only 17 per cent of the total area of Sikkim is cultivable (Annexure Table A-27) while almost 50 per cent is available for livestock farming, as it falls within Classes 4-8 category. With population increases and limited land, opportunities to improve rural livelihoods through cultivation are limited, but livestock and poultry breeding, already an intrinsic part of the rural economy, shows great potential, apart from having beneficial effects on the environment.

If appropriately conducted, livestock farming is an ecologically sound and sustainable activity for a mountainous state such as Sikkim. It uses a minimal amount of land, labour and capital, most farmers rear their livestock under stall-fed condition (which reduces pressure on land due to overgrasing), the grass and legumes planted on the steep slopes provide nutrition for the animals, add nitrogen to the soil and protect the land from erosion, it provides a supplementary source of income as well as high protein food, such as milk, eggs, and meat and organic manure for crop production.

8.1.4 Fisheries

As all other farming activities, fishing in Sikkim is carried out in traditional style with non-mechanised equipment, such as cast-nets and rods, but no fishing crafts. Output has consequently been low, and fresh and canned fish has to be imported from outside the state to meet the local demand.

There are 28 indigenous species (mainly ***mahseer, katli, asla, goonch,*** and ***gardi***) and several 'exotic' species (brown trout, common carp, grass carp and silver carp). Total fish production in the state is 140 tonnes, 60 per cent of which is from captive fisheries and the rest from culture fisheries.[2] However, real growth rates in this sector have more than halved, from 8.01 per cent between 1980-81 and 1992-93 to 3.1 per cent between 1993-94 to 1999-2000 (Table 8.1).

8.2 Agriculture and Horticulture: Issues and Constraints

8.2.1 Production Issues

Limited Land for Farming

Land is one of the most precious resources in the state where, because of the mountainous terrain, high

2. From the *Quenquenniel Livestock Survey.*

altitudes and topography, very little land is available for cultivation or livestock activities. Thus, one of the most important constraints to land-based activities is the limited farmland available. In the tiny state, most of the area is steep, rocky mountainous slopes, and unfit for cultivation. Cultivation is mostly carried out on steep slopes, extensively terraced for maximum use. Of the total geographical area of the state, only 17.18 per cent is available for cultivation, of which less than 9 per cent is irrigated (see Annexure Table A-27). Further, less than 3 per cent of the land in the state has been categorised as Class 1 land,[3] most of the remaining land has been categorised as Classes 4 to 8.[4] In the old classification, only 14 per cent was under cultivation, 36 per cent was forest, 28 per cent barren and uncultivable and 14 per cent under pasture and grassland.[5]

Agriculture increasingly has to compete with other sectors for the limited operational land in the state. As Tables A-28 and A-29 (Annexures) show, area under cultivation of almost all crops has fallen as land is transferred to other uses such as industry, education and tourism.

Land productivity is also affected by the skewed distribution of holdings. Most of the land holdings are very small, with 70 per cent less than 2 hectares in area, and only 10 per cent over 2 hectares.

Traditional Farming Methods

Most farmers use traditional tools and follow traditional practices. Crop cultivation is mainly manual or animal-based. In animal husbandry, animal and poultry breeders rarely experiment with scientific or new practices to increase yield or for disease prevention.

Little Formal Irrigation

Cultivation of agricultural crops is mainly rain-fed, and only a very small area (8.9 per cent of total operational area) is irrigated (Annexure Table A-27), and even less is under assured irrigation. The hilly terrain restricts irrigation to minor projects, which are typically channels linking water sources to the fields. The monsoons continue to play a pivotal role in rain-fed cultivation. In 1998-99, the state suffered from what

FIGURE 8.2

Comparative Fertiliser Use

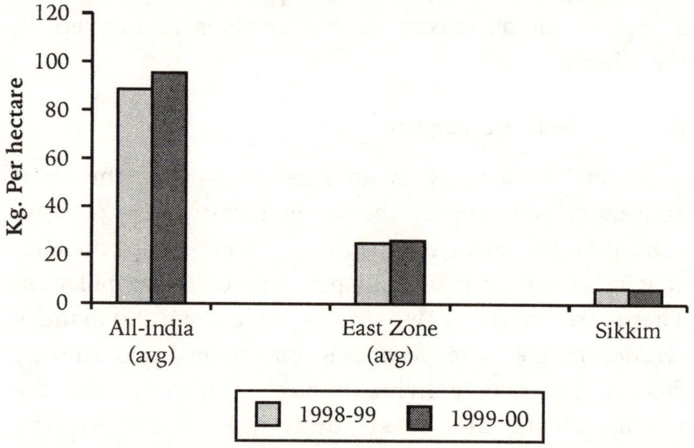

Source: From Table A-30 (in annexure).

was estimated as the severest drought in 25 years. This had an adverse effect on the agricultural economy especially on horticultural crops like large cardamom (an estimated 60 per cent of the crop was lost), ginger, and oranges. Timely monsoons in 1999-2000 and 2000-2001 brought production levels back to normal.[6]

Low Use of Chemicals

Like farmers in most other parts of the country, especially in the northeast, farmers in Sikkim practise 'organic farming' by default. Traditional methods of cultivation are based on the low use of chemicals such as pesticides and fertilisers, which in Sikkim is much lower than the national average and low even in comparison with other northeastern states (Figure 8.2). Weeding is done manually, with little use of herbicides or chemical weed control methods, and fertiliser is usually organic, animal waste, crop residue, rotational legumes, and off-farm organic waste.

The use of pesticides has also been low and diseases account for a substantial proportion of crop losses, which average 15-20 per cent, and in some case are as high as 50-75 per cent of output.[7]

Poor Quality of Inputs

While the government agencies supply some inputs, the large proportion has to be imported into the state

3. Land across the country is broadly classified into 8 categories according to capability: the better quality land is classified as classes 1 to 4, and can be used for crop cultivation, classes 5-8 land is generally suited for non-cultivation activities, such as forestry, agroforestry, silvopasture, perennial grasses, fodder crops, and so on.
4. *Economic Survey of Sikkim.*
5. *Sikkim Perspectives,* p.275.
6. *Economic Survey of Sikkim.*
7. *Sikkim Perspectives,* p.300.

and then transported across long distances, which makes supply expensive and erratic, depending on the weather and transport conditions. The Sikkim State Co-operative Society and Marketing Federation (SIMFED) was set up in 1984 to supply farmers with fertilisers, seeds, poultry and cattle feed, machinery, etc. and to purchase agricultural produce, but in recent years its focus has shifted to the marketing of consumer goods, adversely affecting farm input supply.

Research and Development

There are several research institutes in Sikkim which are supposed to focus on enhancing farm productivity (Box 8.2).

BOX 8.2

Numerous Agricultural Research Institutes

There are several research institutes in Sikkim which have been set up to address the issues of low productivity in agriculture and allied sectors. The largest of these is the Sikkim Centre of the Indian Council of Agricultural Research (NEH Region), which works in collaboration with state departments and other national-level institutes to develop technologies to increase production. An autonomous body of the Ministry of Environment and Forests, the GB Pant Institute of Himalayan Environment and Development (Sikkim Unit) focuses on environmental issues, land, and water resource management, and related areas. The Central Integrated Pest Management Centre (Gangtok) works almost exclusively on pest identification and biological pest control measures, mainly for rice and other staple crops. The objective of the Spices Board is to provide research and marketing support to producers of spices, such as large cardamom. The Indo-Swiss Project Sikkim (ISPS) is a bilateral venture between the Sikkim and Swiss governments, working to improve the livelihoods of small and marginal farmers, through collaboration with departments, such as Animal Husbandry (to improve animal health and the functioning of milk cooperatives) and Horticulture (to increase ginger production and improve cardamom curing methods).

However, research agendas are usually determined by institutions, and much of output relates to conditions in the plains, or in other states in the eastern Himalayas. Very little study is Sikkim-specific, such as, for example, ways to improve the storage quality of the Sikkim orange which will greatly increase its profitability, or methods to increase the supply of breed-appropriate, region-specific feed and fodder.

Institutes are also handicapped by a shortage of trained scientific researchers: the ICAR, for example, is seriously understaffed (of 26 positions for scientific staff, 16 still remain vacant) so no tangible results have been forthcoming at least in horticulture.[8] The veterinary hospital at Gangtok treats around 9,360 cases a year (in 2001-02), with only two doctors and a superintendent. The hospital lacks basic medical equipment like x-ray machines, and medicines are in short supply.[9] There is no full-fledged epidemiological laboratory for livestock disease investigation work, nor are there facilities for producing vaccines and other biological products.

Falling Public Investment

Declining public investment is a cause of concern, especially as it is crucial for infrastructure such as irrigation, agricultural research, markets and communication. Outlay on agriculture and allied activities under the Tenth Plan is 14.81 per cent lower than the outlay in the Ninth Plan. Outlay on irrigation and flood control has been reduced by 24.39 per cent between the two plan periods.[10]

8.2.2 Post-Production Network and Infrastructure

Farm income and opportunities remain depressed because of the poorly developed state of post-production infrastructure and facilities, and the absence of viable marketing structures. Geophysical conditions and lack of storage and warehousing, a good road network and transportation and communication facilities, make for localised markets and dependence on middlemen to provide marketing channels.

Transport

Transport costs are high because of the terrain, the widely dispersed production of small quantities, the cap on transport capacities (5 tonnes a truck), and the transport monopoly of the Sikkim National Transport (SNT).

Access to Credit

Farmers rarely use formal credit networks, yet access to credit is important, especially as the trend is to phase out government handouts and outright subsidies. As in several other states, the availability of rural credit is hampered by the complexities of the loan-

8. IDFC: *Report on Ginger Agri-Processing Zone in Sikkim.*
9. *Manpower Survey*, p.56.
10. Background Note for Annual Plan 2003-04 for Sikkim, Planning Commission, p.13.

disbursement process. Potential borrowers have to make available a variety of documented information before they are considered eligible for credit. The issue is more complicated in Sikkim compared to other states, as land cannot be held as collateral.

Storage and Processing Facilities

The near absence of storage infrastructure in the state adds to post-harvest losses and lower prices for farmers, as the lack of storage facilities erodes their ability to bargain on prices. A very high proportion, around 50 per cent of horticultural crops is lost post-harvest[11] for various locational, climatic, and other reasons. Apart from the monetary loss, this represents a waste of the use of land, labour, and other inputs into the production process.

Poorly Developed Marketing Networks

For horticultural crops such as large cardamom and ginger, there are no *mandis* or wholesale markets trading in specific products in the state. An outcome of the Marketing Regulation Act (enacted during the Ninth Plan) was the wholesale market in Rangpo, but it has met with limited success because it lacks facilities for handling perishable produce.[12] The absence of formal credit systems makes farmers heavily indebted to traders, commission agents and middleman, with little bargaining room on prices. Even were the farmer to get a better price at the wholesale market, the highly dispersed production of small quantities does not make it feasible to transport the produce to long distances.

The marketable surplus of other products is mostly sold through rural markets, and typically involve the trading of small quantities of produce. There are 17 rural markets in Sikkim. They are largely unorganised and not well frequented, given the low purchasing power of the rural populace. While funds have been earmarked in the Tenth Plan for setting up of rural markets/*apni mandis* to tackle the problem, the process is likely to be delayed as the market committees have not been able to raise matching funds.

8.2.3 Horticulture: Specific Constraints

While falling yields in horticulture can be attributed to overall conditions in the sector, additional product-specific constraints on production and marketing for the major horticultural products are analysed below. The absence of a supply chain to link farmers with the market, has kept horticultural production at fairly low levels. There is enough surplus production of the major cash crops, large cardamom and ginger, and of flowers which, if supported by the right kind of infrastructural links, would promote the commercial cultivation of these crops.

Large Cardamom is grown primarily by small farmers, for whom this is the major source of livelihood. More than 65 per cent of planters are poor, marginal landholders (with plantations of less than a hectare), but cultivate only 18 per cent of the total area under large cardamom; 1 per cent of cardamom plantations are over 10 hectares. Both extremes of ownership have problems: the small farmers are handicapped by lack of resources and access to improved technology, and the large farmers by a shortage of labour, which is needed for harvesting.

As Table A-29 (in the annexure) shows, the area under the cultivation of large cardamom has been increasing, but productivity has declined since 1975, and even over the last two years (2001-02 and 2002-03) for which revised estimates were available.

Most of the cardamom plantations in the state have become old, exceeding their economic life of 25 years. Some of the plantations are being replanted, but a shortage of quality seedlings has slowed the process. With deforestation, plantations are becoming devoid of optimum shade, exposing the plants to sunlight which adversely affects yield. Like other crops, large cardamom is cultivated without the benefit of modern technical intervention. Farmers use only organic manure, which depresses yields, but the absence of any organic marketing structure prevents farmers from realising the price benefits of 'organic' production.

The absence of strong marketing links greatly affects farmers' prices, which in any case fluctuate a great deal from year to year. The state needs to leverage its almost complete monopoly of world production to increase exports, and hence revenues, to generate income and employment and improve rural livelihoods. Today Sikkimese producers hardly benefit from the exports, as most of the produce goes through a series of middlemen to the large markets of Delhi, Amritsar, and Mumbai, to be further exported to Pakistan (by far the largest market) and other countries.

11. *Tenth Plan document*, p.44.

12. *Tenth Plan document*.

BOX 8.3

Large Cardamom: The Importance of Good Curing Processes

The quality of large cardamom, and hence its price, is crucially dependent on the curing process. Scientifically cured cardamom commands a higher price, but in Sikkim farmers still use the traditional wood-fired *'bhatti'* for curing. The results are variable, losses can be high and the final quality variable, apart from the environmental disadvantages of being based on large amounts of fuel wood.

Different agencies such as TERI, the Spices Board and the GB Pant Institute have developed, or are in the process of developing, curing technologies that are more energy efficient than the *bhatti* system[13] using fuel-gas technology to dry the produce results in improved quality and a market price that is 10-20 per cent higher than the traditional *bhatti*-cured cardamom. Whatever system is developed and marketed, it has to dovetail with the large cardamom cultivation methods of farmers in Sikkim, so that they accept the new technology.

Source: IDFC. *AEZ for Ginger.*

FIGURE 8.3

Ginger Productivity: Sikkim *versus* India, 1995-99

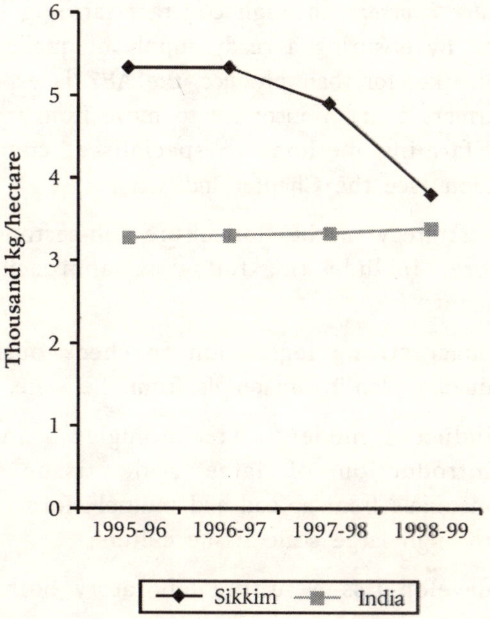

Source: IDFC. *AEZ for Ginger.*

Ginger is cultivated mainly by small and medium farmers, for whom it is a major source of income. Area under production and output has been increasing steadily over the past few decades, but productivity has fallen, especially after the severe drought in the state in 1998-99, and while it is still above the national average yield (Figure 8.3), the gap has narrowed considerably.

One of the most important problems that ginger growers have to tackle is the prevalence of diseases. The department is distributing disease-free seeds, and in areas where farmers groups have been formed, ginger disease control measures are being propagated with some success.

Ginger prices are highly volatile, across seasons and from year to year, and income-smoothening measures are important to promote commercial production of the crop. The variety of ginger that is cultivated in Sikkim is relatively fibrous, and commands a lower price. Research into producing a more marketable variety of ginger that can be grown in the climatic and soil conditions in the state, would be extremely lucrative for farmers.

There are no specific *mandis* for ginger, so marketing is primarily trader-driven. Ginger is sold in its raw form to traders, who then send it to various markets across the country, primarily Delhi (which receives 70 per cent of the exports from Sikkim), UP, Punjab and West Bengal.

Floriculture

The state has not fully explored its natural advantages as a nursery and breeding ground for a variety of exotic flowers and floriculture products. Conducive agro-climatic conditions and the long shelf life of several orchid varieties that flourish in Sikkim make these an ideal floral 'export' for the state. The orchid species native to Sikkim are not as commonly known as the tropical varieties grown in Thailand and South India, and some are extremely rare. Efforts should be made to promote these 'exotic' species in the large urban markets of the country, and for the extremely rare species to link up producers with global specialists in these areas, to facilitate an exchange of technology that could benefit local growers.

Some constraints on the promotion of commercial floriculture created by small plot size and the absence of marketing links with the plains may be addressed by the agri-export zone (AEZ) for floral products the Sikkim government plans to set up near Pakyong in the

13. Lata *et al.*, 1999.

east district. It has entered into a joint venture with a Chennai-based private entrepreneur, to develop the AEZ which is expected to promote the cultivation of flowers and *daler khorsani* through contract farming by local farmers. By ensuring a ready supply of quality inputs and a market for their produce, the AEZ is expected to give farmers a major incentive to move from traditional mixed farming methods to specialised, commercial cultivation (see the Chapter Industry).

The strategy in the floriculture sub-sector should, therefore, include the following approaches and instruments:[14]

- enact strong legislation to check outflow of quality planting materials from the state;
- induct modern technologies including introduction of large scale tissue culture materials from abroad and multiply to supplement through large scale tissue culture;
- develop tissue culture laboratory both in the public and private sector;
- provide large scale demonstration for transfer of technology to the farmers;
- provide good budgetary support as floriculture is capital intensive and the present level of investment will not bring desired changes; and
- provide infrastructure facility for marketing, transport, packaging, and handling.

8.3 Agriculture and Horticulture: Recommendations

Falling yields in agriculture and horticulture attest to the fact that the pace and direction of policy needs to be changed. The overall approach for the government should be to focus on strengthening infrastructure (such as, irrigation, roads, storage and warehousing), promoting a more scientific basis to development (through improved research and extension and awareness-building) and, in general shifting, from the narrow monitoring of inputs into these sectors to evaluating outcomes. Private initiatives should be encouraged in some areas (seeds and seedlings, for example), and community participation strengthened in others (milk supply). The focus for agriculture will be maximising household farm incomes rather than generating food surpluses for self-sufficiency.

14. Lama, 2001.

8.3.1 Increasing Production

Zoning of Land

Given the acute scarcity of operational land in the state, it is imperative that land needs to be clearly demarcated for different uses. There is no land-use plan for the state, but having one will prevent arbitrary transfer of fertile land for non-agricultural purposes.

Better Application of Science and Technology

One of the Tenth Plan objectives is an emphasis on applications of science and technology in agriculture and horticulture. A first step would be to formulate policy to encourage the use of modern technology and more scientific techniques and strengthening the institutional basis for this.

Research outcomes from the several institutes can be vastly improved to provide valuable inputs into agricultural and animal husbandry activities. Research agendas need to focus on current issues and constraints specifically faced by Sikkimese farmers. Research on improved methods or different varieties is effective only to the extent that successful outcomes are efficiently transferred to farmers.

Further, rather than just 'handing over' their findings to the departments, research institutes provide as much information on how to translate these into extension services. Departments, too, have a major role in keeping farmers abreast of relevant recent developments and changes in market conditions. This necessitates the development of a strong chain of information transfer from the research institute to the department, to farmers. While the community information centres (CICs) currently provide information on farm prices and diseases, linking these centres with local rural bodies such as, panchyati raj institutions could provide a stronger link for dissemination of information on new techniques and initiatives.

Inputs

Access to credit needs to be facilitated both by formal and informal methods. Formal networks need to be encouraged to increase credit disbursement to farmers, through self-help groups, co-operatives, or rural banks. Co-opting money lenders into the formal network and regulating them to ensure fair lending also is worth consideration.

- While it is possible to produce cereals in rain-fed conditions, assured irrigation is especially important in the cultivation of vegetables and high-value crops, particularly those earmarked for commercial sale. There are no water tariffs in the state, which leads to inefficient use of existing water. The state needs to enact the Irrigation Act to allow the introduction of such tariffs based on economic costs.
- The non-availability of good quality seeds, seedlings and planting material in time for planting has affected productivity. There is a strong case for reducing the government role in supplying subsidised seeds and promoting private seed producers, either by encouraging certified seed production in farmers' fields or through well-regulated certified nurseries.

8.3.2 Strengthening Post-Production Infrastructure and Facilities

A prerequisite to raising farm outputs is farmers' awareness of the advantages of moving from low-input/low-risk farming to a more market-sensitive system of farming. For this, market signals need to be brought closer to farmers, through vastly improved marketing channels, so that farmers can see the advantages of using better quality inputs and more modern methods and implements. A first step towards bringing crop-related market information closer to farmers is the CICs set up by the IT Department, where prices are posted weekly. However, this initiative is still in its initial stages and of limited applicability as long as the marketing chains remain weak.

Transport and Road Networks

To meet vital transport needs especially for the perishable products, private transporters could be encouraged with adequate credit support through the financial institutions to purchase light commercial vehicles.

Marketing and Infrastructure

The state has enacted agricultural legislation, and regulation of rural markets has to be introduced in phases. One way to improve their functioning would be to assign management of rural and apex markets to elected local bodies, including cooperatives.

To address the lack of a marketing network for large cardamom and ginger, the government plans to enter into MoUs with private entrepreneurs to set up agri-export zones (AEZs) for these major cash crops. The zones will contain infrastructure and facilities to enhance production, establish a supply and marketing link between the farmer and the market, and increase the export potential of the produce through post-harvesting technology such as curing, sorting, packaging, labelling, and even eventually agro-processing (see chapter on Industry).

8.3.3 The Shift to an Organic State

Building on the already low use of chemical fertiliser in the state, the Sikkim government has intentions of declaring the entire state organic by 2009 (Box 8.4).

> BOX 8.4
>
> **Organic Farming: Environmentally Appropriate**
>
> Organic farming is a modern, sustainable farming system which maintains the long-term fertility of the soil and uses fewer resources to produce high quality, nutritious food. It is becoming an increasingly viable alternative to industrial agriculture and in western countries it is expanding at a rapid rate. Soil fertility relies principally on the use of legumes, crop rotations, the application of composted animal manure and ground rock minerals. Weeds are controlled by mechanical methods while pests and diseases tend not to be a problem due to the inherent biodiversity in the system. Artificial fertilisers, pesticides, growth regulators and livestock feed additives are prohibited.
>
> The fall in productivity when converting to organic farming is compensated for by increases in returns, as organic produce commands a higher price. The onus is on the government to make sure that certification is up to international standards, and marketing channels are firmly in place, so that farmers receive the best price their organic produce can command.

Laying the Groundwork a Lengthy Process

The state government needs to formulate policy on organic farming, which is committed to supporting market-related, environment friendly practices, on a long-term basis. It will need to set up basic infrastructure, perhaps enact regulation and set up statutory bodies. Although fertiliser use has been low in Sikkim, it has been increasing steadily in the last few years.[15] Strategy will need to encourage the gradual

15. Department of Agriculture, A Concept Paper and Action Plan 2003-04, Government of Sikkim.

substitution of chemical inputs by organic pesticides, manure, and fertilisers. This can be done through a support and incentives system to encourage farmers to move from using chemical fertilisers and pesticides to organic inputs and biological plant protection measures. Government subsidies for chemical fertiliser will need to be reduced or withdrawn.

A proper scientific base to the process would require comprehensive research into appropriate organic farming methods for Sikkim (such a study has not been done for any part of the country). In fact, the agro-biodiversity of the state is yet to be catalogued and classified.

In the absence of localised research information and support, it would be difficult to convince all farmers to convert to organic farming methods, even if the government is ready to provide both conversion support and continuation or maintenance payments.

In view of the above considerations, the proposal to declare the entire state organic within a five-year period may not be feasible. Given the constraints listed above, such as expensive and extensive groundwork, this will be extremely difficult to regulate, given that farming methods are mainly a lifestyle choice for farmers.

8.4 Animal Husbandry: Analysis and Recommendations

8.4.1 Sectoral Analysis

Milk: In terms of value and quantity, milk is the principal livestock product. It is a source of income for the poorer sections comprising the landless, small, and marginal farmers. In the last two decades there has been an increase in the number of crossbred cows, however, as the most recent livestock census shows, there has also been an increase in domestic varieties (Table 8.2). Milk procurement and marketing in three districts, east, south, and the west, are handled by the Sikkim Milk Union (Box 8.5), but supply still falls short of local demand. A Tribal Dairy Development Corporation to procure and market milk from producers is proposed to be set up in the north district, which had so far been left out of the milk cooperative network. Major steps need to be taken to ensure hygienic standards in milk procurement and storage.

Meat, is the second most important livestock product in terms of value and volume, but its output is lower than the local demand and meat has to be brought in from neighbouring areas. A major source of the demand comes from army personnel stationed in the state, which is met almost exclusively by outside suppliers. Some reasons for low local meat production is the poor quality and limited number of slaughter animals in the state, and controlled meat prices.

Eggs: Poultry-breeding has been actively encouraged by the government as it offers tremendous opportunities for self-employment for weaker sections, such as marginal farmers, agricultural labourers, and those from the scheduled tribes and castes communities. Though poultry is now recognised as a thrust area by the government, it still has a long way to go to become an effective instrument of socio-economic upliftment of rural households. The joint venture between the department and Venketeshwar Hatcheries, the Sikkim Poultry Development Corporation, which commenced in 1992 with the intention of being phased out in a few years time, still continues. This is a commercial poultry breeding and hatchery venture aimed at providing opportunities to unemployed youth to rear broiler and layer birds.

BOX 8.5

Need for Strong Producers' Cooperatives

In 1976, the state initiated a dairy development programme on the lines of Operation Flood. A major player in the programme has been the Sikkim Milk Producers Co-operative Union Limited (SMU), an apex body formed in 1980, to which primary milk societies in the east, west, and south districts are affiliated. The SMU has primary dairy cooperatives formed by farmers.

The SMU's inefficient functioning has affected milk collection, and raised procurement and processing costs. As a result, its market share has fallen, and a large proportion of the demand is being met by 'imports' into the state. Almost since its inception, SMU did not function as a true co-operative: government appointees have always headed the Union, with consequent adverse effects, such as overstaffing, unprofessional management, and poor marketing. The Union's losses have been mounting, from its high administrative, establishment and transportation expenses (which, between 1980-2003, accounted for an average of almost 50 per cent of earnings).[16] In 2002-03, however, the state government amended the Cooperative Act to stipulate that only an elected representative could chair the SMU. The increased involvement of producers in the Union should help strengthen it and make it a more self-sufficient enterprise.

16. ISPS documents.

8.4.2 Constraints and Recommendations

The two broad categories of livestock farming (mentioned in section 8.1.3) need to be tackled differently to increase the income-generating potential of the sector. In the first case, where livestock rearing is a socio-cultural continuum for tribal populations, efforts need to be made to help breeders stay on the land, to prevent their migration to urban areas, by improving their access to health and education, and other services and infrastructural facilities, by providing animal shelters and through improved quality and greater supply of animal feed and fodder.

In the lower regions, where livestock and poultry rearing are part of the mixed system of farming, the current subsistence approach can be made more efficient if commercial fodder production is encouraged, and improved delivery of animal health services and strong marketing and procurement system implemented. Feeding is mainly in stalls. Purchased fodder of higher quality, which is grain or oilseed based, rather than straw based, can make stall-feeding economical, provided commercial fodder production is encouraged and transport costs are kept low; the latter will in turn deepen poultry and livestock markets and increase the demand for livestock products. The growth in incomes also shifts consumption patterns to meat, milk, eggs and fruit. Animal power in land preparation, threshing, etc. will need to give way to motor power technologies.

For this the government needs to strengthen its regulatory role, set up an enabling marketing infrastructure, and improve the interface between research institutes and farmers. It also needs to shift away from its monopolistic provision of feed and fodder and animal health services (some efforts at the latter are currently being implemented).

Livestock and poultry farmers share many of the same constraints that hamper cultivators in the state, such as non-scientific, traditional methods of farming, poor quality of inputs, and lack of adequate research into Sikkim-specific breeds. The absence of a strong marketing structure, including a cold chain, greatly hampers the storage and transportation of perishables such as meat, milk, and eggs, thus constraining their consumption to local areas, which in turn reduces incentives to increase production for farmers. In addition, two major causes of low levels of animal productivity are the poor quality of animal health services and animal feed and fodder.

Animal Health Services

The government is still the sole provider of animal health services, and although it has a wide network of institutions (Table A-33), these have not been able to cope with the demand for medicines and services, especially from more remote villages. Their inability to supply adequate quantities of medicines and veterinary services in time, has often meant financial losses for farmers, and is a major factor in keeping the productivity low.

This inaccessibility of services has had such adverse effects that farmers are willing to pay for timely supply, in the absence of an efficient government distribution system (Table 8.3). A joint survey by the Department of Animal Husbandry and ISPS (2001) found that the main constraint on the animal health delivery system is accessibility of services, which is not surprising in a mountainous state like Sikkim, where many of the farmers live in remote areas.[17]

Based on the survey results, the Department of Animal Husbandry initiated a project to supplement its free provision of animal health services with private provision of medicines for a fee.

Animal Feed and Fodder are vital inputs in this sector sometimes accounting for as much as 60-70 per cent of total cost of production. Good quality feed and fodder is important for livestock health and productivity, but its acute scarcity makes this one of the weakest links in the production chain.

There is shortage of green and dry fodder grasslands which are the major source of green fodder, have

TABLE 8.3

Survey Results: Willingness to Pay for Animal Health Care

(Per cent)

	For Medicines	*For Services*
Willing	90	67
Unwilling	7	27
Unable to respond	3	6
Total	100	100

Source: ISPS (2002). *Medicine Survey Report*. May.

17. Only 21 per cent of respondents were close to an accessible veterinary institution; for 41 per cent a veterinary dispensary was out of reach but not inaccessible; for 5 per cent of the respondents, a veterinary institution was out of reach. Medical shop accessibility was a serious problem. For 77 per cent of the villagers, it is out of reach.

shrunk in area. To increase the availability of green fodder natural pastures and grazing grounds should be developed with suitable species of grasses with high nutritional value. Nutritional value of crop residue can also be enhanced with chemical treatment. The major cause for dry fodder deficit is shortfall in fodder cultivation. Dry fodder supply can be enhanced by research into and planting of good quality fodder seeds. Setting up fodder banks in the high regions will obviate the need for migration to the lower lands in winter.

Animal feed: Well-balanced feed is important to meet specific major nutrient needs for each animal, and for maximum yields, its nutritive value needs to be adapted to the strain of livestock. Most of the ingredients to make concentrated animal feed are not available in the state and have to be brought in from West Bengal. Neither are there processing units for this sector, such as a bone meal plant or a feed mixing and grinding plant. Research is required into the various new technologies in feed processing that help to optimise existing fodder resources.

Marketing Animal Products

As in the case of crops and foodgrain, the development of a strong post-harvest marketing network will be a major incentive for increased production. All three stages for animal products, procurement, transport/marketing, and processing for value addition need strengthening. Marketing perishables such as milk, eggs, and meat will require the development of appropriate infrastructure including a cold chain consisting of milk chilling plants, refrigerated transport, coolers, and a cold storage (see industry chapter for industrial incentives).

Recommendations

- Falling yields and incomes in agriculture and horticulture suggest urgent policy interventions. The overall approach by the government should be to focus on strengthening infrastructure supportive of agriculture and horticulture.
- The focus in agriculture should be maximising household farm incomes rather than generating food surplus for self-sufficiency. This will call for an expansion in the area under assured irrigation, especially in the south district where it is drier, and an improvement in research inputs.
- Research outcomes from the several existing institutes can be vastly improved to provide valuable inputs into agriculture and animal husbandry activities. Research agendas of such institutes should focus on current issues and constraints faced by the local farmers.
- Rather than just handing over their abstract findings to the govt. departments, the research institutes should provide as much information on how to translate their findings into extension services. The departments also have a major role in keeping the farmers abreast of relevant recent developments and changes in market conditions.
- The non-availability of good quality seeds, seedlings, and planting material adversely affect farming in the State. There is a strong case for reducing the government role in supplying subsidised seeds and seedlings and promoting certified private seed producers. Local seed producers are in a far better position to meet local needs.
- While it is possible to produce cereals in rain-fed conditions, assured irrigation is especially important in the cultivation of vegetables and other high value crops. There are no water tariffs in the State, which leads to inefficient use of existing water. The state needs to enact an Irrigation Act to allow the introduction of such tariffs based on economic costs.
- Access to credit needs to be facilitated both by formal and informal methods. Formal networks need to be encouraged to increase credit disbursement to farmers, through self-help groups, co-operatives, or rural banks. There is a suggestion that rural moneylenders be drawn into the formal network and their functioning be regulated to ensure that they do not charge usurious interest rates. This is also worth considering.
- A prerequisite to raising farm outputs is farmer awareness of the advantages of moving from low-input/low-risk farming to market-sensitive system of farming. As a first step towards this, the CICs should be activated to bring crop-related market information closer to the farmers.
- To meet vital transport needs, especially for the perishable products, private transporters could be encouraged with adequate credit support through the financial institutions to purchase light commercial vehicles.
- Regulation of rural markets has to be introduced in phases. One way to improve their functioning would be to assign management of rural and apex

markets to elected local bodies, including co-operatives.

- Building on the already low use of chemical fertilisers in the state, the Sikkim govt. has intentions of declaring the entire state 'Organic' by 2009. A proper scientific approach to organic farming, however, requires considerable research and preparation. Given these constraints, a more gradual and phased shift to organic farming is recommended.
- Livestock and poultry farming are important in the traditional farming system of Sikkim. These activities also suffer from the same constraints that hamper crop cultivation, *viz.* non-scientific traditional farming, poor quality of inputs and lack of adequate research into state-specific breeds. The absence of a strong marketing structure including a cold chain stand in the way of the farmers earning remunerative prices. In addition, two major causes of low levels of animal productivity are poor quality of animal health services, and animal feed and fodder. For the realisation of full potential of this sector and to enrich the rural economy, the above constraints are to be eliminated step by step by appropriate public policies, including public investment.

References

Bhutia, Kunga Gyatso, *et al. Going for Organic Farming in Sikkim: A Concept Paper and Action Plan 2004-05.* Department of Agriculture.

Department of Agriculture. *Area and Production Statistics of Sikkim 2002-03.*

———. Agenda Notes of Sikkim for National Conference on Agriculture for *Rabi* Campaign 2001-02.

———. Agenda Notes for National Conference on Agriculture for *Kharif* Campaign 2001.

———. (various years). *Annual Progress Report.*

Department of Agriculture & Co-operation. *Technology Mission for Integrated Development of Horticulture in the NE States.* Government of India.

Department of Animal Husbandry & Veterinary Services (various years). *Administrative Reports.*

———. *Quenquenniel Livestock Survey.* From the department website.

———. Sixteenth Livestock Census, 1997.

Department of Cooperatives (2003). *List of Co-operative Societies.* December.

———. *Co-operative Awareness Campaign 2001.*

———. *Achievement Report for 1999-2000.*

———. The Sikkim Co-operative Societies Act, 1978.

Department of Economics and Statistics. *Economic Survey of Sikkim*

———. *Manpower Survey.*

Indian Council of Agricultural Research. *Profile of Infrastructure & Achievements.* Sikkim.

Indo Swiss Project-Sikkim (ISPS) (various years). *Annual Report, 2001-02 and 2002-03,* Swiss Agency for Development and Co-operation and Govt. of Sikkim.

———. (2001). Disease Investigation & Health Management System Implementation, December.

———. (2001). Project Document, Phase III, November.

———. (2002). *Medicine Survey Report.* May.

———. (2003). *Cattle Breeding Operations- An Evaluation.* March.

———. MIS for Department of Animal Husbandry and Veterinary Sciences,

———. *Value Addition & Strengthening of Processing Facilities in the Livestock Sector.*

———. *A Study on the Availability of Medicines and Veterinary Services.* With the Department of Animal Husbandry and Veterinary Sciences and Drishti (NGO).

IDFC. *Agri-Export Zone for Ginger in Sikkim.* Food and Agriculture Division.

———. *Agri-Export Zone for Cardamom in Sikkim.* Food and Agriculture Division.

Kaul, G.L. *et al.* (eds.) (1998). *Strategies for Horticulture Development in India.* New Delhi: Department of Agriculture & Co-operation, Ministry of Agriculture.

Lama, Mahendra P. (2001). *Sikkim Human Development Report 2001.* New Delhi: Social Science Press.

Lata, Kusum, Sanjay Mande and V.V.N. Kishore (1999). *Studies on Quality Improvement of Large Cardamom using an Advanced Gasifier-based Dryer.* New Delhi: Tata Energy Research Institute.

National Synergies Limited. *Agri Export Zone for Floriculture & Cherry Pepper in Sikkim, A Proposal.* Chennai.

Planning Commission. *Tenth Plan Document for Sikkim.*

———. Background Note for Annual Plan 2003-04 for Sikkim,

Rai, Suresh Chand, *et al.* (1998). *Sikkim: Perspectives for Planning and Development.* Sikkim: Sikkim Science Society.

Chapter 9

Industry and Trade

9.1 Importance of Industry and Trade

Despite decent growth rate and appreciable levels of human development, unemployment and poverty continue to be issues of utmost concern for the state. The share of the tertiary sector has grown, driven mainly by the public sector, while the share of the primary sector has shrunk with the share of secondary sector remaining stagnant. Within the secondary sector, the share of manufacturing has declined because of an abysmal drop in its growth rate (Chapter 3).[1] Hilly terrain with 80 per cent forest cover, geographical seclusion and inadequate infrastructure have hindered the industrial growth in a state where 80 per cent of the population depend on agriculture and allied activities for their livelihood. As a growing number of educated youths enter the job market along with rural-urban migration, stepping up of the level of economic activities in the state is the only panacea for eradicating unemployment and poverty. Notwithstanding a high share of government expenditure in terms of GSDP, the expansionary impact on the economy remains limited mainly because of high import intensity of expenditure (Chapter 4: Fiscal Management).

The state has a huge potential for industry in areas where the state enjoys a comparative advantage. The major endowments of the state are its nature and natural resources, flora and fauna, and the people. The state has also a huge potential for hydel power. The prospect of opening up of the border trade through Nathu La poses both challenges and opportunities for the state. It is in this context that the importance of industry and trade lies in optimal use of its resources and making the most of the emerging opportunities to realise the state's potential to accelerate growth and ensuring livelihood to all. Furthermore, it is through the promotion of industry and trade which would ensure smooth transition of the state from being overwhelmingly dependent on the public sector to a vibrant economy based on private sector initiative, enterprise, and entrepreneurship.

This chapter deals with industry, its potential and policy prescriptions for the government to act upon. The chapter begins with a critical assessment of the state's potential and handicaps. This is followed by an attempt to identify some core industries that the state should focus on in the short and medium term. A policy framework is spelt out. Since employment generation is crucially linked to the level of economic activity in the state, the chapter ends with employment related issues.

9.2 Status of Industry

As on end March 1996, there were 1683 provisionally registered and 313 permanently registered private sector industrial units, 14 state level public sector enterprises (SLPEs) and no central government units. As per the Economic Survey 2003-04, there are 320 provisionally registered industries and 363 permanently registered. Out of which, only 225 registered industrial units are functioning.

There was a spurt in setting up of the industries during 1999-2000 to avail of the concessions, which was not sustained as mainly the fly-by-night operators set up shops to take advantage of the concessions based regime.[2]

1. The other two components, construction and water and gas supply registered higher growth rates.

2. A rough indication of how the enterprises are doing can be gleaned from the sample of enterprises surveyed. Compared to the other N E states the enterprises in the state were not doing badly. Results obtained from NSS 55th Round indicate a comparative picture of Sikkim among the NE states (Table A-3).

The NSS 55th round survey for non-agricultural enterprises in the informal sector reveals the composition of the industry (Table A-39). Quite expectedly, the shares of trading and hotels and restaurants are higher than all India averages. The shares are low for manufacturing, real estate and health. The industry-wise composition of the workforce also sheds light on the composition of the industries (see Chapter 3).

9.3 'Sickness Syndrome'

The state industry is afflicted with what the *Sikkim Human Development Report* (SHDR) referred to as 'sickness syndrome.' The state is seriously handicapped in many respects, which are generally considered to be essentials for industrial development. The policy packages announced by the state from time to time have mainly focused on giving concessions of various kinds, while the major handicaps, such as inadequate infrastructure, poor connectivity, absence of a marketing network, availability of land continue to remain areas of major concern. A proper assessment of the constraints is imperative to design the policy framework as well as the potential of industrial development in the state and suggest directions.

9.3.1 Size of the Market

It is often argued that insufficient purchasing power or inadequate size of the market acts as a disincentive for the prospective investors. Given the average purchasing capacity of the population, which is rather small by any reckoning, geographical fragmentation of the market, the size of the internal market is limited. Therefore, it is mainly the market outside the state, both within and outside the country that the industries should be looking forward to cater to. However, one additional source of demand within the state would be forthcoming from the tourists. Since the share of government expenditure is pretty high in terms of GSDP, the level of activity and composition of domestic demand are influenced by government spending. However, the multiplier impact remains limited due to relatively high import intensity of expenditure and leakages (Chapter 4).

9.3.2 Input Availability

The choice of appropriate industries should be largely based on the availability of raw materials within the state. Availability of minerals is limited and moreover, minerals based industries may lead to pollution. Even otherwise, the state is not suited for heavy industry. However, the crucial inputs that the state can make available for industry are its manpower, rich varieties of flora and fauna and various horticultural produce. Sikkim has a potential for medicinal herbs (Chapter 8).

Labour is considerably cheap in Sikkim compared to the other north-eastern states (Table A-37). In fact, estimated wage rate from the sample of industries surveyed is lower than that of per capita income of the state. Though this gives a competitive edge to the industry, the flip side is low level of income of the workers in the state.[3]

9.3.3 Land

Hilly terrain with 80 per cent forest cover explains why land is at a premium in the state. One of the most important issues, which comes up for consideration whenever an investor decides to invest in the state is the availability of land as per requirements. Land cannot be sold to the outsiders as per local laws. Suitable plots of land for industries are, unfortunately the fertile ones in the south and east districts near the exit points of the state (Chapter 8). Land in north and some parts of west districts are rugged and not conveniently located, and, therefore not suitable for setting up of industries. Industries have to compete with very little land that is available for cultivation and cattle rearing (Chapter 8).

9.3.4 Poor Physical Infrastructure

Better infrastructure provides better support for the industries and brings down the costs of conducting business. Procuring raw materials, manufacturing and selling products, entail adequate infrastructure. Road, power, and communications are the crucial ones. The *Vision Document (2001)* emphasised that without proper infrastructure in place, it is unlikely that industrial activity in the state would gain momentum. Negative growth for manufacturing notwithstanding various concessional packages is a testimony to this (Chapter 3). Information is scanty both for the small producers scattered mostly in the east, south and west districts as well as for the prospective investors and buyers from outside the state. In fact, in the absence of a marketing network, adequate storage facilities and processing units, the raw materials produced in the state end up getting processed outside the state.

3. Assam and Tripura are the other two states where labour is still cheaper. What is interesting is that the per capita value addition in Sikkim is considerably high. This indicates that per capita non-wage income (which is equivalent to surplus) is pretty high in the state compared to the other north-eastern states.

The supply of power is often deficient and erratic. Due to limited industrialisation, demand for power mainly originates from household consumption. Existing supply of power may turn out to be inadequate if industrial activity picks up.

9.3.5 *Marketing Network*

Poor connectivity, geographical fragmentation and scarcity of information have impeded the development of a proper marketing network. Marketing of products poses a major problem for the producers mainly because of the poor connectivity within the state and also with the outside world. Middlemen often provide crucial links between the farmers and the buyers but at the expense of lower prices for the producers. It erodes competitiveness of the products both in the national and international market (Chapter 7). However, these are some inevitable problems associated with poor road connectivity in a mountainous state like Sikkim.

9.3.6 *Human Capital and Entrepreneurship*

Despite attainment of reasonably high levels of human development, there are areas where there is shortage of skill. People are often found to be inadequately trained to ensure higher productivity, and adopt the latest in science and technology. Particularly, in agriculture and animal husbandry, field level officers are often not adequately trained resulting in poor extension services. Higher yield and generation of surpluses would act as incentives for the farmers as well as make the units viable (Chapter 8).

It is often argued that people of the state lack entrepreneurship. Overwhelming dominance of public sector is argued to have sapped people's enterprise and entrepreneurship. However, entrepreneurship can be inculcated and there are instances that private enterprises can be successful. Though, opportunities for vocational training and entrepreneurial development facilities have come up based on the initiatives of the state government, skill shortages still exist. Quality education is a rare commodity available mainly in the urban areas.

9.3.7 *Law and Order*

Sikkim is a politically stable state with virtually no law and order problem as people are peace loving. The state does not suffer from any labour related problem either. Sikkim probably is the only state in the north-eastern areas, which is free from any insurgency related problems.

9.3.8 *Availability of Loans*

Cumbersome loan disbursement procedure and the dominance of moneylenders have contributed to relatively low credit to deposit ratio in the state. To ensure easy availability of loans to the entrepreneurs at a reasonable rate of interest, the state government has taken initiative with the launching of Chief Minister's Self-employment Scheme. Poor recovery may also deter commercial banks from adopting an investor friendly attitude.

9.3.9 *Problems: What does the Survey Reveal*

The NSS 55th Round Survey results may shed light on the kind and nature of problems the state producing units are facing (Table A-36).[4] For own account enterprises (OAE), shortage of capital and lack of infrastructure facilities seem to be the major hurdles. For larger units, (i.e., establishments) the problems are much less severe. The other major problem being faced by the enterprises is that of competition from larger units. It is mainly the import from other states that the state enterprises have to compete with. It also appears that the larger units need to cope up with shortage and irregular supply of power.

9.4 Identifying Appropriate Industries

Given the fragility of the ecosystem, the approach towards industry should be a cautious one and primarily environment friendly. Industries should be entirely pollution free and effluents should be bare minimum with nature friendly disposal of wastes. The strategy would be to build on state's comparative advantages in terms of raw materials and cheap labour surmounting state's handicaps. In other words, promotion of the industries should be in tune with the development strategy being delineated in this report.

As per the Tenth Five-Year Plan document and the industrial policy of the state, possible thrust areas have been identified in consonance with the long-term development strategy that the state is pursuing. They are as follows:

(a) Agro-based industries including horticulture and floriculture, (b) minor forest-based industries, (c) animal husbandry and dairy products, (d) tourism related industries, (e) information technology including

4. Since the results are based on sample, conclusions derived there from are indicative only.

knowledge based industries, (f) precision oriented high value low volume products, (g) hydel power, (h) tea, (i) education, and (j) hospitality, etc.[5]

However, the state should focus on certain key industries based on their potentials for employment generation, relative comparative advantage, and overall impact on the state economy.

9.4.1 Potential for Agro-processing

Given the large share of agriculture and allied activities in state income, proven potential in producing commercial crops and untapped potential in flora and fauna, potential of agro-based industries is enormous. The primary advantage of agro-based industries is the availability of necessary raw materials in the state.

Floriculture has a high potential as demand in India and abroad would continue to grow.[6] The state produces varieties of orchids, gladioli, anthuriums and rhododendrons. Commercial cultivation is rapidly picking up. However, storage and marketing remain crucial for successful ventures. Given the paucity of land, the possibility of cooperative type cultivation of orchids needs to be explored.

The food processing industry is competitive in the presence of large and established producers. The state may specialise in mandarin oranges, ginger, tea, and cardamom. However, traditional methods of cultivation and poor quality inputs have resulted in low yields (Chapter 8). In terms of prospects, medicinal and aromatic herbs will face an ever-expanding market both nationally and internationally. The varieties of medicinal plants available in the state need to be taken stock of. So far, there has not been any attempt to exploit this potential commercially. Similarly the potential of producing honey can be explored at the individual level. Processing can be at a medium or large scale but the collection has to be from the local farmers who will also be the beneficiaries of the industrialisation. Wool and silk reeling, weaving and processing, and rabbit farming, all these activities may be carried out at the farm level and they may be treated as the primary or secondary sources of livelihood. The objective would be to provide people with multiple sources of income.[7] The marketing constraint seems to have deterred the development of these industries.

9.4.2 Potential for Eco-Tourism

Ideal climate and natural beauty of the state augurs well for the tourism industry in the state (Chapter 10). The green image of the state with emphasis on village tourism has made the state an attractive destination both nationally and internationally. Though the concept of eco-tourism is yet to be found popular among the majority of the tourists who come from West Bengal, the state should continue to assign high priority to it. The multiplier impact of tourism with immense potential for employment generation in a regionally balanced manner would make tourism the leading industry, the state should be focussing on.

9.4.3 Potential for Knowledge Industries

The state has already made great strides in the knowledge-based industries such as information technology. The state can gain from the advantage of skilled manpower, which has shown potential for the IT industry. Moreover, given the climate, promotion of knowledge-based industries would enable the state to bypass most of the handicaps the state is afflicted with. A software technology park is being set up which will have wide-bandwidth, stable power supply and incubation space for entrepreneurs. The department is also promoting IT-enabled services like medical transcription, telemedicine, and computerised braille.

9.4.4 Precision Engineering including Watch Making

Increasing competition in the domestic market has made Sikkim Time Corporation (SITCO), a successful venture, vulnerable in the recent times. However, SITCO does not face any stiff competition from imported watches. However, the producers in the watch manufacturing industry can outsource cheap but skilled labour and congenial climate would be the major sources of attractions for those who would prefer Sikkim. In the recent period, SITCO has gone for diversification in a big way. Manufacturing TV and speakers in collaboration with BPL along with the production of crown jewel are some of the products SITCO has started manufacturing. Skilled manpower at the top level and reduction in transportation costs would be necessary for further growth (Box 9.1).

---

5. This is not an exhaustive list.
6. India is also importing large quantities of flowers mainly from the South East Asian countries.
7. As announced in the Budget for 2004-05, the Anand model may be replicated in the state in a big way given strong local bodies and scattered households and paucity of land.

9.4.5 *Sikkim as a Hub for Education Industry*

Setting up of boarding schools in the Himalayas has contributed to the growth of many hill stations in India. Darjeeling, Mussorie, Shimla would testify this. Promotion of the state as a hub for education would not put strain on state resources other than land, as it has the potential for contributing towards promotion of tourism industry as well. The setting up of the Manipal Institute of Technology is an endorsement of this.

BOX 9.1

SITCO and Sikkim Precision Industries Limited (SPIL): A Mixed Story!

SPIL was set up in December, 2001 by the initiative of the state government for manufacturing ophthalmic lenses at a project cost of Rs. 3.7 crore at Namchi, the south district headquarter. Number of employees employed increased subsequently to 102. After it was found that the demand for ophthalmic lenses was insufficient, the unit started producing power devices in collaboration with BHEL. Industries based on the inherent strength of the state are expected to perform well. A visit to the unit raised pertinent issues, which are important for assessing the potential of the state in producing light, but high value products. The capacity utilisation of the unit in 2002-03 was merely 50 per cent. Since the unit produces only TO 202 chips for BHEL, capacity utilisation depends naturally on the demand for this chip from BHEL. The percentage of acceptance of the products at 93.4 per cent is higher than what is required by BHEL, which is a mere 90 per cent. SPIL has an installed capacity of 100 lakh per annum. The import of cheap products from China may have contributed to the dampening of demand. Though labour is cheap, high transport costs and continuity of workers on the rolls, despite zero production have eroded the profitability. Future seems to be bleak as the unit produces only one type of product, the demand for which depends on the demand from BHEL. Diversification is necessary for survival. Tying up with other electronic giants may be helpful. A pro-labour policy speaks volume of the altruistic nature of the state. In the long run, SPIL may become another sick unit unless serious steps are taken.

On the other hand, SITCO is a success story, which was established in 1977 in collaboration with HMT for assembly of watches. Diversification and aggressive marketing have ensured success. The unit has achieved production of 6 lakh watches per year.

9.4.6 *Sikkim as a Hub for Healthcare Industry*

In line with the argument for development of education industry, the promotion of healthcare industry can also fetch good returns for the state. The ideal climate coupled with easy availability of non-medical support staff can make Sikkim an ideal destination for the healthcare industry. Availability of medicinal herbs and herbal treatment including yoga, meditation, spa and massage, would further contribute to the credence of the state in the healthcare industry. However, till the state acquires air connectivity, the healthcare industry may focus on treatment of those suffering from non-critical illnesses or those who require prolonged treatment or those that are recuperating.

9.4.7 *Handicraft and Handloom Industry*

The handicraft and handloom industry has the potential to promote income and employment generation in a big way. The high quality traditional handicrafts and handloom products enjoy a good market, both nationally and internationally. The traditional crafts like carpet weaving, cane and bamboo crafts, spinning wool, handmade paper and *Thanka* paintings are famous and enjoy government patronage in as far as training is concerned. A proficient manpower base is already available in this field. All that is required is organisation of expertise so that quality and design can be upgraded. Professionals in the field of marketing and supply could work wonders with the traditional industry of Sikkim. However, marketing of product depends on the growth of tourism, promotion outside the state by the government and adequate supply of input and infrastructure support. Gangtok Craft Fair and modernisation of looms are steps in the right direction. Sikkim has to focus on 'product differentiation' as Sikkim faces competition from other north-eastern states.

9.4.8 *Investment Opportunities in the Post Nathu La Trade Route Reopening*[8]

The reopening of the Nathu La trade route after 44 years on July 6, 2006 has brought unprecedented opportunities for Sikkim both in terms of exchange of goods and services and also on cross border investment. There are marked potentials of investment activities on both sides of the border in Sikkim and Tibet Autonomous region of China. Despite so many concessions offered under liberal investment policies by the Government of Sikkim, very few investors have participated in the state in the past. One of the main reasons attributed to the shyness of investment in the state is very limited market options. Therefore, after the

8. Lama, 2005.

Nathu La trade is reopened, Tibet and mainland China will act as additional marketing outlets. This is bound to encourage and trigger investment activities in Sikkim and surrounding areas.

The reopening of Nathu La pass trade route is going to be a major addition in the basket of confidence building measures between India and China. Besides the strategic and commercial gains for the country, Sikkim, Eastern and North East India have much to celebrate in this new vista of cooperation. This is the first major cross border opening for the region as a whole which could bring in massive gains in terms of exchange of goods and services. If integrated with tourism activities particularly the Buddhist circuit, this could be the world's most magnificent eco-tourism sojourn interspersed with nature, culture and economics.[9]

It would be particularly naïve to expect traditional items like yak tail and goat skins to dominate the trade exchange through the Nathu La route. Even Tibet is no more a market for religious/cultural items alone. It is a growing market that absorb cement to latest cars and from *yerchagon bu* to tulips. The composition of products could in fact be much varied than that exists at the bilateral national level as this route could cater to very specific needs and demands in a much quicker and cheaper manner than other national routes.[10]

It will be a mere historical negation and impractical assumption to think this trade as a limited interactions among the communities that inhabit the borders. This was the assumption in the border trade between Nepal and Tibet at Khasa and India and Myanmar at Moreh (Manipur). However, the actual volume, composition and direction of trade in these routes have far surpassed the local communities and local products. They do not at all reflect the border trade phenomenon. Restrictions have only encouraged the illegal and surreptitious aspects of trade. However, given the level of infrastructure on the Indian side and the wretched condition of the road particularly the 50.6 Km stretch between Gangtok and Nathu La, it would be highly unrealistic to expect a brisk trading instantly.[11]

Tourists are likely to make beeline to watch how trade actually takes place at the cross border marts at Sherathang (India) and Renqinggang (China). The trade corridors therefore, need to be highly regulated and its activities synchronised in order to ensure unhindered tourist flow. The income effects on roadside hotels and restaurants, handicrafts and transport and communication and many other backward and forward linkages are likely to be immense. Sikkim could gradually emerge as a dry port.

As usual there are *staus quoists* with insurmountable mindsets. Their arguments against reviving this traditional trade route vary from security to influx of Tibetan refugees and flooding of local markets by cheap Chinese goods to environmental concerns. It were the same mindsets that literally marginalised India in Myanmar where the former once had unparallel historical strongholds, political and social constituency and substantive economic influence. India should have in fact long harnessed these huge cross border opportunities. Prime Minister Manmohan Singh's well acclaimed plea for cross border infrastructure projects in the last SAARC Summit in Dhaka belatedly yet definitely recognises this clamour for lost opportunities.

One should not be unaware of the fact that this local integration strategy of China including with Taiwan, Myanmar, Hong Kong, Vietnam, Thailand, Laos, Indonesia and Korea have paid them handsomely. There are examples galore like that of South China Growth Triangle (SCGT), Greater Mekong Basin Growth Triangle (GMBGT) and Golden Quadrangle. The northern Chinese provinces of Heilongjiang, Xinjiang and Inner Mongolia have been in the forefront of border trading with Russia and other central Asian republics.[12]

While inaugurating the trade marts for Nathu La trade on 6 July 2006, the Chief Minister Pawan Chamling remarked that "we expect that this trade route will change the basic structure of the Sikkimese economy by refocusing on our comparative advantages like scientific harnessing of natural resources, emphasis on ecotourism and other service related activities. We also strongly feel that over the years, Sikkim could be a major trading zone like Singapore. We are therefore, proposing to set up a Special Economic Zone where many of the small and medium enterprise from both India and abroad could be located."[13]

9. Lama, 2006a.
10. Lama, 2006b.
11. Lama, 2006c.
12. Lama, 2006d.
13. Address by Dr. Pawan Chamling, Hon'ble Chief Minister of Sikkim on the Occasion of the Inauguration of Trade Mart at Sherathang (after the Reopening of Nathu La Trade Route) Between Sikkim (India) & Tibet Autonomous Region (China) on Thursday, 06 July 2006 at Nathu La, Information and Public Relations Department, Government of Sikkim, Gangtok, 2006.

Even if Sikkim is not able to produce things that cater to these new markets across the border in the initial stage, it could encourage the location of (within the state) last segment of value chain including assembling, packaging and branding and distribution of any manufactured or any semi-manufactured products meant for exports through Nathu La. This itself will generate substantial income and a major employment opportunity in the state. Over the years, consistent effort should be made to make Sikkim and the surrounding northeastern States as a centre for small and medium enterprises (SMEs) that could cater to multinational companies.

The Confederation of Indian Industry (CII) is setting up a pan-Indian taskforce with leading industrialists from other regions to draw a roadmap for investment activities in North Bengal against the backdrop of reopening of Nathu La trade. The CII is envisaging the strengthening of infrastructure in Siliguri to make it a transhipment hub for all trade through Nathu La. It has also urged the government to speed up work on the 600 km north-south corridor connecting Haldia and Siliguri. The CII has also set up its Shanghai office for larger business activities.[14]

The Nathu La trade related investment could be on diverse areas including construction materials, food processing units, and forest products. There are ample opportunities for investment in Tibet autonomous region in areas of agriculture, forestry, animal husbandry and aquaculture, chemical industry, mining, building material and printing industry; Two way investment in food & medicines industry; tourism, trade and service industry, infrastructure and culture.

9.5 Policy Initiatives—Present and Past: A Critical Analysis

In the 'New Industrial Policy' announced during the Ninth Plan period, special emphasis was given to small scale sector and cottage industries. The Industrial Policy (2003) outlines the present policy statement of the state for the Tenth Plan period. In addition, various types of concessions given by the centre for the north-eastern states are applicable to the state as well. Combined effect of both the central and state industrial policies would have considerable effect on profitability of the enterprises. A 'White Paper' on industrial development and sick industries was tabled in the state legislative assembly in 1998. Notwithstanding, past experience has been disheartening. During the eighties, those who set up units to take advantage of the prevailing policy regime loaded in favour of fiscal concessions, turned out to be `fly-by-night' operators. Industries set up purely to take advantage of fiscal concessions will be motivated by short term objectives detrimental to the long-term interests of the state. Steps are to be initiated to prevent this from happening again. There are instances of success stories among the SLPEs (such as SITCO and Sikkim Distilleries) as well as instances of successful entrepreneurship without any assistance from the government, for example, 'Tripti Bakery.' A number of sick industrial units have been revived.

However, certain policy guidelines may be indicated. Given the state's potential, the present performance of the state industry is way off the mark. Though there are instances of successes, there are more instances where the units are sick and facing closure. While the concessions based policy is a prerequisite to enable the industries to overcome the constraints encountered typically in a hilly state, improvements in the basic infrastructure facilities, such as connectivity and marketing network, should be given top priority.

While most of the SLPEs are in a bad shape, performances of some of them are satisfactory. The state's decision regarding the sick units is awaited. However, the promulgation of the Disinvestment Policy (2003) has provided a policy framework to act on the sick enterprises. With the withdrawal of central subsidy scheme in 1988 by the Government of India, the state lost its attractiveness to the investors. Budgetary provisions are required for successful implementation of the scheme. It may also be noted that the state should sift the applications and discourage those with short-term interests. Budgetary assistance is also required for the rehabilitation of sick units, in case they are found viable. What is lacking is a prompt action by the government as this puts pressure on the budgetary situation of the state. An outlay of Rs. 10 crore have been set aside for this purpose during the Tenth Plan period.

As per the new industrial policy, Sikkim Industrial Promotion and Incentive Act 2000, incentives and concessions have been provided for the investors (Box 9.2). It also appears from the budget that the thrust is on providing fiscal incentives. The government had meetings with CII, ASSOCHAM, and FICCI to find out the possibility of private investment in the state. Some of the policy directions that the state can think of initiating are discussed in the following section.

14. *The Telegraph*, Siliguri, July 15, 2003.

BOX 9.2

Sikkim Industrial Policy

Notwithstanding several attempts by the government to promote industries in the state, the performance has been unsatisfactory. However, unmistakably there are some bright rays of hope. A comparison with the 2000 policy is imperative to ascertain what went wrong and how the pitfalls of the earlier policy regime are being surmounted. It has been empirically observed that industries are attracted towards the state on the basis of location, connectivity, power, availability of cheap input, an enabling framework and market. Concessions are actually arising on the cake. For Sikkim, concessions based policy package is necessary. The question, which remains to be answered is whether the sub-optimal performance is a reflection of a failure of the policy package or is it due to the inherent weaknesses of the state. Success depends on entrepreneurship and a pro-active government.

The Sikkim Industrial Promotion and Incentive (Amendment) Act, 2003.

The elements of concessions are:

Subsidy on state capital investment: to be provided on total investment to both new as well as those carrying out modernisation activities.

Subsidy on captive power generating sets: government shall subsidise up to 25 per cent of the cost for purchase of power generating sets. For local entrepreneurs, subsidy will be 50 per cent subject to a maximum of Rs. 2 lakh.

Special incentive to pioneer unit.

Special incentive for women entrepreneurs: additional state capital investment subsidy of 5 per cent subject to a ceiling of Rs. 5 lakh which constitute more than 50 per cent of the workforce in the industry.

Stipendiary support to EDP: stipend at the rate of Rs. 5001 per month per trainee shall be provided for training 100 youths annually.

Reimbursement of stamp duty and registration fee: small scale, village, and cottage industrial units will be reimbursed in full amount paid towards the said taxes.

Local employment promotion grant: the government will reimburse annually up to 30 per cent of the realistic wage bill for local employees.

Subsidy on cost incurred on quality control measures: cost of laboratory unit for the purpose of quality control and ISI certification subject to a maximum of Rs. 10,000.

And consultancy measures, study tours and in plant training power.

Special incentives for agro and food processing industries.

Allotment of land: Cost of land development to the tune of 25 per cent for small-scale industries.

And State transport among other things. State capital investment provides for subsidy, which varies across the size of the industries, such as, artisan and tiny scale units, small-scale units and medium and large-scale units. Local entrepreneurships and investment in the area of identified sectors are encouraged.

Besides these, as per North East Industrial Policy, there are income tax and excise tax concessions. It may however be noted that Income Tax of GoI is not applicable in the state.

Source: SIDICO (2003). *New Industrial Policy and Other Concessions for the State of Sikkim*

9.6 Newer Approaches

Policy directions should be in tune with the objective of the state to create an enabling policy framework for fostering eco-friendly industrial development with special emphasis on employment generation. Focus only on policy making will not be effective. Provision of infrastructure and empowerment of individuals through skill formation will be complementary to each other for sustained industrialisation. Policies directed towards individuals would be referred to as micro-level policy and those aiming to create an enabling framework would be referred to as macro-level policy.

9.6.1 Micro-level Policy Making

Provision of Inputs and Information

The first step for promotion of industries based on local entrepreneurship would be to provide inputs and information to the entrepreneurs. This is how cost and uncertainty of doing business in the state can be reduced. Identified individuals desirous of undertaking investments may be provided with the requisite inputs preferably at a price, credit, and information regarding production and marketing of products.

Role of Community Information Centre (CICs) and the Local Bodies

As hinted above, given household specific characteristics, the focus should be on enrichment of each and every household through identification of multiple sources of income. The rural local bodies (PRIs) may take a stock of the situation in their respective constituencies to identify the production potential of households.[15] Ultimately, the objective should be to integrate each and every household within a supply chain of, for example, medicinal herbs, or, orchids to the overall procurement from that area. The CICs may disseminate information to the potential investors as well as potential buyers regarding the availability and price of raw materials in the respective areas.

Emphasis on Skill Formation and Development of Entrepreneurship

To ensure success of the local initiatives, proper training in respective areas is a prerequisite. Depending on the areas, the potential entrepreneurs should be required to undergo training for conduct of business. In a highly competitive world where the latest in the science and technology is effecting rapid changes in the world, basic training in computers, language proficiency and commerce are necessary. Vocational training or manpower development should continue to be given priority. Information about trained personnel at the *panchayat* level/district level should be collated and used for selecting people for giving loans/seed capital. Since the regions vary in terms of their comparative advantages and deficiencies, choice of streams/disciplines in vocational training should be accordingly determined. Skill formation in consonance with the demand for skills expected to be forthcoming in the course of growth of the identified industries is required.

The stress on inculcating entrepreneurship has to be viewed in the context of redefining the role of the government. However, jobs in the public sector have been made available from time to time mainly on the basis of patronage, giving wrong signals to young aspirants that jobs are indeed available in the government. Surely there are areas where the government needs to expand its participation and activities particularly in the social sector, the demand for which is unlikely to be met merely by redeployment of surplus staff. There have been many initiatives in the recent past mainly at the behest of SIDICO to train people and provide them with loans/seed capital so as to enable them to undertake business ventures. Training programmes are also organised to take care of this by organisation such as, Small Scale Industrial Service Institute (SSISI), NABARD, and SMIT on a regular basis.

9.6.2 Macro-level Policy Making

However, individuals with necessary skills and capital can be successful only in a business environment, the development of which requires provision of land, development of growth centres, and attracting big investors with requisite knowledge and expertise. To avoid over-industrialisation, which can disturb the fragile ecological balance of the state, environmental accounting/auditing should be undertaken. It is also necessary to find out how much is the capacity of the state to ensure sustainable development because after all it is the 'green image' of the state, which will foster tourism, education, and hospitality industry. Some of the suggestions are given below.

Developing the Growth Centres

Growth centres should be developed on a priority basis. This is how the state can surmount two major constraints—land and infrastructure. This will also help in reaping the economies of scale in disposal and treatment of effluents, provision of power and other physical infrastructure in an environment friendly and efficient manner. The tardy growth of the growth centres is mainly because of non-availability of land and inadequate resources to purchase land. However, it has been agreed in principle that the cost of land should be included in the project cost. Two more industrial estates have been identified in other parts of Sikkim under the electronics and fruit processing sectors. Rs. 3 crore has been allocated during the Tenth Five Year Plan for this purpose.

The state government has already identified areas for setting up of growth centres. The new industrial policy, provides a list of locations for setting up of the new industrial units.[16] However, the response of the state

15. One household can go for production of medicinal herbs, whereas the other one may be more suitable for dairy farming.

16. Recently even this policy remained on paper when an investor who expressed his willingness to invest in floriculture in a growth centre near Gangtok could not be provided with the land. Worth mentioning is the recent initiative of the government to buy land for setting up industries in Marchak in the East district. The government has sanctioned Rs. 15 crore for this purpose.

machinery has been far from satisfactory. What is required by the government is to show genuine willingness to make land available to the investors. The government has already declared Rangpo-Gangtok, Meli-Jorethang and Jorethang-Rishi as industrial corridors for giving the land to the investors on a leasehold basis.

The developed land will be allotted on a leased basis for a period of thirty years. The state government will subsidise the cost of land depending on the nature of industries. For small-scale industries, it is 25 per cent, export-oriented units and units managed by local entrepreneurs at the rate 30 per cent and large and medium units at the rate of 15 per cent. Other than this, one more option the state can think of is, to ensure that the landowners are made partners in business.

Investment Board

The state has constituted a high level Board of Investment (BoI) headed by the Chief Minister himself to facilitate the investment proposals in a friendly and straightforward manner under its single window policy. This Board needs to be further strengthened by inducting members from private sector and other professionals in areas like legal actions, finance, environment and technology management. It may also entertain complaints and grievances and seek their redressal. The Board may also advise the respective departments and ensure better coordination among the departments and explore both the domestic as well as international market. This information would help building up the marketing network and alleviate uncertainty from the minds of the investors. For successful ventures, preparation of the project reports may be insisted upon or at least the committee should guide the loan applicants or investors if the amount exceeds, Rs. 50 lakh.

Procedures have been simplified to make it more investor friendly. What was, however observed, is the lack of coordination among the departments and speedy disposal of cases/files. It was also observed that if implementation is time consuming, the investors might even withdraw. The state must be vigilant about this aspect.

Inviting the Market Leaders

In certain areas, the state can invite the market leaders where large investments are the requisite required to make them competitive. Furthermore, the leaders can bring with them expertise and knowledge. Exploring the market would cease to be a problem for these enterprises. This would be relevant for industries such as education and healthcare industry, production of medicinal herbs.

Provision of Loans

The upper limit for grant of loan is Rs. 90 lakh for an individual units, which often turns out to be inadequate for setting up of medium sized plants. What is more important is the tendency to set up *manihari* shops or, grocery shops with the loan amount. The impact on value addition and employment is limited from such trading activities. However, the inclusion of Sikkim in the NEC means that there is one more institution (NEDFI which has a branch office at Gangtok) to channelise resources. This will hopefully ease the credit constraint for industrial development in the state. The performance of SIDICO has been commendable. The strategy should be to enhance the quantum of loanable funds to be given as loans so that greater number of loan seekers can be covered.

Allocation under the Eleventh Five Year Plan

Adequate allocation as per sanction and its utilisation has to be ensured for industry during the Eleventh Five Year Plan.

Marketing Network

Marketing network requires setting up of an institutional set up both within the state as well as tying up with the potential customers outside the state so that the producers, traders and retailers constitute a network for the purpose of conducting business. Guaranteeing market through better roads and marketing network is probably the best motivating factor for the investors.

Recommendations

- There are tremendous investment opportunities in areas like: educational institutions; professional-technical institutions like medical, IIT, engineering, information technology; and management institutions; banking-financial institutions; hydel power; medicinal plants and herbal medicines; organic farming; trading activities within the country and across the border; transport and communication; science and technology including biotechnology; health; manpower development; horticulture; floriculture; mountaineering and trekking; agriculture and allied activities; industries including small and medium enterprises (SMEs) and tourism.

BOX 9.3

The AEZs for Large Cardamom and Ginger

The AEZs will provide a continuous supply chain for farmers across identified contiguous production areas. Farmers growing ginger or large cardamom will be grouped into identified producer blocks, which will be linked to rural markets or *apni mandis* (7 in the large cardamom producing areas and 11 in the ginger areas). These in turn will be linked, depending on their location, to the wholesale market at Rangpo and the one proposed to be set up at Melli.

To strengthen the export potential of these crops, the zones, to be located at Rangpo/Singtam, and Melli, will have post-harvest handling and storage facilities for both the products and their processing. Laboratory facilities will be provided to test water, soil, and quality of the produce, and agri-information centres will disseminate market information to farmers *via apni mandis*. A ginger processing plant will be set up at Singtam fruit processing factory, with a grading and packaging unit to prepare the produce for export.

The advantages of this approach are several: apart from the value addition effects on income and revenues, there is the demonstration effect that the introduction of modern facilities of processing, quality production analysis, storage and packaging will have on farmers' awareness and motivation.

Organic farming once it takes off in the state can avail of the facilities of the AEZ to ensure greater standardisation and improved quality, and commercial packaging and labelling for sale through supermarkets and organic chains.

The success of the AEZs will hinge on the awareness created among the farmers prior to the establishment of this infrastructure, about the beneficial effects of the entry of large investors. So far, farmers have been reluctant to rejuvenate or replant old plants, preferring to live off the declining incomes from the old plants. The setting up of an AEZ, which guarantees a market for the produce is likely to encourage replanting at a faster rate. It would be beneficial if the AEZ identified the final destination and supplied directly to them to maximise benefits to the state. The average price of exports to Pakistan is Rs. 1.14 lakh per tonne, while to UAE it is 2.5 lakh per tonne and Singapore it is Rs. 3.73 lakh per tonne. The price at the main market in Sikkim in Singtam varies from 0.9 to 1.75 lakh per tonne, depending on the quality.

Source: IDFC documents.

- In order to harness these opportunities the most crucial issue is that of providing all the investment facilitating measures including the provision of land by the State. The Board of Investment set up by the State Government has to be made proactive with substantive powers so that the decisions related to investment and other business ventures can be taken in a forthright manner.
- Disinvestment and privatisation in/of the scores of sick industries have to be carried out on an urgent basis.
- The State government must examine the case for setting up of Special Economic Zone (SEZ) against the backdrop of the reopening of the Nathu La trade route. This can serve as the major point for the both the export oriented activities and also a launching pad for investment ventures across the border.
- The State Government must work towards meeting the various actions suggested by the Nathu La Trade Study group towards harnessing the opportunities generated by the reopening of this trade route. These include the following:

2005-2010: Initiation of trading on both sides backed by existing and some additional infrastructures. Meanwhile start building wider and deeper infrastructural facilities.

2010: Trading on a larger scale start taking place based on upgraded and more developed infrastructures

2012: Integration of trade with tourism for which a fresh bilateral legal framework needs to be concluded to facilitate the movement of tourists across the border.

Package Tours: During 2012-2015, only Indian and Chinese tourists are permitted to cross the border through Nathu La on a package tour basis.

Open Tourism: 2015 onwards movement among Indian and Chinese tourists both on package and individual basis.

2015: Inclusion of movement of freights to and from the neighbouring countries including Bangladesh, Bhutan and Nepal through this route.

2018 onwards: *SAARC* tourism, integrate with tourism activities of third countries of the region including Bangladesh, Bhutan and Nepal. Open for all the tourists to cross the border.

Besides these the following measures must be undertaken on an urgent basis:

i) Drastic revision in the list of exports and imports so as to match the market realities on both sides of the border.

ii) Putting in place the most modern trade facilitating measures including customs, banking, warehousing, insurance, etc.

iii) A strong regulatory framework to oversee the entire trading and tourism operations.

iv) A constant monitoring of the likely impact of trading activities on smuggling, environment, social interactions and other security parameters.

- The State must start preparing itself for the sale/ export of huge surplus power likely to be generated in the next few years.
- Growth centres should be developed on a priority basis. This is how the state can surmount two major constraints—land and infrastructure.

References

Lama, Mahendra P. (2005). *Sikkim-Tibet Trade via Nathu La : A Policy Study on Prospects, Opportunities and Requisite Preparedness.* Prepared by Nathu La Trade Study Group for the Government of Sikkim. August.

———. (2006a). "Passing the Yuan", *Hindustan Times.* July 4.

———. (2006b). "The Forward Policy and South Asia", *Himal Southasian.* Kathmandu. September.

———. (2006c). 124 "Decentralised trade: Nathu La and China's "Local Integration" Strategy, *Tribune,* Chandigarh. October 17.

———. (2006d). "The Dragon's Local Turn: Hu's South Asia Visit Fits in with China's South Asia Plans", *DNA (Daily News and Analysis)*, Bombay. 20 November.

Chapter 10

Tourism

10.1 The Potential for Tourism

Tourism is well positioned to become a major source of employment and income generation in Sikkim. The state has rich natural and cultural resources, which have yet to be developed to their full tourism potential. The government has a clearly enunciated commitment to promoting ecotourism, village tourism and adventure tourism, which are increasingly becoming the new leisure time activities across the world. The central government has also considerably relaxed the permit systems, making it far easier for foreign and domestic tourists to travel to hitherto unexplored parts of Sikkim (Box 10.1). The reopening up of the Nathu La pass, with Lhasa only 527 km away on a motorable road, is expected to have a major effect on tourist traffic, as tourists from both sides of the border transit through the state as well as make it a target destination. The World Tourism and Travel Council has predicted that India is poised for high growth in tourism traffic: travel and tourism demand is expected to grow by 8.8 per cent per annum, in real terms, between 2004 and 2014.[1] Sikkim is in a good position to take advantage of this growth.

BOX 10.1

Relaxation of Entry Permits

While foreigners still require inner line permits to travel in Sikkim, rules for acquiring these permits have been eased. Foreigners can get inner line permits from any Indian mission abroad, any tourism office in the four metropolitan cities and at the border checkpoint at Rangpo. These permits can also be extended up to 45 days, at intervals of 15 days, by superintendents of police in any of the four districts of the state. The stipulated number of foreigners in a group applying for adventure tourism permits has also been reduced from four to two.

Source: Government of Sikkim website.

10.2 Importance for Balanced Growth: The Multiplier and Leakages

Tourism not only creates jobs in the tertiary sector, it also encourages growth in the primary and secondary sectors of the economy. This multiplier effect of tourism, in its simplest form, is the number of times money spent by a tourist circulates through the state's economy (Box 10.2). Money spent in a hotel helps to create jobs directly in the hotel, but it also creates jobs indirectly in other sectors. The hotel, for example, has to buy food from

BOX 10.2

Estimating the Tourism Multiplier

The total impact of tourism may be analysed in terms of direct, indirect, and induced benefits. The direct employment and income effects refer to the incremental income and employment generated in different sections of the tourism industry as a direct result of tourist spending. The indirect effects refer to the incremental effects in sectors supplying inputs to tourism. These input-supplying industries, in turn, require raw materials and intermediate supplies which they source from other industries, thus creating employment and income in the latter, and so on. The increased incomes in tourism and related sectors lead to increased consumption and demand in consumption in goods sectors, and this is the induced effect of tourism spending. The total effect (the sum of the direct, indirect and induced effects) is a multiple of the direct effect and is termed as multiplier.

Source: Tata Economic Consultancy Services (TECS) (1998). *Tourism Master Plan.*

1. WTTC: Travel and Tourism Economic Research, India 2004.

local farmers, who may in turn, spend some of this money on fertiliser or clothes. The demand for local products increases as tourists often buy souvenirs, which increases secondary employment. The multiplier effect continues until the money eventually 'leaks' from the economy through imports—the purchase of goods from outside the state.

Clearly, the multiplier's effectiveness on local employment and incomes is directly related to the extent to which demand can be met from within the state. The low level of industrial activity and agricultural surpluses in Sikkim mean that leakages from the regional economy are high as most of the goods and even services have to be 'imported' from outside the state to meet the tourism demand. The Tata Economic Consultancy Services study estimates the tourism multiplier in Sikkim at between 1.3 and 1.48.[2] In contrast, the tourism multiplier for the country has been estimated at approximately 3.5.

Its tremendous unexploited potential and the multiplier effect make tourism a vital part of any strategy in Sikkim that aims at enhancing income and employment, and in the process boosting of revenues. It is especially important given the limited scope for any large-scale expansion in industry and agriculture, the bottoming out of the government sector as sole provider of employment, and the limited infrastructure currently available for any significant expansion of 'other services' in the near future. Further, by promoting 'non-mass' tourism—such as eco-tourism, adventure sports and village-related activities—the tourist sector could serve a much needed goal of keeping people on the land, and placing some restraint on the rapid urbanisation process that is overwhelming urban environments in the state.

The Chief Minister's speeches and the recommendations of *Sikkim: A People's Vision,* which have been adopted for implementation, are a clear indication that the government recognises the contribution that travel and tourism can make to the state's economy, both in terms of wealth creation and employment generation. The steps the state government has taken to harness the state's tourism potential are a further reflection of its commitment to the sector. Nevertheless, there seems to be a lack of appreciation of the full scope of the industry and its potential as a catalyst for the development of other areas of economic activity, such as agriculture, manufacturing or financial services. It has become imperative that the tourism industry in the state is developed to play all these roles; it is, however, equally imperative that development be judiciously carried out to ensure that it is sustainable, economically, socially, and environmentally.

10.3 An Analysis of Tourist Traffic

In recent years, there has been an increase in efforts to boost tourist traffic to the state by government agencies, private operators and the two industry associations, Travel Agents Association of Sikkim (TAAS) and the Sikkim Hotels and Restaurants Association (SHRA). However, these have had marginal success: tourist numbers have not increased to any large extent (Tables 10.1A and 10.1B) and the pattern of tourist traffic has largely remained unchanged.

10.3.1 Current Patterns

- ***Volume:*** The total number of tourist arrivals has remained almost the same over the five-year period, 1997 to 2002 (Table 10.1).

The data in table 10.1 which shows tourist arrivals from two different official sources raises an important issue—the discrepancy in numbers indicates that the system of gathering data on tourist arrivals has not been streamlined. The statistical cell of the tourism department is responsible for collating this information. The large discrepancy in foreign tourist arrival data is particularly surprising, as these numbers can be estimated fairly accurately based on the number of permits issued. Domestic arrivals are mostly broad estimates, as there appears to be no systematic process by which hotels and lodges routinely submit occupancy figures to the department, from which arrivals can be calculated.

- ***Seasonality and Duration:*** Tourist arrivals into the state are seasonal and tend to cluster around April-June and October, as these are the 'holiday season' months in West Bengal, the source of the overwhelming majority of tourists. Efforts by the Tourism department to stretch the tourist season beyond these months have had some success, as tourists visits are spread almost continuously from March to October, barring the monsoon months of July and August.

  The average duration of tourist visits tends to be short, on average around three days, mainly because most of them originate from the areas around the state. For tourists from further afield, Sikkim is often an 'add-on' destination to Bhutan

2. TECS (1998). *Tourism Master Plan.*

TABLE 10.1

Differing Estimates of Tourist Arrivals in Sikkim

	1997	1998	1999	2000	2001	2002	2003	2004
*Tourist Arrivals in Sikkim, 1997-2002**								
Domestic	1,40,821	1,20,103	1,35,273	1,40,151	1,44,278	1,36,506	NA	NA
Foreign	8,812	8,985	98,219	11,320	8,176	7,726	NA	NA
Total	1,49,633	1,29,088	1,45,094	1,51,471	1,52,454	1,44,232	NA	NA
Tourist Arrivals in Sikkim, 2000-2004#								
Domestic	1,16,500	1,33,158	1,39,085	1,44,203	1,46,923	1,60,789	1,76,759	2,01,250
Foreign	8,068	6,111	8,563	8,794	7,757	8,539	10,954	11,232
Total	1,24,568	1,39,269	1,47,648	1,52,997	1,54,680	1,69,328	1,87,713	2,12,482

Sources: *: *Sikkim: A Statistical Profile, 2002,* Directorate of Economics, Statistics, Monitoring and Evaluation, Govt of Sikkim.

#: Annual Reports, Tourism Department, Government of Sikkim.

and Darjeeling, and for this reason too the number of days spent in this state are limited.

- ***Destinations:*** Most tourists, an estimated 70 per cent, visit the east district; the other most popular district is the west where an estimated 15 per cent visit, and 10 per cent visit the south district.[3] The proportion of people visiting the south is likely to increase with Namchi being developed as an important tourist spot after the recent construction of the Guru Rimpoche statue on the outskirts of the town, which has become a must see destination for local and out-of-state visitors.
- ***Policy Implications***: Tourist patterns in the state raise important pointers for policy focus: broadening the source base of tourists will, apart from increasing the volume of traffic, have a beneficial effect on lengthening the average duration of stay and tourist season. The advantages of promoting the state as a tourist destination for the winter months of December and January (following the example of Shimla and Chail) are several: this would allow more efficient year-round use of tourism infrastructure, which would result in lower prices during the 'season months', as well as provide more regular income for those in the hospitality industry.

10.3.2 Projections of Tourist Traffic

In recent years there have been two tourism development plans for the state,[4] which have estimated tourist traffic growth, and based on this have estimated the infrastructure requirements for the next decade or so. A third study is being finalised which will also make recommendations for sustainable tourism development. The recommendations in the report by Tata Economic Consultancy Service (TECS) in 1998, which covered the period from 2001 to 2011 are in danger of becoming outdated and hence irrelevant. A study by Horizon covers a 20-year period from 2002 to 2021. The Horizon study estimated that tourist traffic will be 4.01 lakh in 2011, against the TECS projection of 3.72 lakh in the same year; Horizon goes on to project total tourist inflow of 16.2 lakh by 2021.

The TECS forecast which covers 1997 to 2011 uses an explanatory variable to forecast future traffic using income method (GDP growth at 5.5 per cent and population at 2 per cent till 2000 and 1.8 per cent thereafter)—based on the fact that population grew at 2.2 per cent over the last three decades) to arrive at a domestic tourist arrival figure of 3.33 lakh in 2011. The foreign tourist pattern is volatile, so the estimated arrivals were based on Sikkim's share in Indian tourist arrivals of 0.6 per cent, which gives the foreign tourist arrival figure of 0.384 lakh in 2011. The total tourist arrivals projected for 2011 is thus 3.71 lakh tourists. The Horizon study projects are based on a pure time series growth rate, and yields a higher total tourist arrival figure of 4.01 lakh for the comparable year 2011, and 16.23 lakh in 2021 (Table 10.2).

However, when we compare the projected TECS figures for 2001 against actual arrivals, the former are far

3. Horizon Study, p.145.
4. Tata Economic Consultancy Service, January 1998 and Horizon Industrial Consultancy Services, New Delhi in November 2002.

TABLE 10.2

Projected Tourist Arrivals in Sikkim, TECS *versus* Horizon

Year	Horizon Projections			TECS Projections		
	Foreign	*Domestic*	*Total*	*Foreign*	*Domestic*	*Total*
1996				7,508	1,10,555	1,18063
2001				13,766	1,63,870	1,77,636
2002	8,533	1,61,615	1,70,148			
2003	9,386	1,77,700	1,87,086			
2005	11,357	2,15,110	2,26,467			
2006	12,493	2,36,621	2,49,114	23,637	2,36,424	2,60,061
2007	13,742	2,60,283	2,74,025			
2009	16,628	3,14,942	3,31,570			
2011	20,120	3,81,080	4,01,200	38,419	3,33,324	3,71,743
2013	26,608	5,03,979	5,30,587			
2015	35,189	6,66,512	7,01,701			
2017	46,538	8,81,462	9,28,000			
2019	61,547	11,65,734	12,27,281			
2021	81,396	15,41,683	16,23,079			

Source: TECS and Horizon Studies.

higher, especially for arrivals. While 2001 was a particularly bad year for foreign tourist travel, it may be worth asking if the two projections (in particular those by the Horizon study) are too optimistic.

10.4 Overall Strategy for Developing Tourism

The overall strategy for expansion in tourism should fit in with the sustainable development paradigm envisaged for the rest of the economy, so that the sector becomes a major source of employment, income, and revenue, to be focused on:

- **Sustainability:** Development of tourism in the state has to be sustainable—environmentally, culturally and economically. The topography and environment makes it inevitable that the focus has to be on 'non-mass' tourism, such as eco-tourism, adventure tourism, village tourism.
- **Shift in government role**: Rather than being a provider of accommodation and transport services, the government has to strengthen its role as a facilitator, promoter, and regulator for the sector; and
- **Active participation by non-government agencies:** Non-government agencies, such as industry associations, NGOs (especially working in the environmental sphere) and private individuals need to take over several operational functions currently being dispensed by the government.

10.5 Sustainability: Focus on Non-mass Market Tourism

Sustainable tourism has several, often seriously debated, definitions. According to the Federation of Nature and National Parks, sustainable tourism is 'all forms of tourism development, management, and activity that maintain the environmental, social and economic integrity and well-being of natural, built and cultural resources in perpetuity.'

For Sikkim, traditional mass-market tourism would be environmentally and physically unsustainable. The focus has to be on environmentally friendly segments, such as ecotourism, rural, and adventure tourism.

10.5.1 Ecotourism

Ecotourism has many different interpretations, but it can generally be defined as responsible travel to natural areas that conserves the environment and sustains the well-being of local people.[5] Traditional travel makes no commitment to conservation or natural area management, merely offering travelers an opportunity to visit exotic

5. Definition by The International Ecotourism Society (TIES).

BOX 10.3

Different Facets of Sustainability in Tourism Development

Sustainability in the process of tourism development has to be ensured on various fronts:

- *Environmental sustainability* means that tourism development does not cause irreversible changes in a destination's ecosystem.
- *Social and cultural sustainability* refers to the ability of a community to absorb the effects of tourism (both from the industry and tourists) without the creation of social disharmony. It assumes that a given community is able to retain or adapt their own distinctive cultural traits in the face of cultural pressure from visitors.
- *Economic sustainability* is ensured when economic gains from tourism can provide an appropriate income level to the local community (against the inconveniences caused by tourism activities) and to cover all the costs of any special measure taken to satisfy the tourists.

The different aspects of sustainability are not in competition, but are equally important. High economic profits cannot be an excuse for damage to social or natural resources; similarly, the relative fragile nature of the ecosystem cannot create a planning environment where economic considerations are not fully taken into account.

BOX 10.4

Two Ecotourism Initiatives in the State

Ecotourism was introduced in Sikkim a few years ago, and ever since has been gathering momentum. Sikkim Industrial Development Corporation (SIDICO) in conjunction with the Voluntary Health Association of Sikkim (VHAS) promotes eco-tourism in two remote villages, Rong in the south district and Lading in the west district. An interesting finding from these projects is that success in involving villagers in the development work and effecting changes among the community is inversely related to accessibility to government funding. In Lading, which is more remote than Rong, and thus had lower recourse to government resources, the project was able to secure higher levels of village participation.[6]

In another eco-tourism project in Assam Lingzey (near Gangtok) run by project KEEP (Khedi Ecotourism and Eco-development Promotion) local residents offer rooms in their homes for home-stays and work as guides for trekkers traversing the Khedi route and for day-long hikes through the village and neighbouring areas. By involving visitors in their traditional way of life, the project encourages the local Bhutia people to retain the traditional features of their homes, local customs, and sensitises village inhabitants and visitors to the importance of environmental preservation.

places and experience these cultures before they change or disappear. In contrast, ecotourism works through partnerships with local people, to protect the natural environment and to help promote understanding of other cultures. Its main aim is to ensure that local communities are the major beneficiaries.

10.5.2. Village/Rural Tourism

Closely related to ecotourism are the areas of rural and village tourism. This is one segment that has plenty of potential in Sikkim, with its distinctive, attractive cultural landscapes with small villages, rivers, and waterfalls—unique landscapes in peaceful setting for tourists in search of relaxation and recreation. In a broader context, rural tourism covers farm tourism or agritourism, and services include accommodation, local cuisine, local festivals and events, outdoor recreation, involvement in local handicrafts or agricultural activities, visits to neighbouring religious and historical sites, etc.

10.5.3 Adventure Tourism

Sikkim's unique selling point as an adventure tourism destination is that it is home to some of the most remote and challenging, and least traversed trekking trails. However, a detailed study of the trekking routes and facilities in the state listed in the *Trekking Master Plan*[7] lists several potential areas of environmental damage caused by unregulated trekking and camping activity: many of the routes, especially the Yuksom-Goechala trail, are functioning beyond their carrying capacity. There is

6. P.D. Rai. *Ecotourism*.
7. Trekking Master Plan, INTACH, State Tourism Development Corporation, Sikkim Government.

BOX 10.5

Integrating Trade and Tourism through Nathu La Route

Tourism is Sikkim's major strength. It has the potential of acquiring a status of the backbone of Sikkimese economy and society. Therefore, a conscious attempt should be made to gradually integrate trade through Nathu La with the movement of tourists across the border. Historically also trade was done alongside tourism, mainly pilgrimage. A significant exchange of tourists takes place between Nepal and Tibet through the land route of Kathmandu-Kodari highway. Tourists are likely to make a beeline to watch how trade actually takes place between India and China at Sherathang and Renqinggang respectively. Like Nathu La, one can expect Sherathang and the proposed Nathu La museum to be rather prime attractions for tourists in Sikkim. Equally a large number of tourists can come from the Chinese side.

The Tibet tourism is on a developing stage. It was only in the post 1980 period that Tibet was opened up to foreigners. Globally known as the "roof of the world", Tibet lately has focused on 'ecotourism.' There are over a hundred high quality tourist attractions within the TAR. Annually there are over 6000 pilgrims who make their way from India to this region. Most of them make their way to this region *via* the Nepal-China border town of Khasa (Tatopani). For the Indian tourists the Pulan Port at Taklakot (in Uttar Pradesh, India) is the only accessible port of entry. Nathu La would be logistically more economic, historical, and culturally a better port of entry.

On a very simple assumption also the charges on tourists visiting Sherathang and Nathu La could generate a revenue of Rs. 1.81 crore in 2006, and Rs. 3.47 crore in 2010. The income effects on roadside hotels and restaurants, handicrafts, and transport and communication and on other backward and forward linkages are likely to be immense.

Moreover, Sikkim could be the hub connecting all the major Buddhist destinations in India and neighbouring countries—Bodh Gaya in Bihar, Rumtek in Sikkim, Tawang in Arunachal Pradesh, Lumbini in Nepal, and Taktsang in Bhutan to Jokhang and Potala in Lhasa. This is likely to be further strengthened by the proposed air link between Bagdogra and Kathmandu.

The other most attractive areas of interests for the people of Tibet Autonomous Region and nearby areas will be the health and educational facilities that are available in, and around Sikkim. The entire Sikkim-Darjeeling belt has been famous for educational institutions and the quality of education they impart. The huge surge in demand for English speaking students and professionals in China could, in fact, trigger a beeline for educational institutions in Sikkim and surrounding districts.

However, the present diplomatic arrangement does not allow the use of Nathu La route as a transit point to visit various parts of Tibet and mainland China. A separate international agreement needs to be in place.

Source: Lama, 2005.

BOX 10.6

Ripple Effects of Village/Rural Tourism

In a state with few options for rural employment, village/rural tourism can prove one way to stimulate economic growth of less developed regions, improve the living standards of local people and help stem the flow to urban areas. If developed in a sustainable fashion, rural tourism can be an appropriate tool to revitalise stagnant rural areas and to ensure their sustainable future through creation or retention of jobs, increased diversity of employment, revival and preservation of different traditions— arts and crafts, medical practices, festivals and dances, and landscape and conservation of nature. It often provides an incentive (and some of the funding) for infrastructural development, which in turn, contributes to the growth of other rural economic activities.

Rural tourism development has negative and positive influences on the sociocultural characteristics of rural destinations. The positive effects are: encouraging more efficient use of available resources, beneficial socioeconomic change, heritage protection and conservation of the rural environment, and increasing social contact for local people and opportunities to learn from other cultures. The negative impacts could include environmental outcomes and sociocultural changes that place pressure on the local community, change their rhythm of life, threaten their privacy or result in the inauthentic presentation of local customs and traditions for tourists' wishes.

noncompliance with any environmental code of conduct (garbage and plastic litter on trails, overnight debris at campsites and huts, so on), inadequate water supply, sanitation services and parking facilities, and haphazard construction of multi-story hotels at the entrance to the sites. Maintenance costs are high in these areas, because heavy snow and rainfall and landslides routinely damage the infrastructure.

10.6. Recommendations

10.6.1 Shift in the Role of the Government

There are several areas that need urgent and active involvement by the government, in the absence of which tourism will remain in its current stagnant state. The broad recommendation is that government agencies (Tourism Department, STDC, and related bodies) move out of operational areas, such as the direct provision of tourist accommodation and transport services, and focus on establishing an enabling framework for a sustainable 'take-off' in tourism. Broadly, there are three roles in tourism development that the government needs to strengthen—as a facilitator, promoter and effective regulator.

Government as Facilitator

Planning and Development

An important first step will be to announce a development plan for tourism. Several such plans have been commissioned by the government[8] but not implemented, and now run the risk of becoming outdated. What is needed is a Tourism Master Plan (based on the Tata's report) with clearly defined roles for all the government agencies involved, as well as for private service providers, industry associations [Travel Agents Association of Sikkim (TAAS), the Hotel and Restaurant Owners Association], and representatives from ecotourism projects, CBOs working with local communities, and local communities themselves.

The sparse supply of tourism infrastructure means that it is spread very thinly across the state, and its use has to be maximised. This is possible through the creation of 'tourism zones' (as the regional clustering of tourist sites often does not conform to administrative boundaries). Each tourism zone will have a separate development plan, prepared with inputs from experts in the field of area planning, building, and landscape architecture.

A development agency could be assigned to each zone (or important tourist destination), and would be responsible for setting up essential infrastructure for the area, such as interconnecting roads, power, and basic municipal services. Successful tourism planning and development is based on cooperation and coordination among government departments and agencies. A major hurdle faced by private entrepreneurs seeking to construct tourism assets and infrastructure in the state, is land acquisition, which often entails clearances from various departments (such as the Urban Development and Housing Department, the Department of Forests, and so on).[9] Similarly, the development and supply of saleable tourist handicrafts would need inputs from the Directorate of Handlooms and Handicrafts. A central function of the tourism development agency would be to provide such coordination, and to balance diverse interests, for which it would need to have representatives from local communities, private bodies, and top-level state agencies.

Formulating Appropriate Policy

A clear tourism policy will need to be formulated based on the underlying strategy in the tourism master plan. To protect the long-term prospects for this sector, planning will need to focus closely on the ecological, sociocultural and economic impact, with special emphasis on the promotion of alternate forms of tourism.

Ecotourism is one area in which, experience from other states shows, bureaucratic processes often hamper innovation. To prevent this from occuring in Sikkim, a clear and facilitative role for the government needs to be defined. Ecotourism policy and planning will be integrated with overall tourism policy for the state, in which the roles of government departments will be specified to prevent arbitrary and uncoordinated decision making.

Increasing Allocations

Government resources allocated to the sector are still very low, and there are inadequate incentives to encourage private investment in the industry. Total outlay on tourism in the Tenth Plan (Rs. 2,500 lakh, or 1.2 per cent of total outlay) is lower than total outlay in the Ninth Plan (Rs. 4,000 lakh) of which only Rs. 1,733 lakh, or 43 per cent was spent.[10] Given the central role tourism is expected to have in generating employment and income, proportional expenditure needs to be raised substantially,[11] as low public investment could severely hamper the sector's potential, especially as over

---

8. Tata Economic Consultancy Service (1998). Horizon Industrial Consultancy Service (2002). and a forthcoming update to the TECS plan by the ADB in 2004.

9. The difficulty in obtaining these clearances is cited as major reason for the low utilisation of central funds during the Ninth Plan: of the Rs. 687 lakh sanctioned, schemes worth only Rs. 258.24 lakh were executed; only 9 of the 95 schemes could be completed (Horizon study).

10. Background Note to Annual Plan 2003-04 for Sikkim, Planning Commission, New Delhi.

11. Other countries allocate the following shares: Singapore, 9.1 per cent; Hong Kong, 7.4 per cent; Malaysia, 5.1 per cent; Sri Lanka, 4.0 per cent; and China, 3.8 per cent, WTTC, 2004.

one-fifth of the Tenth Plan outlay (Rs. 528 lakh of Rs. 2,500 lakh) is earmarked for direction and administration, and of that a major proportion is for wages and salaries.

Enabling Infrastructure

A major hurdle to the expansion of tourism is access to and within the state. There are no airport or rail services, so travel is only by road, and entry to the state is almost exclusively through one highway, the NH 31A helicopter service from Bagdogra to the helipad is generally erratic, depending on the weather and volume of traffic, and expensive. The construction of an airport in Pakyong in conjunction with the Airports Authority of India has been stalled over transfer of funds. The road network of Sikkim, as in all hill states, requires constant maintenance. Roads connecting several of the tourist destinations are in poor condition, and act as a deterrent to tourists.

Roads connecting major tourist destinations have to be ranked by priority and upgraded to international standards to provide all-weather access, an important prerequisite to lengthening the tourist season. One method would be to invite private sector investors on a 'build, operate and transfer' (BOT) basis, which has been successfully done in other states, and made economically viable through the introduction of toll systems.

Other infrastructure-related inputs from the government would be standardising nomenclature, and specifying a list of approved spellings for all tourist destinations and towns. Different spellings of Tsomgo Lake (Changu, Tsangu, Dzongu and so on) in travel brochures, advertisements, and signposts to the destination have led to confusion among tourists. Clear and uniform signage for all tourist sites, buildings, parks, institutes, etc., are important. At present some have no visible boards that allow visitors to clearly see where they are.

Preserving Natural Habitats

The state has some of the finest, most pristine mountain locations, but haphazard development, lack of infrastructure planning and non-enforcement of environmental regulation have begun to adversely affect their tourist appeal. This applies to some of the most popular tourist destinations, such as the Tsomgu lake (see Box 10.6), and only the government can step in to halt the process and make sure that other areas do not suffer the same fate.

This is particularly important in trekking and adventure sports areas. Information on trekking regulations at road-heads and along the route, strictly enforced high penalties for noncompliance with rules, making guides and porters responsible for enforcing the rules, local policing of the treks, etc., may help stem the drift towards environmental degradation of these areas. Environment-related information specific to Sikkim should mandatorily be displayed on all tourism-related websites, signposts at strategic locations and tourism publicity pamphlets.

Reliable and Appropriate Statistics and Database

Reliable and comprehensive data and statistics are a vital input into policy planning. As table 10.1 shows, data from official sources vary even on the basics, such as tourist arrivals, quite apart from other critical statistics like tourism-related expenditure and income generated, revenue earned, and so on. The Tourism Department is developing a new format for better data collection on tourist arrivals, but it needs to set up a database and keep it updated with as accurate data as is possible, on all aspects of tourism-related activities.

Government as Promoter

Promoting the 'Sikkim' Brand

Tourism is an increasingly competitive business, and given Sikkim's low visibility on the 'tourist map' of India, strong branding and marketing of the state's attractions is necessary. Only the government can promote the entire state as a tourist destination (along the lines of 'incredible India', the branding of the entire country as a place to visit). Branding of states has been done successfully by governments in Rajasthan and Kerala, and the STDC (or tourism department) could use a variety of media avenues to similarly highlight Sikkim's unique qualities as a tourist destination.

Enabling E-Tourism

Travel within the state is almost exclusively through operators or hotel owners. While these agencies have done an admirable job in developing itineraries to suit visitors to the state, globally there is an emerging trend towards 'e-tourism'—especially by the adventure travellers who are likely to target a destination such as, Sikkim. Rather than resorting to pre-organised options, individuals like to fashion their own journeys through information gathered from travel magazines and guides and increasingly through the Internet; often such visitors travel without any prior itinerary.

To tap into this growing market; far more comprehensive information on travel, accommodation, destinations, dates of festivals and flower shows, and so on needs to be made available on the internet. One way to do this is by expanding the existing government website on Sikkim tourism into a full-fledged regional tourism destination database. This can be done in conjunction with private software companies, which will also help small and medium-sized enterprises develop e-marketing skills.

Government as Regulator

This is one of its most important functions, and the government needs to ensure that clear guidelines are in place for providers of all travel and tourism-related services, such as accommodation, food, tour operators, adventure sports, homestay arrangements, trekking, adventure tourism, and so on. More importantly, it needs to enforce the guidelines, rules and regulations in a uniform and transparent manner, with strict penalties for noncompliance. Expansion of tourism, especially into source markets that have so far been untapped will require far more active regulation.

Certification of Accommodation

Registration of accommodation needs to be strictly enforced. At present, there are several new functioning hotels which have not been cleared by the Department of Urban Development and Housing. Environmental standards (such as hygiene, environmental disposal of waste, aesthetic construction, and so on) need to be developed and all accommodation needs to be inspected and certified annually on compliance with these standards. Complainants should have recourse to an independent authority to file grievances, which should be dealt with promptly and transparently, with high penalties.

Transparency of Rates and Services

The rapid increase in the number of taxis operating within Gangtok and to popular tourist destinations (such as Tsomgu lake) and the resultant increase in congestion, noise and pollution have already begun to adversely impact on the travel experience, and needs to be checked before consequences become irreversible. The government could consider limiting or even reducing the number of taxi licences issued, while simultaneously promoting minibus travel to popular sights from convenient locations in Gangtok or Namchi.

Better public access between major tourist towns by public transport would also be desirable, to reduce traffic congestion and increase access. For example, bus services between the most important district towns in the state, Gangtok and Namchi, are only once or twice a day; the situation is probably worse between other towns.

Taxi operators are required to display tariffs clearly and abide by them, a practice that is not adhered to especially in high tourist season. Further, providers of all types of accommodation—hotels, resorts, homestays, village and ecotourist projects—should be required to clearly display their tariffs and services—or face punitive action for noncompliance.

Transparency of tariffs and amenities is especially important in new projects, such as ecotourism and village tourism projects that have been initiated. These are relatively new forms of tourist ventures, and given the uniqueness of each project, transparent and public display of rates for treks, tours, home-stays, village visits and so on will add to their credibility. While the expectation is that alternative forms of tourism will largely be self-regulating, some amount of central monitoring would help ensure that these ventures are a continued success.

10.6.2 Ensuring Sustainability

It is important to note that focusing on new forms of 'alternative' tourism is not enough to minimise the negative effects or maximise the positive impacts of tourism. The whole sector must be developed and managed in a way that it does not damage the natural and sociocultural environment.

Ecotourism

Promoting the ecotourism potential of the state requires a departure from the traditional approach and will require careful planning. Policies on tourism and areas related to the environment and rural development will have to include ecotourism principles at the regional and state levels, supported with excellent coordination among government, CBOs, local communities, and other stakeholders. Decisions will need to involve local communities concerns, and focus on increasing benefits to them through tourism activities. Local communities should have a 'voice' in planning decisions and in initiating eco-tourism ventures in their areas, through institutionalised processes, like local community institutions (Panchayati raj institutions).

A clearly formulated ecotourism policy is needed, based on economic use of natural resources with appropriate inputs, viable projects and community participation. This is an important way to conserve and develop a region, but accurate estimates of its impact are still unknown. So far visitor arrivals have formed the basis of planning for these activities, however organisations working in these areas can jointly identify indicators that will help in planning and management. In the absence of any national norms for ecotourism, the state will need to develop standards for ecotourism facilities (lodges, home-stays, etc.) and activities (trekking, rafting, etc.) that are region-appropriate, in consultation with private providers and civil society organisations.

Village Tourism

The recent focus on this segment of the tourism market *via* the incentives announced by the Chief Minister could have very beneficial effects on rural economies in the state. A related initiative by the UNDP/central government project on endogenous tourism has identified the village of Lachen in the north district as one of the 31 sites in the country to be developed as a model for 'endogenous tourism'. The state could draw on the experience of countries such as Indonesia and Malaysia, which have successfully and lucratively promoted village tourism. Their experience indicates the importance of appropriate location, aesthetic, vernacular styles in construction, and the provision of basic, essential amenities. Rather than funding all households in a village to construct rooms for lodging visitors, a more effective way of ensuring participation would be to involve providers through some form of financial commitment, so that they have a stake in maintaining service and quality standards.

An important factor to be kept in mind, when planning policy from the standpoint of villagers, is that the provision of rural tourist services is unlikely to become the sole source of income, as demand is seasonal, occupancy rates are low and investment for creating or improving tourist facilities often high. Village and rural tourism can be seen only a seasonal and partial source of income, particularly in the initial stages of functioning, and can be supplemented with other year-round tourism-related, income-generating activities, such as, creation of handicrafts, processing and preserving of local fruit.

Trekking and Adventure Tourism

To ensure that the state remains a popular adventure destination, trekking tourism could be developed and managed carefully, with active involvement from representatives from NGOs (such as ECOSS and VHAS), private stakeholders (such as TAAS and the SHRA), government departments (such as Tourism and Forests), and local communities. The two main areas that should be focussed upon are, increase in the access to information on trekking and preservation of the environment.

Increasing availability and access to information

A first step is to collect and disseminate detailed information on trekking routes and suggested itineraries through tourist information centres. There should be a registered organisation of guides and porters; information on the organisation and rates for each trekking itinerary should be available centrally as well as at the road head. Trekking tourism is a specialised activity and its appropriate promotion requires specialised human resources.

Preserving the environment

Trekking permits should be issued according to the carrying capacity of the area and infrastructure along the trails, such as campsites, should be minimal and environment friendly. Construction should be based on local materials, blended with the surroundings and retaining the scenic surroundings. Emergency shelters can be located between campsites especially for the high altitude treks. Localised radio communication for the emergency operations should be installed in the wilderness trek routes.

Entry tariffs for trekking trails are low (Rs. 100) and need to be increased to around Rs. 500 (for foreign tourists) and Rs. 200 (for domestic tourists). Funds can be ploughed back into maintaining the infrastructure, trail and park conservation, such as afforestation, cleaning water bodies, improving benefits to guides and porters.

10.6.2 Role of Other Agencies

Given the crowded agenda and limited resources of state government agencies, comprehensive development of this sector depends crucially on active participation by non-government stakeholders.

The Private Sector and Industry Associations

The private sector has a critical role in developing quality products and services geared to international and domestic demand. It should expand the development of quality hotels, travel agencies and transport services, while the government needs to relinquish responsibility for areas that are best managed by private enterprise. A major task for industry associations would be grading accommodation: central government guidelines exist on grading four and five-star accommodation; state tourism departments develop their own guidelines for grading various types of accommodation. In Sikkim the onus is on the hotelier to apply for a grade, but most hotels have not done so.

Non-governmental Organisations (NGOs)

Historically there have been relatively few NGOs functioning in the state, but recent years have seen increased activity in some areas such as environmental impacts of development, ecotourism projects focussing on marginalised mountain communities, and training and skill development in related fields.

Many of these NGOs are well placed to initiate, develop, and supplement government's efforts in tourism development. An emerging area of strength is research into and dissemination of environment-related information, such as fragility of the ecosystem, conservation measures, protection of rare and endangered species, and so on.

Many of them, such as the Ecotourism and Conservation Society of Sikkim (ECOSS) and Voluntary Health Association of Sikkim (VHAS) actively work for mountain communities, and are ideally placed to interact closely with travellers to more remote areas, and to providers of services there. Two areas they can contribute to are: providing basic training and skill development to tourism service providers in villages on various aspects of hospitality; and helping to develop complex tourist products to cater to the needs of different tourist segments in rural areas.

Their experience and inputs would be valuable in the development of trekking guidelines. The neglect of the trekking environment is also a result of a lack of environmental awareness both by trekkers and guides. Periodically the Tourism department conducts training courses for guides, but this could be outsourced to specialised institutes. ECOSS and related organisations can expand their programme for training guides and porters to include short awareness courses on the use and maintenance of hiking and camping equipment, first-aid especially for high altitude sickness which affects many first-time trekkers in Himalayan altitudes, hygiene and environmental awareness such as segregation of disposable and non-disposable waste, and expanded map-reading skills, besides familiarisation with all the trekking routes in the state.

With the proposed focus on village and rural tourism, local communities will perforce become active participants. Many of them will become providers of hospitality related services, accommodation and food, while others would get seasonal employment as guides to local festivals, religious and historic sites, or around agricultural activities. The knowledge and experience of local communities can be harnessed to provide information on local flora and fauna, to make travellers aware of the unique environment and heritage of the state. However, expanded tourist activity in these remote areas means that rural communities must also be made aware of the importance and relevance to their sustainable livelihoods of responsible tourism and eco-trekking. This will help them become partners in preserving and maintaining these natural habitats.

10.7 Agreement with China[12]

The Nathu La Trade Study Group has recommended integration of trade with tourism between Sikkim and the Tibet Autonomous region of China, by 2012. For this a fresh bilateral legal basis needs to be concluded to facilitate the movement of tourists across the border. The Group also recommended that 2018 onwards this tourism linkages should be extended to "SAARC tourism thereby integrating" tourism activities of third countries of the region including Bangladesh, Bhutan, and Nepal. This means opening of all the SAARC tourists to cross the border through Nathu La.

The trade-tourism integration will call for the signing of a separate treaty/protocol between India and China. The Government of Sikkim in collaboration with other north-eastern states and West Bengal should put forward proposals for integrating tourism with trade to the union government at an appropriate level so as to achieve the goal by 2012. The state government should also initiate discussion with the union government on lifting restrictions on the entry of tourists from mainland China, Bangladesh, and Myanmar, into Sikkim. Networking of the tourism related institutions in Sikkim and other states of India and in Nepal, Bhutan, and China may be initiated by including Gangtok-Lhasa Bus Service.

A modern museum that would house all the artifacts, archival material, memoirs and other objects related to various missions, agreements, physical exchanges regarding Nathu La trade could be set up at Nathu La.

12. Lama, 2005.

References

ECOSS (Eco-Tourism & Conservation Society of Sikkim) (2002). *Survive* Magazine.

———. *Annual Report 2002-03.*

Horizon Industrial Consultancy Services (2002). *A 20-Year Perspective Plan for Sustainable Tourism Development in the State of Sikkim.*

INTACH (Indian National Trust for Art & Cultural Heritage). *Trekking Master Plan for Sikkim.* STDC, Sikkim.

Khedi, Eco-Tourism & Eco-Development Promotion (KEEP). *Annual Report 2002-03.* Pastanga, Gaucharan.

Lama, Mahendra P. (2003). *Sikkim Human Development Report 2001.* New Delhi: Social Science Press.

———. (2005). *Sikkim-Tibet Trade via Nathu La: A Policy Study on Prospects, Opportunities and Requisite Preparedness.* Prepared by Nathu La Trade Study Group for the Government of Sikkim.

———. (2006). "Trade is only the Bginning of the Story", *Indian Express,* June 18.

Tata Economic Consultancy Services (TECS) (1998). *Tourism Master Plan 1977-2011.*

Tourism Department. *Annual Report 2002-03.*

———. *Sikkim: Land of Mystic Splendor* and other publicity materials

World Travel and Tourism Council (2004). Travel and Tourism Economic Research, India (website)

Websites:

1. *www.censusindia.net*
2. *www.envis.nic.in*
3. *www.mountain.org* (The Mountain Institute)
4. *www.mtnfourm.org* (The mountain forum)
5. *www.northeast.nic.in* (DONER website)
6. *www.planningcommission.nic.in*
7. *www.sikkim.nic.in*
8. *www.sikkiminfo.net*
9. *www.sikkiminfo.net*/ecoss (ECOSS website)
10. *www.tourismofindia.com*
11. *www.uneptie.org*
12. Vhai.org (voluntary health association of India)

Chapter 11

Rural Development

Areas other than the bazars and their surroundings are defined as rural areas in Sikkim. Almost 90 per cent of the people belong to these areas. The latest district and subdivision wise village profile of Sikkim is given below in Table 11.1.

TABLE 11.1

Village Profile in Sikkim

State/District	*Sub-division*	*No. of Villages*
Sikkim	Total	454
North	Chungthang	8
	Mangan	46
	Total	54
West	Gyalshing	71
	Soreng	51
	Total	122
South	Namchi	98
	Ravong	47
	Total	145
East	Gangtok	83
	Pakyong	28
	Rongli	20
	Total	131+2*=133

Note: *–There are 2 uninhabited villages.

Source: Census of India, 2001.

The main objective of the chapter is to make an in-depth study of the emerging issues for rural development, analyse the efficacy of the policies for rural development, identify the gaps and give some useful suggestions to fill up the gaps.

The chapter is organised as follows:

11.1 attempts to sketch the economic profile of rural Sikkim and gives the current status of the major poverty alleviation and income generation schemes in the state;

11.2 gives a detailed account of the rural infrastructure and related policies implemented in the state;

11.3 gives an account of community development and panchayati raj institutions and the measures taken to empower the decentralised structure;

11.4 critically analyses the efficacy of the policies and programmes implemented for rural development in Sikkim and identifies some gaps;

11.5 gives some useful recommendations.

11.1 Economic Profile of the Rural Sector

Poverty and unemployment are the twin blocks of rural development in Sikkim. Unfortunately, independent estimates of poverty for the state are not available. Planning Commission estimates of BPL population replicating Assam gives 40.04 per cent as the figure for BPL population in rural areas in all north-eastern states which is higher than the all India average of 27.09 per cent.

11.1.1 Analysis of Some Basic Statistics

We start with a district level analysis of the percentage distribution of total workers, main workers, marginal workers and non-workers from 1991 and 2001 censuses (provisional figures).

The main findings suggest:

- The proportion of total workers in rural Sikkim has increased over the last decade, all the districts show the same trend except for the west, where the overall proportion has fallen;

TABLE 11.2

District-wise Percentage Distribution of Workers in Rural Sikkim

State/District	Total Workers		Main Workers		Marginal Workers		Non-workers	
	1991	2001	1991	2001	1991	2001	1991	2001
Sikkim	**41.74**	**49.74**	**40.68**	**39.57**	**1.06**	**10.17**	**58.26**	**50.26**
North	43.95	58	42.84	42.78	1.11	15.22	56.05	42
East	38.31	49.71	36.88	37.99	1.43	11.72	61.69	50.29
South	42.95	53.49	41.95	43.73	1	9.76	57.05	46.51
West	45.06	43.17	44.51	36.66	0.55	6.51	54.94	56.83

Source: Census of India, 1991, 2001.

- The proportion of main workers has fallen in the state; a similar trend has been recorded for north and west, for east and south it has risen;
- The proportion of marginal workers has drastically increased over the decade in the state; a similar trend is recorded in all the districts;
- The proportion of non-workers has fallen in the state; similar trend is recorded in all the districts except for the west where the overall proportion of non-workers has increased.

The following table gives an overall ranking of the districts in terms of proportions of workers' category in Sikkim in the past two decades.

From the above analysis it is clear that the pattern of growth in employment over the decade is not very healthy. A fall in the proportion of main workers and a drastic rise in the proportion of marginal workers accompany the rise in the proportion of total workers. East and south, with relatively greater concentration of industries and tourism opportunities (reasons being partly political and partly economic) have witnessed a slightly better pattern with a rise in the proportion of main worker. In the north the proportion of total workers has risen, with the most pronounced rise (in terms of percentage points) in the proportion of marginal workers mostly because of recent growth of tourism in the district. Situations have drastically deteriorated in the west in order to get an idea about the trends of change in the main worker categories in the state's initial phases of development, we analyse the economic tables of 1981 and 1991 censuses. There is:

- an overall decrease in the share of rural cultivators; a drastic fall is recorded in the female category;
- a slight fall in the share of manufacturing, etc. (household), construction;
- a fall in the share of other services;
- a rise in the shares of rural agricultural labourers, manufacturing etc. (non-household), transport & communication, and trade & commerce (with rural male category showing stronger trends);
- a slight rise in the share of mining and quarrying; and
- an increase in the share of forestry, fishing.

BOX 11.1

Some Interesting Observations on the Basis of 1981 and 1991 Censuses

- In north, as opposed to the general trend, there is a rise in the share of cultivators which is more pronounced for females, a rise in the share of other services, a slight rise in manufacturing etc. (household); there is a considerable fall in the share of forestry and livestock, non-household manufacturing and trade and commerce.
- Though the share has fallen over the years, cultivation, among the work categories, has the highest share both in 1981 and 1991 for all the districts. Mining and quarrying has the lowest share in 1991 in all the districts and in 1981 for east and south. In 1981, west and north did not have mining and quarrying at all, the share of transport was the lowest.

Comparing 1981 and 1991 censuses, we can infer that there are signs of growth of the secondary and tertiary sectors in the economy. However, agriculture remains the most important sector capturing the highest share; within this sector the trend can be explained by the fact that the young cultivator generation is having other sources of income and more land is tilled by hired labour. Sectors like mining and quarrying have started developing showing the state's effort to tap its resources properly, a rise in the share of forestry sector can also be explained by the developmental activities in forestry, tourism, and fisheries. These inferences give clear indications that the rural economy, in the initial phases of development with high dependence on agriculture, was ready to move ahead with growth in the other sectors.

Data on main work categories for 2001 census is not available. But 2001 census data on the proportion of main workers show a downward trend, which means that the current policies of the state could not contribute to sustain the growth process initiated in the past. To be more precise, the sectors, which showed signs of growth, did not get enough support from the state in terms of policies so that they can generate adequate employment opportunities.

11.1.2 Schemes and Programmes[1]

Let us have a look at the present status of the main employment generating policies in the state.

- Sikkim Rural Development Agency (SRDA) implements Swarnjayanti Gram Swarozgar Yojana (SGSY) in the state to organise rural youth into self help groups for taking up self-employment through training and infrastructure development; the latest accounts show that targets have been fulfilled;
- The Sampoorna Grameen Rozgar Yojana (SGRY) I (DRDA level) and II (GPU level) are implemented in the state with targeted APL and BPL population; latest accounts[2] show that the targets are being fulfilled to generate 11 lakh mandays with distribution of 8634 metric tonnes of foodgrains investing 913 lakh in 2003-04.

BOX 11.2

Sikkim Rural Development Agency (SRDA)

Local level planning is facilitated by the scheme of rural development agency came in to being. SRDA has four District Administrative Agencies (DAA) and these agencies are further divided into DAA blocks. The east has 30 DAA blocks, west 10, north 6, and south 10. SRDA is also entrusted with the task of implementing and monitoring the poverty alleviation and employment generation programmes.

11.2 Rural Infrastructure

This section attempts to assess the conditions of the important components of infrastructures in rural Sikkim. The section is divided into two parts, the first part deals with housing and related infrastructure facilities like water supply, sanitation and electricity; the second part deals with connectivity in rural Sikkim.

11.2.1 Rural Housing, Water Supply, Electricity and Sanitation

As per 2001 census, 18.86 per cent of the rural households in Sikkim have thatched roof, 11.57 per cent have asbestos roof and 67.83 per cent have concrete houses. Some of the important statistics derived district-wise from censuses 1991 and 2001 (Table 11.4) on roof materials used over the decades will throw some light on the standard of living and its changes over a time period.

We have considered three commonly used roof materials in Sikkim. The findings show that the proportion of

- thatched houses has fallen;
- asbestos houses has risen; and
- concrete houses has risen drastically in the rural areas in all the districts.

West as a district has shown the highest proportions of fall in the thatched category and rise in the concrete category (in terms of percentage points). Some of the basic amenities like access to electricity, sources of drinking water and latrine are also studied. Figures derived from census 2001 gives that about 48 per cent of the total households and 37 per cent of the rural households in Sikkim have access to drinking water. Statistics derived from the last two censuses reveals that the proportion of rural households having all the above mentioned facilities has increased over the decades in all the districts excepting north where the proportion has fallen (Table 11.5).

The case of the north district can be explained by the fact that number of rural households below poverty line have increased mainly due to migration at a rate higher than that in the other districts.

The above analysis indicates that within the rural sector there is an overall improvement in the standard of living. With newer tourism destinations developing in North, West and South districts, there is an increasing number of new settlements there. Given the stagnancy in employment generation (in spite of the clear accounts of the income generating programmes), a large part of this improvement can be attributed to housing and other policy initiatives.

1. *Annual Progress Report,* Rural Management and Development Department, 2003-04.
2. Ibid.

TABLE 11.4

District-wise Percentage Distribution of Rural Households by Main Categories of Roof Material®

Districts	*Year*	*Percentage of Rural Households with Grass Leaves, Reeds, Thatch, Wood, Mudun-burnt Bricks, Bamboo*	*Percentage of Rural Households with Asbestos Cement Sheets Houses*	*Percentage of Rural Households with Concrete Houses*
North	1991	46.55	1.43	4.02
	2001	24.54	7.84	65.89
East	1991	27.97	0.33	42.42
	2001	14.43	18.42	64.86
South	1991	47.02	0.67	5.25
	2001	19.01	8.89	70.42
West	1991	56.14	0.65	4.71
	2001	23.76	4.94	70.33

Note: ® three categories thatch, asbestos, and concrete, which account for 98 per cent of the houses in rural Sikkim, are considered.

Source: Census of India 1991, 2001.

TABLE 11.5

Percentage Distribution of Rural Households with Access to Drinking Water, Electricity and Latrine

District	*Year*	*Percentage of Rural Houses*
North	1991	93.13
	2001	90.38
West	1991	96.38
	2001	98.25
South	1991	89.38
	2001	94.11
East	1991	65.89
	2001	68.38

Source: Census of India, 1991, 2001.

Schemes and Programmes

Let us have a look at the present status of the major policy initiatives taken by the government to improve the status in each of the above-mentioned facilities.

Rural Housing[3]

Schemes for rural housing can be divided under three main heads, *viz.*:

- *Indira Awas Yojna* (IAY): both components (1448 new constructions and 593 upgradations) have successfully fulfilled the financial and physical targets investing 310 lakh saving 20 lakh of the allocated amount;
- Rural Housing: benefited 12000 families so far and fulfilled physical and financial targets for both its components *viz.* Financial support to people and distribution of GCI sheets investing an amount of 10 lakh;
- Model Village: construction of rural houses in 30 constituencies; 900 houses built so far investing 1000 lakh targets are yet to be achieved.

Rural Water Supply[4]

Rural Water Supply programmes have covered 1583 habitations fully and 96 habitations partially, out of 1679 habitations in Sikkim in April 2004. The objective is to satisfy the norm of 40 lpcd to all the habitations. The major programmes implemented include:

- Accelerated Rural Water Supply Programme, which has achieved the physical and financial targets;
- Rural Water Supply Programmes under PMGY and state plan, which have achieved the physical target by exceeding the financial constraint under PMGY by 2.5 lakh;
- Traditional Water Source Development Programme financed by Eleventh Finance Commission, which is not yet complete, but resources are spent;

3. Annual Progress Report, Rural Management and Development Department, 2003-04.
4. Ibid.

- Revival of traditional sources under Prime Minister's programme, which are yet to be completed with one-third of the resource being spent.

There are provisions for construction of rainwater and roof water harvesting structure in the west district, a water testing laboratory has been set up in the east. But unfortunately the community based programmes like *Swajaldhara* is yet to be initiated in the state.

Rural Energy[5]

The Integrated Rural Energy planning Programme (IREP) and schemes under the new and renewable sources of energy is being implemented by Sikkim Renewable Energy Development agency (SREDA). The programmes include

- Biogas: a scheme shared with the Ministry of Non-conventional Energy for construction of biogas plants under which 3354 plants have been constructed in the state; targets are not fully achieved;
- Solar Photovoltaic Program (SPV): a scheme shared with Ministry of Non-conventional Energy with five components *viz.*, village electrification, solar home lights, solar street lights, solar power plants, and solar water heater; under progress with targets partly achieved in power plants component and almost fully achieved in water heater component;
- Rural Energy Programme: a SREDA scheme distributing LPG connections to BPL population; targets fulfilled.

11.2.2 Rural Connectivity

One of the major investment heads in a hill economy like Sikkim is on connectivity. Hill areas are connected through rural footpaths, motorable roads and bridges, which facilitate the economic activities in the state. Construction of foot-bridges like suspension, RCC, steel and log bridges in the rural areas are necessary for inter village communication.

Between 1997-2001, 123 bridges and 1682.5 km of footpaths were constructed incurring an expenditure of 362 and 2016.07 lakh respectively.[6] Exact figures on present length of rural roads and number of bridges are not available.

Schemes and Programmes

The state has launched[7]

- A new programme under PMGSY for upgradation of roads from which a large number of habitations in the rural areas are expected to be benefited; invested 513 lakh out of 3550 lakh allocated for 21 projects to construct 106 km, work is under progress;
- There is a provision for compensation of land under PMGSY which is shared by the state; invested 15 lakh.
- Some amount in NLCPR also finances rural bridges; 315 lakh out of 345 lakh has been spent, no record on physical achievement is available.

11.3 Community Development and Panchayati Raj Institutions

The Sikkim Panchayat Act, 1993 with successive amendments in 1995 and 1997 attempted to give a set of guidelines for decentralisation of local governments in the state. The reform process of the local level governance started late in 2002, in Sikkim. However, the effects of the 73rd and 74th constitutional amendments are quite visible in the state.

There is a two-tier *panchayati* system in the state. The government has been actively involved in strengthening the administrative set up of the *panchayats*, both at the district and village levels. Table 11.6 below gives an account of the *zilla* and *gram panchayats*, wards, members, village libraries and community information centres (CICs) in the state. This includes the two traditional *zumsas* in Lachen and Lachung in the north district and their pipons.

There are 4 *zilla panchayats* with 100 elected members; for 453 villages there are 166 *gram panchayats*, at the ratio of roughly one *panchayat* for every three villages (the ratio for all Indian states taken together is 1:2). These 166 *gram panchayats* are divided into 905 wards (roughly 5 wards in each *panchayat*) with one elected member in each ward. In order to have a good representation in both the tiers of the *panchayats*, with SC, ST, OBC candidates and women candidates there are reservation schemes in the state, the detailed figures for which are given in table A-40.

5. Annual Progress Report, Rural Management and Development Department, 2003-04.
6. Rural Development Department, Sikkim.
7. Annual Progress Report, Rural Management and Development Department, 2003-04.

TABLE 11.6

District-wise *Zilla* and *Gram Panchayats* and Related Infrastructure (Number)

Districts	Zilla Panchayat Members	Gram Panchayats	Panchayat Wards/ Panchayat Members	Panchayat Ghar	Village Libraries	CICs in Panchayat	Total No of CICs
North	20	20	103	15	20	2	8
East	31	50	273	25	50	4	12
South	24	45	255	37	45	6	9
West	25	51	274	25	51	8	11
Total	100	166	905	102	166	20	40

Source: Annual Administrative Report, RDD, Sikkim.

11.3.1 Decentralised Participatory Approach

In order to empower rural communities, the emphasis is on adoption of decentralised, participatory and beneficiary driven approaches designed to improve the delivery of rural services such as drinking water, sanitation, connectivity, micro credit, education and health to the poorest and vulnerable sections of the societies. Community management for sustainable use of natural resources and common property resources is also included in the agenda.

The state government has now embarked on the process of multi-level intervention by building up right procedures and bringing about necessary technical and administrative changes. The following steps are proposed:

- 70 per cent of the state budget is allocated for development of rural areas;
- Women have been given 33.5 per cent reservation at all levels;
- *Gram panchayat kendras* have become centre offices where field functionaries of all line departments are posted under the administrative control of *panchayat* President;
- GPUs and ZPs now have the power to prepare, sanction, supervise and implement schemes of Rs. 3-10 lakh in their own area;
- The government has provided an amount of Rs. 10 lakh to all 166 GPUs and Rs. 50 lakh each to the four ZPs in 2003-04. Apart from this some departments have provided funds separately to the *panchayats* for development projects;
- District Planning Officers, Joint Directors, Deputy Directors and Assistant Engineers are posted in all the ZPs and 9 sub-divisional officers along with other staff have been posted in all the sub-divisions;
- Capacity building training is made mandatory to all the *panchayat sabhapatis*, *sachivas*, and rural development assistants;
- All government institutions like primary schools, PHSCs, VLO centres, libraries, CICs, rural tourism, minor irrigation works, community centres, playgrounds, within a GPU is put under the control of the president of the GPU;
- All plans and schemes to be passed in the *gram sabhas* and district planning committee meetings to ensure transparency and accountability;
- Any problem at the village level can be addressed at the *gram prashasan kendra*.
- As per policy directives of the government, the sectoral outlay of the funds of a GPU is as follows:

• water supply repairs	15 per cent
• social forestry	10 per cent
• welfare programme for women and children	10 per cent
• setting up of individual cottage industry units	30 per cent
• investment in *Smriti Van*	10 per cent
• investment in medicinal plants/herbal medicines	10 per cent
• miscellaneous	15 per cent

A detailed account of actions taken by departments as per government directives on decentralisation and devolution of financial powers in Sikkim is given below:

TABLE 11.7

Government Directives on Decentralisation and Devolution of Financial Powers in Sikkim

Department	*Panchayat*	*Institution to be Transferred*	*Manpower Deployment*	*Modalities*
Education	*Gram Panchayat*	Lower primary school	Headmaster, teachers, members, staff	Management & Supervision, Disciplinary Powers, Maintenance of School Buildings, Salary to be paid by parent Department, School managing Committee
		Primary school	Headmaster, teachers	Chairman-president, GPU, Member-local elderly people, Member secretary-headmaster
	Zilla Panchayat	Junior high school	Headmaster, teachers, staff/language teacher	Overall management & supervision, disciplinary powers, salary to be paid by parent department, maintenance of school buildings, school managing committee, chairman-member, ZP, member secretary-headmaster
		Asst. Dir. Posted in *Zilla* Office	Asst. Dir. of Education	Will be on deputation to ZP Salary to be paid by parent department
Forest	*Gram Panchayat* unit	Block office	Block officer	Directly under GPU issue of marking order for fallen treetransit permit to be issued for local transportation from the field to the residence
	Zilla Panchayat	Asst. Conservator of Forest	Asst. Conservator of Forest	Will be on deputation to ZP Salary to be paid by parent department
Animal Husbandry	*Gram Panchayat* Unit	Stockman Office, GPU		Salary to be paid by parent department
	Zilla Panchayat	Stockman Office		Will be on deputation to ZP Salary to be paid by parent department
Agriculture	*Gram Panchayat* Unit	VLW Office under GPU	VLW will be under GPU	Salary to be paid by parent department
	Zilla Panchayat	Horticulture officer Jt. Dir. Agri/Horti		
Health	*Gram Panchayat* unit	PHSC	Multipurpose health worker, Staff	Maintenance of PHSC overall supervision, management and Control salary to be paid by health department.
	Zilla Panchayat	PHCCMO	Doctors under the control of ZP report to ZP	Supervisory power Dual control
Land Revenue	*Gram Panchayat* unit	VLO office	VLO under direct control of GP	Salary to be paid by parent department
Industries	*Gram Panchayat* unit	Inspector	Directly under the control of GPU	Salary to be paid by parent department
Cooperative	*Gram Panchayat* unit	Inspector	Directly under the control of GPU	Salary to be paid by parent department
Irrigation	*Gram Panchayat* Unit	Jr. Engineer	Directly under the control of GPU	Salary to be paid by parent department

Source: Annual Administrative Report, RDD.

11.3.2 Schemes and Programmes

To make the process of democratic decentralisation effective some schemes are designed in the state in the following areas:

- *Panchayat* infrastructure: A sanction of Rs. 95 lakh for construction of 10 *panchayat ghars* by the state government; 7 are constructed investing slightly over 80 lakh;
- Skill Development: Training programmes for capacity building of newly elected *panchayat* personnel in State Institute of Rural Development (SIRD) *karfektar* in the state and National Institute of Rural Development, in Guwahati, and Hyderabad.

11.4 Schemes and Programmes for Rural Development: A Critical Analysis

11.4.1 Allocation

Let us start with the plan allocations of the state on rural development for the last two five year plans.

Comparing figures for Ninth and Tenth Five-Year Plans (Table 11.8 below) it is clear that it has decreased considerably, both in absolute and percentage (of total plan outlay) terms.

Analysis of the last few annual plans during (2000-2004) will throw some light on the allocations for the schemes (Tables A-41 and A-42):

For SGSY, the absolute allocation amount remains stable over the last two plans at 80 lakh, starting from 50 lakh in 2000-01, no change in percentage share (2.5 per cent):

- For SGRY, absolute amount remains the same at 300 lakh starting in 2002-03, percentage share has slightly increased;
- For inter-village communication we find a downward trend in both the absolute amount and the percentage share of allocation in the annual plans, it declined from 300 lakh to 250 lakh in absolute amount and 14.8 per cent to 7.8 per cent during 2000-2004.
- For rural housing an upward trend has been recorded in both the absolute amount (from 762 to 2050 lakh) and the percentage share (37.6 per cent to 63.9 per cent)
- Rural water supply and sanitation has shown an upward trend in terms of allocation;
- For IREP the absolute amount has increased from 25 lakh to 230 lakh in, percentage share has increased from 4.9 per cent to 7.2 per cent.

It is clear that in order to tackle the financial constraints, there is a decrease on the allocation for rural development. The state has channeled resources on housing, water supply and sanitation, and energy programmes at the cost of inter-village communications. The poverty alleviation programs have shown stable allocations except for the allocation on Jawahar Gram Samridhi Yojana (JGSY), which has increased over the past few years.

TABLE 11.8

Plan Allocations for Rural Development

(Rs. Lakh)

	Ninth Plan	*Tenth Plan*
Absolute	11026	7000
Percentage	6.88	4.23

Source: Ninth and Tenth State Five Year Plans.

11.4.2 Achievements

The physical achievements of the programmes shown in the latest progress report are too bright to be realistic. Table 11.9 below summarises the targets and achievements recorded by the Rural Development department for the year 2003-04.

The SGRY (I&II) is claimed to generate 11 lakh man days in the current year. SJSY is claimed to form 72 self-help groups, and creating 1942 *swarozgaris*. But it is clear from first hand experiences of the visits to the state and the past records of the physical achievements of these programmes (Table A-43) that the employment generating programmes are not taking off in the state. The existing figures on massive unemployment also hint at massive leakage in the system.

Policies aimed at providing housing and other related infrastructure are performing comparatively better. It is clear that the government is emphasising on creating basic household amenities in the state. But the long run impact of the housing programmes, particularly the model village component, can be questioned on the ground whether the beneficiaries would be able to maintain such structures. Water Supply and sanitation programmes are yet to cover all the habitations. Energy programs are building up environmental consciousness but both the quality and quantity should be ensured.

11.5 Recommendations

This section spells out some recommendations for strengthening the base of rural development in Sikkim.

- For focused and more effective policies accurate poverty estimates are needed because in most of the cases the below poverty line population is the target group for rural development. These estimates will help in smoothening the resource mobilisation process.
- Short term targets to be set to achieve development goals for the rural sector.
- Service delivery to poorer sections to be assured : proper monitoring by *panchayats* is needed particularly to ensure the efficacy of the employment generating schemes.
- Cultivation is the major occupation in Sikkim but surprisingly there is a very biased structure of land distribution and the authorities are absolutely silent about any revision of the laws regarding land distribution and transfer. This

TABLE 11.9

Targets and Achievements of Employment Generating Schemes in Sikkim 2003-04

Programs	*Target*			*Achievement*	
	Financial		*Physical*	*Financial (Rs. lakh)*	*Physical*
	Cash (Rs. lakh)	*Foodgrains (Metric Tonnes)*			
SGSY					
Individual	145.27		1942 nos	145.27	1942 nos
Self Help Groups	11.58		72 Groups	11.58	72 Groups
Training	3.69			3.69	
Infrastructure Development	49.28			49.28	
Skill Training	20.47			20.47	
Total	230.30			230.30	
SGRY I					
Centre	385.87	4684			
State	118.00				
Total	503.87	4684	5.89 lakh man days	4684	5.89 lakh man days
SGRY II					
Centre	317.68	3850			
State	112.00				
Total	429.68	3850	4.99 lakh man days	3850	4.99 lakh man days

Source: Annual Administrative Report, RDD, Sikkim

issue should be taken up immediately. Revision of Revenue Act 1 will eliminate many distortions in the system.

- Technical education and vocational courses can act as quicker sources for income. The IT department has come up with training programmes on animation and related subjects in which the young students have utilised their creative talent and used it as a source of livelihood. Courses of these kinds should be encouraged.
- Training programmes for porters, tourist guides to be initiated.
- Cut in funds on rural connectivity is not justified on any ground because lack of proper infrastructure in the hilly and difficult terrain of the state will impede the process of development. Investment on rural connectivity can generate long chains of positive impact on the economy of the state.
- Strengthening of rural marketing chains is one of the issues, which demands special attention. The transmission of information to the farmers through CICs should be made more effective by giving proper training to the farmers to enable them to utilise the system fully. Rural co-operatives should be made more powerful.
- More emphasis on handicrafts: consolidation of craftsmen training
- Rural R&D activities are dormant in the state. Revitalising ICAR in Sikkim should be one of the most important steps. Other institutes like GB Pant, Sikkim Manipal, should also be motivated in this regard. The efficacy of the policies of rural development is also judged in terms of the positive externalities they generate on the rural economy. Rural R&D can generate the strongest chain of positive externalities over time. CAPART can be consulted in this regard.
- Mobilisation of funds for rural R&D: inclusion of private sector and NGOs.
- Revised recruitment policy in ICAR
- Private sector, NGOs participation should to be encouraged.
- Developing patent system to protect rights: revitalise the patent information centre in the state
- To make rural development a complete and well-knit process, convergence of the policies of different departments is needed. There should be a good coordination between departments so that they can

formulate policies with a greater degree of compatibility.

- In order to make the 73rd and 74th amendment work in a more efficient way in the state the infrastructure of the *panchayats* needs to be improved. More *GP ghars* need to be constructed so that each GP has its own share. *Panchayat* members should be trained to use CICs so that the villagers can learn from them and take advantage of the facility. Number of CICs should increase over time; at least one CIC should be there for each *panchayat ghar*.
- Community based conservation programmes like *swajaldhara* to be initiated soon.
- Sensitising village folk about community development: NGOs to play an active role.
- *Panchayats* to play the role of investigators in locating the gaps in implementation of policies, discontinuation of projects, etc.
- *Panchayat* and NGOs to form more self help groups
- There is total absence of monitoring and evaluation of the rural development schemes and programmes both at macro and micro level. In such a a situation, it is very difficult to assess the progress made by any such projects.
- There are very many areas where resources can be better utilised by improving the coordination between the various departments working in the rural areas. It is necessary to set up a district level coordination committee of all the rural development projects.

References

Annual Administrative Report 2001-02, 2002-03, Dept. of Information Technology, Govt. of Sikkim.

Annual Progress Report of Rural Management and Development Department, 2003-04; Govt. of Sikkim.

Annual Report 2002-03, Ministry of Rural Development, GOI.

Background Notes for Discussions of Annual Plan 2003-04, Govt. of Sikkim.

Basic Rural Statistics (1996). Govt. of India.

Bhasin, Veena (1989). *Ecology, Culture & Change: Tribals of Sikkim Himalayas*, Inter-India Publication.

Census of India, 1981-Sikkim-Series-19, Portrait of Population Sikkim./Sikkim: C.O.P., 1988; vi: p.132.

———. *1991-Series-22-Sikkim*, Part-III-B-B: Economic Tables. — Sikkim: Dir. of Census Oper., 1997; vii: p53.

———. *1991-Series-22-Sikkim*, Part-III-B-B: Economic Tables. — Sikkim: Dir. of Census Oper., 1997. vii,p.398.

———. *1991-Series-22-Sikkim*, Portrait of Population Sikkim. C.O.P., 1997; xiii: p.155.

———. 1991-Series-22-Sikkim, Sikkim State District Profile 1991. New Delhi: C.O.P., 1999; X: p88.

———. *2001*, Primary Census Abstract.

Das, B.S. (1996). *The Sikkim Saga*. New Delhi: Vikas Publishing House.

Dasgupta, Manas (1992). *Sikkim: Problems & Prospects of Development*. Indus Pub. Co.

Directives of Govt. of Sikkim on Democratic Decentralisation and Devolution of Financial Powers to PRIs, Department of Rural Devvelopment, Govt. of Sikkim.

Economic Survey of Sikkim 2003-04, Directorate of Economics and Statistics, Govt. of Sikkim.

Guidelines, DRDA Administration, Department of Rural Development, Govt. of Sikkim.

Lama, Mahendra P., *Sikkim Human Development Report, 2001*. New Delhi: Social Science Press.

Lama, Mahendra P. (*ed.*) (1994). *Sikkim: Society, Polity, Economy, Environment*, New Delhi: Indus Pub. Co.

Manual of Panchayat Law, Department of Rural Development, Govt. of Sikkim.

Planning and Development Deptt., Govt. of Sikkim, Ninth and Tenth Five Year Plans.

Project Report-Mapping of Suitable Areas for Mandarin in East District, Sikkim using Remote Sensing & GIS Technology, Prepared by Space Applications Center (ISRO), Space Remote Sensing Application Center, Sikkim, and Dept. of Horticulture, Govt. of Sikkim.

Rai, Suresh Chand, *et. al.* (*eds.*) (1998). *Sikkim: Perspectives for Planning and Development*. Sikkim Science Society.

Release of Funds to Local Bodies (PRIs) District-wise for Developmental Schemes, Department of Rural Development, Govt. of Sikkim.

Selvarajan, E, *et. al.*, *Rural Development: Programmes & Externalities*. New Delhi: Serial Publication.

Sikkim—A Statistical Profile, Govt. of Sikkim.

Sikkim Govt. Gazette, July, 2002, Govt. of Sikkim.

Sikkim State Annual Plan, 1999-2000, 2000-2001, 2001-2002, 2002-2003.

Chapter 12

Development of Forest Resources

12.1 Background

Sikkim has traditionally followed a growth path that is sustainable both economically and ecologically. The very morphology and sociology of the state is fragile—both in terms of the geographical location as well as in terms of sociocultural makeup. The State Forest Department was set up in 1907 and the forests were demarcated into:

- reserved forests (left in their pristine state for their crucial ecological functions);
- *khasmal* forest (forest areas in the vicinity of villages from which people meet their timber and fuelwood requirements); and
- *gorucharan* forest (areas for cattle grazing and fodder collection).

In the early 1970s, it was estimated that of the total surface area of 7,096 sq. km in Sikkim, forests occupied 1,944.05 sq. km. (27.4%) excluding slip reserve and road reserve forests for which figures were not available. Within this also, forests occupied nearly 805.69 sq. km in the northern zone, while in the intensely cultivated eastern and western zones forests cover only 527.59 and 610.7 sq km., respectively.[1] The last base line survey of forest resources in the state was done in 1988, which found the forest cover to be 44 per cent.

However, the actual forest cover of the state was only 45 per cent of the total geographical area as in 2001 (Figure 12.1).

The Forest Survey of India (FSI) estimated the forest cover to be around 42.8 per cent of the geographical area. The state has a policy of environment, forest and land use as well as a state forest fire management

FIGURE 12.1

Trend in the Ratio of Forest Cover to Geographical Area in Sikkim

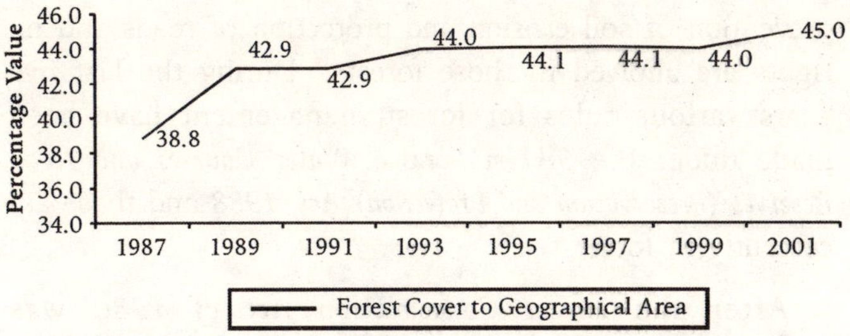

Source: Department of Forest, Wildlife and Environment, Govt. of Sikkim.

TABLE 12.1

District Wise Forest Cover (Sq Km): 2001

District	*Geographical Area*	*Forest Cover*	*% of Total Geographical Area*
East	954	670	70.23
West	1160	712	61.06
North	4226	1301	30.79
South	750	510	68.00
Total	7090	3193	45.04

Source: IPRD, Government of Sikkim.

policy. These along with the *National Forest Policy 1988* form the basis of forestry development and protection. However, a 20-year State Forestry Action Plan (SFAP) has been prepared under the National Forestry Action Programme, 1994-95 (NFAP) which provides guidelines for the preparation of a management plan for all the forests and ecosystems of the state. According to this Plan, *inter alia* top priority has been given to the

1. Debnath, 1974.

strengthening of policy, legislation, and institutional framework.[2]

12.1.1 Legal Framework and Institutions

Sikkim has had several traditional forest laws. The forest manual served as a statute book since 1909 when it was first compiled. Since then, it has been supplemented from time to time. According to this manual, no rights and concessions to the people exist as far as reserve forests are concerned. As far as private estate forests are concerned, all rights, of course, devolve upon the owner landlords and their tenants. For *khasmahal* forests, people have the right of free supply of timber and firewood but this can be availed of only after obtaining formal permission from the Forest department. In *gorucharan* forests the local people have the right of free grazing and collection of deadwood and fodder. Slip reserve and road reserve forests are maintained by the state for the prevention of soil erosion and protection of roads and no rights are allowed in those forests.[3] During the last five years various rules for forest management have been made under the *Sikkim Forests, Water Courses and Road Reserves (Preservation and Protection) Act, 1988* and these are currently in force.

After the *Forest Conservation Act of 1980* was implemented in Sikkim, the state required permission for any activity in the forest area. Legal diversion is now possible only for the public forests while for the private forest land this permission is not required. The state has an array of laws and policies in areas of forest, land and environment and wastes management.[4]

12.1.2 Institutional Infrastructure

Besides the Forest department, there are institutions like Botanical Survey of India, Geological Survey of India, GB Pant Institute for Himalayan Environment and Development and even Indian Council of Agricultural Research which are working on forest and environmental related issues in Sikkim. NGOs like Green Circle, WWF, like Kanchenjunga Conservation Committee are also creating awareness towards environment and ecology in the state. However, during our field visits to the state, one could see visible signs of poor coordination among these various institutions looking after the forest and environmental issues. This included conservation awareness, approaches to physical conservation, research, planning and evaluation. Besides inefficient use of resources, this has brought about a considerable degree of overlapping, duplication, and unaccountability in their functioning and other routine activities.

For example, there are different lists of vanishing species of flora and fauna available in these institutions. In many cases, the listing is done in pure botanical and scientific language. These lists are never circulated to the people in general and grassroot workers, in particular. As a result only few scientists, forest officials and academics know about the endangered species in the state whereas the real protectors and custodians like village communities, students, and non-governmental organisations find it difficult to access this crucial knowledge base.

12.1.3 Forest Revenue

Forest has never been a major source of revenue for the government both because of the strict conservation techniques and the regulated price of forest and allied produce. The total expenditure for the conservation and development of forest is much more than the total revenue received from the forest resource. Although there has been a gradual increase in the total revenue realised from various sources of forestry sector in the state in the last one decade, revenue from the major sectors including timber, charcoal, and firewood has been fluctuating and declining (Table 12.2).

The Forest department fixes the rate of royalty of different forest produce depending on the importance of the produce, the extent of their availability in the forest and their market value. The forest produce like sand and

TABLE 12.2

Percentage Share of Major Forest Produce to Total Revenue Realised from Various Sources of Forestry Sector

Years	*Timber*	*Firewood*	*Charcoal*	*Total*
1997-98	2.95	0.53	0.61	4.09
1998-99	0.90	0.14	0.12	1.16
1999-00	0.54	0.20	0.11	0.85
2000-01	0.45	0.13	0.03	0.60
2001-02	3.34	0.03	0.06	3.42
2002-03	2.80	0.26	0.04	3.10

Source: Computed from the *Annual Administrative Report, 2002-03*, Forest Department, Government of Sikkim

2. *Handbook on Environmental Law and Policy for Sikkim, 1999.*
3. Debnath *op. cit.* pp.216-17.
4. *Handbook on Environmental Law and Policy for Sikkim.*

stone, medicinal herbs, are not sold by the department. Only royalty per unit value/number is fixed by the department for collection of the same from forest. Royalty is also realised for timber in the form of trees/logs from the villagers who require timber for their bonafide use, from reserve forests.

Though the department's pricing of forest produce has been based on the cost of extraction and transport, royalty and storage and handling charges put together, the sale price has been many times lower than the market price. More importantly, the sale price once fixed has not been revised regularly. For instance, timber price per cu. ft. fixed in 1990, continues to be the same.[5] This unrealistic pricing of the forest produce requires a serious reassessment and needs to be re-examined on the basis of market valuation.

The forest revenue has not been taking into consideration many tangible and intangible benefits that are particularly difficult to quantify. Even though these benefits are not accounted for and calculated, they accrue to the people and the state. In a direct manner, the forest supports over 5 lakh people and over 3-lakh livestock population including cattle, buffalo, sheep, goat, yak, horse, pony, mule, and pig.

Except the logging and sale of other forest resources like stone, and sand, that too in a highly subsidised manner, the revenue which could have been generated through the sale of fodder, timber, etc are never calculated as the income generated by the forest in the state. On top of this, the illegal and unaccounted extraction of fuel wood, fodder, timber—which has been much more than the legally processed—do not figure in the official records of revenue receipts. Many of these produce is literally taken 'free' and 'freely' by the people which amounts to a revenue loss amounting to several crore rupees every year.

Besides these direct and tangible benefits, there are intangible benefits like air and water, which largely help in continuing the regenerative process in the state. The green cover is also critical to sustainable livelihoods like, animal husbandry, tourism, hydel power generation, and many other economic activities. Even the environmental benefit (including prevention of soil erosion led disasters) which has been accruing to the state and the people through the maintenance of forest resources is never quantified. This has in fact, undermined the need and scope for investment in the forest areas. The forest resources have served as a major infrastructure catering to both the general needs and that of tourists etc. Therefore, investment in the forestry as a distinct sector is rather crucial, particularly when this provides sustainability to the general physical environment.

12.1.4 Forest Budget

The budget allocation to the Forest department has been rather dismal which has been adversely affecting both the regenerative process through afforestation, and investment on forest planning and management. For instance, the plan allocation in 1995 was Rs. 4.25 crore and Rs. 5.55 crore in 2003, hardly an increase of 30 per cent which is also more or less offset by the inflationary trend during the period. This budget is not sufficient at all. The department has to pay around Rs. 2 crore as wages to the workers per annum and around Rs. 2.50 crore in plan salaries. The present plan budget does not provide for any meaningful forest development in the state. Had it not been the 100 per cent centrally sponsored field activities like plantations, the forests resources would have faced a tremendous pressure. This has been the case with the wildlife related activities as well.

12.2 Emerging Issues

12.2.1 Deforestation Hazard

For a fragile ecosystem like that of Sikkim, deforestation has been the most critical environmental danger. Unlike plain lands, in primarily hill and mountainous state like Sikkim, the reasons for deforestation have been much more diverse and are sometimes deeply related to traditional consumptive habits, practices, and patterns. This is more so because of the very limited availability of cultivable land. As the population increased there has been a considerable clearance of land for cultivation at least upto the altitude of 2,000 metres. The depletion of forest resources have a wide ranging impact on ecological balance leading to extinction of rare flora and fauna, soil erosion, changes in the climatic conditions, desertification, landslides and flood. Organised gangs have also been operating in some parts of Sikkim, particularly in the bordering districts (with West Bengal).

However, the main reasons behind steady deforestation in the past could be attributed to energy needs, land diversion for development activities,

5. The Forest Department attributes this to the fact that sale of timber is carried out from the utilisation wing of the department as a welfare measure rather than on commercial basis.

commercial deforestation, forest fires, grazing and natural calamities (exclusively discussed in the following section). The traditional sources of energy in rural Sikkim, *viz.*, firewood, animal dung, crop residues, are still the only or major energy sources to the overwhelming populace. The environmental degradations arising out of persistent over dependence on the biomass and the adverse health effects of biomass cooking, particularly in confined spaces are now taking alarming shapes.

Fuel wood continues to be the main source of energy accounting for more than 85 per cent of total energy consumption. In rural areas, of all the districts, forest wood continues to be the predominant source of fuel for cooking. In the urban areas too, at least in two districts of west and north, wood is the main fuel for the purpose of cooking. Unlike popular belief that electricity is increasingly replacing the conventional sources of energy, it is found that not even one per cent of urban and rural population use it as a cooking medium. LPG consumption in the north is still relatively much lower thereby indicating their dependence on forest resources.

Development led diversion of land from the forest area has been another major source of deforestation in Sikkim. Sometimes the difficult terrain makes it inevitable to encroach into the forestland. This has been there in Sikkim for long. Till March 1998, it is estimated that over 590 hectares of forestland was diverted for the development-related activities. In 1998-1999 alone 10 hectares were diverted. For the *Teesta V Project*, a total of 147 hectares needed to be diverted. (Table 12.3).

Out of the total diverted land so far, over 35 per cent has gone to road buildings mostly by the army and Border Road Organisation (BRO). The other diversions have taken place mainly due to hydel projects and transmission related activities (26%) and construction (29%). Sikkim is believed to have the best record of compensatory afforestation (CA). Whatever deforestation is done for the purpose of development projects by diversion of forestland, CA is recorded to have been carried out. So far approximately over 1000 hectares of CA is said to have been done. This has more than offset the deforestation caused by acquisition of land for development activities.

However, the diversion of land recorded in the table 6 accounts for only formal and legal diversion. The informal and illegal diversion could be many times bigger than this. The *Forest (Conservation) Act, 1980* stipulates that an equivalent extent of non-forest land has to be provided for any type of forestland lost due to any of the development projects.

The commercial deforestation in Sikkim broadly originated in the 1951 scheme of 'floatation of timber.' Under this scheme, timbers used to be floated through the rivers both in log and sawn forms. This scheme was found to be very handy, as the transport cost involved was

TABLE 12.3

Approved Cases of Diversion under the Forest Conservation Act 1980 including Compensatory Afforestation (CA) up to 1988

Projects	*Number*	*Forest Area Approved for Diversion (hectare)*	*Compensatory Forest Non-land (hectare)*	*Afforestation in Forest Land (hectare)*
Irrigation	5	4.4	11.5	
Roads	15	8.7	503.3	5.9
Hydro-electric Project	6	59.3	240.0	18.0
Quarrying of Minerals	2	2.4	6.0	
Transmission Line	9	92.6	9.5	2.5
Water Conductor Channel	1	0.6		
Building Complex and Playground	8	127.0	5.7	
Cremation Ground	1	0.1		
Plantation	1	80.0		
Water Supply Scheme	2	18.1	32.6	
Microwave Repeater Station	2	0.4		0.2
War Memorial	1	0.1		
Total	54	593.8	1,008.6	26.6

Source: Computed from data supplied by the Department of Forests, Government of Sikkim.

minimum. However, there were massive losses of forest resources mainly because of the flood in the riverine belt and ill timing of the launching of timber. For instance, during 1959-60, out of a total of 1,10,000 cubic feet of timber floated in two consignments, 86,000 cubic feet were lost in floods, and only 24,000 cubic feet of timber could be salvaged.[6] However, the commercial deforestation has steadily gone down after the present government put a complete ban on tree felling in mid-1990s.

Another major source of subtropical biodiversity destruction including forest has been the forest fire caused either accidentally or by villagers for growing fresh grasses for fodder. The villagers also burn debris and slash their agricultural fields and sometimes the fire escapes to the forests from the adjacent fields. Some fires are deliberately lit by graziers and poachers. The extent of forest fire depends on the terrain, direction of wind and dryness of the forest areas, and the general weather condition. The prolonged drought from September 1998 to April 1999 caused extensive forest fires. Almost all the forests of the Teesta and Rangit valley in east, south and west experienced forest fires in this period and several young plantations including the naturally regenerated *sal* forests were affected. The extent of damage of ground flora has been estimated from 500 to 1000 hectares. Though the burnt ash adds manure to the soil, which helps the growth of plants that come up after the fire, the damage caused on the flora, fauna, soil binding capacity by the ground flora and some of standing tree crop together amount to several lakh of rupees each year.

Grazing has been found to be a major factor leading to deforestation. The government noted the depredatory and degrading menace of grazing in the reserve forests by multitude of cows, buffaloes, yaks, sheep and goats. A great many fragile forest ecosystems throughout the state are under immense threat of destabilisation and disequilibrium. Consequently, the diversity and richness of Sikkim's floral and faunal wealth is also seriously at stake. A total ban on grazing was effected in 1995 by the present government.

12.2.2 Vanishing Species

One of the most debilitating impacts of deforestation and human encroachments has been the steady depletion of some of the very well known plant and animal species in Sikkim. There are several efforts to identify and protect these vanishing species both at the state and the union level. However, despite all these, one does not find a very well-thought out strategy to carry out this gigantic, yet critical task. The near absence of non-governmental organisation in these activities have made it more like a governmental concern rather than the peoples' popular concern.

The red panda was declared the state animal by the government in 1984.[7] Of the 155 odd mammals known to exist in this Himalayan state, as many as 39 have been declared endangered or rare under schedule I of the *Wildlife (Protection) Act 1972*. These include the red panda, cast Himalayan *thar*, musk deer, snow leopard, jungle cat, tree shrew, Tibetan wolf, red fox, Indian wild dog, hog badjer, Tibetan sheep, *bharal, serow, kiang* and *gorla*. Many of them have been sighted in parts of Kanchenjunga National Park. Besides the red panda, musk deer and bharal (blue sheep) are other two animals sighted rarely during the last decade. Alpine musk deer is reported to be found in 12 locations in the high altitude areas of north and west Sikkim. Demand for musk, obtained from its pod, has made this animal rare.

There are various sources of information regarding the endangered, rare and threatened plants in Sikkim. Some of them vary drastically in both identifying the affected species and attributing the exact status and the causes for being so. The state and union government agencies, independent research organisation, local non-governmental environmental organisations and international bodies have separate listings of these species. Many of them are endangered species listed in schedule I to the *Wildlife (Protection) Amendment Act, 1991* and appendices of CITES. A scientist attached to the GB Pant Institute in Gangtok remarks, "A baseline information would help much in conserving many of the plants....much has to be done in terms of researches. The flowering and fruiting of most of the species are hitherto not known or recorded and this particular aspect remains to be crucial in terms of conservation of biological diversity for the region. Unless measures are taken to update reproductive and regenerative information the work on germ plasm preservation will also fall short."[8]

A survey and study revealed that many plant species could not be collected after its first collection and have

6. Debnath *op. cit.*, pp.219-22.
7. Many people believe this declaration was made by Chogyal of Sikkim in the late 1960s.
8. Rai, 1993: 10.

dwindled considerably perhaps due to over collection for ornamental value and medicinal uses. Therefore a well coordinated, concerted and urgent effort must be made to inventorise the rare, threatened, and endemic plants of the state with their phenological data, associates, soil texture, and causal factors of rarity, so that adequate steps could be taken to conserve them.

So far no systematic efforts have been made in this direction. What is more crucial is the protection, conservation, and regeneration aspects of it. For this, people have to be made aware of the implications of further destroying the already endangered. People in the state do not know about the endangered species as the scientific knowledge and the conservation have remained exclusively with the scientists and forest officials.

BOX 12.1

Case of Biopiracy in Sikkim

In July 2001, two foreign nationals were arrested for trying to smuggle out moths and beetles from the Khangchendzonga National Park. They were caught red handed with more than 1,000 specimens of these insects and other tools used. They were booked under Section 35(6) of the *Wildlife (Protection) Act 1972* and kept in judicial custody for more than a month. Subsequently, a detailed investigation and complaint (charge sheet) was filed. The case was later transferred to the *lok adalat*, subsequently compounded, and all seized items confiscated.

Source: Department of Information and Public Relation, Govt. of Sikkim.

12.2.3 Natural Calamities

i) Landslides

Sikkim, which lies in the lower Himalayas, is characterised by deep valleys and steep mountain ranges. There is no published data on the geo-environmental studies of Sikkim. However, this region is characterised by instability of the ground resulting in earthquakes and frequent landslides. Earthquakes are of small and medium scale. This zone is also highly mobile in the Himalayan sector. According to the continental drift theory a few thousands years ago north Sikkim was a part of Thespian Sea which rose up with its sediments as the Himalayan range. This happened due to a collusion between the Indian Plate and the Eurosian Plate. Therefore, the rocks and hills are very young, soft, and fragile. The process of neo-tectonism is also said to be working in the region (the mountain building movements).

Heavy rains are a bane of life in the hills of Sikkim. Practically every year, torrential rains lash the state leaving behind a trail of deaths and destruction. The enormity of natural hazards, such as landslides and floods, is gaining alarming proportions. Excessive monsoon rains is just one of the causes triggering these calamities. The more important cause is anthropogenic or human-induced changes in the ecosystem.

Three factors prevailing in Sikkim Himalayas further exacerbate the destabilising impact of high rainfall. Firstly, hills in the region are extremely fragile. The strata consist of sandstone, shale, mica schist and quartzite, which are in disintegrated condition in many places and folded and thrusted with a number of fault planes. Secondly, the topography is such that it leads to enormous erosion, landslides, and toe cutting. Thirdly, and most importantly, huge land use changes and development intervention have taken place in the state. Sikkim has suffered extensive deforestation in the last 200 years.[9]

Contrary to our popular belief that forests conservation has a positive correlation with the non-occurrence of landslides, there are instances in Sikkim to show that even very dense forests have faced one of the worst landslides in the past. The Thekeiberg and Changecenti areas in the east districts and Rang Rang Reserve Forest in the north district, have had one of the worst landslides in the densely forested areas of Sikkim. Any engineering manipulations or the usual strategy of vegetative cover cannot check this type of landslide. It is therefore more of geological formation which is responsible for landslides.

Earlier people used to have small houses and light construction. But now with the building of huge houses, roads, water supply schemes and hydropower projects and biotic interference in the form of indiscriminate felling of trees, the stress condition incapacitates the carrying capacity. This is what happened in the now dreaded Chandmari landslide in 1997. Way back in 1954, the *Sikkim Darbar* while recognising this building menace as a major hazard had notified that "construction of buildings whether temporary or permanent is permitted along either side of the road without obtaining the prior sanction of the *Darbar* in writing."[10]

9. Centre for Science and Environment, 1991.
10. Forest Department Notification No: 2375/F, 1954.

ii) Floods

Two major rivers Teesta and Rangit have been the symbols of Sikkim's rich natural and cultural heritage. Teesta is considered to be the wildest river in the Himalayas, and prone to cloudbursts, landslides, and flash floods. The Teesta has the highest sediment yield of all the Himalayan rivers and brings down approximately 98 cu m of silt per hectare per year of its catchment area. Thus, it releases the highest denudation rate estimated for any river valley in the world. Teesta meets several tributaries, which have steeper slopes and tiny catchment areas. These streams bring down large quantities of silt, boulders and water at high velocity. They play a major role in causing floods during rainstorms. Several of them flow into the Teesta in an opposite direction. At their confluence, there is enormous turbulence and silt deposition. The narrow gorge of the Teesta tends to widen at such points because of the large silt deposits. But during the rest of its course, the rivers velocity is very high because of its narrow channel. The entire watershed is, therefore, conducive to quick run-off leading to flood peaks of short duration. The high floods, in turn, accentuate landslides and toe erosion.[11]

Because of these factors, the Teesta was considered wild and unpredictable even when its catchment was clothed with dense forests. "Up to the close of the 18th century, the Teesta flowed into the Ganga. But after the destructive floods of 1787, in which a large part of the Rangpur district was laid waste, it suddenly turned eastwards and joined the Bramhaputra."[12]

In October 1968, rainfall between 600 mm to 1200 mm lashed the Darjeeling-Sikkim Himalayas for three days continuously when the ground was already saturated after a long monsoon. It is estimated that some 2,000 landslides took place. Numerous bridges (28) were washed away and rail traffic was disrupted for 32 days. Rangpo's lower market, which was well above the river before 1968, came under 2 m of sand after the flood and is now almost at the same level as the river's flood plain. Further, downstream, enormous silt came down the Tar *khola* and the road leading to the bridge across it was badly damaged.

The severity of the flood was unprecedented in the recent history of Sikkim. The damage done to the economy, particularly in the field of road and bridges was extensive. The planners were so depressed by the flood of 1968 that they slashed down the budget proposals of Rs. 2.35 crore for 1968-69 to the revised estimates of Rs. 1.75 crore only. Since it was not possible to carry on works on many schemes due to flood, the revised estimates were lowered so that the year's financial targets might be achieved.[13]

12.2.4 Folk Medicinal Practices

Sikkim is famous for all kinds of practices related to traditional medicines both because of the strong socio-religious fervour and the availability of a rich variety of plants and animals. However, very little attention has been given to the importance of protecting the intellectual property rights of indigenous peoples, whose traditional knowledge has often been the source of products introduced into the international market. The 'bio-partnerships' for sustainable development is therefore, very critical in this Himalayan state.

An emerging facet of biodiversity conservation is the medicinal and therapeutic value of plant and animal extracts. The rich possibilities of commercial exploitation of these biodiversities could be assessed from the fact that the herbal products are said to account for nearly half the medicines prescribed in the US and this trend is set to grow. *The Economist* published from London reported that annual sales of herbal products in the US are in the order of $4 billion. Sikkim has a wide and undiscovered development frontier in the scientific and commercial harnessing of these resources.

Most of the rural folk and a significant proportion of educated people living in urban areas have persistent faith on herbal charms that are indigenous to Sikkim. Local plant-based drugs can easily be seen in most of the rural houses and rural markets. Some of the popular plant drugs used since time immemorial for the respective purposes are as follows:

- *Azambari-buti (panax pseudoginseng)* for longevity;
- *Eephedra gerardiana var. Sikkimensis* for treatment of asthma;
- Juice of leaves of *drymaria cordata* in high fever, cold and throat trouble;
- Roots of *dichora febrifuja* for treatment of malaria and other fevers.
- *Elshcolzia blanda* and *mahonia Nepalensis* in eye-trouble and eczema;

11. Centre for Science and Environment, 1991.
12. Chandra, 1975.
13. Debnath *op. cit.*, p.187.

- *Urtica parviflora* (young inflorescence) as a clearing and invigorating agent after childbirth by local womenfolk.

Studies that have been done on the botanical resources of Sikkim in the past have hardly emphasised on the vast potential of studies on ethno-medico-botany particularly in the context of both rich heritage of indigenous medical practises and the fast changing international regime on intellectual property rights.

More pertinently, in all these practices the rural folks with well founded traditional technological experiments and bases are engaged. For many of them, it is the single important source of livelihood. These traditional practices have, in fact, been the source of many unknown medical practices today across the world. In the absence of any monitoring of the flow of knowledge from these remote areas to the pharmaceutical laboratories in the cities, one really does not know what innovations were introduced to make these practices commercial and popular. This brings in larger question of at what stage the intellectual property rights of a Sikkimese faith healer was infringed upon.

Though the state Forest department rules out any surreptitious activities, many of the environmental activists do mention about the quiet way these medicinal plants are exported to different cities of India and abroad by some known and unknown syndicate sometimes with a tacit connivance of the people in the helm of affairs. This phenomenon is silently eating away the sinews of Sikkimese biodiversity, yet very few in the civil society and the government seem to be seriously concerned. This is going to be more serious as the world is gradually turning to traditions, old practices and "ethnic orientation" where the pressure on biodiversity is going to be unprecedented. The economic reforms led pressure on the bio-diversity again brings us back to our fundamental surroundings and interactions. In the new scenario, however, the villains are biotechnological companies having very scanty respect for sustenance of traditional practices and occupations.

12.2.5 Intellectual Property Rights and Sikkim

No sooner the Trade Related Intellectual Property Rights (TRIPS) became effective under the new World Trade Organisation, a predominantly biodiversity rich state like Sikkim has started confronting very serious issues varying from patenting to livelihood. This has squarely challenged its rights over such resources, which they thought so far were its exclusive domain.

A widely debated issue has been as to what extent the patenting of genetic resources would be detrimental for Himalayan states like Sikkim. It is primarily an agricultural economy and therefore, heavily dependent on genetic resources for upgrading and maintaining agricultural stocks. Privatisation of genes under the new regimes of TRIPS, leading to license fees for their use would not only result in the absurd spectacle such as to pay for the use of their own property, but would also increase the already strained research and conservation budget in the state. Scientific research would suffer, leading to diminishing technological capacity, thereby both exacerbating the technology gap and increasing dependence.

Ecologists and biologists are concerned about another dangerous offshoot of gene patents i.e. genetic erosion. In fact the increasing privatisation and patents will lead to an even greater narrowing of the genetic base. Plant varieties carrying a few economically important traits like high yields or resistance to a particular disease, have been and will continue to be marketed aggressively by the patent or plant breeding rights (PBR) holders. This leads to only few varieties being grown for a crop, displacing older varieties.[14]

This is an area where the state of the art technology and knowledge regarding the true value of biological resources is limited. The Science and Technology department in the state is oblivious of all these developments. Sikkim could in fact set up an institution to work on the issues of biodiversity research and conservation for the entire Eastern Himalayas and the North East by pooling together knowledge, expertise and resources in the region. This would create a sophisticated source of biotechnological knowledge and bank of genetic resources and a genetic pool. It could make use of the technical manpower that the region produces. Each segment of this region could then have access to the knowledge and technology banks to make the best, sustainable use of its biological resources or to protect them where they are threatened with extinction.

12.2.6 Climate Change

The worldwide phenomenon of global warming due to the impact of green house effect and *El Nino* led climate change has also been recorded in many parts of the

14. Sahai, 1995.

Himalayan regions particularly in the past few years. A study carried out by Kathmandu based South Asian Association for Regional Cooperation (SAARC) Secretariat showed that there is likely to be an increased ice melting in the Himalayas because of increasing impact of the greenhouse effect. Further, the changes in rainfall patterns could inundate vast areas of the flood plains of the Ganga-Brahmaputra-Barak basins thereby multiplying the miseries and sufferings of millions of people.[15]

The entire eastern Himalayan zone had an unbelievably warm and pleasant winter in 1998-99. Many people in fact missed the usual winter conditions like fog, chill, frost and snow. Environmentalists have largely attributed this unique climatic behaviour to the global warming and the resultant changing global climate. Winter is usually the time when forest cover is under cold spell and gets some regenerative space. However, this long spell of dryness leads to forest fire, affect young seedling, drying up of water sources and grazing areas get high and dry. In other words, the entire natural cycle is disturbed.

This had visible adverse effect on the economy of Sikkim including drinking water, *rabi* crops and cash crops like cardamom, ginger, and orange cultivation. According to the Agriculture Department, the total rainfall between October 1998 to March 31, 1999 was 93.34 per cent less than the rainfall in the last 25 years in the state. Cardamom bushes which had survived all kinds of climatic depredations for the last six to eight decades also got dried to the hilt. The state government sent a proposal to the central government for relief to the estimated crop loss of Rs. 49.34 crore. This phenomenon is increasingly seen over the last few years now.[16]

12.3 Joint Forest Management

In the past, there were some attempts to evaluate some of the forest projects that were implemented and its impact. The Bureau of Economics and Statistics (BSE) did one such evaluative study on forest plantation (under the Social Forestry, Departmental Plantation and Rural Fuel Wood Plantation Schemes) in 1988. The study covered three plantation locations from each of the four districts. This study made following significant revelations:[17]

- During the three fiscal years of 1985-86 to 1987-1988, the overall survival rate was 38.5 per cent.
- The species recommended by the Forest department were not in tune with the scheme of plantation. Over 71 per cent of the trees survived were not in conformity with plantation envisaged for rural fuel wood plantation scheme.
- For all the plantation the saplings were procured from forestry nursery and no fertiliser or manure were used while planting the saplings or on subsequent dates.
- A difference of almost 55 per cent was found in the cost of plantation and cost per plant as worked by the BSE and the one announced by the Forest department.
- In most of the plantation locations the saplings have been found to be covered with weeds and shrubs. This might have resulted in higher mortality rates as well as under growth of planted saplings.

One of the belated but a positive initiative taken by the Forest department is the initiation of Joint Forest Management (JFM) project in the state in 1998. It was primarily taken up after the JFM's success story of South Bengal, especially when the Arabari village became well known. The notification that introduces JFM mentions that "the *Khasmal* and *Gorucharan* lands in the state have been considerably degraded in most of the areas due to over exploitation of the forest produce without caring for the future."

For the first time, it constituted Forest Protection Committees involving the residents of the adjoining villages. Such committees may be given 25 per cent of the net income derived from the forest crop (including non-timber forest produce and medicinal plants) so protected after meeting the 'bonafide' demands of the local villagers in respect of fodder and fuel wood from fallen and dry twigs.[18]

The JFM has been extended to Khasmal, Goucharan and degraded forestlands that are sensitive to severe biotic interference and damage to forest crop with the help of Forest/Village Protection Committees (VFCs) involving

15. SAARC Secretariat, *Regional Study on Green House Effect and its Impact on the Region, 1992* and *Regional Study on the Causes and Consequences of Natural Disasters and the Protection and Preservation of the Environment, 1992*. South Asian Association for Regional Cooperation (SAARC), Kathmandu, Nepal.
16. *Wichar*, 1999.
17. Bureau of Economics and Statistics, Evaluation Study of Forest Plantation, Planning and Development Department, Government of Sikkim, October 1988, pp.11-14.
18. Government of Sikkim, Joint Forest Management, Notification No 2/F dated 26.6.1998, Department of Forest, Environment and Wildlife.

the residents of the adjoining villages. In this connection VFCs have been constituted consisting of concerned villagers and the officials from the Forest department. Until 2002-03 there were 139 VFCs scattered across the districts of the state for the purpose.

Apart from joint forest management committees, forests in Sikkim are also managed through eco-development committees (EDCs). Such is particularly true in case of the natural vegetation and related resource bases adjoining national park, wild life sanctuaries and biosphere reserve. Accordingly, the above committees have been formed consisting of the villagers in the adjoining villages and forest officials. As of today 32 EDCs have been formed around the sanctuaries and national parks in the state with majority of them in the East District in this regard. Micro-planning and capacity building has been carried out. It is also that the EDCs have been active in apprehending medicinal plant smugglers and fire fighting. Together, the joint forest management committees and eco-development committees are protecting over 14,000 hectares of forestlands in Sikkim. (Table 12.4).

The village community complements the efforts of the official machinery by certain obligations like keeping the forests free from grazing by cattle, not removing forest produce without permission and not practising agriculture on forestlands. In return, the community committing itself to protection of the forests become entitled to enjoy usufructuary rights over forest produce and a share in the profits of sale of such produce by the department.[19]

TABLE 12.4

Joint Forest Management in Sikkim

District	Area under Protection (Hec)	No. of VFCs till July 2003	No. of EDCs till July 2003
Joint Forest Management			
North district	2700	27	-
East district	2900	49	-
South district	2400	30	-
West district	2300	33	-
Total	10300	139	-
Eco-Development			
North-east district	2000	-	16
South-west district	2100	-	16
Total	4100	-	32
Grand Total	14400	139	32

Source: Annual Administrative Report, 2002-03, Dept of Forest.

12.3.1 Role of NGOs

Sikkim is one state in the eastern Himalayas where the concept of development-related NGOs and community-based organisations (CBOs) crept in very late and rather slowly. It is largely a phenomenon of the 1990s. This in a way shows the increasing consciousness among the Sikkimese about the development-related problems brought about by a massive induction of public funds in the last 25 years. The state and the government as the sole custodian of development certainly brought about a massive change in the state both in terms of development and in improving the living standard of people. On the other hand, this process also brought about a lot of imbalances and distortions in the socio-economic fabric of the state. This could certainly cause environmental dislocations also.

BOX 12.2

Moving Towards Success

The forest protection committee of Upper Namchebong–Nimtar has been protecting 5 hectare of degraded Pricklakha Reserve Forest under the guidance of Pakyong Range Forest, East Sikkim. Plantation of mixed species with emphasis on medicinal plants started in early 2003. The survival rate of the saplings has been over 80 per cent till April, 2004. This formal protection will end in 2007 when it will be finally handed over to the villagers. Villagers of the adjoining villages are for the first time witnessing such active participation. The committee president, Meera Lepcha mentions that the forest officials have been really working hard in the project. These officials have been instrumental in convincing the people that rights over the forest resource have to be followed by duty to protect the same. As a result villagers have been in the centre of the project. Urmila Subba, Block officer, Pakyong range has been involved in the project since its inception. She finds a definite change in the outlook and attitude of the villagers. She mentions that "the villagers have become aware of the environmental hazards due to deforestation, the committee is also constructing footpaths, checking landslides and doing other forest-related activity. There has been no conflict whatsoever between the villagers and forest officials with respect to the functions of the committee and decisions taken in this regard. Based on the visit to the plantation site and discussions with the stakeholders

19. Krishnan, 1999.

The absence of any monitoring and evaluation mechanism in the state made it more difficult for the government and the state to exactly locate the distortions and imbalances in the development process. The state badly needed some institutions to give it a strong sense of direction and in identifying the priorities. This is where the role of NGOs was felt by at least the enlightened Sikkimese.

By now, there are quite a few NGOs working in Sikkim. Besides the Gangtok based *Green Circle* and *Concern Citizens*, there are *Sadbhavana Samiti* in Singtam, and *SOYA* in Samdung, *Paryawaran Sangrakshan Sangh, Sikkim Youth Welfare Association* in Gyaltshing which are quite well known in their respective fields of operation.

The Khangchendzonga Conservation Committee is another community-based organisation in Yuksam in west Sikkim which helps to mitigate adverse impact of tourism, conserve natural and cultural resources and provide training to community stakeholders, educate visitors, monitor resources and advocate for appropriate policy changes. It supported local plantations of native tree species and also conducts training in responsible trekking

BOX 12.3

Nathu La Trade Route Concerns

The Nathu La Trade Study Group has highlighted some major concerns related to reopening this trade route for cross border trade. There has been a steady increase in the number of tourists interested in trekking and mountaineering. Though these expeditions generate a lot of local income and employment, its adverse impact on the fragile mountain environment is enormous. In Sikkim, the opening up of Changu lake has suddenly exposed the pristine resort to human influx. The shops, vehicles, garbage and animals around the lake certainly do not go well with the carrying capacity of the lake site. Given the way the concerned Government agencies have maintained this area, it will soon become another dirty and dilapidated resort. Over 70 per cent of the medicinal plants are located in the alpine areas where regeneration is very difficult. It is a long process. The recovery cost is very high. The plantation cost is exorbitant. Therefore, the main emphasis in the alpine areas should be on protection of the already existing vegetation. It is in the sustainability of high altitude areas that the environmental security of Sikkim lies embedded and the long term viability of Nathu La trade route depends upon.

The carrying capacity in certain places and stretches like Gangtok, Singtam, and Changu are already under tremendous pressure both because of the population growth, tourist arrivals, buildings and hotels, and vehicular movements.

The biggest challenge to the state today comes from the destruction of vegetation in the high altitude areas. This along with the impact of global warming could emerge as a major threat to the mountain ecology thereby entailing a serious problem on the hydrological and other resources. There has been increasing instances of biopiracy in Sikkim. The movement of people for Nathu La trade exchange could also lead to more exposures of these bio resources thereby leading to their unregulated exploitations.

There are concerns related to the threats to glaciers. Most glaciers in Sikkim originate from the Kanchendzonga, or their "five big treasures of ice" and in turn give birth to streamlets. Sikkim's largest glacier, Zemu, has also retreated by 3-4 km. If the glaciers continue to recede, it could spell disaster for Sikkim's fragile economy and may even lead to devastating floods and ultimate dryness in river Teesta. This could be rather disastrous for the hydel power plants that are being planned to be located on the Teesta basin. It could also change the entire hydrological map of the eastern Himalayan regions including that of north east India, West Bengal and neighbouring countries like Nepal, Bhutan, and Bangladesh.

Issues related to infrastructure projects led dislocation of village areas, landslides in fragile areas, air pollution disturbance to major and minor tributaries are also relevant. These infrastructures, if not planned in a long term manner could damage reserved forests and plantations, wild life, religious places, utility lines like telephone and electric poles, and transformers existing in semi urban/urban areas. The present highway from Sevoke to Gangtok and the JN Road from Gangtok to Nathu La mostly pass through the forest and rural areas. It is also stated that the national highway from Rangpo to Gangtok fall under zone-IV of the seismic zonation map with high earthquake damage risk.

For instance, a comprehensive social screening and assessment exercise conducted on the proposed improvement of the existing single lane of national highway from Sevoke to Rangpo (52.0 km) and its widening to 2-lane national highway standard road revealed that it is likely to affect 450 properties of which 70 are *pucca*, 350 semi-*pucca* and 30 *kutcha*. Thesalso include 5 religious structures. The cost of rehabilitation and resettlement is estimated to be Rs. 3.5 crore.[20]

Source: Lama, 2005.

20. The Final Feasibility Report for Segment A (Vol. I) by Archtech Consultants Pvt. Ltd of India and Halcrow Group Ltd of UK on behalf of Sikkim Industrial Development & Investment Corp. Ltd. (SIDICO, February 2004, p.1-18).

practices for locally based porters in major trekking trail. It is also felt that a whole lot of NGOs have mushroomed in the last few years. Some of them have doubtful backgrounds. The haphazard mushrooming of NGOs may ultimately overshadow some of the genuine NGOs purposefully involved in the grassroot development process in the state. Without disturbing their freedom to work, there must be some independent non-governmental mechanism to promote and regulate NGO activities in the state. This monitoring can reduce overlapping, repetition, resource wastage, and clash of activities. However, unhealthy political interventions may stunt the growth and dampen the spirit of the NGOs.

However, a large number of people are still unaware about the JFM. The question of acceptability and adaptability have not really come up as most of them are yet to understand the conceptual framework and its socio-economic implications.

Therefore, the JFM programme could be more seriously injected into the communities by making them aware of the successes in other states of the country through organising exposure visits of the farmers to these areas. This also calls for protracted motivation programmes and constant monitoring. Driving force in the entire concept of JFM should be its very philosophy of peoples' participation. The JFM should in fact be tagged with already introduced programmes like *Smriti Van*, which also aims at involving people at the grassroots level. This could be done only after convincing the people that they will have some kind of economic return in the long run. This can go a a long way in making plantation and forestry sustainable.

Simplified guidelines will have to be prepared for JFM. The villagers need to be encouraged to plant more and more trees in the private wastelands. The NGOs, on the other hand, should be encouraged to organise awareness camps to educate people for protection of environment and forests, benefits of the JFM scheme, prevention of natural calamities like landslides and drought etc. In areas where village forest committee is given the forests adjacent to the villages, their confidence has to be gained by providing them the basic minimum services and empowering them.

12.3.2 Capacity Building in Forest Management

Capacity building is an essential aspect of afforestation and other forest related activities. In Sikkim, there has been a major gap in the manpower development and availability. The non-gazetted officers and other field officials are never exposed to any training or modern techniques and technologies in terms of forest related activities. They still look at the entire gamut of forest-related issues and problems from a traditional perspective of management.

They are not equipped to deal with the changing dimensions of forest management. Only the Indian Forest Service officers are exposed to the latest dimensions but they are mostly in Gangtok. The present level of manpower availability in the Forest department needs to be used more effectively. Instead of inducting very many new people, the department should provide the existing manpower with the facilities like refresher courses, short-term training and skill improvement training in various forestry institutes and other professional institutions in and outside the country.

The central institutions are primarily meant to supplement the activities of the related state departments by means of broader research, better technological intervention and drawing experiments and resources from other national and international institutions. At the moment there seem to be no harmony or coordination among various agencies engaged in forest related activities.

The Meteorological Department, BSI, GB Pant, ZSI, ICAR should be given clear mandate to work with the state departments. These mandates should not mismatch with the fact that the actual protection and afforestation are done by the state department. Therefore, without diluting the autonomy, a mechanism should be worked out to make these central institutions partly accountable to the counterpart state institutions. This should be more so because the state extends these central institutions all the required facilities.

The thrust should be on the forestry research including wild life, new technological interventions in the forest management and conservation projects with added emphasis on preservation of traditional practices. There are positive initiatives which need to be consolidated further. Similarly the wildlife research is doing fairly well particularly in the collection of wildlife data. The wildlife wing has worked with WWF-India, Sikkim unit in the baseline survey of Pangolakha Forest area and the Sikkim Biodiversity & Ecotourism Project, a sister organisation of the Mountain Institute which runs interesting ecotourism programmes in the national parks and sanctuaries. These interventions are directly related to capacity building both within and outside the state departments.

12.4 Recommendations

1. The forest and other natural resources could be a major source of revenue for the state. The entire orientation of the management of these resources need to be changed. They can be made use of in the state more meaningfully by undertaking the following measures:
   - enhance the rate of timber and non-timber forest products drastically to make it more realistic with the market price and the demand trends; and
   - drastically cut down the number of people working in the forest department by engaging more village communities in the conservation activities.
2. The poor coordination, low productivity, and dismal usefulness of most of the central institutions working on forest, agriculture, and environment located in Sikkim should be immediately put to a halt. They should be made more purposive and useful. This should be done in the following ways:
   - Besides the national goals, their main focus should be on the state's development and environmental needs. Accordingly the present manpower in these institutions need to be drastically redeployed;
   - the annual report of all these central institutions located in Sikkim must be made compulsory and should very clear indicate chapters on activities they are doing for the benefit of the state.
3. Conservation Strategies/Techniques:
   - Forestry, if it is linked to the rural development will benefit a large number of people. Despite JFM, people view that afforestation is still not a public benefit scheme and is essentially imposed by the governmental agencies. If afforestation is made a part of the rural development schemes, people will get an earning out of it and will naturally start protecting the forests. One way would be to link afforestation with the food for work programme so as to match generation of income, employment, and environmental protection.
   - The names of vanishing/threatened/extinct species should be accessible to the people at all levels in simple and friendly local terms along with their attached importance. This should be accompanied by very practical suggestions/ training/awareness campaigns on how to conserve and protect these species.
   - On the medicinal plants and herbs front the prime need of the time is to: a) develop a well planned strategy to explore medicinal plant-wealth of the state; b) find out the method of propagation; c) encourage sustainable harvesting of plants from the wild and cultivation; d) involve small farmers and communities in the cultivation; and e) conduct phyto-chemical, pharmacological and pharmacognostic studies on the commercially exploitable species.
3. Institutional Interventions:
   - National Institute for Natural Resources Management: In view of the richness of the state in natural resources including water, minerals, medicinal herbs and plants, a national level institute for Natural Resources Management should be set up to facilitate fundamental research on natural resources management. It would also be a centre of conservation techniques. In view of the very complex issues emerging out of the World Trade Organisaton (WTO) provisions and trade practices and globalisation process-led newer challenges to natural resources management, a national institute located in Sikkim would cater to the entire north east and the adjoining Himalayan regions so vital for ecological balance. The proposed institute should have research centres dedicated to biotechnology and creation of gene banks both for conservation and commercial harnessing.
   - National Institute of Adventure and Himalayan Eco Tourism Management: With the opening up of the trade route through Nathu La, there will be a further spurt in tourism activities in the state. Already the state has rich adventure tourism facilities which need to be further garnered. Since the pilgrimage route to Kailash Mansarovar will be shorter and more convenient from Sikkim, the state expects to ultimately integrate trade with tourism and other service sector related activities. The emerging concept of sub-regional cooperation including BIMSTEC and South Asia Growth Quadrangle would further intensify the tourism-related activities in and around Sikkim.

- There is no biodiversity data bank at the moment and no status report of the plant species. Scientific monitoring of biodiversity should be initiated largely based on participatory process at the grassroot level. Specific places may be identified like a botanical garden at Rumtek mainly to serve both as gene sanctuary and a recreational resort.

Environment management plan involving plantation in adequate numbers in association with both governmental and non-government organisations must remain a consistent activity. Enhancement of environmental aspects have to be considered giving due attention to the following aspects:

- by stabilisation of slopes/preservation measures;
- by proper landscaping at junctions and available areas;
- by enhancing the cultural properties along the highways;
- by enhancement of highway side water bodies; and;
- redevelopment of burrow areas located on public land.

References

Bandhyopadhyay, M.K. (1998). Glacier Variation in the Himalaya, *Geographical Review of India.* Vol. 60(4): 381-491.

Banerjee, Bireswar (1998). "Use and Misuse of Water Resources in India", *Geographical Review of India.* Vol. 60(3): 248-260.

Basu, Ranjan (1998). "Bio-diversity in India and Relevance of GATT-Expectations and Apprehensions", *Geographical Review of India.* Vol. 60(1): 21-32.

Bureau of Economics and Statistics (1988). *Evaluation Study of Forest Plantation.* Government of Sikkim: Planning and Development Department. October pp.11-14

Centre for Science and Environment (1991). "Floods and Flood Plains and Environmental Myths", *State of India's Environment, A Citizen's Report 3.* New Delhi.

Chandra, Harish (1975). "Landslide in Teesta Valley", in Proceedings of seminar on *Landslides and Toe Erosion Problems with special reference to Himalayan Region.* Calcutta: Indian Society of Engineering Geology.

Department of Forest (2002). *Annual Administrative Report, 2001-02.* Govt. of Sikkim.

———. (2003). *Annual Administrative Report-2002-03.* Govt. of Sikkim.

Debnath, J.C. (1974). "Development of the Sikkimese Economy under Planning (1954-71)". Thesis submitted to Calcutta University for D. Phil Degree. Darjeeling: North Bengal University. p.282.

Forest Department Notification No: 2375/F, Gangtok, 21 September 1954, quoted in Mahendra P. Lama, *Sikkim Human Development Report,* 2001.

Government of Sikkim. Joint Forest Management, Notification No 2/F dated 26.6.1998, Department of Forest, Environment, and Wildlife.

Gurung, Bejoy (2002). *The Medicinal Plants of the Sikkim Himalaya.* Sikkim: Jasmine Bejoy Gurung.

WWF for Nature-India (1999). *Handbook on Environmental Law and Policy for Sikkim.* New Delhi. March.

Khawas, Vimal (2003a). "Joint Forest Management in India with special reference to Darjeeling Himalaya". Mountain Forum online document, *www.mountainfourm.org.*

———. (2003b). "Environment and Rural Development in the Darjeeling Himalayas: Issues and Concerns", *Spatio-Economic Development Record.* Vol. 10(2): 27-33, March-April.

———. (2002). "Environment, Common Property Resources and Rural Development in India". *www.geography.org/sustainable.*

Krishnan, N.R. (1999). "Where People Help Themselves", *The Hindu,* September 26. p.24.

Lama, Mahendra P. (2001). *Sikkim Human Development Report,* 2001. New Delhi: Social Science Press.

———. (2005). *Sikkim-Tibet Trade via Nathu La: A Policy Study on Prospects, Opportunities and Requisite Preparedness.* Prepared by Nathu La Trade Study Group for the Government of Sikkim.

Rao and Saxena (1994). *Sustainable Development and Rehabilitation of Degraded Village Land in Himalaya.* Dehradun: Bishen Singh Mahendra Pal Singh.

Rai, L.K., Pankaj Prasad and E. Sharma (1999). *Conservation Threat to some Important Medicinal Plants of the Sikkim Himalaya.* Elsevier Science Ltd. *www.elsevier.com/locate/ biocon.*

Rai, L.K. (1993). "Vanishing Plants of the Sikkim Himalayas", *SSS Newsletter,* Gangtok, January-June.

Rasaily, M.M. (1970). "Sikkim: Its Flora and Fauna, Part I", *Sikkim Herald,* May, 29, Gangtok.

SAARC Secretariat (1992a). *Regional Study on Green House Effect and its Impact on the Region.* Kathmandu, Nepal.

———. (1992b). *Regional Study on the Causes and Consequences of Natural Disasters and the Protection and Preservation of the Environment.* Kathmandu, Nepal.

Sahai, Suman (1995). "The Patenting of Genes and Living Organisms: The South's View", Paper presented in seminar on *Environmental Concerns in South Asia.* New Delhi: JNU. April 10.

Suresh, A. and Puran Chand (2004). "Trade Related Aspects of Intellectual Property Rights: An Evaluation", *Kurukshetra.* 52(6): 21-26. April.

Wichar, Gangtok, 22-28 May, 1999.

Chapter 13

Urban Development

Although Sikkim is still primarily an agrarian state, its pace of urbanisation in recent years has been rapid, mainly because of growing rural-urban migration. Migration essentially stems from differential opportunities between the rural areas and urban centres, both in terms of employment and access to quality social sector services, such as education, and health. Declining productivity in land-based activities accompanied by expanding administrative and commercial activity in towns have shrunk employment prospects in the rural areas. Urbanisation is likely to continue in the medium term, as the scale of development continues to differ between the urban and rural areas.

13.1 The Current Pattern of Urban Growth and Development

The number of urban centres has increased from only one (Gangtok) in 1961, to nine notified urban towns today. Most recent census figures (2001) show that over 11 per cent of the population now live in urban areas (Table 13.1), with Gangtok accounting for 48.5 per cent of the total urban population. There are also 55 villages that display peri-urban characteristics, which have been designated as rural marketing centres (RMCs).

TABLE 13.1

Urbanisation in Sikkim, 1951-2001

Year	*State Population*	*Urban Population*	*Urban Population as % of Total Population*	*Growth of Total Population*	*Growth of Urban Population*
1951	1,37,725	2,744	1.99		
1961	1,62,189	6,848	4.22	17.76	149.56
1971	2,09,903	19,668	9.37	29.42	187.21
1981	3,16,309	51,084	16.15	50.69	159.73
1991	4,06,457	37,006	9.10	28.50	-27.56
2001	5,40,493	60,005	11.10	32.98	62.15

Source: Census of India, various years.

Between 1991 and 2001, the overall urban growth was low in some towns (Gangtok registered only 16 per cent growth, Gyalshing 15 per cent growth, while Nayabazar registered a decline of 5 per cent), while relatively smaller towns such as Mangan, Jorethang, and Namchi added more than 50 per cent to their population over the decade and Singtam and Rangpo (marketing centres), grew by 40 and 25 per cent, respectively, although their overall share of urban population declined (Table 13.2).

The main reason for the influx into Gangtok and the other three district headquarters is the expansion of administrative activities. In the last few decades, the increase in the size of the government has meant a steady stream of people moving into the major administrative towns in search of 'secure' jobs in the government. These towns, especially Gangtok, are also attractive for job-seekers because they are hubs of tourist-related activities. Other towns and rural market centres owe their growth mainly to the expansion of local commercial activity.

13.1.1 Urban Population Underestimated

These growth rates do not give an accurate picture of the urbanisation process because the 'notified' urban boundaries are not accurate geographic indicators of the extent of urban development. Official urban population figures would be far higher, if they included the area contiguous to several towns, which are highly urbanised but still classified as 'rural.' In fact, the dramatic fall in total urban population between 1981 and 1991 (Table 13.1) is a result of the redemarcation of the boundaries of Gangtok to exclude a large section of its periphery,

TABLE 13.2

Population of Towns in Sikkim

City/Town	*District*	*Total Population*		*Per cent Change*	*Per cent of Total Urban Population*	
		2001	*1991*		*2001*	*1991*
Gangtok	East	29,162	25,024	16.54	48.60	68.00
Upper Tadong	East	14,670	7,941*		24.45	
Rangpo	East	3,724	2,980	25.00	6.21	8.05
Singtam	East	5,431	3,868	40.41	9.05	10.45
Mangan	North	1,248	803	55.42	2.08	2.17
Jorethang	South	2,968	1,939	53.10	4.95	5.24
Namchi	South	978	630	55.24	1.63	1.70
Gyalshing	West	828	717	15.48	1.38	1.94
Nayabazar	West	996	1,045	-4.69	1.66	2.82
Total		60,005	37,006			

Note: * In 1991, Upper Tadong was designated a rural area.

Source: Census of India, various years

which reduced its population by around 60 per cent. If Gangtok and the surrounding urbanised revenue villages with distinctly urban characteristics (known as the Greater Gangtok Area) are taken as a whole, the urban population would be an estimated 1 lakh in 2001,[1] which is more than the total urban population of the state, and almost one-fifth (18.5 per cent) of the total state population.

13.1.2 Rapid Urbanisation without Urban Development

The rapid expansion of urban areas has not been matched by appropriate planning and management, investment in expansion of systems or maintenance of existing ones, or improvements in service delivery. There are no land-use maps and few master plans for the towns, and whereever they are in existence, are not being implemented. Most importantly, the haphazard and unmanaged growth of most towns has placed unsustainable pressure on urban environments through spiraling pollution and congestion, unauthorised high-rise construction with increased risk of landslides, and urban service networks that can no longer keep pace with the population growth.

The process of urbanisation is likely to continue as the population of the state increases and the disparity in health and education services and job opportunities continues. In recognition of the situation, the Chief Minister recently announced that the state was moving towards a goal of zero rural-urban migration by improving employment prospects in the rural areas,[2] however for the present, the problems are likely to continue.

The next section discusses major development issues arising from unplanned growth that now confront planners for Gangtok. Many of these issues are becoming increasingly relevant for the other rapidly expanding urban centres, which are going down the same path of haphazard development.

13.2 Gangtok: An Appraisal of the City's Development

In 1991, the state government reclassified the limits of Gangtok, to exclude a large proportion of its peripheral areas, which resulted in a shrinking of its 'notified town area' by 60 per cent, and a fall in its population to a mere 25,000 inhabitants, with 65,000 residents outside the boundary in 16 contiguous urbanised 'villages'.

Land ownership lies at the heart of the redemarcation as, according to a Sikkim legislation, land outside designated urban areas can only be owned by specified groups of people. Buying and selling of land within municipal limits is much easier (or freely permitted), so municipal limits were shrunk to curb the amount of land that could be freely transacted. The redefinition of Gangtok's boundary had a significant impact on its

1. ILFS: *Proposal for the Preparation of a Comprehensive Gangtok City Development Plan.*
2. Background Note for Sikkim's Annual Plan 2002-03, Planning Commission.

physical planning and management and on the provision of services, which ultimately affects its environmental sustainability.

13.2.1 Physical Planning and Spatial Management

There has been no urban local body (ULB) in Gangtok since the municipality was suspended in 1985. In the absence of a ULB, two departments, Urban Development and Housing (UDHD) and Public Health Engineering (PHED), have the primary responsibility for managing development, which includes physical planning, growth management and providing core civic services. The UDHD also issues trade and taxi licences and bazaar contracts, and collects various forms of taxes, fees, and fines. Several other departments and institutions share responsibility for policy formulation and implementation.

Despite the commissioning of at least three master plans for Gangtok, there is still no notified master plan for the city, or for any of the towns in the state.[3] The absence of a landuse plan, with zoning regulations, has resulted in haphazard growth, in a ribbon pattern all along the highway, NH 31A which passes through the centre of the city. To ease the congestion and other urban pressures, the state government has planned several construction projects, such as parking lots, a satellite township near Gangtok, and a capital complex for the state administrative offices. But each initiative is disconnected and needs to be linked into a holistic long-term development plan.[4]

13.2.2 Environmental Issues

The rapid growth in construction activity and vehicular population has placed a question mark on the sustainability of Gangtok's development along the current path.

- ***Construction*** in the city has been mainly guided by the presence of roads, and in the absence of a landuse map, no area has specifically been assigned any particular use. Inappropriate construction has placed severe stress on the civic infrastructure, denuded forest cover and in general threatened the geomorphology of the landscape. Intense, indiscriminate building activity, such as construction beyond prescribed limits, especially vertically, in geologically weak areas, over *jhoras*, and on steep slopes has led to erosion of the fragile topsoil and building collapse, and exacerbated the risk of landslides. Many of these buildings are in contravention of UDHD regulations, but the punitive fines levied by the department have been no deterrent.
- ***Traffic***: The rapid increase in the number of vehicles in recent years (Table 13.3) has meant congested roads, increasing vehicular and noise pollution and a severe shrinking of space for pedestrians as vehicles park on the pavements. The only national highway in the state, NH 31A, passes through the centre of the city and attracts a large volume of traffic, but the tightly packed commercial and residential construction lining the highway precludes any widening. There is no public transport system in the city—local commuting needs are met through private taxis and personal vehicles, and the consequent explosion of vehicle population has caused the inevitable environmentally damaging consequences. There are plans to increase car parking facilities in the capital. But with limited land, parking space can never keep pace with the vehicle population, and the lasting solution has to be a limit on the number of vehicles in the city.
- ***Jhora Contamination:*** A major source of environmental degradation is the contamination of *jhoras* through the large-scale dumping of solid waste in the *jhoras* and sewerage overflows (Box 13.1).[5]

TABLE 13.3

Growth in Vehicular Traffic

	Total No. of Vehicles @		*New Vehicles Registered*	
Vehicle Type	*1979-80*	*1991-92*	*2000-01**	*2002-03#*
Two-wheelers (scooters/ motorcycles) SK01	256	1,645	606	227
Cars, van, jeeps (private and government) SK02	47	2,858	745	821
Taxis SK04	197	1,146	676	652
Trucks SK03			226	325
Total	533	6,474	2,253	2,025

Sources:@–Bureau of Economics and Statistics and Motor Vehicles Department, Government of Sikkim, from the RITES, *Master Plan for Gangtok, 2020;*

*–Transport Department, Government of Sikkim website;

#–*Economic Survey of Sikkim,* Planning Department, Government of Sikkim.

3. A part from the 2003 IL&FS Master Plan for Gangtok, an earlier master plan was prepared by GILCON which was later revised by RITES in 1997.
4. A holistic development plan has been proposed by IL&FS (IL&FS: Proposal for the Preparation of a Comprehensive Gangtok City Development Plan, December 2003).
5. AUSAID: Jan 2002.

BOX 13.1

Pollution through Contaminated *Jhoras*

The city has a series of main drains or *jhoras* fed by perennial springs, which drain the water from the catchment area, ultimately into the Teesta river at Singtam. These *jhoras* are gradually being choked, or built over. Solid waste is commonly deposited in them, which leads to blockage and overflow, reduces their carrying capacity, and contaminates the water and underlying soil. Some of the waste dumped into the *jhoras* is washed away during the monsoon, but during the non-monsoon months, it collects and festers and has adversely affected environmental hygiene and public health. During the monsoons, *jhoras* often cannot handle the garbage and extra soil material, which overflows and pollutes the drinking water in the pipelines that run alongside the *jhoras*.[6]

The UDHD is responsible for cleaning *jhoras*, but while doing so, waste material is dumped on the banks, which slips back into the streams. One solution that is being explored is fencing the *jhoras* to block people from throwing garbage in, especially in the central areas of Gangtok.

The UDHD manages solid waste collection, but its vehicles cover only a small proportion (6 per cent) of households mainly from the central areas; the majority (57 per cent) dumps their waste into the *jhoras* (Table 13.4).

13.2.3 *Physical Infrastructure*

The quality of basic services in an urban environment influences its economic, social, and physical health. The Greater Gangtok Area is served by several departments and institutions: the PHED provides water supply and sanitation services to the urban areas and some rural areas, UDHD provides solid waste management, the Rural Development department looks after part of the rural water supply and sanitation, and drainage is the responsibility of the Irrigation department. Service provision is divided between the 'notified town area' and the peripheral 'rural' areas, and the artificial boundary between the two has fragmented service delivery. It has also resulted in loss of revenue, when a primarily urban body (the PHED) supplies services to 'rural' areas at low or nonexistent rural user rates. The lack of communication and interdepartmental coordination has prevented the development of critical interlinkages and has adversely affected efficiency.

TABLE 13.4

Solid Waste Disposal in Gangtok

Disposal Arrangements	*Per cent of Households*
Dumping in street bins	13
UDHD Vehicle	6
Dumping in street	7
Burning	3
Dumping in *jhoras*	57
Dumping in open spaces	14
Total	100

Source: TARU (2000). *Gangtok Socio-Economic and Health Study Report.*

Further, these departments and institutions are subject to different regulations and legislation, often with no clear delineation of responsibilities on service provision. For example, there is overlapping jurisdiction on regulatory powers and enforcement; there is also overlapping responsibility when one department lays down the physical infrastructure, while another manages its functioning.

Regulation is lax, and existing rules are not enforced systematically or impartially. Service standards are poorly defined or nonexistent, and there is hardly any monitoring and reporting of performance.

- ***Drainage:*** As in all hill towns, proper drainage is critical in Gangtok to maintain the stability of its fragile slopes. More than a quarter of the GGA (26 per cent) has no drainage, one-third is drained through open concrete channels and only 22 per cent has access to drainage pipes.[7] The city streets are lined with box-type drains which carry water to the *jhoras*, and these often overflow especially during the monsoon because of inadequate capacity and blockages. Drains are not well maintained, and not cleaned frequently enough. This results in often severe soil and road erosion, local flooding, landslides, and in some cases the collapse of buildings.
- ***Sewerage:*** Gangtok is one of the few hill towns to have a piped sewer system and a sewage treatment plant. Established in 1980, and maintained by the PHED, the gravity-based system covers only about 25 per cent of the total population.[8] Sewage is transported to a treatment plant at Adampool, where it is treated and discharged into the river. However, the system and treatment plant are poorly

6. RITES: *Master Plan for Gangtok, 2020.*
7. TARU (2000). *Gangtok Socio-Economic and Health Study Report.*
8. ILFS report.

maintained. Further, leaking pipe joints in the system, especially during the monsoon, allow sewage to seep through and contaminate the groundwater and soil. As a result of the leakages, only a proportion of the sewage reaches the treatment plant, the consequence of which is that the plant operates at less than 30 per cent of its design capacity. Faults in the system have had severe repercussions on public health: gastro-intestinal disease affects up to 60 per cent of households with 140,000 cases reported annually, and coping costs are an estimated Rs. 150 lakh an annum.

- ***Water Supply***: The main water source for Gangtok is the stream, Rateychu, 16 kilometres from the city. The PHED operates and maintains the gravity-based water distribution system and the water treatment plants. With the boom in construction and tourist activities, there is a shortage of water supply (only 37 per cent of users receive 24-hour supply), physical losses are high (almost 80 per cent of water supplied is unaccounted for, mainly because of unauthorised connections and system faults) and water contamination is widespread. A survey carried out by AUSAID in 1999 estimated that the PHED billed only 28 per cent of the water users in the Gangtok urban area. There are no formal methods of rainwater harvesting in the state, where almost 70 per cent of rainfall occurs during the monsoon months.
- ***Solid Waste:*** The needs of the population have by far outstripped the provision of solid waste services, such as street bins and landfill sites. The low frequency of emptying public bins means that even the few that do exist are usually overflowing; similarly, the capacity of the landfill site can no longer handle the garbage generated. The UDHD has plans to set up a composting plant at the landfill site but little progress has been made on this venture.

13.3 Other Urban Areas

13.3.1 Other Towns

Apart from Gangtok, there are eight 'notified urban towns,' Upper Tadong in the capital area, and seven others: Mangan, Namchi, Gazing, Rangpo, Ravangla, Nayabazar/Jorethang, and Singtam. Many of the towns are growing rapidly as commercial and tourism hubs: Namchi, Gayzing, Ravangla and Mangan today attract a large number of tourists. Between 1991 and 2001, some of the larger towns grew at over 50 per cent (Jorethang, Mangan and Namchi) (Table 13.2). Namchi is fast emerging as the second most important town in the state.

However, several towns, even those far smaller in size than the capital, are beginning to face many of the problems outlined above that are affecting the development of Gangtok. Drainage arrangements, for example (Table 13.5) are still inadequate in all the urban areas across the state: only 57.9 per cent of all urban homes have appropriate drainage of wastewater.

13.3.2 Rural Marketing Centres

There are 55 villages that display peri-urban characteristics which have been designated as rural marketing centres (RMCs). These centres, which till recently had low population levels have begun to expand, and the expansion is most prominent in RMCs located near clusters of villages, which have begun to function as commercial and economic centres.

However, RMCs too have begun to experience shortages of service supply or a complete lack of supply. For example, none of the centres have a water treatment plant and the water supply systems in several RMCs need to be expanded and upgraded to keep pace with population growth.[9]

13.4 Recommendations

The main aim of urban development would be to ensure improved living conditions for urban residents within a framework of sustainable and environmentally sound planning. This will require appropriate advance planning and regulation of urban growth, based on geo-technical and environmental conditions, and ensuring

TABLE 13.5

Drainage Connections for Wastewater in Urban Areas

Type of Drainage	*Households*	
	Total	*Per cent*
Running	7,542	57.9
Open	4,717	36.2
None	756	5.8
Total	13,015	100

Source: Table H-10: *Census of India 2001.*

9. From the PHED Annual Report.

efficient transport systems and services, based on appropriate resource use. The latter will involve an expansion in coverage and access to quality services (including water and environmental services) to all urban residents, especially the poor and vulnerable.

13.4.1 Urban Planning and Development

- ***Master Plans and Land use***: The state government has announced its commitment to preparing a master plan for each town (and *bazaar*, as centres of economic activity). As discussed above, several master plans for Gangtok already exist, and there is even one for Ranka, the town that has been proposed as a sattelite to Gangtok.[10] The RITES report and the ILFS plan are fairly comprehensive documents for Gangtok, and based on these, a master plan for the city can be finalised, preferably with inputs from various stakeholders, including civil society representatives, to ensure that development is environmentally sensitive and sustainable. A time-line for preparing master plans for the other towns and major RMCs is needed, which should be strictly adhered to.

  The legal tool for guiding urban development is a land use plan, which is a vital input into the master plan. The land use plan will zone areas for different uses—commercial, industrial, recreational, community and residential—in line with the projected growth of the city. A core pre-requisite to strategic planning would be the accurate mapping of the urban centres in the state, and a re-demarcation of the boundaries to reflect this.[11]

- ***Development Authorities***: The planning and coordination of towns are currently managed by different departments, with unsatisfactory outcomes as detailed above. Given the long-term nature of master plans, there needs to be a development authority at least for major towns. The authority should have the power to acquire land, develop and sell property, and perform other functions necessary to develop the urban area according to the master plan.[12]

- ***Elected Municipal Bodies***: In keeping with the *74th Constitutional Amendment (1992)* all towns are required to have elected urban governance bodies. Local bodies have been given a constitutional status by the amendment, and as the third tier of government have the responsibility for planning of social and economic development and safeguarding the interests of the weaker sections. So far none of the towns in the state have a municipal authority, that will perform these vital tasks, as well as other functions such as levying and collecting property taxes and other taxes and fees.

- ***Regulatory Framework:*** A strong autonomous body (along the lines of the Environmental Protection Agency in the United States), ideally the municipality, could help formulate regulation and oversee the compliance of urban laws and regulations relating to environment and health. These rules need to apply across a range of urban issues, such as *jhora* contamination, illegal construction, safe disposal of medical and chemical waste, vehicular pollution, monitoring the air and water quality, and so on (some of these tasks are currently performed by the State Pollution Control Board). To prevent placing the entire urban landscape at risk, construction of buildings beyond permitted limits has to be made illegal.

13.4.2 Tackling Environmental Issues

- ***Traffic:*** Serious efforts have to be made to reduce the number of private vehicles; and taxis, especially in Gangtok. Measures could include imposing a steep vehicle tax on each vehicle, limiting or even reducing the number of taxi licenses, creating more vehicle-free zones, and promoting a well-managed user-friendly public transport system. The winding narrow roads preclude the operation of large buses, but mini-vans which run on the commonly used routes, especially to areas of dense commercial or administrative activity, at peak traffic hours could help ease the noise, air pollution, and congestion. The provision of vehicles to government employees needs to be reduced, as some states have done. Buses can be introduced to transport employees to and from work: apart from economising on expenditure, this will also improve office attendance and punctuality.

---

10. *Integrated Urban Development Plan for Ranka, 1997.*
11. In recognition of this fact, the RITES and ILFS master plans for Gangtok apply to the Gangtok Urban Area, which comprises the notified town area and the surrounding areas that receive the same sanitation facilities from government departments as the notified town area.
12. Details of the constitution and role of such development authorities are given in the RITES report.

- ***Aesthetic Development:*** The state's continued tourist appeal depends on preserving its natural scenic resources, and any plan for the main towns must be based on retaining the architectural features and original characteristics of the area. Much of the recent buildings in Gangtok and other towns have been based on materials and styles of the larger cities of the plains. Apart from being inappropriate for the climate and topography of Sikkim, they impinge on the aesthetics of the Himalayan landscape. Building rules could be formulated to promote a return to traditional building styles and materials, more in harmony with the surrounding landscape, which would promote pride in traditional culture among the Sikkimese. Even overbridges, footpaths, parking lots can be built aesthetically, rather than as concrete functional appendages to the existing infrastructure. Flat roof structures, exposed RCC columns and bare concrete exterior buildings should be discouraged.

  The state can leverage its advantage as a natural habitat for flowers and plants to beautify its urban spaces: efforts could be made to plant shrubs and flowers in public places, and to develop scenic walks on the peripheries, in short to make this truly an 'orchid state'.

- ***Dispersing Development:*** Gangtok is the centre of all urban activity in the state—commercial, administrative, educational, health and tourism. Future planning has to disperse development to other urban centres to decongest the capital. Proposed new educational institutes, hospitals, or research institutes should be located in other towns, which will boost development in the hinterland and peripheral regions. A satellite town for Gangtok is proposed to be set up in Ranka, which is expected to take some of the pressure off the capital. An excellent proposal is to move some major government offices to the office zone in the new town (around 35 per cent of the workforce in Gangtok is employed in government and semi-government offices;[13] several offices are scattered around the city, even in residential buildings), which would ideally decongest the capital.

13.4.3 Improving Civic Services

Almost all the service systems are in need of maintenance and repair and networks need expanding to meet current and projected demand for services. For this, basic requirements would be imposing and implementing economic user fees and monitoring service quality and environment impacts. In addition, improved civic services will require the following:

- ***Reliable Data:*** Appropriate policy formulation requires accurate, comprehensive and up-to-date data. Most of the information on water supply and other services even in the Gangtok area is based on sample surveys or outdated numbers. As an important first step, departments responsible for supply need to map, record, and analyse the coverage and performance of the existing systems and supply networks. This will provide a base for projecting demand and steps that need to be taken within the next 15 years till 2020.

- ***Better Governance***: This will require a clear, comprehensive regulatory framework for all services, which aims at protecting consumers' rights and which has well-defined responsibilities for each service agency. Given the overlapping and undefined domains for the departments functioning in the sector, ideally an autonomous legal entity needs to be constituted, with clearly defined responsibilities, operating within the above regulatory framework.

- ***Cost Recovery:*** An effective system of assessment, billing, and cost recovery, based on actual service costs, will need to be introduced in respect of all the urban civic services which are not in the nature of public goods. Political will is needed to implement a user pays system, and its success will depend on the extent to which the public can be made aware of the ultimate benefits of such a system.

- ***Selective Privatisation:*** Many towns need a waste management strategy to cope with present and future demands on the system of waste collection and disposal in an environmentally sustainable manner. A strong case can be made for privatising solid waste management in some of the densely populated areas, such as the centre of Gangtok.

13. RITES report.

References

Department of Roads and Bridges. *Mid-term Appraisal Report for Tenth Plan 2002-2007*. Government of Sikkim.

Gangtok Urban Water Supply and Environmental Sanitation Project (2004a). *Study Report on Community Engagement and Regional Excellence*. AUSAID.

———. (2004b). *Sectoral Assessment Reports on Community Engagement, Water Supply System, Solid Waste Management, Sewerage, Institutional Arrangements*. March 26.

IL&FS (2003). *Proposal for the Preparation of a Comprehensive Gangtok City Development Plan, Approach and Methodology*. Govt. of Sikkim. December.

Public Health Engineering Department. *Annual Report 2001-02*, Govt. of Sikkim.

———. *Draft Tenth Five-Year Plan (2002-07) and Proposals for Annual Plan 2002-03*. Govt. of Sikkim.

RITES (1997). *Master Plan for Gangtok, 2020, Draft Final Report*, Urban Development & Housing Department, Government of Sikkim. May.

Urban Development & Housing Department (various years). *Annual Report*. Government of Sikkim.

Chapter 14

Development of Scheduled Castes and Scheduled Tribes

This chapter traces the path of development of the scheduled castes, scheduled tribes, and other backward classes of Sikkim. We would attempt a thorough analysis of the data from the last three censuses to get an idea of the basic socio-economic indicators and their changes over the last three decades for SC and ST communities. For OBCs, the data sources accrue from the official records of the Welfare Department of the State and Commission for Backward Classes. Schemes and policies designed to promote development of the communities are critically analysed. The chapter would also give some constructive suggestions to facilitate the development process.

The chapter is organised as follows:

14.1 gives an account of the ethnic groups in Sikkim with a historical note on their evolution;

14.2 analyses some basic statistics on the scheduled castes and tribes of Sikkim derived from the past three censuses;

14.3 gives an account of the schemes and programmes implemented for the development of the SC and ST communities;

14.4 analyses the main functions of SABCCO, a government body set up to facilitate the flow of financial resources as loans from different sources to the target group;

14.5 gives an account of the initiatives taken by the state for the development of these communities; and

14.6 gives a set of recommendations as an agenda for further development of the communities.

TABLE 14.1

Ethnic Groups in Sikkim

Race/Caste	*Total*
Lepcha	5,762
Bhutia	4,894
Limbu	3,356
Gurung	2,921
Murmi	2,867
Rai/Jimdar, etc.	2,020
Khamba	1,963
Kami	1,670
Brahman	1,414
Mangar	901
Chhetri	829
Newar	727
Darzi	287

Source: Official Census of Sikkim, 1891.

14.1 Ethnic Groups in Sikkim

14.1.1 A Brief Historical Note

Lepchas, Bhutias and Nepalese ethnic groups primarily constitute the population of Sikkim. The first official census of Sikkim, published in 1891, presents the following figures in Table 14.1 for different groups of population:

After 1891, only *lepchas*, *bhutias*, and *limbus* are taken as distinct ethnic groups, while all other groups mentioned above were regarded as various castes of the nepali society.

The oldest inhabitants of Sikkim or the autocthones are the *lepchas*. No historical records exist to show how they came to inhabit this region. They are believed to have migrated *via* Assam and upper Burma. They have their own language known as Rong. *Lepchas* are cultivators as well as food-gatherers and hunters and practice shifting hill cultivation. The *lepchas* do not have caste distinctions but they are divided into groups by birth and marriage. As for marriage, they follow community endogamy and clan exogamy but are now having alliance with the *bhutias* except for Dzongu area where rules are stricter. Bride price in cash and kind are common. Divorce is a rare phenomenon. Their love for music and dance is well known. Education is not discriminatory so far as sex is concerned.

Before the advent of the *bhutias* in 1642, the land was mainly in the hands of the *lepchas*. In 1642, the bhutia rule started in Sikkim under the influence of Tibetan theocracy. It was a first attempt of racial assimilation by *bhutia* immigrants. They were successful in promoting intermarriages with the *lepchas* and converted the spirit-worshipper *lepchas* into Lamaist Buddhists. The immigrant *bhutias* were mostly traders and herdsmen, settled in higher altitudes and drove away the *lepchas* to valleys and forests. Owing the bhutia rule, the ownership of cultivable land had been under the control of *bhutia* landlords and aristocrats in the names of feudal kings. The *lepchas* were mostly tenant cultivators and the monopoly over land was shifted from the hands of *lepchas* to the *bhutias*.

The name *bhutia* is derived from their original habitat 'Bhot' (Tibet). The main *bhutia* sub-tribes are *drukpas*, from Drukul/Bhutan, the *chumbipas*, from Chumbi valley (eastern Tibet), the *dhopthapas*, from Dhoptha (south Tibet), the *tromopas* from Do-mu. They are spread all over Sikkim but their main concentration is in the north. They have a distinct language of their own named, *Bhutia*. Marriage is endogamous at the community level. In older times, the boy's side used to give a token amount of two rupees to the bride's father, now the bride price is much higher. Divorce is a rare phenomenon. The *bhutias* mainly depend on agriculture, dairy farming, and pastoralism. Land is their main source of income. In Lachen and Lachung, the *Bhutias* still maintain the traditional village *Zumsas* where the Pipons act as headmen elected by the villagers and are believed to solve all problems. The *bhutias* are Buddhist by religion. They are great enthusiasts of art and sculpture. Education is favoured for both boys and girls.

With the signing of the anglo-chinese convention at Calcutta in March 1890, Sikkim became an acknowledged protectorate of British India. The British contact brought in a new kind of administration, revenue system, forest reservation rules, and development of the area by improving the communication network. Nepali immigration was encouraged, as labour was needed for construction of roads and extension of agriculture. The ethnic composition of Sikkim changed rapidly as the Nepalese multiplied in number from 51 per cent of total population in 1891 to 75 per cent of the total population in 1947. With the modified lease system of land, a new land settlement pattern also developed with a new lessee landlord class among the nepalese. Nepalese were considered to be better cultivators, industrious and hard working labourers. They settled down in wastelands and also by clearing unoccupied forests. Gradually they acquired land from the *lepchas* and *bhutias* and the large-scale nepalese immigration exerted pressure in changing the land settlement pattern and agricultural techniques as well.

Lepchas and *Bhutias* got the constitutional status of scheduled tribe after Sikkim's merger with India.

BOX 14.1

Two New Scheduled Tribes: *Limbu* and *Tamang*

The word *Limbu* is derived from Li meaning bow and Abu meaning shooter. Their original homeland was supposed to be in the Tsang province of Tibet from where they migrated to eastern Nepal before they came to Sikkim. They are considered as one of the earliest settlers in Sikkim. Their main concentration is in western Sikkim but they are also found in the south and the east. Their villages are situated in the sparsely forested slopes at an average altitude of 4000–6000 ft. Community endogamy and clan exogamy are the marriage rules in the community of *Limbus*. Land is their main resource. Their traditional occupation was pastoralism and animal husbandry. Now they mainly practice terrace cultivation. They also engage themselves as agricultural labourers. The women contribute to the family income by collecting firewood and fodder. Limbus have a rich oral tradition. Folk songs are sung by both sexes. They are more closely linked with the tribal communities of *Bhutias* and *Lepchas* than any other Nepali speaking community in Sikkim.

The word *Tamang* might have been derived from their principal occupation of horse-trading. Land is their major resource. Though traditionally they had been traders, some of them engage themselves as terrace cultivators, agricultural labourers, milk-sellers, animal rearers, etc. Endogamy in community and exogamy at the clan level are the common norms for marriage. *Tamangs* maintain their identity through their faith in Buddhism, speaking their own language *Tamang*, and practicing their own festivals and rituals. They do wood carvings and decorate the *gumphas*. They also perform dance with music during religious festivals.

14.1.2 Scheduled Castes

Four castes have the constitutional status of scheduled castes in Sikkim *viz. damai, kami, majhi,* and *sarki*. All these castes belong to the nepalese community. All of them mostly follow endogamy at the community level and exogamy at the clan level, have the system of bride price in cash or in kind, are non-vegetarians, follow hinduism as their religion, belong to the *shudra varna* and do not discriminate between genders as far as education is concerned. The phenomenon of divorce is rare but provision for compensation is there in case there is one. Widow remarriage options are common.

Damais are identified as *darjis* or master tailors according to their traditional occupation. They are scattered throughout the State, with greater concentration near the markets. They do not have a separate dialect than Nepali. The other occupations of the community are those of porters, vendors and agricultural labourers. Very few of them own land. Some have an interesting profession of playing nine musical instruments in marriages. *Kamis* and *sarkis* are placed higher among the *shudras* than *damai*. This community is known for their passion for music.

Kamis, the *Vishwakarmas* or traditional blacksmiths and goldsmiths, are mostly found in the south district. Apart from making items of gold and iron they involve themselves in terrace cultivation, business, milkselling, etc.

Majhis are the traditional boatmen. Other professions of this community include business and contract-supply. Few own land, many of them work as agricultural labourers, terrace-cultivators, wood-workers, milk-sellers, truck-drivers and labourers. They sing folk songs and perform folk dances.

Sarkis are traditional shoe-makers and tanners but now most of them are agricultural labourers. A few are engaged as vendors and construction labourers.

TABLE 14.2

District-wise Distribution of SCs and STs in Sikkim

District	*Total SC Population*	*Total ST Population*	*Percentage of SC*	*Percentage of ST*
North	879	21,772	2.1	53.1
West	5,747	23,829	4.7	19.3
South	6,262	20,483	4.8	15.6
East	14,277	45,321	5.8	18.5
Sikkim	**27,165**	**1,11,405**	**5**	**20.6**

Source: Census of India, 2001.

14.1.3 Other Backward classes

About 40 per cent of the total population belong to OBCs. On the recommendation of the Mandal Commission in 1994 the communities who attained the status of OBCs were *bhujel, gurung, limbu, mangar, rai, sunuwar, tamang*. (*limbu* and *tamang* were added to the list of STs recently.)

Three communities *thami, jogi,* and *dewan* were added in 2000 as OBCs of the state of Sikkim.

14.2 Analysis of Some Basic Statistics

14.2.1 District-wise Population

Census 2001 gives the following district-wise figures of SC and ST population in Sikkim.

Total SC population is highest in the east district followed by south, west and north respectively. The east district also has the highest ST population followed by west, north and south respectively. This can be explained by the fact that opportunity for employment is the highest in the east district, which attract most of them.

Table 14.3 summarises the ranks of the districts (with rural-urban classification) in terms of SC, ST population concentration. The percentage of SC population is highest in urban areas of west (9.2 per cent), highest concentration being recorded in urban areas of Soreng subdivision (9.8 per cent). The percentage of ST population is highest in rural areas of north (53.8 per cent), highest concentration being recorded in rural areas of Mangan subdivision (57 per cent). We can generally infer that the STs are mostly concentrated in the rural areas, the SCs in the urban areas; their traditional occupational patterns support this phenomenon.

14.2.2 Caste/Tribe-wise Population

Table 14.4 summarises the district-wise percentage of each caste and tribe.

TABLE 14.3

Ranks of Districts (with Rural-Urban Classification) in Terms of SC, ST Population Concentration

Ranks of Districts	*1*	*2*	*3*	*4*
SC Population	Urban West	Urban South	Rural East	Rural North
ST Population	Rural North	Rural West	Rural East	Rural South

Source: Census of India, 2001.

TABLE 14.4

District-wise Profile of Each Caste/Tribe as Percentage of Total SC/ST Population

State/ District	*Year*	*SC*				*ST*	
		Damai	*Kami*	*Majhi*	*Sarki*	*Bhutia*	*Lepcha*
Sikkim	**1981**	**32.71**	**62.57**	**1.36**	**3.30**	**66.10**	**33.89**
	1991	29.64	63.26	1.22	3.32	65.40	33.30
North	1981	29.38	68.25	0.13	1.88	45.93	54.06
	1991	32.94	62.11	0.09	0.27	41.76	57.82
East	1981	32.86	62.85	1.43	2.81	77.27	22.73
	1991	29.47	64.16	0.95	2.55	76.23	21.68
South	1981	33.21	60.95	2.52	3.30	70.49	29.50
	1991	30.05	61.34	2.95	4.13	69.33	30.35
West	1981	32.46	62.39	0.08	4.98	59.27	40.72
	1991	28.86	63.41	0.22	5.03	62.07	36.50

Source: Census of India, 1981, 1991.

FIGURE 14.1

Gender-wise Percentage Composition of SC, ST in Sikkim

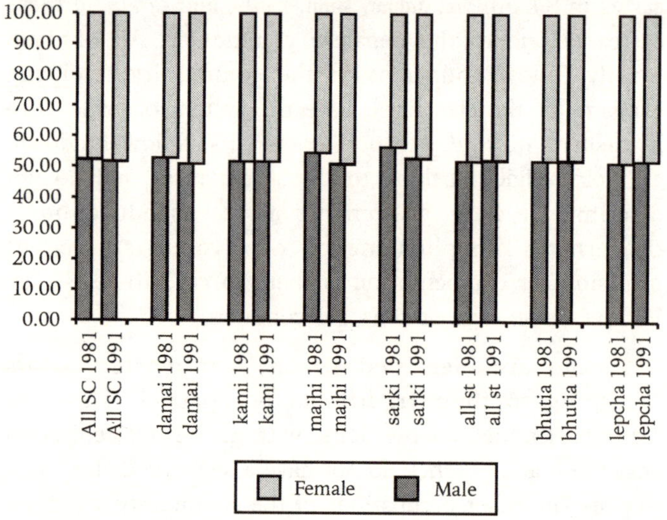

Source: Census of India, 1981, 1991.

In Sikkim, among the SCs *kami* as a caste has the highest proportion followed by *damai, sarki* and *majhi*. *Kami* and *Damai* constitute more than 95 per cent of the community population for both 1981 and 1991. Among the tribes in Sikkim, *bhutias* have a greater proportion than the *lepchas* within the tribal community. However in the north district, the *lepchas* outnumber the *bhutias*. The conclusions hold true for both the years.

14.2.3 Gender Analysis

Gender analysis for 1981 and 1991 shows that for all the castes as a whole and individually, percentage of male (female) population has slightly fallen (risen). For the tribes, the trend is opposite with slight increase (decrease) in the percentage of male (female). The analysis roughly suggests absence of any discriminatory behaviour against females in SC communities.

14.2.4 Literacy

Table 14.5 throws some light on the literacy figures.

TABLE 14.5

Literacy Rates by Gender and by Caste/Tribes for Each Category

SC/ST	*Total* 1981	*Total* 1991	*Male* 1981	*Male* 1991	*Female* 1981	*Female* 1991
All SC	28.06	41.16	66.4	72.99	61.66	68.18
Damai	30.97	47.14	68.04	77.01	62.93	70.03
Kami	27.23	38.27	66.13	71.15	61.1	67.12
Majhi	24.5	31.01	61.85	66.33	62.65	67.69
Sarki	16.56	26.92	57.12	69.71	59.44	67.21
All ST	33.13	48.41	70.47	76.56	62.66	71.84
Bhutia	22.59	51.04	69.16	77.94	63.43	73.09
Lepcha	30.16	43.35	69.02	73.94	61.15	69.41

Source: Census of India, 1981, 1991

For the castes, overall there is a considerable rise in literacy rates over the two decades. This is reflected both in male and female categories, the effect being more pronounced for females. Ranking among the castes in terms of literacy has slightly changed over the decades: *Damais* have the highest literacy rate in both the censuses, *sarkis* used to be the most illiterate caste in 1981 who has come up in 1991 above the *majhi* community. In the female category, in 1981, *kami* women were behind *majhi* women, in 1991, *sarki* women have progressed to have an equal status with *kami* and *majhi* women. For STs also there is a considerable rise in the literacy rates. *Bhutias* progress more than the *lepchas* over the decades in both the categories of male and female.

14.2.5 Employment

Percentages of total main workers in SC population has slightly fallen overall and has either fallen slightly or remain stable for individual castes. Percentage of total main workers has fallen (by more percentage points than SCs) for ST population, overall and for individual tribes. The findings are summarised in Table 14.6.

Analysis of the Economic tables for the two censuses gives some interesting results, which are summarised in

TABLE 14.6

Total Main Workers as Percentage of Total SC/ST Population

SC/ST	*1981*	*1991*
All SC	42.40	37.70
Damai	39.36	34.38
Kami	43.80	39.02
Majhi	38.96	41.50
Sarki	46.52	40.68
All ST	44.51	39.49
Bhutia	43.45	39.41
Lepcha	46.59	39.60

Source: Census of India, 1981, 1991.

Table 14.7. For SCs there is a fall in the share of cultivators, manufacturing-processing-servicing-repairs in household industries, other services; a slight decrease is recorded. In the share of mining and quarrying some categories recorded a rise in their share, such as, agricultural labourers, forestry, manufacturing, processing in non-household industries, trade and commerce; there is a slight rise in the share of construction too.

These observations suggest that for SCs

- among the census category of main workers there is an increase in the share of the tertiary sector;
- within the primary sector, there is almost an equiproportionate fall in the share of cultivators and rise in the share of agricultural labourers;
- Within the secondary sector there is a fall in the share of household industry with a less-than-proportionate rise in the non-household-industry; and
- A fall in the share of other services suggests that there is a trend away from the traditional occupations of the respective communities. This is true for all the castes excepting *Damai*.

Individual caste analyses show visible trends in development for *sarkis*; there are drastic changes in the occupational pattern. Share of cultivators has drastically reduced; shares of transport, construction and other services have fallen whereas these in manufacturing (household+non-household) have increased considerably; slight increase is also recorded in the share of trade and commerce.

For the STs, the share of cultivators has fallen; there is a rise in the share of agricultural labourers, manufacturing-processing (non-household industry), trade and commerce, transport; slight rise has been recorded in the area of forestry. Tertiary sector has progressed very slowly. Within the primary sector there is a considerable fall in the share of cultivators and rise in the share of agricultural labourers.

These observations suggest that for STs:

- The land owning class now has other sources of income from alternative occupations and more land is being tilled by hired labour.
- This suggests that a greater proportion of the target group is relying on outside options rather than self-employment.
- Tertiary sector has started growing.
- Slight rises in the share of construction shows a positive change in the attitude of people who rank construction labour the lowest of all occupations.

TABLE 14.7

Percentage Distribution of SC, ST Households with Source of Drinking Water, Electricity, Latrine in Sikkim

Category	*SC*	*ST*
Total	70.6	80.48
Rural	67.1	78.46
Urban	93	98.16

TABLE 14.8

Percentage Distribution of SC, ST Households Availing Banking Services and having At Least One of the Census-Specified Assets

State/ District	*Total/ Rural/ Urban*	*Percentage Availing Banking*		*Percentage having at Least One Asset**	
		ST	*SC*	*ST*	*SC*
Sikkim	Total	32.33	43.51	54.59	22
	Rural	27.67	38.68	50.92	17
	Urban	73.18	74.60	86.76	55

Note: *–Census specified assets: radio, television, telephone, bicycle, motorcycle, car.

Source: Census of India, 2001.

BOX 14.2

Some Interesting Facts

- The Revenue order No. 1 of 1917 (in confirmation of an executive order passed in 1897) prohibits any alienation of land of the *bhutia* or *lepcha* community by other communities in Sikkim.
- The *Kyi-dug* constitutes the social organisation of the bhutias which is generally identified with a territorial clan like thomorva, ardowa, or khampa. The main function of the *Kyi-dug* is to help its clan members in times of need. For instance if any death occurs, every family is expected to send a member to help in cremation. If a family fails to do so *Kyi-dug* would impose a fine on the family. The members from amongst themselves elect its office-bearers.
- Lachen and lachung in north Sikkim have an organisation called zumsa in existence from very early times. It is very unusual and almost a communistic government where carrying of load for visiting government officials to allotment of land to different members is decided upon by the entire village folk. The village headman (Pipon) is elected by adult members from each family for a term of two years. Besides the *zumsas*, there is another body called gyemni for aiding and advising the Pipon in functions involving the community as a whole. The *zumsas* are approved as rural self-government in the state.

14.3 Schemes and Programmes for Development of SC, ST, and OBC Communities

Combining the plan allocations for the Social Welfare department for the period 1997-98-2003-04 and a compendium of achievements of Social Welfare department (Welfare Division), Government of Sikkim, we can have a fair idea about the financial aspects of the schemes and programmes undertaken for SC, ST, OBC development in the state. The allocation figures in the Ninth and Tenth Five-Year Plans for the Social Welfare department are Rs. 2250 and 1800 lakh respectively, showing a fall in allocation by 450 lakh. In percentage terms also, in the Ninth Five-Year Plan the share of the Social Welfare department was 1.40 per cent of the total plan allocation whereas in the Tenth Five-Year Plan it declined to 1.09 per cent showing a decrease by 0.31 percentage points. Analysing the allocation under major heads for SC, ST, OBC development, we find a declining trend in most of the categories in absolute as well as percentage terms.

- Allocation on scholarship schemes was 39 lakh in the year 1997-98 which declined in the two subsequent years to 30, and 26.9 lakh, recorded an increase in 2001-02 to 58 lakh, then again declined to 50.5 and 33.5 in the next two years. The allocation under this head in 2003-04 is even less than that in 1997-98;
- Among the other categories of education, allocation on vocational training has increased steadily from 8 lakh in 1997-98 to 30 lakh in 2002-03 and then declined to 21 lakh in 2003-04;
- Allocation on SC, ST, OBC hostel buildings, residential and ashram schools has increased from 50 lakh in 2000-01 to 130 lakh in 2002-03, an amount of 50 lakh have been allocated in 2003-04 for construction hostels for OBC boys and girls, the allocation on construction of residential schools for OBCs shows a drastic increase from 33 lakh in 2002-03 to 150 lakh in 2003-04;
- Allocation on pre-examination coaching centres is almost stable over the years after showing a sharp increase in 1999-2000;
- The share of special central assistance to tribal sub-plans shows a mixed trend over the years, from 99.5 lakh in 1997-98 it first declined to 50.25 lakh in 1999-2000 and then increased to 162 lakh in 2001-02 and then again declined to 108 lakh in 2003-04;
- The grant under Article 275 (1) remains stable at around 33 lakh in 2003-04 from 33.46 lakh in 2001-02;
- Allocation on research and monitoring remains the same (1 lakh) as it was in 1997-98, after increasing to 10 lakh in 2001-02 and then declining to 2.5 lakh in 2002-03.

The physical achievements are listed in Table A-45.

The Departments, apart from the Welfare department, instrumental in channelising the funds under special central assistance or grants under Article 275(1) to special component plans or tribal sub-plans are education, agriculture, floriculture, animal husbandry, STCS and SIMFED.

Apart from the two categories of schemes mentioned above, there are centrally sponsored schemes, some of which are totally funded by the centre, others are sponsored partly by the centre and the state at agreed proportions. Some of the recent projects under these schemes are listed below:

TABLE 14.9

List of Schemes Shared

Schemes	*Sharing Proportion of Funds/Funds*
Construction of Hostel at PNGSS School for OBC Students at Gangtok	50:50
Construction of Residential School/ Hostel for OBCs at Namchis	50:50
Upgradation of Merit for SC and ST students	100%
Coaching and Allied schemes for SCs and STs.	100%
Pre-Matric Scholarships for OBCs	50:50
Post-Matric Scholarships for OBCs	100%
Atrocity Awareness	Rs. 2,81, 000

Source: Compendium of Achievements, Social Welfare Department, Sikkim.

14.4 Sikkim Scheduled Castes, Scheduled Tribes and Other Backward Classes Development Corporation (SABCCO)

SABCCO was established under the *Companies Act Sikkim 1961* in 1996. The corporation is a fully government undertaking under Welfare department with a share capital of Rs. 10 crore. It avails financial assistance by way of loans from apex corporations *viz.*, National Scheduled Tribes Finance and Development Corporation, National Scheduled Castes Finance and Development Corporation, National Backward Classes Finance and Development Corporation for financing income-generating schemes for the target group. These corporations identify beneficiaries and the viable schemes as per needs of the beneficiaries, disburse loans, monitors the utilisation of loans, and are responsible for the timely recovery of the loans. However statistics are not available on the loan recovery experience of the corporation.

The schemes for assistance can be in any of the following areas:

- agriculture and allied;
- artisan and traditional occupation;
- technical trades;
- hotel/guest house/lodge/restaurant;
- small business; and
- transport services.

The corporations offer term loans for a wide range of incomes but do not finance infrastructure development schemes unless such schemes directly generate income. It also extends assistance to NGOs to promote micro-credit schemes at the grass-root levels. Loans sanctioned are disbursed only after execution of requisite security related documents, A processing fee @Re 1 per cent on the sanctioned loan amount is to be deposited with the corporation.

14.5 Initiatives taken by the State

14.5.1 The SCs and STs (POA) Act 1989

An Act to prevent the commission of offences of atrocities against the members of the scheduled castes and the scheduled tribes, to provide for special courts for the trial of such offences and for the relief and rehabilitation of the victims of such offences and for connected matters.

Provision of the scheduled castes and scheduled tribes (POA) Act has been translated into the regional languages and widely circulated among *panchayats*, collectorate offices, NGOs, and members of SC and ST families. In order to improve awareness about this act some publicity material has been displayed through hoardings at important public places like courts, police stations, district headquarters describing the different situations where the Act is applicable and the expected remedial action from the government including relief, and compensation.

14.5.2 Reservation Schemes

The following scheme for reservation of posts under the Govt. of Sikkim and PSEs are applicable in the State:

SC - 6 per cent

ST - 23 per cent

OBC - 21 per cent

Scheme for relaxation of the upper age limit is as follows:

SC - 5 years

ST - 5 years

OBC - 3 years

TABLE 14.10

SABCCO Coverage

Year	*No. of Beneficiaries*			
	SC	*ST*	*OBC*	*Total*
1998-99	42	105	213	360
1999-2000	120	338	542	1000
2000-01	202	153	497	852
2001-02	29	86	100	215
2002-03	45	139	132	316
2003-04	76	90	155	321

Source: Compendium of Achievements, Social Welfare Department, Sikkim.

BOX 14.3

SABCCO in a Nutshell

1. Authorised share capital: Rs. 20 crore.

2. Paid-up share capital: (Rs. in lakh as on 31.03.05)

SJ, E&W	*Min.SJ&E*	*Min.TA*	*Total*
GOS	GOI	GOI	
624.87	132.18	19.12	776.17

(Rs. in lakh as on 31.03.05)

3. Loan sanctioned:	*SC*	*ST*	*OBC*	*Total*
(a) Physical	419	1055	1156	2630
(b) Financial	394.63	1221.98	1010.29	2626.90

4. Recovery from beneficiaries: (Rs. in lakh as on 31.03.05)

SC	*ST*	*OBC*	*Total*
141.12	459.91	411.49	1012.52

(Rs. in lakh as on 31.03.05)

5. Term loan from apex corps:

NSFDC (SC)	*NSTFDC (ST)*	*NBCFDC (OBC)*	*Total*
281.83	883.84	769.67	1935.34

(Rs. in lakh as on 31.03.05)

6. Repayment to apex corps:

NSFDC (SC)	*NSTFDC (ST)*	*NBCFDC (OBC)*	*Total*
266.15	524.16	578.3	1368.61

7. Rate of interest on loans
   - (a) Scheduled castes and scheduled tribes: 7 per cent per annum
   - (b) Other backward classes:
     - (i) loans below Rs. 1 lakh 7 per cent per annum
     - (ii) loans above Rs. 1 lakh 10 per cent per annum

8. Recovery percentage:
   - (a) from beneficiaries: 51 per cent
   - (b) repayment to apex corps: 85-90 per cent

Table 14.10 shows the beneficiaries of the loans disbursed by the corporations in the past five years

14.6 Recommendations

The recommendations are made on the basis of the existing socio-economic trends visible in the community and the existing policies of the state. These recommendations intend to fill up the gaps in the policies to make them instrumental in directing the existing trends to desirable directions.

- Education is one sector that can prove to yield the maximum return in the developmental process of a community at their initial stages of development. Fall in expenditure on account of education is not justifiable on any grounds.

- In order to have real trickle-down mechanism for SC/ST/OBC with reservation at the primary level education, the quality of the teaching staff should also be maintained. A very low proportion of teachers in Sikkim is trained. A permanent basis of recruitment for non-Sikkimese teachers is needed to ensure this quality.
- Emphasis should be given to vocational and technical training. Scholarship schemes should be coupled with some scheme of assurance that enables them to start their own enterprises after completion of the course. For instance, SABCCO can give some concession in the interest rate to the best student who wants to start his own unit for handicrafts (the handicrafts training centres face this problem after training students they cannot provide them the assistance so that the student becomes self-employed). In this way the government can have sustained rates of returns as future flows of income to the state on whatever it invested on scholarship schemes.
- Revival of handicrafts industries. Improved low-cost technology input using natural dyes for basic processing of wool to be developed.
- Alternative sources of income to younger sections e.g. in ecotourism, yak-safaris, handicrafts, nature guides, mountaineering guides. The communities should be sensitised and trained about the new sources of employment; NGOs to actively participate.
- Easy access to information: Training needed to use CICs.
- Information base for aspirants of higher studies in the rural areas; use CICs to access information on education opportunities.
- There is an immediate need for convergence of policies. Departmental network involved in channeling government's resources for the same purpose should be well coordinated to minimise loss of resources.
- Data record system should be improved. Proper assessment of the policies can only be done on the basis of detailed record. For instance, establishment of SABCCO is a welcome move but their activities as a financial intermediary could not be judged as time series data is not available on the recovery of loans. The relevance of the POA Act cannot be assessed due to lack of data on the number of victims and account of atrocities.
- One valid ground for the criticism of the reservation policy is the inclusion of *bhutias* in the reservation list. Bhutias form the creamy layer and indicators also support the fact that they are by far the most developed among all the communities.
- Immediate action should be taken to revise Revenue order No.1. This revision will help eliminating many distortions in the developmental process. Sensitisation programmes to be launched to make people aware of the positive aspects of amending the order. Long-term lease system. can be one option. The Government can protect the interests of the original landholders by giving them an appropriate share of the resources generated from the activities carried out in their land. New legal handles can be developed to make the system work in a different way.
- Some of the schemes initiated by the government were discontinued. An example is the angora rabbit project at Rabong (North). Before taking up a project a proper cost–benefit analysis should be done so that resources are not wasted with the discontinuation of the project.

Index of Abbreviations Used

SJ.E&W:	Social Justice, Empowerment & Welfare Department.
Min. SJ& E:	Ministry of Social Justice & Empowerment.
Min.T&A:	Ministry of Tribal Affairs.
GoS:	Government of Sikkim.
GoI:	Government of India.
SC:	Scheduled Castes.
ST:	Scheduled Tribes.
OBC:	Other Backward Classes.
NSFDC:	National Scheduled Castes Finance & Development Corporation, New Delhi.
NSTFDC:	National Scheduled Tribes Finance & Development Corporation, New Delhi.
NBCFDC:	National Other Backward Classes Finance & Development Corporation, New Delhi.

References

Annual Plans, Social Welfare Department, Welfare Division, Government of Sikkim 1999-2000, 2000-2001, 2002-2003.

Bhasin, Veena (1989). *Ecology, Culture & Change: Tribals of Sikkim Himalayas.* Inter-India Publication.

Dir. of Cen. Oper. (1988). *Census of India-1981.* "Sikkim-Series-19, Portrait of Population". pp.vi, 132. Sikkim.

————. (1997). "Series-22-Sikkim, Portrait of Population". *Census of India-1991.* pp.xiii; 155. Sikkim

————. (2000). "Series-22-Sikkim, Part-VIII(i): Special Tables on Scheduled Castes". *Census of India-1991.* pp.v; 212. Sikkim.

————. (2001). "Series-22-Sikkim, Part-IV-B(i)(a)-C Series: Language Table C-7". *Census of India-1991.* pp.v, 38. Sikkim.

Census of India-2001, Primary Census Abstract.

Dasgupta, Manas (1992). *Sikkim: Problems & Prospects of Development.* New Delhi: Indus Pub. Company.

Das, B.S. (1996). *The Sikkim Saga*, Vikas Publishing House.

Directorate of Economics & Statistics. *Economic Survey of Sikkim 2003-04.* Govt. of Sikkim.

Govt. of Sikkim. *Sikkim State Annual Plans 1999-2000, 2000-01. 01-02. 02-03.*

————. *Sikkim—A Statistical Profile.*

Lama, Mahendra P. (*ed.*) (1994). *Sikkim: Society, Polity, Economy, Environment.* New Delhi: Indus Pub. Company.

————. (2001). *Sikkim Human Development Report.* New Delhi: Social Science Press.

National Commission for SC & STs, Reports-1993-94.

Planning & Development Dept. *Ninth Five Year Plan-1997-2002.* Govt. of Sikkim.

————. *Tenth Five Year Plan-2002-2007.* Govt. of Sikkim.

————. *Draft Tribal Sub-Plan for Scheduled Tribes under Ninth Five-Year Plan (1997-02).* Govt. of Sikkim.

————. *Draft Tribal Sub-Plan for Scheduled Tribes under Tenth Five-Year Plan (2002-07).* Govt. of Sikkim.

————. "Compendium of Achievements of Social Welfare Dept. (Welfare Division)". *Ninth Five Year Plan (1997-2002).* Govt. of Sikkim.

Rai, Suresh Chand, *et al.* (*eds.*) (1998). *Sikkim: Perspectives for Planning and Development.* Sikkim Science Society.

Reports of National Commission for SC & STs, 1993-94, 1994-95, 1995-96, 1996-97, 1997-98.

Singh, K.S. (*ed.*) (1993). *People of India: Sikkim.* Calcutta: Seagull Book.

Sikkim Scheduled Castes, Scheduled Tribes, and Other Backward Castes Development Corporation Limited (SABBCO). *List of Financial Assistance Extended by Corporation to Beneficiaries as on March 31, 2002.*

Social Welfare Dept. *Annual Plan 1999-2000.* Welfare Div., Govt. of Sikkim.

————. *Statistical Profile of Scheduled Tribe.* Govt. of Sikkim.

Annexures

TABLE A-1

Baseline Information on Biodiversity in Sikkim

Plants		*Animals*	
Wild	*Domesticated*	*Wild*	*Domesticated*
Medicinal Plants in high to low altitudes including insectivores (*Drosera, Utricularia*)	Crops (Grains, Pulses) e.g. Maize, *Jhao, Gau,* Rice, *Kodo, Kalo Dal, Batamas,* Beans (*TIBI*), *Ghiu-shinbi, Masoor*	Lowland e.g. Barking Deer, Peafowl, Leopard, Langur, Kalij, *Luinche, Chamera*	Cow (*Gai*): Indigenous: e.g. *Siri* Exotic: *Jersey* and other hybrids
Wild Vegetables, Flowers e.g. *Bethu, Khendu, Tho, Sisnu, Simrayo,* Bamboo shoots, Ferns, *Nakima*	Vegetables e.g. Potato, Cabbage, *Saag,* Radish, Peas, *Phapar, Kenyum (Latte saag), Dalda saag,* Pumpkin	Temperate e.g. Goral, Shapi, Serow (*Jharal*), Bear, Musk Deer *Danphe, Monal,*	Yak Dzo
Mushrooms e.g. *Karsha, Seysha, Yarcha Gombuk*	Exotic Vegetables e.g. Broccoli, Brussels sprouts, Squash	Trans-Himalayan e.g. Nayan, Kiang, Snow leopard,	Sheep: Highland *Bhenglu* Lowland *Bheda*
Wild Fruits e.g. *Lapsi, Pomsi, Kusum, Kiwifruit,* Mango, *Hippophae*, Strawberries,	Fruits e.g. Apple, Orange, *Naspati, Aarucha, Aru,* Banana, Papaya, Guava, Jackfruit,	Butterflies, Moths, Beetles, Molluscs, Dragonfly, other insects on land, in water	Goats: Highland *Chengra* Lowland *Baakhra*
Wild Nuts e.g. Okhar, Katus,	Nuts	Fishes (22 wild species, I exotic)	Domestic Fish e.g. Goldfish, Carps
Rhododendrons, Junipers (religious/dhoop)	Herbs e.g. *Dhania, Pudina, Tulsi*	Frogs, Toads	Horse
Spices/Seasoning/Herbs e.g. *Elaichi, Tejpatta,* Rampo, Timbur, Chimphing	Spices/Seasoning e.g. Haldi, Adua, *Lasun, Tori, Methi,* Chilli,	Snakes, Lizards e.g. Python, Cobra, *Chepara* (Lizard)	Donkey, Mule
Fuel/Firewood trees	Domesticated Bacteria and other micro flora (in *Kinema, Gundruk, Sinki, Chang, Cheeses*)	Earthworms, Spiders,	Buffalo
Timber Trees		Crabs	Pigs (local and exotic)
Fodder Trees, Fodder Grasses	Exotic Fodder Grasses e.g. Kyu-Kyu Grass,	Soil nematodes	Poultry: Indigenous: *Bustee* Exotic: Leghorns,
Lichens		Micro fauna	Guinea Pigs, Rabbits e.g. Angora, Albino, Chinchilla
Mosses		Wolf, Fox, Jackal, Wild dog	Dogs e.g. Feral, Tibetan mastiff, Lhasa Apso
Algae e.g. *Chusha*		Lesser Cats	Cats: Feral cats
Orchids	Hybrid Orchids	Wild birds	Pigeons: Feral Blue Rock
Naturalised exotics e.g. *Digitalis,* Dhupi		Honey bees (rock bees *Apis dorsata,* 'Pudka', 'Khetauri')	Domestic Honeybees *Apis cerana indica*
Natural Dyes e.g. *Rumex* sp.	Mulberry bush	Wild Silk Moths	Domestic Silk Worm
Fibres e.g. Argeli			
Weeds e.g. *Eupatorium (Banmara)*			

Source: Sikkim Biodiversity Strategy and Action Plan (SBSAP), Sikkim.

TABLE A-2

Sustainability Issues Relevant for Sikkim

- Illicit Felling
- Wildlife Poaching including NTFP and Medicinal Plants
- Biopiracy
- Poaching incidences by Assam Rifles and GREF
- Lack of Awareness
- Plantation in private lands
- Firewood and fodder demand
- Increasing demand for medicinal plants
- Demand for wild edibles (ferns, nettles, roots, tubers fruits, flowers etc).
- Landslide control
- Requirement of seedlings
- Alternative energy
- Requirement of LPG
- Requirement for biogas
- Livelihood issues
- Ecotourism enterprise
- Lack of capacity
- Lack of publicity
- Improvement of trekking trails
- Agriculture and horticulture development
- Decline in soil fertility
- Requirement for food preservation and processing technologies
- Increased introduction of exotic/hybrid flora for commercial purposes; No state level gene bank
- Animal Husbandry initiatives
- Husbandry of high yielding livestock (local and exotic/hybrid)
- Decline in yak breeds
- Decline in indigenous sheep varieties
- Mules for army and tourists, employment potential, especially during road blocks
- Improvement of existing breed of livestock for more meat, milk, etc. to decrease the existing pressure on forests
- Need for better marketing of milk and milk products from temperate and trans-Himalayas where yak, sheep, goat and cow population occurs
- Lack of cheese processing plant in livestock dominated areas of trans-Himalayas
- Micro enterprise development
- Revival/protection of indigenous handicrafts and handloom
- Infrastructure development
- Communication problems, damage to environment in trans-Himalayas
- Essential services
- Health issues in remote areas encompassing nutritive foods including traditional diet, medicinal plants conservation and use, traditional medicinal systems, diverse agricultural produce, foods from the wild
- Improvement of drinking water source
- Culture and traditional knowledge conservation
- Reduction of vehicular emissions
- Efficient garbage management
- Biodiversity conservation

Source: Sikkim Biodiversity Strategy and Action Plan.

TABLE A-3

Bodies Involved in Participatory Approach to Sustainable Development

Organisation	*Role and Initiatives*
BSI, Sikkim Himalayan Circle, Gangtok	Flora documentation & research
CWC, Tadong; Superintending Engineer	Water resource study, monitoring
Village level institutions like *Panchayats*, Joint Forest Management Committees, Eco Development Committees, Watershed Committees, Pipons.	Administration and conservation at village level
NGO's based in Sikkim and India	Promoting conservation and livelihoods
GBPIHED, Tadong, Gangtok, Sikkim Government College, Tadong	Research & Development
International donors (AUSAID, UNDP, GEF, World Bank etc.)	Funding programmes
Geological Survey of India, GoI, Gangtok; Director	Geological research, glacier study
SHRA	Hospitality industry facilitates ecotourism
ICAR Research Complex	Agriculture & Animal Husbandry Research
IOC (liquid petroleum gas or LPG bottling plant), Bagey Khola, Bardang; Manager	Providing alternatives to firewood
Khadi Commission	Apiary and allied cottage industry
Manipal Institute Central Referral Hospital, Tadong, Gangtok	Manipal University Bio-medical waste management
Traditional Health Practitioners	Repository of indigenous knowledge of biodiversity resource use
National Institute of Orchids, Pakyong; Director	Orchid breeding centre
NHPC: Rangit HE projects, legship, South Sikkim; Teesta HE projects, tista stages 5, Singtam	Hydroelectric power projects in river valleys
Spices board	Large cardamom research
State pollution control board	Industrial pollution control
TAAS	Streamlining of travel agencies
District collectors:	Enforcing Law and coordinating development
Telecommunications	Connectivity to remote biodiversity rich areas
Departments of Government of Sikkim, Agriculture Department Animal Husbandry and Veterinary Services Dept., Government Institute of Cottage Industries, Horticulture, Floriculture Departments, Industries (temi tea, labott glass, fruit preservation, distilleries & breweries, Science & Technology Department, Information Technology Department, SIDICO/SABCO	Livelihood generation
Department of Food & Civil Supply, Education Department, Health Department, Forest, Environment & Wildlife Department, Police Department	
Buildings & Housing Department, Irrigation & Flood Control Department, Motor Vehicles Department, Public Health and Engineering Department, Power Department Roads & Bridges Department, Rural Development Department, State Trading Corporation of Sikkim, State Tourism Development Corporation, Tourism Department, Urban Development & Housing Department. Essential services	Infrastructure development

Source: SBSAP, Sikkim.

TABLE A-4

Steps Towards Sustainable Development

- A Comprehensive State Policy on Forests, Environment and Land use, 2000, passed by the State Government: Budget in the field of Forest, Environment and Wildlife enhanced by 5 per cent.
- Compulsory environmental education.
- Environment impact assessment, Management plan, and Catchment Area Treatment Plan for all the hydro-electric projects: Rathong Chu hydro-electric project abandoned and closed.
- CM Online website launched to strengthen eco-governance; 40 community information centres set up all over the state.
- Scaling of important peaks like Kanchenjanga for mountaineering expeditions banned: so are commercial activities on natural lakes and wetlands.
- Use of non-biodegradable materials banned by legislation: no plastic or polybags.
- Integrated afforestation and Integrated Watershed Management Programme; Constitution of Watershed Development Committee under IWDP being implemented through the *zilla parishad;* emphasis on fuelwood and fodder plantation to reduce biotic stress on natural forests.
- *Smriti Van* programme in all the districts.
- State Award: *Rajya Van Sangrakshan Evang Pariyavaran Puraskar.*
- State Biodiversity Strategy and Action Plan under the National Biodiversity and Action Plan: enacting State Biodiversity Act Wireless communications created and strengtened to protect Forest, Environment and Wildlife Infrastructure like check posts, arms and amunitions.
- Massive power decentralisation: Rs. 50 lakh transferred from the state and central pool of resources to each of the *panchayat* units, Rs. 2 cr. to each *zilla panchayat*; 5 per cent of the funds to be used for afforestation and conservation activities.
- All *panchayats* to maintain classified *panchayats* biodiversity register to record every species in their area.
- Planting 100 trees in the names of sons and daughters: one tree equivalent to Rs. 1 lakh after 20 years.

Source: State Government Documents.

TABLE A-5

Allocation in Different Sectors in Five Year Plans

(Rs. Lakh)

Sectors	*Ninth 5 yrPlan*	*Tenth 5 yr Plan*
Fisheries	270	200
Forestry and Wildlife	4892	3500
Soil and Water conservation (forest)	2525	900
Ecology and Environment	405	500
Mines and Geology	300	300
Science and Technology	825	600
Information Technology		800
All Sectors	160280	165574

TABLE A-6

Percentage Allocation in Different Sectors in Five Year Plans

(Rs. Lakh)

Sectors	*Ninth 5-yr Plan*	*Tenth 5-yr Plan*
Fisheries	0.17	0.12
Forestry and Wildlife	3.05	2.11
Soil and Water conservation (forest)	1.58	0.54
Ecology and Environment	0.25	0.30
Mines and Geology	0.19	0.18
Science and Technology	0.51	0.36
Information Technology	0.00	0.48
All Sectors	100.00	100.00

Source: Ninth and Tenth Five Year Plans, Sikkim.

TABLE A-7

Persons Engaged in the Public and the Private Sector: A Comparative Analysis (%)

	Public sector	*Private sector*
Assam	4.15	4.22
Manipur	3.81	3.86
Meghalaya	3.44	3.62
Mizoram	4.67	4.67
Nagaland	3.81	4.00
Tripura	3.84	3.87
Sikkim	**6.84**	**NA**
India	2.61	2.79

Source: Directorate General of Employment & Training, Ministry of Labour, *Statistical Abstract 2002*, CSO.

TABLE A-8

District-wise Distribution of Workers in Sikkim

	North	*East*	*South*	*West*
Total workers	9.0	44.4	26.5	20.2
Main workers	8.3	43.5	27.0	21.3
Marginal workers	11.9	47.9	24.5	15.7
Cultivators	7.0	28.9	36.9	27.2
Agricultural labourers	12.4	47.7	15.8	24.1
Household industry	8.8	46.8	16.3	28.1
Other workers	10.8	62.0	16.1	11.1
Memo: Percentage of population	7.59	45.29	24.33	22.79

Source: Census 2001.

TABLE A-9

Percentage Distribution of Workers in Sikkim 1999 and 2001

		Rural		Urban	
		1991	*2001*	*1991*	*2001*
Main workers	Male	50.58	50.75	53.24	51.92
	Female	29.6	26.89	17.7	19.4
	Total	40.68	39.57	38.08	37.21
Marginal workers	Male	0.34	6.99	1.29	4.35
	Female	1.87	13.78	0.88	1.99
	Total	1.06	10.17	1.22	3.28
Total workers	Male	50.90	57.74	54.53	56.27
	Female	31.47	40.67	18.73	21.42
	Total	41.74	49.74	39.20	40.49
Non workers	Male	49.10	42.26	45.47	43.73
	Female	68.53	59.33	81.25	78.58
	Total	58.26	50.26	60.80	59.51

Source: Census 2001.

TABLE A-10

Changing Composition of the Workforce

(as a % of Total Population)

	Main Workers			Marginal Workers			Non-workers		
	1981	*1991*	*2001*	*1981*	*1991*	*2001*	*1981*	*1991*	*2001*
Arunachal Pradesh	49.6	45.2	37.8	3.0	1.0	6.2	47.4	53.8	56.0
Assam	NA	31.2	26.7	NA	4.9	9.1	NA	63.9	64.2
Nagaland	47.5	42.3	35.4	0.7	0.4	7.2	51.8	57.3	57.4
Manipur	40.3	38.6	30.4	2.1	3.6	13.2	56.8	57.8	56.4
Meghalaya	43.4	40.3	32.6	2.5	2.4	9.2	54.1	57.3	58.2
Mizoram	41.7	42.1	40.8	3.7	6.8	11.8	54.6	51.1	47.4
Sikkim	**46.6**	**40.4**	**39.4**	**1.7**	**1.1**	**9.3**	**51.7**	**58.5**	**51.4**
Tripura	29.6	29.1	28.5	2.6	2.0	7.7	67.7	68.9	63.8
India	33.4	34.1	30.4	3.3	3.4	8.7	63.2	62.5	60.9

Source: Census 2001.

TABLE A-11

Distribution of Estimated Number of Workers by Tabulation Category

(per cent)

	Persons	*Male*	*Female*
Manufacturing D	18.6	21.1	9.1
Construction F	2.2	2.8	0.0
Trading and repair services G	47.1	43.3	61.2
Hotels and restaurants H	18.9	18.6	19.8
Transport, storage, communications I	4.9	5.9	1.1
Financial intermediation J	0.0	0.0	0.0
Real estate renting K	0.7	0.9	0.1
Education M	3.0	2.0	7.1
Health & social work N	0.3	0.3	0.4
Other community social and personal services O	4.3	5.0	1.4
ALL	100	100	100

Source: NSS 55th Survey.

TABLE A-12

Per Thousand Distribution of Persons of age 15 years and above by Broad Current Weekly and Daily Activity Status (CWS and CDS) for all Size Class of Towns

	Self-employed	*Registered Employed*	*Casual*	*Total*	*Unemployed*	*Not in Labour Force*
Arunachal Pradesh						
CWS	99	212	66	376	11	613
CDS	99	209	62	369	11	620
Assam						
CWS	208	193	49	451	53	496
CDS	183	187	45	415	57	528
Manipur						
CWS	269	147	44	461	33	506
CDS	239	142	40	421	31	548
Meghalaya						
CWS	120	256	76	452	22	527
CDS	117	252	74	443	22	536
Mizoram						
CWS	268	180	102	550	15	434
CDS	230	178	83	491	18	490
Nagaland						
CWS	111	335	16	462	50	487
CDS	95	333	14	442	50	508
Sikkim						
CWS	188	283	48	519	45	437
CDS	180	283	44	507	42	451
India: CWS	198	195	78	470	30	500
India: CDS	187	192	66	446	37	518

Notes: Sample of all size classes (1+2+3) taken together. Sikkim has only size class 3 towns with population less than 50,000.

Source: NSS Survey (55th Round on Employment and Unemployment, 1999-2000).

TABLE A-13

Unemployment Rate: Various Indicators

	Usual Status			*Usual Status (Adjusted)*		
	Male	*Female*	*Persons*	*Male*	*Female*	*Persons*
Rural	35	20	31	32	19	28
Urban	67	10	76	6	100	75

Usual Principal Status Among the Youths (15-29) Years

	Male				*Female*				*Persons*			
	15-19	*20-24*	*25-29*	*15-29*	*15-19*	*20-24*	*25-29*	*15-29*	*15-19*	*20-24*	*25-29*	*15-29*
Rural	74	84	131	102	0	103	25	50	49	89	95	84
Urban	221	132	154	156	0	495	167	299	167	234	156	190

Per 1000 Distribution of Households by Usually Employed (Principal Status) Persons of 15 Years and above

	None		*Only 1 Male*		*Only 1 Female*		*Only 1 Male and 1 Female*		*Others*	
	All	*FH*	*All*	*FH*	*All*	*FH*	*All*	*FH*	*All*	*FH*
Rural	81	106	338	187	38	378	250	140	294	190
Urban	70	560	557	0	37	233	162	35	174	172

Source: Sikkim and the North Eastern States: *A Statistical Abstract–2001* (based on *NSS Report No. 458: Employment and Unemployment Situation*) published by Directorate of Economics and Statistics, GoS.

TABLE A-14

Central Assistance and States' Own Resources in Tenth Plan in North-East States

(Rs. crore)

State	States Own Resources	Central Assistance	Total
1. Arunachal Pradesh	492.07	3396.25	3888.32
2. Assam	-1212.37	9527.60	8315.23
3. Manipur	-362.42	3166.42	2804.00
4. Meghalaya	-23.71	2323.15	2299.44
5. Mizoram	-346.93	2399.44	2052.51
6. Nagaland	-366.82	2594.47	2227.65
7. Sikkim	95.50	1560.24	1655.74
8. Tripura	491.55	4008.45	4500.00
Total (NE-States)	-1328.63	27415.78	26087.15
All States	306771.77	253844.01	560615.78
NES—as per cent of Total	-0.43	10.80	4.65
Manipur as per cent of NES	27.28	11.55	10.75

Source: *Draft Tenth Five-Year Plan (2002-2007)*, Vol. III, State Plans–Trends, Concerns and Strategies (Planning Commission).

TABLE A-15

Additional Resource Mobilisation by the State Government: Own Tax Revenue

(in Rs. Lakh)

Measures taken in	1997-98	1998-99	1999-00	2000-01	2001-02
1997-98					
Sales tax	200.0	206.0	207.0	210.0	211.0
1998-99	-	-	-	-	-
1999-00					
Taxes on vehicles			6.0	6.0	6.0
Entertainment tax			10.0	11.0	11.0
Excise			151.0	160.0	160.0
2000-01	-	-	-	-	-
2001-02					
Sales tax					50.0
Total ARM from Taxes	200.0	206.0	374.0	387.0	438.0

Source: Memo to TFC.

TABLE A-16

Additional Resource Mobilisation: Non-Tax Revenue

(in Rs. Lakh)

Measures initiated in	1997-98	1998-99	1999-00	2000-01	2001-02	2002-03 (RE)
1997-98						
1998-99						
Housing (License fees)		15.07	17.07	17.86	18.33	
1999-2000						
PHE			10.0	11.0	11.0	
Power			105.0	111.0	115.0	
Lottery			900.0	950.0	950.0	
Road (SNT)			9.0	9.0	9.0	
2000-01						
Animal Husbandry				5.0	5.0	
Health				10.0	10.0	
Education				60.0	60.0	
2001-02						
Lottery						6700.0
2002-03	-	-	-	-	-	-
2003-04	-	-	-	-	-	-
Total ARM from Non-tax	0.0	15.07	1041.07	1173.86	1178.33	6700.0
Total ARM Tax & Non-tax	200.0	221.07	1415.07	1560.86	1616.33	6700.0??
Total ARM as a percent of GSDP	0.31	0.28	1.68	1.71	1.65	6.36

Source: Memo to TFC.

TABLE A-17

Arrears of Tax Revenues

(in Rs. Lakh)

Taxes	Actuals (As on 31st March)					
	1998	*1999*	*2000*	*2001*	*2002*	*2003 RE*
Sales Tax	128.94	243.77	236.25			
State Excise			116.95			
Stamps & Registration				1.93		
Other Taxes	5.57				113.14	
Non-taxes: Power	717.63	836.84	1160.34	1198.73	1273.0	1298.0

Source: Memo Vol II p 72.

TABLE A-18

Deficits and Debt

(as a percentage of GSDP)

	1990-91	*1995-96*	*1997-98*	*1998-99*	*1999-00*	*2000-01*	*2001-02*	*2002-03*
Revenue deficit	-13.41	-12.47	-6.34	7.03	-0.22	-10.90	-14.63	-22.02
Capital outlay	21.53	21.02	16.47	11.74	11.23	16.56	21.56	27.01
Net lending	0.52	-0.22	0.17	0.02	0.01	-0.12	-0.10	-0.06
Fiscal deficit (=1+2+3)	8.64	8.33	10.37	18.78	11.02	5.54	6.84	4.95
Primar deficit	4.18	2.30	3.67	11.66	2.43	-3.70	-2.42	-5.25
Debt	60.05	57.44	54.76	64.55	80.63	80.18	82.61	81.87

Source: Finance Accounts and Budget Documents.

TABLE A-19

The Progress of Rural Local Governments (PRIs) in North East States (February 2002)

State	*Panchayats Elections*	*District Planning Committee*	*SFC-Recommend-ations*	*Devolution of Funds, Functions and Functionaries*	*Merger of DRDA/ZP*
Arunachal Pradesh	Not held	Constituted	Not constituted	Not applicable yet	Not yet
Assam	Held in Jan.02	Not constituted	Accepted in part	No action	No merger yet
Manipur	GP&DP-Jan.97	In 2 districts	Accepted	22-functions, 4-functionaries	No information
Meghalaya States	73rd Constitutional Amendment Act is not applicable as the traditional system of local Government exists in these				
Mizoram	-Do-				
Nagaland	- Do-				
Sikkim	October 97	Yes	Accepted, 2nd SFC constituted	Funds-24,Function-24 Fuctionaries-24	Status not reported
Tripura	July 99	Yes	Accepted, 2nd SFC constituted	Functions (12) only	Status not clear

Source: Draft Tenth Five Year Plan (2002-2007), Vol. III, State Plans-Trends, Concerns and Strategies (Planning Commission).

TABLE A-20

Year-wise Enrolment in Various Levels of Schools

Stages	*2001*			*2003*			*2004*			*2005*		
	Boys	*Girls*	*Total*	*Boys*	*Girls*	*Total*	*Boys*	*Girls*	*Total*	*Boys*	*Girls*	*Total*
Pre-Primary	12205	11003	23208	11095	9945	21040	10264	9410	19674	8657	7827	16484
School Enrolment												
Total (I to V)	38837	38166	77003	38573	38226	76799	39502	39083	78585	40053	40225	80278
Total (VI to VIII)	11779	12843	24822	11551	13251	24802	12585	14,964	27549	13360	15801	29161
TOTAL (IX To X)	4236	4014	8246	4606	4682	9288	4489	4658	9147	4810	5356	10166
Total (XI to XII)	2520	2057	4577	2937	2807	5744	3253	2878	6131	*	*	*
Grand Total Class I to XII	57372	57080	114648	57667	58966	116633	59829	61583	121412	58223	61382	119605

Note: * Enrolment for Classes XI & XII will be available later as Enrolment is under way for these classes.

Source: Data supplied by the Department of Human Resource Development in August 2005.

TABLE A-21

Profit and Loss Account of Sikkim Power Department

S.N	*Component of Expenditure*	*1998-99*	*1999-00*	*2000-01*	*2001-02*	*2002-03*
	Energy generated	53.53	49.52	43.11	29.11	40.32
	Energy purchased	73.14	82.94	89.79	120.58	120.70
	Total availability	126.67	132.46	132.90	149.69	161.02
	Energy sold		89.38	87.72	65.19	73.27
A	Income (Rs. crore)					
1	Revenue receipts from sale of electricity	6.76	8.25	10.04	11.84	13.31
2	Misc revenue					
3	Other revenue if any					
	Total A	6.76	8.25	10.04	11.84	13.31
B	Expenditure (Rs. crore)					
1	Fuel	0.78	1.10	0.10	0.22	0.36
2	Purchase of Power	3.00	3.00	3.00	3.00	24.31
3	O&M Expenses	8.52	10.31	11.80	11.84	11.80
4	Establishment andAdministrative Expenditure	7.84	9.03	6.80	6.70	6.84
5	Depreciation					
6	Other Misc Expenditure					
	Total B	20.14	23.44	21.70	21.80	43.31
C	Operating income (A-B) Rs. Crore	(-)13.38	(-) 15.19	(-) 11.66	(-) 9.96	(-) 30.0
D	Interest due					
E	Net Surplus (Deficit) (CD) Rs. crore	(-) 13.38	(-) 15.19	(-) 11.66	(-)9.96	(-) 30.00

Note: Gap = Non-plan expenditure minus revenue receipts.

Source: Computed from *Annual Reports,* Power Department, Government of Sikkim.

TABLE A-22

Financial Projection: Profit and Loss Accounts

(Rs. crore)

Particulars	*2004-05*	*2006-07*	*2007-08*	*2011-12*
A. Income				
Revenue receipts from sale of power	111.02	118.25	145.79	200.57
Miscellaneous revenue	1.10	1.22	1.28	1.55
Subsidy (Agriculture/consumers)	0.00	0.00	0.00	0.00
Other subsidy if any	0.00	0.00	0.00	0.00
Total (income)	112.12	119.47	147.07	202.12
B. Expenses				
Fuel	0.53	0.58	0.61	0.74
Cost of power purchased	77.29	77.29	77.29	77.29
Repair and maintenance	15.75	18.37	19.84	26.99
Employees Cost	8.14	9.50	10.26	13.95
Administration and Genl. Expenses	0.56	0.63	0.67	0.84
Less: Capitalisation (13%)	1.13	1.32	1.42	1.92
	101.14	105.05	107.24	117.90
Gross Operating Surplus (A-B)	10.99	14.41	39.82	84.23
C. Depreciation	21.17	26.11	28.00	41.03
D. Interest and finance charges	6.92	11.02	12.78	17.97
Less: IDC	0.90	1.26	1.48	2.15
Total B+C+D	128.33	140.92	146.56	174.75
Net surplus/Deficit (A-B-C-D)	-16.20	-21.46	0.50	27.38
Sales MU	531.63	561.47	645.41	883.75
Average cost of supply *(Rs./kWh)*	2.41	2.51	2.27	1.98
Average tariff including misc. revenue	2.11	2.13	2.28	2.29
Profit/loss *(Rs./kWh)*	-0.30	-0.38	0.01	0.31

Note: Demand is forecast on 'Business as Usual'; transmission and distribution losses to be reduced to 38 per cent by 2006-07 and 15 per cent by 2011-12 (current level of losses is 55 per cent); no tariff increase is envisaged as transfer of free power to the corporation is considered; and sale of power outside the state at Rs. 2/unit.

Source: Author's computations.

TABLE A-23

Category-wise Estimated Demand (MU)

Consumer Category	*2001-02*	*2006-07*	*2011-12*	*Overall Growth (%)*
Domestic	29.75	57.13	112.69	14.2
Commercial	18.83	37.00	63.94	13.0
Industry (LT & HT)	9.35	13.68	30.29	12.4
Public lighting, water works and others	12.52	20.16	32.47	10.0
Total sales (net T&D losses)	70.45	129.35	239.39	13.0

Source: Author's computations.

TABLE A-24

Demand Projections: 'Business-as-Usual' Scenario

Particulars	*Tenth Plan (2006-07)*	*Eleventh Plan (2011-12)*
Energy Requirement (MU)	209	282
Peak Demand (MW)	60	80
Capacity Required (MW)	100	135
Existing Capacity (MW)	119/91	119/91
Additional Capacity Required (in winter) (MW)	9	44

Source: Author's computations.

TABLE A-25

Demand Forecast: High Demand Scenario

Particulars	*Tenth Plan (2006-07)*	*Eleventh Plan (2011-12)*
Energy requirement (MU)	438	678
Peak demand (MW)	106	141
Capacity required (MW)	180	235
Existing capacity (MW)	119/91	119/91
Additional capacity required (in winter) (MW)	89	144

Note: Number of industries likely to materialise.

Source: Author's computations.

TABLE A-26

Comparison of Demand Forecasts

Category	*2001-02*		*2004-05*	
	Actuals	*16th EPS*	*ASCI Study*	*16th EPS*
Domestic	29.75	57.98	44.13	61.80
Commercial	18.83	17.71	28.14	19.11
Public lighting and others	15.52	18.30	16.64	19.35
Industry (LT&HT)	9.35	57.48	12.44	62.77
Total demand	70.45	151.55	101.45	163.03

Source: Author's computations.

Annexure for Power

Recommendation from the Centre for Infrastructure Management & Regulatory Studies, Administrative Staff College of India (ASCI), Hyderabad on restructuring the power sector in Sikkim

The study has suggested corporatisation of this sector by reorganising the generation, transmission, and distribution units into strategic business units. This report suggests two alternatives without unbundling of the sector.

Alternative I

Transfer all generation, transmission, and distribution assets and personnel of Power Department to SPDCL. Set up strategic business units (SBUs). The power sector to be reorganised as SBUs within the Corporation and they are not legal entities but would maintain separate accounts.

Generation

- the generation SBU will be responsible for:
- all new projects would be taken up by the corporation directly as per the government policies for domestic consumption and export;
- operation and maintenance of existing generating stations;
- R&M works in the existing generating stations;
- all the activities connected with power generation;
- sale of power to the transmission SBU;
- one chief engineer may head the generation SBU and will be chief executive of the generation SBU; and
- minimum regulation.

Transmission

Transmission SBU will obtain power from the generation SBU, central stations and other sources and sell to distribution SBU at 11 kV from 66 and 132 kV substations.

The transmission SBU will be responsible for:

- operation and maintenance of the 66 kV and 132 kV system including substations;
- operation of the power system in coordination with eastern regional load dispatch centre;
- planning of new transmission, sub-transmission lines and substations;
- construction of new transmission, sub-transmission lines and substations;
- loss reduction in transmission and sub-transmission network;
- management will fix transfer price for sale of energy by generation SBU to transmission SBU; and
- transmission charges regulated by ERC.

Distribution

The distribution SBU would be responsible for:

- purchase of power from the transmission SBU;
- management of distribution network (11kV and LT);
- expansion of supply to new consumers;
- sale of electricity to consumers;
- metering, billing and revenue realisation from consumers;
- distribution tariff will be regulated by ERC;
- consumer service;
- assessment of demand (demand forecast) in the state;
- planning for power supply to meet the demand;
- reduction of distribution losses (technical and non technical); and
- management will fix transfer price from transmission SBU to distribution SBU.

Though entire distribution segment suggested to be organised as on SBU, the three circles could in turn be organised as SBUs/ profit centres to improve the performance and customer service.

Each SBU to sign MOU with the management covering:

- responsibility of the unit;
- targets for various activities of the unit;
- management of the unit;
- devolution of administrative and financial powers; and
- other provisions to make the unit accountable.

Alternative II

- Transfer only generation assets to SPDCL along with personnel later.
- Distribution is the most critical activity requiring immediate attention, transfer of generation alone to SPDCL will not improve the sector.

This report provides a clear road map for reform implementation

- approval of financial restructuring plan for the power sector;
- identification of assets and liabilities and personal to be transferred to the corporation;
- transfer scheme for transfer of assets, liabilities and personnel;
- management structure for the corporation;
- appointment of Board of Directors;
- operationalisation of the corporation; and
- specific time-bound programme to electrify all villages/ households.

It also discusses both the objectives and issues in financial restructuring including.

- asset liability mismatch;
- current assets and current liabilities-mismatch;
- overdue payments to lenders/suppliers; and
- employees related liabilities (unfunded liabilities)

It provides options to meet the liabilities of the existing employees' liabilities including creation of a pension fund operated by a trust and transferring employees on deputation and recovering the liabilities from the Corporation in due course.

The ASCI report makes the following projections wherein the state will have a net surplus of Rs. 27 crore by 2011-12 (see Annexure Table A-21).

In order to realise the above situation the report suggests that the following policy decisions be taken by the state government:

- operationalisation of SPDCL by transfer of generation, transmission, and distribution simultaneously or only Generation initially;
- transfer of all personnel to the corporation on 'as-is-where-is basis' or need based;
- decision on surplus manpower;
- payment of pension etc., to the existing employees by state government/creation of a trust;
- transfer of employees on deputation and recover provident fund, pension contribution from corporation in due course;
- takeover of all current liabilities by the state government;
- free power from central projects to be passed on to the corporation-corporation has to pay income tax on surplus/ profit;
- or, allow to be sold by the state government at market rate outside the corporation and pay subsidy to the corporation if required, and what tariff levels should be maintained; and
- financial support to the corporation by the state government during transition.

It imposes conditions for success as follows :

Demand and Supply Scenario

- demand projection are made up to 2011-12; and
- power supply scenario is comfortable with share from central generating stations including free power.

Efficiency Improvement

- T&D loss to be brought down from 55 per cent to 15 per cent by 2011-12

a. Tariff Policies

- no tariff increase is considered for financial projections up to 2011-12; and
- tariff to be rationalised to reduce cross subsidy.

TABLE A-27

New Land Classification and Land Use, 2001-02

New Classification	*Area (hectares)*	*Per cent of Area Total Operational*	*Per cent of Total Geographic Area*
Irrigated	11,310	8.90	1.53
Unirrigated	49,310	38.81	6.67
Non-agricultural use	6,220	4.90	0.84
Barren land	8,980	7.07	1.21
Forest/Jungle/ Bushes	17,340	13.65	2.34
Grasses	4,120	3.24	0.56
Uncultivated fallow land	8,540	6.72	1.15
Area under cardamom	21,220	16.70	2.87
Total operational area	1,27,050	100	17.18

Note: The state has a geographical area of 739,600 hectares. The table shows revised land-use data based on full enumeration at the *panchayat* level during 2001-02. In the old classification, operational area was 111.3 thousand hectares.

Source: Economic Survey of Sikkim, 2003-04, Planning Department, Government of Sikkim.

TABLE A-28

Foodgrain and Oilseed Output, Area and Yield, 1975-2003
(Output in Thousand Tonnes; Area in Thousand Hectares; Yield: kg./ hectare)

Crop		*1975-76*	*1985-86*	*1995-96*	*2001-02**		*2002-03*	*% Change 2001-02 (Actual) to 2002-03*
					Reported	*Actual*		
Rice	Output	10.0	17.1	21.7	23	13.4	12.9	-3.7
	Area	11.4	15.5	15.9	15.6	10.4	10.0	-3.8
	Yield	877.2	1,100.0	1,372.6	1,474.4	1,293.8	1,252.5	-3.2
Wheat	Output	0.2	11.2	15.3	11.3	5.5	5.5	0.0
	Area	0.2	7.4	8.4	7	4.4	4.4	0.0
	Yield	1,000.0	1,516.2	1,817.6	1,614.3	1,245.3	1,245.3	0.0
Maize	Output	16.5	49.3	56.6	54.4	50.9	49.4	-2.9
	Area	28.5	39	39.9	39.4	38.8	38.7	-0.3
	Yield	579.0	1,262.8	1,416.0	1,381.2	1,312.0	1,275.3	-2.8
Other Cereals	Output	4.5	7.0	8.1	8.1	4.8	5.5	14.6
	Area	7.2	7.8	8.3	8.3	6.8	6.9	1.5
	Yield	1,755.6	2,885.8	3,192.5	3,153.4	2,473.7	2,655.6	7.4
Total Cereals	Output	31.2	84.5	101.6	96.8	74.6	73.3	-1.7
	Area	47.3	69.7	72.6	70.3	60.5	60.3	-0.3
	Yield	659.3	1,212.3	1,402.6	1,378.0	1,234.4	1,215.0	-1.6
Total Pulses	Output	0.7	4.6	5.9	5.6	3.7	3.6	-2.7
	Area	1.7	5.5	6.7	6.3	5.1	5.0	-2.0
	Yield	411.8	836.4	878.9	884.1	720.5	715.0	-0.8
Total Food Grain	Output	31.9	89.1	107.5	102.4	78.3	76.9	-1.8
	Area	49.0	75.2	79.3	76.6	65.5	65.4	-0.2
	Yield	1,071.0	2,048.7	2,281.5	2,262.2	1,954.8	1,930.1	-1.3
Total Oilseeds	Output	0.7	5.6	7.6	7.8	4.0	6.4	60.0
	Area	1.5	6.7	9.7	10.1	6.7	9.0	34.3
	Yield	466.7	828.4	784.5	773.3	607.5	713.7	17.5

Note: * Area and output data was revised. 'Actual' figures are based on the revised data and on 100 per cent enumeration with the *gram panchayat* as the unit instead of the district.

Source: Department of Agriculture, Government of Sikkim.

TABLE A-29

Horticulture: Total Output, Area and Productivity, 1975-200
(Output in Thousand Tonnes; Area in Thousand Hectares; Yield in kg./hectare)

Crop		*1975-76*	*1985-86*	*1995-96*	*2001-02**		*2002-03*	*% Change 2001-02 (Actual) to 2002-03*
					Reported	*Actual*		
Orange/Citrus Fruit	Output	3.6	12.1	8.7	4.3	2.7	6.1	129.7
	Area	1.4	4.6	6.6	6.7	1.6	4.3	167.3
	Yield	2,571.4	2,630.4	2,396.0	7,500.0	1,665.8	1,436.8	-13.7
Total Fruits	Output	4.7	18.2	12.0	32.0	4.4	9.1	108.0
	Area	1.9	9.1	9.2	15.3	2.5	6.7	175.1
	Yield	1,620.6	2,011.1	2,102	2,091.5	1,775.5	1,342.3	-24.4
Vegetables	Output	5.0	23.9	28.0	24.2	10.5		
	Area	1.0	3.8	5.8	5.2	2.3		
	Yield	5,000.0	6,289.5	4,482.0	4,631.0	4,725.1		
Potatoes	Output	8.0	26.4	24.0	25.5	11.9		
	Area	2.4	5.0	5.5	6.2	2.7		
	Yield	3,333.3	5,280.0	4,000.0	4,112.0	4,828.7		
Large Cardamom	Output	2.3	3.9	3.6	4.67	4.1	4.3	6.4
	Area	11.1	20.9	23.5	23.5	21.2	24.2	13.9
	Yield	230.0	186.6	191.5	233.0	191.5	179.1	-6.5
Ginger	Output	2.0	10.9	29.0	24.0	23.3	25.4	9.2
	Area	0.5	2.3	4.5	5.1	3.3	4.8	47.1
	Yield	4,000.0	4,739.1	5,333.0	4,705.0	7,119.4	5,275.0	-25.9
Cut Flowers (lakh)	Output	..	..	8.0				
	Area			0.4				
	Yield			3,000.0				
Misc	Output	12.4	42.3	58.2				
	Area			28.6				
	Yield			1,478.0				

Note: * Area and output data was revised. 'Actual' figures are based on the revised data and on 100 per cent enumeration with the *gram panchayat* as the unit instead of the district.

Source: Department of Horticulture, Government of Sikkim.

TABLE A-30

Comparative Fertiliser Use: Sikkim *Versus* Selected States
(kg. per hectare)

	1998-99	*1999-2000*
Sikkim	6.53	6.19
Arunachal Pradesh	2.52	2.54
Nagaland	3.25	3.55
Manipur	84.16	91.99
Mizoram	10.47	20.55
Tripura	21.32	19.45
Meghalaya	17.8	16.27
Assam	19.62	27.66
India (average)	88.62	95.33
East Zone* (average)	25.21	26.21

Note: *East zone includes Bihar, West Bengal, and Orissa apart from the eight north-eastern states.

Source: *Agricultural Statistics at a Glance*, Directorate of Economics & Statistics; *www. Agricoop.nic.in.*

TABLE A-31

Livestock and Poultry Population (Total Number)

	1997	*2002**	*% Change*
Buffaloes	1,899	2,118	(+) 11.53
Goats		1,23,841	(+) 49.31
Horses	5,436	1,682	(-) 69.05
Yaks	3,140	5,719	(+) 82.13
Rabbits	357	3,329	(+) 832.49
Poultry	2,19,552	2,22,297	(+) 1.25

Note: *Provisional data, 17th Livestock Census.

Source: Department of Animal Husbandry and Veterinary Science, Government of Sikkim.

TABLE A-32

Sources of Dry Fodder and Deficit, 1997

(thousand metric tonnes)

Source of Grain/Dry Fodder	*Availability*	*Requirement*
Forest	250	305
Natural Grassland	475	850
Agricultural Holdings	920	1,645
Fodder Cultivation	480	1,770
Total Dry Fodder Supply	2,125	4,070
Deficit		47.79%

Source: Sixteenth Livestock Census, 1997, Department of Animal Husbandry, Government of Sikkim.

TABLE A-33

District-wise Distribution of Veterinary Services (31 March 2001)

	North	*East*	*South*	*West*	*Total*
Veterinary hospitals	3	4	2	3	12
Veterinary dispensaries	4	8	6	5	23
Disease investigation Laboratories	1	2	1	1	5
Artificial insemination centre	-	11	6	18	35
Stockman centres	7	21	22	15	65
Livestock checkpoints	-	2	1	1	4
Veterinary doctors	5	34	5	7	51

Source: Annual Administrative Report (2000-01), Department of Animal Husbandry and Veterinary Services, Government of Sikkim.

TABLE A-34

Geographical Distribution of the Industries in the State (as on March 2000)

Particulars	*Unit*	*North*	*East*	*South*	*West*	*State*
Provisionally registered	No.	25	244	51	66	386
Small scale units	Unit	6	276	54	31	367
Permanently registered	No.	-	-	-	-	-
Small scale units						
Cottage industries	No.	1	19	6	10	36
Medium scale industries	No.	-	3	-	-	3
PSUs		-	3	-	-	3
Joint sector undertaking		-	-	-	-	-
Non-functioning units		3	65	10	9	87

Source: Sikkim: A Statistical Profile, 2002.

TABLE A-35

Structure of Industries

Particulars	*1997-98*	*1998-99*	*1999-2000*	*2000-01*	*2001-02*
Small Scale industry: Units registered	13	9	19	9	9
Estimated number of workers employed ('0000)	55	69	257	143	54
Entrepreneurship development programme conducted	1	1	1	5	1
Participation of entrepreneurs	36	31	13	185	25

Source: Sikkim: A Statistical Profile, 2002.

TABLE A-36

Proportion Per Thousand of Enterprises by Problems Faced by Them (combined for tabulation category)

	Own Account Enterprise		*Establishments*		*All Enterprises*	
	India	*Sikkim*	*India*	*Sikkim*	*India*	*Sikkim*
No specific problem	289	254	337	384	295	277
Shortage of capital	431	564	318	314	417	520
Lack of lighting capacity	24	6	26	26	24	10
Problem of power cut	17	9	68	83	23	22
Lack of infrastructure facilities	173	459	136	353	168	441
Local problem	194	221	145	176	188	213
Competition from Larger units	160	185	249	162	171	181
Non availability of Labour	5	1	20	10	7	3
Labour problems	5	1	30	10	8	3
Raw material/ fuel not available	34	15	25	38	33	19
Non recovery of Service charges	93	74	74	38	91	68
Others	52	4	35	17	50	6
Sample	162973	1181	34664	361	197637	1542
Estimated ('000) A 200	38799	11	5613	2	44412	14

Note: Own account enterprises: undertaking run by household labour, usually without any hired worker on a 'fairly regular basis.' Fairly regular basis means the major part of the period of operation of the enterprise during last 365 days. Establishment: Those enterprises, which have got at least one hired worker on a fairly regular basis, are called establishments.

Source: NSS 55th Round, salient features, informal sector.

TABLE A-37

Estimated Annual Value of Emoluments Per Hired Worker and Value Added Per Worker

State	*Emoluments Per Hired Worker (All Enterprises Combined) (in Rs.)*			*Value Added Per Workers (in Rs.)*	
	Salary	*Group Benefits*	*Total*	*Method 1*	*Method 2*
Arunachal Pradesh	25567	100	25667	69842	84319
Assam	13150	112	13262	24471	24647
Manipur	21687	1211	22899	25035	25167
Meghalaya	18442	69	18511	26113	26847
Mizoram	21876	581	22458	57803	58677
Nagaland	18290	39	18329	25203	27130
Sikkim	14140	86	14226	29071	30048
Tripura	11562	159	11721	16801	22634
India	19089	611	19700	23977	24242

Note: 1 Factor income approach; 2: Product approach.

Source: NSS 55th round, salient features, informal sector.

TABLE A-38

Proportion (per thousand) of Enterprises by Growth Status

State	*Expanding*	*Stagnant*	*Contracting*	*Not Applicable*	*No Response*
Arunachal Pradesh	302	631	58	0	8
Assam	198	749	50	3	0
Manipur	286	651	59	4	0
Meghalaya	237	740	11	11	0
Mizoram	240	680	8	72	0
Nagaland	320	651	30	0	0
Sikkim	252	545	59	143	1
Tripura	300	654	37	8	1
India	180	667	91	61	1

Source: NSS 55th round, salient features, informal sector.

TABLE A-39

State-wise Distribution of Estimated Number of Enterprises by Tabulation Category (%)

	Own Account Enterprises		*Establishments*		*Enterprises*	
	India	*Sikkim*	*India*	*Sikkim*	*India*	*Sikkim*
Manufacturing D	31.8	23.2	34.2	15.9	32.1	21.9
Construction F	4.4	4.7	2.8	0.4	4.2	3.9
Trading and Repair Services G	39.7	53.9	35.3	29.5	39.1	49.7
Hotels and Restaurants H	3.5	6.7	7.2	28.1	4.0	10.5
Transport, Storage, Communications I	9.1	3.3	7.1	15.4	8.9	5.4
Financial Intermediation J	0.3	0.0	0.7	0.0	0.4	0.0
Real Estate Renting K	1.5	0.3	3.6	1.5	1.7	0.5
Education M	1.0	0.9	3.1	4.9	1.3	1.6
Health & Social Work N	1.6	0.3	2.8	0.4	1.8	0.3
Other Community Social and Personal Services O	7.0	6.7	3.2	4.0	6.5	6.3
ALL	100.0	100	100.0	100	100.0	100

Source: NSS 55th round, salient features, informal sector.

TABLE A-40

Reservation of Seats in *Zilla* and *Gram Panchayats*

Districts	Total					Women				
	Total	SC	ST	OBC	GEN	Total	SC	ST	OBC	GEN
Zilla Panchayat										
West	25	0	3	12	10	7	0	0	0	7
South	24	1	4	10	9	7	2	0	2	3
East	31	4	7	7	13	8	2	3	2	1
North	20	0	19	1	0	6	0	0	6	0
Total	100	5	33	30	32	28	4	4	10	11
Gram Panchayat										
West	274	17	57	127	73	110	22	5	38	45
South	255	16	50	95	94	86	35	2	18	31
East	273	19	73	73	108	89	36	4	22	27
North	103	1	95	7	0	31	0	1	29	1
Total	905	53	275	302	275	316	93	12	107	104

Source: Rural Development Department, Govt. of Sikkim.

TABLE A-41

Rural Development: Allocation in the Annual Plans

(Rs. Lakhs)

Categories	1999-2000	2000-01	2001-02	2002-03	2003-04
Jawahar Rozgar Yojana	121				
Swarnjayanti Gram Swarozgar Yojana		50	50	80	80
Employment Assurance Scheme	244	254	254		
Integrated Rural Development Programme	116				
Jawahar Gram Sammridhi Yojana and Allied Programmes		76	76	90	300
a) *Jawahar Gram Samridhi Yojana*		20	20		200
b) *Indira Awaas Yojana*		46	46	70	80
c) *Indira Awaas Yojana* (conversion)		10	10	20	20
Sampoorna Grameen Rozgar Yojana				300	300
New and Renewable Sources of Energy		34	34		
Integrated Rural Energy Programme	25	25	25	230	230
Inter Village Communication		300	700	200	250
Water Supply and Sanitation		525	1000	1320	
Rural Housing		762	1900	2000	2050
Model Village				1173	1100
Total	506	2026	4039	4220	3210

Source: State Annual Plans.

TABLE A-42

Rural Development: Percentage Allocation in the Annual Plans

(Rs. Lakhs)

Categories	*1999-2000*	*2000-01*	*2001-02*	*2002-03*	*2003-04*
Jawahar Rozgar Yojana	23.9	0.0	0.0	0.0	0.0
Swarnjayanti Gram Swarozgar Yojana	0	2.5	1.2	1.9	2.5
Employment Assurance Scheme	48.2	12.5	6.3	0.0	0.0
Integrated Rural Development Programme	22.9	0.0	0.0	0.0	0.0
Jawahar Gram Sammridhi Yojana And Allied Programmes	0	3.8	1.9	2.1	9.3
a) *Jawahar Gram Samridhi Yojana*	0	1.0	0.5	0.0	6.2
b) *Indira Awaas Yojana*	0	2.3	1.1	1.7	2.5
c) *Indira Awaas Yojana* (conversion)	0	0.5	0.2	0.5	0.6
Sampoorna Grameen Rozgar Yojana	0	0.0	0.0	7.1	9.3
New and Renewable Sources of Energy	0.0	1.7	0.8	0.0	0.0
Integrated Rural Energy Programme	4.9	1.2	0.6	5.5	7.2
Inter Village Communication	0	14.8	17.3	4.7	7.8
Water Supply and Sanitation	0	25.9	24.8	31.3	0.0
Rural Housing	0	37.6	47.0	47.4	63.9
Model Village	0	0.0	0.0	27.8	34.3
Total	100	100.0	100.0	100.0	100.0

Source: State Annual Plans.

TABLE A-43

Achievements At a Glance

Jawahar Rojgar Yojana & Jawahar Gram Samridhi Yojana

Jawahar Rojgar Yojana		*Jawahar Gram Samridhi Yojana*	
Year	*Achievements*	*Year*	*Achievements*
1997-98	2.65 lakh man days	1999-00	2.15 lakh man days
1998-99	6.13 lakh man days	2000-01	3 lakh man days
		2001-02	3.39 lakh man days

Integrated Rural Energy Program (IREP)

Sikkim Renewable Energy Development Agency (SREDA)

Item	*1997-98*	*1998-99*	*1999-2000*	*2000-01*	*2001-02*	*2002-03*
Biogas	174	200	181	200	250	302
Improved *Chullah*	5114	5869	5045	5107	5015	2046
Solar Water Heater	23000					3(500 LPD)
Solar Lights						200
a. Home Lights		70		50	100	
b. Solar Lantern		50		100	300	
Energy Parks					3	

Source: IPR, Govt. of Sikkim, RDD (SREDA), Govt.of Sikkim.

TABLE A-44

Economic Profile: Percentage-wise Classification of Main Workers by Category and Caste/Tribe

	Cultivators		*Agri-Lab*		*Forestry-Fishing etc*	
SC/ST	*1981*	*1991*	*1981*	*1991*	*1981*	*1991*
All SC	54.84	52.66	5.10	8.89	1.15	2.54
Damai	46.18	46.54	5.27	8.68	1.23	2.53
Kami	58.50	55.53	4.89	9.05	1.12	2.61
Majhi	61.86	27.05	1.03	5.74	1.03	6.56
Sarki	60.50	60.31	8.19	10.15	0.71	1.54
All ST	66.45	62.93	1.95	4.81	2.55	2.78
Bhutia	57.99	56.66	2.22	4.68	3.07	3.25
Lepcha	81.83	75.70	1.45	4.91	1.61	1.87

	Mining-Quarrying		*Man-Proc HHI*		*Man-Proc NHHI*	
SC/ST	*1981*	*1991*	*1981*	*1991*	*1981*	*1991*
All SC	0.25	0.15	5.53	3.65	7.90	8.87
Damai	0.17	0.16	8.11	1.63	13.64	9.98
Kami	0.24	0.10	4.67	4.66	5.65	8.02
Majhi	2.06	3.28	1.03	0.00	2.06	30.33
Sarki	0.36	0.00	0.71	2.46	2.85	6.15
All ST	0.02	0.08	0.86	0.57	1.46	2.13
Bhutia	0.02	0.11	1.24	0.75	1.92	2.59
Lepcha	0.01	0.02	0.17	0.23	0.60	1.29

	Construction		*Trade-Commerce*		*Transport/Storage/Communication*	
SC/ST	*1981*	*1991*	*1981*	*1991*	*1981*	*1991*
All SC	8.13	8.82	0.75	2.17	2.06	3.13
Damai	8.79	9.94	0.72	2.00	2.85	3.95
Kami	9.36	8.04	0.72	2.12	1.58	2.93
Majhi	11.34	7.38	2.06	4.92	3.09	3.28
Sarki	15.30	13.23	1.07	1.54	4.27	1.54
All ST	5.71	5.72	2.00	3.13	0.81	1.67
Bhutia	8.12	7.53	2.91	4.23	1.06	2.12
Lepcha	1.33	1.93	0.34	0.93	0.35	0.78

	Other Services	
SC/ST	*1981*	*1991*
All SC	13.02	9.12
Damai	13.13	14.59
Kami	13.29	6.95
Majhi	15.46	11.48
Sarki	6.41	3.08
All st	17.59	16.18
Bhutia	20.50	18.08
Lepcha	12.28	12.33

Source: Census of India, 1981, 1991.

TABLE A-45

Physical Achievements at a Glance

1. Vocational Training

Particulars of Vocational Training	*Year*	*No. of Candidates*
One Year Advanced Course in Computer Training at CCCT-Deorali	1997-98	20
One Year Shorthand and Typing Course at Holy Cross Institute	1997-98	30
Three Months Driving Course at Mani Auto Institute, Kalimpong	1998-2000	63
Cutting Tailoring Training to SC/ST and OBC Candidates at Rongli, E.Sikkim	2000-01	110

2. Vocational Training

Particulars of Vocational Training	*Year*	*No. of Candidates*
Six Months Diploma in the Field of Repairs of Electronic Products at Nam-Nang, Gangtok	2000-01	22
Cutting Tailoring Training to SC/ST and OBC Candidates, Namchi	2001-02	63
Six Months Extension in the Field of Repairs of Electronic Products (Advance Course)	2001-02	22
One Year Diploma in Information Management at Aptech Computer Centre, Gangtok	2001-02	27
Six Months Software Education on IMPACT, SSI-Tadong	2001-02	24
Three Months Vocational Training in Making Stuffed Toys Making Course Organised by SC Entrepreneur's Service Co-operative Society Ltd., Gangtok	2001-02	23
Total	1997-2002	404

2. Central Assistance to Special Component Plan (2001-02)

Name of Scheme	*No. of Beneficiaries*
Distribution of Agriculture Tools at Taraythang	110
Distribution of Blacksmiths' Tool to All Four Districts	100
Distribution of Agriculture Tools to All Four Districts	200
Distribution of Sewing Machines to All Four Districts	200
Distribution of Milk Cane to All Four Districts	150
Total	760 families

3. Central Assistance to Tribal Sub-Plan (2001-02)

Department	*No. of Beneficiaries (families)*
Agriculture	2685
Horticulture	2220
Floriculture	604
Other Expenditures	632
Total	6811

3. Schemes Implemented for Welfare of OBCs

Name of Scheme	*No. of Beneficiaries*
1999-2000	
Distribution of Cream Separator	49 nos.
Distribution of Milk Can	40 nos.
3 Months Motor Driving Training at Mani Auto Institute, Kalimpong	15 candidates
2000-2001	
Distribution of Cream Separator	49 nos.
Distribution of Milk Can	40 nos.
3 Months Motor Driving Training at Mani Auto Institute, Kalimpong	15 candidates
2001-2002	
Distribution of Milching Cows at Dentam, West	51 nos.
Distribution of Piglets at Lower Sichey, East	41 nos.
Distribution of Milching Cows at Sorang, West	16 nos.

contd. ...

contd. ...

2001-2002	
Postmatric Scholarship to OBC Students (for the first time)	1 nos.
Prematric Scholarship to OBC Students (for the first time)	918 nos.

4. Scholarship Schemes to SC, ST and OBC Students

Items	*Unit*	*1997-98*	*1998-99*	*1999-2000*	*2000-01*	*2001-02*
Pre-matric Scholarships	SC Students	2758	598	1645	1614	1974
	ST Students	3659	3569	568	2385	4132
	Total	6327	4167	2213	3999	6106
Post-matric Scholarships	SC Students	113	72	96	98	101
	ST Students	216	260	132	142	493
	Total	329	332	228	240	594

Source: Compendium of Achievements, Social Welfare Department, Sikkim.